The World of Wilderness

The World of Wilderness

Essays on the Power and Purpose of Wild Country

Edited by T. H. Watkins
and Patricia Byrnes

ROBERTS RINEHART PUBLISHERS

in cooperation with

THE WILDERNESS SOCIETY

Published by
ROBERTS RINEHART PUBLISHERS
Post Office Box 666, Niwot, Colorado 80544

Published in the UK and Ireland
Roberts Rinehart Publishers
Trinity House, Charleston Road
Dublin 6, Ireland

Printed in the United States of America

Distributed in the U.S. and Canada
by Publishers Group West

Designed by Gerard A. Valerio, Bookmark Studio

Composed in Garamond Old Style and Centaur
by WESType Publishing Services, Inc.
Printed on 60# Enviro-Text by Bookcrafters
Bound by Bookcrafters

Contents

The Poetry of An Idea

J ust a little over thirty years ago, on the afternoon of September 3, 1964, while the White House Press Corps and a phalanx of politicians and administration officials looked on in the Rose Garden, President Lyndon B. Johnson took pen in fist and scrawled his signature across a piece of sunlit paper called The Wilderness Act. Smiling, he then handed out commemorative pens to a number of observers, including Interior Secretary Stewart Udall, Senator Clinton B. Anderson, and Alice Zahniser and Margaret Murie—the widows of Howard Zahniser and Olaus Murie, pioneers of the Wilderness Act, who had both died before they could participate in the moment that had just validated much of their lives.

The presidential pens were talismans, for the men and women here knew that they had just borne witness to an important moment in history, the triumph of an idea that had evolved over nearly five centuries. It had begun when Europeans "first burst into this silent, splendid nature," as James Bryce once described the moment, and encountered a land and a collection of peoples that challenged the certitudes of human dominion significantly for the first time since the first human jammed the first dibble stick into the first patch of cultivatable earth to begin the journey toward what we still insist is civilization. Even as the new culture ground its way westward from the Atlantic coast, eating up land and overwhelming resident cultures with equal dispatch, it left in its wake an almost inchoate sense of loss.

The native American cultures—the first peoples of the continent who were now being displaced—could have told the new people what they were losing, had anyone been willing to listen. They could have learned, for instance, what Brave Buffalo, a Sioux, had learned as a child:

When I was ten years of age I looked at the land and the rivers, the sky above, and the animals around me and could not fail to realize that they were made by some great power. I was so anxious to understand this power that I questioned the trees and the bushes. It seemed as though the flowers were staring at me, and I wanted to ask them, "Who made you?" I looked at the moss-covered stones . . . but they could not answer me. Then I had a dream, and in my dream one of these small round stones appeared to me and told me that the maker of all was Wakan tanka, and in order to honor him I must honor the works in nature.

To honor the works in nature was the *leitmotif* of native American cultures, however much they may otherwise have varied one from the other. A Hopi or Navajo beginning the complex weave of ritual in a kiva to ensure a good corn harvest, California Yahi Indians chanting in their sweat huts to cleanse themselves of illness, a Cheyenne hunter giving thanks to the spirit of the buffalo he has just slain—all these were acting out the protocols of interdependence, satisfying the human need to propitiate disaster and promote security in the only way available to them.

It was not the new culture's way, and it did not listen. Not for a long time, anyway. We—for it was these United States that became the chief proprietor of that new culture's legacy—proceeded through most of our own history to view the land as a commodity, something to be used and, if necessary, used up in the pursuit of acquisition and power. By the middle of the nineteenth century, the consequent wreckage of land and wildlife lay all around us; and some began to wonder just what it was that had been lost—and at what price to the future?

One such was Henry David Thoreau, the maverick philosopher of Concord, Massachusetts. In "Walking," an essay published in 1861, Thoreau etched a thought that has since become part of the national memory: "The West of which I speak is but another name for the Wild, and what I have been preparing to say is, that in Wildness is the preservation of the World." Three years later, George Perkins Marsh, a Vermont statesman and self-taught naturalist, gave such concerns a certain practical air. In *Man and Nature* he told of the vanished civilizations of the Old World that had doomed themselves when they abused the wildness out of which they had been born. Were we, he wondered, in danger of doing the same?

There was reason enough for worry. True, we had set aside Yellowstone National Park in Wyoming as early as 1872, and in 1890 did the same for Yosemite and Sequoia in California, and with the Forest Reserve Act of 1891 and the Forest Organic Act of 1897 had attempted to keep the remaining public forest lands from being completely stripped by cut-and-run loggers. For the most part, however, we paid little heed even to our own prophets, moving into the twentieth century confident that the abundance of natural resources with which this country had been blessed was inexhaustible. Even so, other voices began to be heard along the way—John Muir, the hairy wood sprite who founded the Sierra Club in 1892; Gifford Pinchot, the young forester who seduced the cooperation of President Theodore Roosevelt in the creation of the U.S. Forest Service in 1905 as an agency of steward-ship; Stephen Mather, the former borax king who became the first director of the National Park Service in 1916; Robert Sterling Yard, head of the National Parks Association, who sent out from his home in Washington, D.C., blizzards of newsletters, broadsides, articles, and books in defense of wild country. And perhaps a few dozen more citizen conservationists in an age that did not welcome the message that wilderness was, at the very least, a responsibility to be attended with care, and, at the very most, a legacy to be loved and preserved for its own sake.

There were not many wilderness advocates in the early decades of this century, nor would their numbers increase dramatically until well after World War II. Yet the energy of passionate belief, a high level of literary skill, experience in public communication, and professional expertise com-bined to give those few voices an effectiveness far beyond their number. Their cause was further strengthened by the fact that not a few of these early adherents enjoyed a tenure within the federal bureaucracy itself. Indeed, it was two young government foresters who began to shape the outlines of ad-ministrative reality for the idea of wilderness preservation not long after the end of World War I.

In 1919, Arthur Carhart, a landscape architect for the Forest Service, urged his superiors to consider a time in the not too distant future when "the scenic spots where nature has been allowed to remain unmarred will be some of the most highly prized scenic features of the country," and proposed that some areas in the national forests be kept in an undeveloped condition. Carhart was joined in this notion by Aldo Leopold, a graduate of the Yale School of Forestry and a regional forester in New Mexico. In years to come, it would be Leopold who would give the wilderness idea philosophical con-tent with his "land ethic" in *A Sand County Almanac,* published posthu-mously in 1949. "We abuse land because we regard it as a commodity belonging to us," he would write then. "When we see land as a community to which we belong, we may begin to use it with love and respect." And, he said, it was "raw wilderness" that "gives definition and meaning to the human enterprise."

But even before this, Leopold had given the idea form: in 1924, he per-suaded the Forest Service to set aside as administratively designated wilder-ness a 540,000-acre roadless area in Gila National Forest in New Mexico—

the first federally designated wilderness area in our history. L. F. Kniepp, chief of the Forest Service's Division of Lands and Recreation, liked the idea so much he initiated a survey of other areas that might also become designated wilderness; in 1929, he formulated regulations whose goal was to establish various "primitive" areas to be kept in as pristine a condition as possible. By 1932, there were 63 such primitive areas established.

Enter another young forester with wilderness ideas. His name was Robert Marshall, the rich son of a successful New York attorney (and major figure in the creation of the six-million-acre Adirondack Park in upstate New York). Until his death in 1939, young Marshall could continue to burrow from within the government—first in the Forest Service, then in the Bureau of Indian Affairs, where as director of forestry he established more than 4.7 million acres of roadless and wild areas on sixteen Indian reservations. Then, back in the Forest Service as the new head of the Division of Lands and Recreation, he restricted roads and other development on 14 million acres of national forests and personally financed a detailed mapping survey that built upon Kniepp's earlier work. There were, Marshall concluded, about 45 million acres of roadless areas in the contiguous 48 states that could and should be preserved. But in spite of the presence and commitment of people like himself in the bureaucracy, he had little faith that left to its own devices the government could do the job that had to be done. "There is just one hope of repulsing the tyrannical ambition of civilization to conquer every niche on the whole earth," he had written as early as 1930. "That hope is the organization of spirited people who will fight for the freedom of the wilderness."

In that hope, Marshall joined with Aldo Leopold, Robert Sterling Yard, and a handful of other "spirited people" to found The Wilderness Society in 1935. And it was The Wilderness Society, under its president, Olaus Murie, and its executive director, Howard Zahniser, that provided the early leadership in the movement toward wilderness preservation that began to accelerate after World War II—even as expanded federal road-building, dam construction, and logging began to vindicate Marshall's skeptical view of the government's commitment to protection. A particular bone of contention was the Bureau of Reclamation's 1950 announcement that it intended to build water-storage and power-producing dams that would flood major portions of Dinosaur National Monument in Colorado-Utah. Led by The Wilderness Society and the Sierra Club, conservationists banded together and ultimately managed to defeat the proposal. But even in the earliest stages of the fight, this singular demonstration of how far the bureaucracy had fallen from grace persuaded the preservationists outside the government that administrative assurances of protection were no longer enough. Zahniser articulated a common sense of impatience in March 1951 when he told a gathering at the Second Wilderness Conference that it was time to act:

> It behooves us to do two things. First we must see that an adequate system of wilderness areas is designated for preservation, and then we must allow nothing to alter the wilderness character of the preserves. . . .
>
> As soon as we have a clear consensus of conservationists we should most certainly press steadily for the . . . congressional establishment of a national wilderness system backed up by an informed public opinion. A bill to establish a national wilderness preservation system should be drawn up as soon as possible with the joint cooperation of the federal land-administering agencies and conservation organizations. . . .
>
> Let us try to be done with a wilderness preservation program made up of a sequence of overlapping emergencies, threats, and defense campaigns! Let's make a concerted effort for a positive program that will establish an enduring system of areas where we can be at peace and not forever feel that the wilderness is a battleground!

The fight against the Dinosaur dams took most of Zahniser's time and energy, and it was not until the dams were blocked by Congress in 1956 that he was able to answer his own clarion call and write the first of many, many drafts of a wilderness bill and have it introduced in the House and Senate simultaneously in the fall of that year. Over the next eight years the bill staggered from committee to committee, through reintroduction after reintroduction, revision after revision (the first version of the bill was rewritten no fewer than 66 times, most of the work done by Zahniser himself). Finally, in 1964, a final version was agreed upon in conference committee between the two houses of Congress, passed, and sent to President Johnson for his signature on September 3.

Like Olaus Murie, who died in 1963, Howard Zahniser was gone by then, having collapsed and died on May 5 before he could see his child made real. The language of the act's preamble, however, remained much as he had written it in his first version; its staid poetry stands taller than any other monument Zahniser might have been given (or might have wanted):

> In order to assure that an increasing population, accompanied by expanding settlement and growing mechanization, does not occupy and modify all areas within the United States and its possessions, leaving no lands designated for preservation and protection in their natural condition, it is hereby declared to be the policy of the Congress to secure for the American people of present and fu-

ture generations the benefits of an enduring resource of wilderness. For this purpose there is hereby established a National Wilderness Preservation System to be composed of federally owned areas designated by Congress as "wilderness areas," and these shall be administered for the use and enjoyment of the American people in such manner as will leave them unimpaired for future use and enjoyment as wilderness. . . .

A wilderness, in contrast with those areas where man and his own works dominate the landscape, is hereby recognized as an area where the earth and its community of life are untrammeled by man, where man himself is a visitor who does not remain. . . .

Like the Omnibus Civil Rights Act signed earlier in 1964 and the Voting Rights Act signed a year later, the Wilderness Act of 1964 was nothing short of revolutionary—an attempt to enshrine in law a principle designed to change the way we live in the earth. But if the Wilderness Act institutionalized an idea, it did not immediately do much in the way of creating a system. What it did do was establish the administrative structure within which wilderness areas could be designated. As a kind of "starter," it designated 9.1 million acres of wilderness on various national forest units that already had been administratively identified by the Forest Service as deserving protection. The rest would have to come after the federal land-managing agencies surveyed their respective territories and made recommendations to Congress as to which areas qualified as candidates for wilderness designation. Such recommendations might or might not be followed by legislation. Moreover, Congress had the power to bypass agency recommendations.

It was a cumbersome process at best, but slowly, with many fits and starts and in spite of shifting political winds, bureaucratic complexities, and conflicting needs and desires on the part of the American public, a National Wilderness Preservation System took shape. Now, in the thirtieth anniversary year of the act's passage, it can truly be said that such a system exists. There are now more than 100 million acres of designated wilderness in the national parks, national forests, wildlife refuges, and the lands administered by the Bureau of Land Management.

Every state west of the Mississippi River except Iowa and Kansas is graced with more or less wilderness (Nebraska has a paltry 12,735 acres, while Alaska enjoys nearly 56.5 *million* acres, most of it designated with passage of the Alaska Lands Act of 1980), as are most states east of the river. As wilderness areas now, the names sing across the landscape of this new American map: Drift Creek and Bull of the Woods, Raven Cliffs and Gospel Hump, Never Summer and Eagles Nest, Rich Mountain and Hells Canyon,

Mud Swamp and Big Blue, Apache Creek and Russell Fjord, Welcome Creek and Dark Canyon, Little Frog Mountain and Devils Backbone. Hundreds more compose a litany of the hope and irony and poetry that Americans have always put on their land, embracing every kind of landform, from windswept granite mountain peaks where almost nothing but lichens can grow, to swamps and bogs swimming with the diverse fecundity of life; from desert riverine habitat to old-growth forests, waterless alkaline flats to alpine lakes, seashores to saline emptiness. The creatures that crawl, walk, swim, or fly through this abundance of wild country include all of the known forms of surviving wildlife on the North American continent, many hundreds of them threatened or endangered. Altogether, they represent the most diverse and beautiful and spectacular examples of wildness ever protected by any people anywhere.

This much we have saved, or have tried to, and it is worth the celebrating. But there is much left to protect. A pretty good rule of thumb among conservationists is that there remain about 100 million acres of wilderness on the public lands of the United States that can and should be placed under the protective mantle of the Wilderness Act. Other lands—like the complicated patchwork of private, state, and federal lands that dominate the landscape of the New England states—while no less in need of protection, may require innovative programs to preserve their natural integrity. By whatever means it takes, the wild or nearly wild country left in the United States should be given protection as soon as possible.

The essays gathered in this book may help to explain why. All of them were first published over the past thirteen years in *Wilderness,* the quarterly magazine of The Wilderness Society, in an attempt to illuminate the power and purpose of wilderness—not just as an aesthetic that satisfies the human need for natural beauty, but as the living, breathing, functioning heart of the natural system that sustains all life, including human life. It is, of course, an argument that has been presented repeatedly and with varying degrees of literary respectability in the pages of *Wilderness* ever since its founding as *The Living Wilderness* in 1935. Like the organization it represented, the magazine knew what it wanted from the beginning and went after it with a bright zealotry that brings to mind the old Western adage: "You can't stop a good man who knows he's right and just keeps on a-comin'." For nearly sixty years, through eight editors, one name change, and vicissitudes of format and frequency, the magazine has fixed its sights on the land-management agencies of the federal government in an often militant, always fervent, and remarkably successful effort to ensure the protection and preservation of wild country. No other conservation publication in the land has been so unremittingly single-minded over so long a period of time.

So what we offer here is in an old tradition but with something of a new context—the increasingly complex mix of science, politics, and economics that now characterizes the conservation movement (and its opposition) wherever you find it. We Americans are too large and various a people and we have learned too many new ways to put our environment (and with it, our lives) in peril. We fumble too often and too ineptly toward the safe middle ground of compromises that destroy in the name of a spurious balance. We move too swiftly and too devastatingly over too much landscape for any of us to rest easily in the traditions of the past.

What we have tried to do in this book, then, is assemble what we believe to have been some of the best conservation writing published in recent years into a kind of literary primer for a new age of preservation. We begin with Charles Little's beautifully rendered explication of the continuing validity of Aldo Leopold's land ethic as the principle that should inform and direct our relationship to the land and its creatures. The late Wallace Stegner then outlines with wit, clarity, and wisdom the often troubling history behind our possession and use of the American land. Bryan G. Norton and David Rains Wallace offer graceful and wonderfully informed scientific excursions into the labyrinths of two modern issues that are too often viewed with as much ignorance as enthusiasm: the meaning and function of biodiversity and the definition and ecological importance of wetlands. Then Charles E. Little and Christina Bolgiano respectively take a close look at two of the most glamorous and singularly misunderstood North American predators for which the preservation of wild habitat is essential—the wolf and the mountain lion—with some artful emphasis on the tangled sociological and psychological intricacies of the human relationship to both.

Having presented some of the ethical and ecological arguments for wilderness preservation, we then get down to specifics: the preservation of what has so far been left unprotected or, at best, imperfectly protected, in a number of especially significant areas—from the slickrock country of southern Utah to the rolling tundra of Alaska's Arctic National Wildlife Refuge, from the old-growth forests of the Pacific Northwest to the "river of grass" in Florida's Everglades.

There has been progress (or at least, movement) in some areas since many of these essays were published. Much of this has resulted from the arrival of a new and more environmentally conscious presidential administration in January 1993, though not all the early actions of President Bill Clinton and his people were greeted with unanimous applause by the conservation community. Most environmentalists cheered the appointments of former Arizona governor Bruce Babbitt as Interior Secretary; George T. Frampton, Jr., former president of The Wilderness Society, as Assistant Secretary for Fish, Wildlife, and Parks; Jim Baca, former chief of lands for the state of New Mexico (though Baca later resigned over questions of policy), as director of the Bureau of Land Management; and Roger G. Kennedy, former director of the National Museum of American History, as director of the National Parks Service.

Other moves were viewed more darkly. In July 1993, for example, a year and a half after Norman Boucher's chapter on the Everglades appeared in the winter 1991 issue of *Wilderness,* Secretary Babbitt helped to negotiate a "statement of principles" between the sugar industry and the government that included a suspension of federal litigation that would have forced the industry to reduce significantly the nutrient pollution of the Everglades ecosystem from sugar cane farming operations.

Efforts to save the Everglades, Jim Webb, The Wilderness Society's regional director for Florida, says, may finally have "emerged from the twilight of pollution litigation," but they have now entered the equally murky world of "ecosystem management," with cooperation among federal and state agencies now touted as the way to build a viable system of restoration that will ensure the future of the region's water supply. Webb has his doubts: "Discussions about ecosystem management have never saved one creature or its home. Until we develop standards, audit tracks, and develop ways in which to *assure* performance in ecosystem management, we can keep on talking about systematic restoration of the Everglades, and it will keep on being systematically destroyed. Everything the Everglades loses deprives us of restoration choices. Making integrated, system-wide plans is now far ahead of the demonstrated capacity of our various governments to execute them. This is the time when conception meets reality; this is when the tough work begins."

Even more has taken place in the Pacific Northwest since the publication of John Daniel's "Long Dance of the Trees" in the spring of 1988—itself the first major investigation by a national conservation publication of an issue that would come to dominate environmental news in the 1990s. At the end of 1990, The Wilderness Society issued the first of a series of GIS—Geographic Information Systems—studies of the remaining old growth in the national forests of the region. These studies, undertaken two years before, utilized Landsat imagery from space, aerial photography, and on-the-ground investigations to determine that there was only about one-third as much old growth left as the U.S. Forest Service had been claiming for years. The Forest Service at first dismissed The Society's figures, then later admitted that they were far closer to reality than its own, much less sophisticated, estimates.

In the meantime, a so-called "God committee" appointed under the provisions of the Endangered Species Act of 1973, declared that the northern spotted owl, indigenous to old-growth forests, was a threatened species and recommended the creation of "habitat conservation areas" in old-growth forests to preserve the owl's habitat. A federal judge ordered the suspension of all logging in such areas until a management plan to preserve the owls could be developed by the U.S. Fish and Wildlife Service. The timber industry complained that the suspension of logging would eliminate tens of thousands of jobs. Conservationists countered that the industry in the region was in a state of decline because of market forces, not environmental laws; that as many as 26,000 jobs already had been lost through modernization of mills, the export of unmilled logs, and the move of many timber company operations to the fast-growing pinewood plantations of the South.

That, roughly speaking, was the situation when President Clinton took office in January 1993. Almost immediately, he held a so-called "timber summit" in Portland, Oregon, well-covered, to say the least, by the media. The president promised a solution and a few months later offered one—a detailed, long-range plan for the management of the nearly 23 million acres of national forest land in the region. Unfortunately, the president's "preferred alternative"—Option 9 in the list of alternative plans included in the final report—satisfied neither the timber industry (too restrictive) nor the environmental community (too careless of protection of both old-growth forests and wildlife habitat). At this writing, the Clinton administration has committed itself to its preferred alternative, while conservationist lawsuits have persuaded the courts to issue injunctions that promise to keep the remaining old-growth forests uncut for the near future; the hope is to force the administration back to the drawing board.

For the most part, however, what these regional essays document is unfinished business, as unfinished now as it was when they were first written. In Utah, for instance, the same BLM lands are still unprotected, still threatened by the same interests, and while some of the players have changed (Wayne Owens, for instance, the representative who first introduced the Utah Wilderness Bill, was defeated in his bid for the Senate in 1992, and Maurice Hinchey of Massachusetts has taken up the banner of his cause), the same bitter struggle between the intransigent warriors of the past goes on today with the same passion that John G. Mitchell outlined with such style in the fall of 1988—although now the stakes have been raised to 5.7 million acres of wilderness proposed by the conservationists.

For Montana, yet another wilderness bill (the sixteenth attempt) was introduced in the summer of 1993, but the gaggle of interests who fought it this time around were just as determined to kill it as any of those who appeared in Dyan Zaslowsky's fine survey in the summer of 1987. In the summer of 1994 the bill stalled, apparently dead where it stood. So was similar legislation for Idaho, though in this case, conservationists were just as glad to see it die, since it would have protected minimal wilderness.

In Alaska, the good news is that President Clinton has announced his opposition to any drilling for oil and gas on the coastal plain of Arctic National Wildlife Refuge, that the state of Alaska apparently has backed off from its vigorous pursuit of so-called "rights" to submerged lands, and that the U.S. Forest Service finally has voided its timber contract with the Alaska Pulp Company. The bad news is that the Forest Service contract with the Ketchikan Pulp Company remains in force, that the subsistence question is just as confused and confusing today as it was when I attempted to unravel it in the winter of 1990, and the problems of monitoring how well the Forest Service adheres to the "buffer zone" restrictions on logging in Tongass National Forest remain horrendous.

The national parks of Alaska, still pressured by the sheer numbers of visitors in places like Denali, are now visited by yet another assault by the perennially exploitive state government of Alaska: the attempted use of an old federal law regarding rights-of-way along ancient abandoned roads. This would serve as a means of punching highways and other inappropriate access routes into the heart of wild country in an effort to boost tourism even more (and to do the same in BLM and national forest lands in order to get at natural resources). Conservationists in and out of Alaska continue to face problems as outsized as the Great Land itself.

The land essays included in this book, then, still have the character of dispatches from the field of battle. An old battle. More than twenty years ago, geographer-philosopher Daniel P. Luten said that so long as the national tradition of utility over all else prevailed, "the cause of the American landscape is a losing battle, to be fought from barricade to barricade, but always backward. When will the tide turn?" He was speaking out of a long history, some of it repeated in these pages, and both his complaint and his question are voiced regularly today. The battles have been necessary, even inevitable, and admittedly there is something almost perversely appealing, if somewhat simple-minded, in the idea of Absolute Good (us) locked in sweaty combat with Absolute Evil (them). The confrontation always has given birth to a good deal of satisfactory passion and the kind of rhetoric that glows in the dark.

But listen again to the question: When *will* the tide turn? And then to a kind of answer: Not for so long as the barricades still stand. As long as we continue to misunderstand the land so profoundly that battles have to be waged over its preservation, there can be no true conservation victories, for each victory becomes just another barricade that must be held. We must accept and embrace the deepest implications of Leopold's land ethic. "All ethics so far evolved," he wrote, "rest upon a single premise: that the individual is a member of a community of interdependent parts. . . . The land ethic simply enlarges the boundaries of the community to include soils, waters, plants, and animals, or collectively, the land." With Leopold's criteria as our guide, what we must learn in our bones in the decades that follow is that the world of wilderness is not merely a phrase: it is a definition of this planet's essential being, and if we reduce wilderness to a meaningless remnant, we will have diminished by precisely that much the character and quality of life itself.

—T. H. WATKINS
Washington, D.C.
December 1994

The World of Wilderness

CHARLES E. LITTLE

In a Landscape of Hope

T he land ethic of the future—if there is a future, and there will be none without the land—will have to be an ethic not to serve the political economy, but to serve the land whether it is economic or not: an ethic that advances that *land's* reasons for being. This is what Aldo Leopold has taught us, and I believe it. But it's hardly the case at present. In fact, as far as land is concerned, the present is a flop. If you do not believe this, go home again.

I did.

At the foot of the San Gabriel's talus slope, where the vineyards (and orange groves and truck farms) fructified in the 1930s, there has been a narrow, two-lane concrete highway. A canopy of fragrant eucalyptus trees had shaded the road as it meandered through the valley, and shaded, too, the long strung-out column of tramps looking to do chores for food in those days when there was no money. They came to our settlement along California State Route 118, a wide place where there was a grocery, and a post office, and Jack's gas station, and even a tiny library. In springtime the tramps would come through the gate of our bright-green picket fence to sit on the back steps of our old house, a block off the highway, and eat sandwiches my mother had prepared for them. I would watch them from my perch on a low limb of the great pepper tree that shaded the yard, and they would say, "Howdy, boy," to me, like Woody Guthrie. And, "You some tow-head, you are," in a thick drawl from Oklahoma or Arkansas or the Texas Panhandle, and then they'd tip their hats and say, "Thank you Ma'am," to my mother and wink at me and be on their way to the next little town along the highway where produce trucks and flivvers stuffed with furniture and children and hope chugged along in some dance choreographed by the economics of the land in those years.

The hope was the amazing thing. And the faith: faith that new land could be found that would not wear out and turn to dust.

Eventually, I found our old house. For I wanted hope, too. But the bungalow's stucco was now mottled and flaky, the pepper tree gone, the picket fence with it. The house itself was standing precariously on the edge of a cliff—a cliff of concrete surmounting the freeway, the new six-laner that now cut through my valley.

I looked down on the three eastbound lanes where, I think, Mr. Lee's place was, a small chicken ranch now hovering in memory about 20 feet above the streaming traffic. I wondered where all this machinery was going and had a vision of the great river of cars disappearing at the edge of the earth after a million miles of shopping centers, eroded fields, pastures grown to brush, suburban-kitsch office buildings, clear-felled forests, drive-in banks, dammed rivers, muddy lakes, festoons of high tension wires, and Wendy's and Hardee's and Arby's disappearing into a taupe-colored distance.

Mr. Lee had always told us not to put our finger through the chicken wire lest the Leghorn rooster, who was cranky, come peck at it. And so we would put our finger through the chicken wire, and rooster would come and peck it, and we would yowl, and Mrs. Lee would give us a cookie.

Aldo Leopold wrote when I was two: "To build a better motor we tap the uttermost powers of the human brain; to build a better countryside we throw dice."

Zoom zoom zoom go the cars along the freeway. We put our fingers through the wire. We roll the dice. The land disappears. Mrs. Lee is no longer there to give us a cookie. And Mr. Leopold is dead.

Is there a "land ethic" in heaven? I hope so for Aldo Leopold's sake, since he despaired of there being one here on earth. He despaired on the first published version of his remarkable essay on the land ethic, which appeared in the October 1933 number of the *Journal of Forestry*. And the despair was unallayed by the passage of years. In the final version of the essay, appearing in *A Sand County Almanac,* written after the war and the atom bomb, Leopold bitterly concluded that "No important change in ethics was ever accomplished without an internal change in our intellectual emphasis, loyalties, affections, and convictions. The proof that conservation has not yet touched these foundations of conduct lies in the fact that philosophy and religion have not yet heard of it."

And that is our text for today: because the fact is that philosophy and religion *did,* eventually hear of conservation and of the land ethic that is its
philosophical cornerstone. In fact, the land ethic is something of an intellectual growth industry these days. And therefore might *we* be justified in predicting a different future for the land than could Professor Leopold? Despite
the blasted landscapes of the present, might not ethical considerations finally be set into the grain of our future public and private decisions about
land use and conservation? Or shall we keep on tossing the dice, again and
again, until the land craps out?

If you are looking for hope, please attend to the word of the U.S. Catholic
Bishops in their recent (November, 1984) pastoral letter, "Catholic Social
Teaching and the U.S. Economy":

> The biblical vision of creation has provided one of the most enduring legacies
> of church teaching, especially in the patristic period. We find a constant af-
> firmation that the goods of this earth are common property and that men and
> women are summoned to faithful stewardship rather than to selfish appropriation
> or exploitation of what was destined for all. Cyprian writes in the middle of the
> third century that "whatever belongs to God belongs to all," and Ambrose states
> "God has ordered all things to be produced so that there would be food in com-
> mon for all, and that the earth should be a common possession of all." Clement of
> Alexandria grounds the communality of possession not only in creation but in
> the incarnation since "it is God himself who has brought our race to communion
> (*koinonia*) by sharing himself, first of all, and by sending his word to all alike and
> by making all things for all. Therefore everything is in common." Recent church
> teaching, as voiced by John Paul II, while reaffirming the right to private prop-
> erty, clearly states that Christian tradition "has always understood this right
> within the broader context of the right common to all to use the goods of the
> whole creation."

Applied to land, this is as clear an ethical pronouncement as one could
wish. To some it is shockingly clear. At a meeting held to discuss the implications of the Bishops' letter for managing land resources, a government
economist confessed his dismay. "I have a Ph.D. in economics," he said.
"And in all my studies, I have never seen as radical an economic document
as this."

You see, we commonly take land to be, mainly, an economic "input":
with labor and capital, a "factor of production." The Great Plains are an
input into the agriculture industry. The timbered Northwest is an input to
the forest products industry. The wilderness fastness is an input to the recreation industry. And my valley was an input to the real estate industry.

Leopold made this curiosity familiar, describing it as a kind of resource Babbittry. I personally know people who go around muttering "land is a factor of production" all day long, without even realizing what they are saying, just as some of us say grace at dinner, "God is great, God is good/And we thank Him for this food," without wondering who *really* owns the land that makes the food. And the table. And the china and silver and tablecloth, too. At this level of inquiry, it's hard to understand land ownership in any but the most transient and inconsequential sense. Ownership: this is the linchpin in the whole business of land ethics, of course, as the Bishops so forthrightly assert.

A real philosopher I know (Sara Ebenreck, who has a Ph.D. in ethics from Fordham) tells of the young chief of the Western Cayuses who in 1855 protested the selling of the tribal lands. "I wonder if the ground has anything to say," he asked the governor of the Washington Territory. "I wonder if the ground is listening to what is being said?"

Owning land—in the monopolistic, exploitative sense, not in Jefferson's sense that all should be allowed "a little portion"—has always seemed a bit like owning the air through which we pass, or the waters that fall or flow or tidally undulate. Land *moves*, like air and water. And we move through it in our brief lives. It opens before us and it is well to wonder, after we have passed: do other travellers and voyagers find it good? What does the ground say? I am often astonished when people talk about the need for a land ethic as if it were an argument about table manners. It is not. It is an argument about violence, as Leopold made plain in the very opening lines of his essay. The stewardship of land is a form of not raping it.

"How do you feel about not-raping?" asks the fellow next to us at the cocktail party, for he has somehow discovered that we are the holder of strange views.

"Well, I'm all for it," I guess we are supposed to say. "There ought to be a whole lot more not-raping going on. We got to get the word out."

"Still," says the fellow at the cocktail party, fingers glistening with chicken grease from the barbequed wings of a factory-made Leghorn, "you can overdo the idea of not-raping. After all, we have to be practical. This is a free country. A man has his rights. I'm sick and tired of all those dogooders running around complaining all the time. Let's stand up for America."

But we are called to stand up for the land, too.

Another, earlier, statement by the Catholic Bishops—those whose sees are in the American heartland—asserted that the Bible and the tradition of the church make manifest these ten principles of land stewardship:

4

1. The land is God's.
2. People are God's stewards on the land.
3. The land's benefits are for everyone.
4. The land should be distributed equally.
5. The land should be conserved and restored.
6. Land use planning must consider social and environment impacts.
7. Land use should be appropriate to land quality.
8. The land should provide a moderate livelihood.
9. The land's workers should be able to become the land's owners.
10. The land's mineral wealth should be shared.

An ecumenical group of North Carolina churchmen called the Land Stewardship Council writes in its "Ministry Statement" of 1981 that:

> We are all Creatures of God. We and the land are the work of God's creative love. The strong basis for the traditional Jewish-Christian concept of stewardship can be seen in numerous places in the Scriptures. The Bible describes the proper relationship that people should have with the land and with each other. This is expressed plainly, for example, in Psalms 24:1—"The earth is the Lord's and all that is in it, the world and all that dwell therein." In Leviticus 25:23, God says that no land should be sold in perpetuity "because the land is mine;" to me you are "aliens and settlers."

In Minnesota, an outfit called the Land Stewardship Project has created its own bible. Put together by Joe and Nancy Paddock and Carol Bly, poets and writers, the book is a compendium of long and short quotations by other poets and writers interspersed with the editors' own insights. (The book, by the way, belongs in every conservationist's library and is available from the Project's headquarters at 1717 University Avenue, St. Paul, Minnesota 55104.) Black Elk, the Oglala Sioux holy man, is here. And Isaiah. And E.F. Schumacher. And Walt Whitman. And scores more you haven't heard of, and don't need to.

Joe Paddock, in his poem, "Black Wind":

> This vast
> prairie, its hide of sod
> stripped back, black
> living flesh of earth
> exposed.
> Our way

has made thieves
of the wind and rain.
Listen,
listen to the wind moan
through the bone-white dead
cottonwood limb: *Half gone!*
Half gone! Half gone! . . .

In all of it, though, there is the amazing hope.

We are, like the Chinese (from Confucius to Mao), a nation in love with axioms. Our homes and offices are littered with them: from "Be It Ever So Humble. . . ." to "The Buck Stops Here." We wear them on our T-shirts ("A Woman's Place is in the House . . . and the Senate") and the bumpers of our automobiles ("Thank You For Not Laughing At My Car"). My own grandfather, a printer, used one on a magazine he published to promote his business. Under a lithographed team of horses straining at the plow were the words, "Work, Son of Adam, and Forget It."

But axioms are not ethics. Ethics, it seems to me, is work: the work of a society trying to live up to its beliefs. A land ethic proposes restraint in land use, deferred reward from exploitation of the resource base, concern for posterity so that future generations will get as much or more from the land as we. It is a social goal, this land ethic of Aldo Leopold, and it must be expressed in "policy." And not only the abstract, big-P Policy of Principle, but the workaday little-p policy of legislation, of statute, of government regulation and management practice.

While the land ethic has recently laid claim to our consciousness to a degree that might have heartened Professor Leopold, there are other social goals that tend to complicate the effort to create and implement the legislation needed to make it actual. Some of these goals—individual liberty, social justice, scientific progress—are much on the lips of those whose economic ox would be gored by the actual application of a land ethic in policy. They insist that the goals they espouse are in conflict with a land ethic. In fact, so persuasive have the opponents of a land ethic been with this tactic that of all industrial democracies, the United States (which has the most to gain from it) has the least effective legislation to protect its land base.

Whether the arguments are in opposition to wilderness designation, establishing wild and scenic rivers, conserving soil and water resources, planning for urban development, or limiting the conversion of prime farmland, the exploiters of land are adroit at using the rhetoric of the social reformers of yesteryear.

6

John Locke (1632–1704), who gave us the outline for a liberal constitutional government, provides the most relevant example. Lock proposed the concept of "natural rights"—these being life, liberty, and property.* They are natural because they would inhere to mankind in a "state of nature." He said that government was valid only with the consent of the governed, and that it was the "natural right" of men to "dispose of their persons and possessions as they think fit." We now listen to modern day philosophers of the political right asserting their own anarchic version of Lockean liberalism, as in, "It's my land and I can do with it what I want."

Locke, an urbane Londoner, was, in effect, the originator of "individualism" of the kind that is now thought to be an uniquely American characteristic. In its most simplistic form, the American individualist is contemporaneously embodied by the Marlboro Man who rides the plains alone and inhales deeply despite warnings by the Surgeon General. Only slightly more subtle are the landowners who believe that moral responsibility stops at property lines.

How does the Lockean individualist view, American-style, comport with the Bishops communitarian philosophy of land use? The answer is, not very well. And here is the first of several conundrums that arise when we wish to apply the land ethic to policy. It is deepened, at least so it would seem on the surface (and we shall return to this point later), by Thomas Jefferson's small-d democratic insistence on the individual right of land ownership to provide for one's own welfare and subsistence.

Thus are we caught in a trap of our own manufacture. By appealing to authority without sensitivity to the historical setting in which the reform-minded concepts to which we mindlessly cling were created, we allow the moral teachings of the past to be perverted by those who would use them cynically. According to Eugene C. Hargrove, a professor of philosophy at the University of New Mexico, a landowner cannot honestly justify his position that he is absolved of social responsibility by asserting a natural right of land ownership to do with his land whatever he might choose. This is a claim, says Hargrove in the Summer 1980 issue of *Environment Ethics,* that neither Locke nor Jefferson would have been comfortable with given present-day circumstances in which the perverse exploitation of land is exacerbated by lim-

---

*In the Declaration of Independence, Jefferson's "inalienable" rights are "life, liberty, and the pursuit of happiness." Jefferson believed that property, including ownership of land, was a right, and he championed it in every respect. But Garry Wills says the word "property" did not survive in the Declaration because Jefferson, influenced by the Scottish philosopher Francis Hutcheson, felt that property "*follows* on society rather than precedes it. Thus he places it among the 'adventitious' rights rather than the 'natural' ones." See *Inventing America* (New York: Random House, Vintage Books Edition, 1979), pp. 229–239.

itations on its quantity. Both men thought of the American frontier as virtually endless.

Locke and (less often) Jefferson are not the only authorities patriotically invoked in defense of unethical land use. Jeremy Bentham (1748–1832), another reformer, proposed that the basis for all legislation was "the greatest happiness for the greatest number." At one time, this radical thought stood in contrast to policies that benefited only the nobility in England. Today, in America, Benthamite utilitarianism is used to justify everything from ski lifts in national forests to governmental sponsorship of the use of poisons in agriculture. Another reformer, Adam Smith (1723–1790), hoped to benefit the masses with his theories expounded in the *Wealth of Nations.* Here it is written that if individuals undertake their "industry" primarily for their own gain, then they will benefit society by "an invisible hand" that frequently produces a better result in serving society's needs than would governmental intervention in order to improve the public welfare. Ever since, industrialists and others have taken the work of the great Scottish economist as license for greed and antisocial behavior in general, and specifically to excuse a failure to think of land resources in terms other than immediate gain from exploitation.

These days The Free Market is having its best run since Coolidge, and "trickle down" is no longer a cause for sniggering by limousine liberals. Adam Smith, in an agrarian age, said that government could not do very much to affect the welfare of individuals in society. And if a twentieth century John Maynard Keynes proved him wrong, and if a fifty-year history of just the opposite created the wealthiest and strongest, as well as the most decent, nation on earth, then so what?

If you want a course in selective Anglo-American intellectual history, all you need to do is attend a hearing—in Congress or at Town Hall—on any legislation or ordinance designed to protect the land resource base, on policies that would give substance to the *idea* of a land ethic, which, while much on the lips, is scarcely on the books.

In such sacred places as these you will hear Mr. Bentham, who wants to construct a theme park in the last remaining unspoiled marsh in the state's coastal zone, insisting, "Listen, I'm a *people* person." Or Mr. Locke, who wants to build a 3,000-unit townhouse development on some prime farmland, complaining, "I don't need a bunch of conservationists telling me what I can do with my land." Or Mr. Smith, whose nuclear power plant is to be sited atop the local fault line, crying, "Jobs, jobs, jobs!"

They are, each of them, historically correct, having got hold of some solid philosophical precepts. But they are tragically wrong, too. And the dilemma doesn't bode well for the future of the land ethic.

What do we build on then? Most important are the citizen-effort models, of course: the heartening case histories of those who earnestly try to express the land ethic in terms of civic action in small as well as large ways. Perhaps the small ways are better for purposes of inspiration. It is one thing to fight hard for the highly visible conservation goal, such as, say, the protection of the Alaskan wilderness. But it takes nothing away from that achievement to remember that smaller victories (albeit equivalently partial) may be even more expressive of the internal change of intellectual emphasis, loyalties, affects, and convictions that Aldo Leopold said was the sine qua non of a functioning land ethic.

For example, a land ethicist I know, Tom Lamm, who works out of Black Earth, Wisconsin, is helping to organize small farmers to do, finally, what politicos from FDR on down have been afraid to do: make soil erosion against the law. A recent account of the work of the Soil Stewardship Task Force in the *Wisconsin State Journal* quotes the farmers who make up the task force as saying that "Regulations must be set in place to control abusive soil eroders who have not, and will not, respond to technical assistance and financial incentives alone." It is the small farmers, Lamm believes, who have the largest sense of land stewardship and who must therefore take the lead in making laws about the care of the land. Otherwise its future is left to real estate investors and other absentee owners to whom land is mainly surface and not the magical thing that a real dirt farmer knows it to be.

There are a good many people like Tom Lamm who give us hope and inspiration. The fact is, I have a rolodex full of them. Eddie Albert continues to celebrate "green acres" in soil erosion work. Ned Ames gives away money for a foundation to preserve natural areas. George Anthan writes articles for a major midwestern newspaper on farmland preservation. Malcolm Baldwin, when at the President's Council on Environmental Quality, rescued from certain oblivion the Agricultural Lands Study, which alerted the nation to the loss of farmland. John Banta guards the legal standing of the Adirondack Park Agency, which protects some six million wilderness and semi-wilderness acres in New York State. Others in the B section are land ethicists too: Batcher, Beale, Beamish, Beard, Beaton, Beaty, Becker, Berg, Berger, Bergland, Berrett, Berry, Bodovitz, Boon, Borgers, Borrelli, Boswell-Thomas, Bray, Brinkley, Brooks, Brown, Browne, Burch, and Burr. And it goes on like that through Zinn, Zitzmann, and Zube. Zinn is a geographer who works for the Congressional Research Service and edits a newsletter on coastal zone resource management. Zitzmann is a recently retired land use planner from the Soil Conservation Service. Zube, at he University of Arizona, is a leading figure in landscape aesthetic analysis. Poets and planners, Pooh-Bahs and panjandrums. But land lovers all.

Why isn't this enough, these examples, to show that progress in land ethics is afoot, and that eventually all will be well? We have, to be sure, a wilderness policy (although it operates only on the federally owned lands). We have a recreation policy (though emasculated by budget and staff cuts at the federal level). We have a soil erosion policy (albeit weak and pusillanimously voluntary). We have wildlife policies, and historic preservation policies, and we have various state and federal policies to protect places of special significance such as the coastal zone. But, alas, there is no overall policy for *land*.

Leopold insisted on dealing with land whole: the system of soils, waters, animals, and plants that make up a community called "the land." But we insist on discriminating. We apply our money and our energy in behalf of protection on a selective basis. Not of land, but "natural areas." Not of land, but "prime farmland." Not of land, but "wilderness." Leopold briefly compares the evolution of the land ethic with the evolution of ethics concerning children in our society. Child labor laws are now applied to all children, and recently the rights of children not to be beaten by their parents have been asserted. Would we say, for example, that we have an ethic for the protection of children in our society but that it pertains only to some children—perhaps those whose noses do not run—and not to others? The question this raises for land and its future is: if an ethic is selectively applied, is it still an ethic? Or is it just a hobby?

The idea of a hierarchy in land quality is, nevertheless, *the* basic tenet of the conservation and environmental movement. We do not see this as an ethical flaw in our thinking but necessary to the organization of our actions. We preserve prime farmland because it is the most productive in terms of dollars flowing into the agriculture industry. Therefore, we are casual about other lands. Recently, we have been plowing up great swaths of thin prairie soils in the High Plains, soils that should never have been the "sillion shine" of the plowshare. Great center-pivot irrigation rigs crawl over the land like weirdly articulated steel insects, sucking up the irreplaceable reserves of water in the Ogallala aquifer, the great multi-state underground lake that when exhausted will leave the land defenseless against the wind that even now piles the sandy soil against the fences, like dunes.

In urban areas, we commonly assume that we must ruin one landscape to preserve another. A beautiful apple orchard becomes uglified by tasteless development because we wish to save a marsh, and we assume, incorrectly I believe, that since all development is ugly, let ugliness reign except in the marsh. The skunk cabbage thrives, but do we? What hierarchical perversity has led to the tawdriness of the so-called "gateway" communities at the entrances to our national parks? How is it that the beautiful village of Taos can

be well-managed and its historical artifacts protected, and yet the road leading to it so blaspheme the surrounding landscape?

But is there no "normative" landscape? Aren't some places better than
others, even so? On the other hand, ethologists tell us that all animals have
an instinctive habitat preference. *Homo sapiens* is an animal species, therefore
humankind has a habitat preference just as imbedded as that in, say, a
meadow mouse. Now the anthropologists take over. What is the preferred
habitat for man? Well, look no further than the place where man arose,
where he emerged as a species. What place is that? The archeologists have
the answer: the Great Rift Valley in East Africa. Well, what was it like there
a couple of million years ago? It was a savanna, say the paleontologists. Short
grass and scattered trees. Campsites by the lake or best of all where the river
runs into the lake. And was that really the good life? Sure, say the prehisto-
rians. A gatherer-hunter spent maybe twenty hours a week gathering and
hunting and doing other work necessary to his survival. The land was abundant, the landscape provided safety, the climate was ideal (not as dry then as
it is now). So most of the time was taken up with peaceable intellectual, social, and artistic pursuits. Normative landscape? It is, of course, the Garden
of Eden, paradise (which in Persian means garden). Where is it today? Why,
in the landscaped estates of the wealthy. On golf courses. On wilderness cal-
endars that show alpine meadows rimmed with trees and mountains (as did
the mountains rise tens of thousands of feet, to Kilimanjaro, as a backdrop
to the Great Rift Valley). And, at the end, the normative landscape is where
we are laid to rest. Short grass and scattered trees in manufactured savannas
called memorial parks.

On the other hand, other landscapes are good, too. What is better than a
bustling, unblighted city neighborhood, a tidy suburb, an apple orchard
framing a white farmhouse, a sea-pounded cliff, a deep hemlock forest, an
unspurious fishing village, a desert where the cholla and saguaro give spiny
protection to a community of strange creatures? Any place is a good place if
it is allowed to be true to its inherent nature. Land lovers understand such
speculations, understand them to be the eternal argument of culture versus
the genes.

Scott Buchanan, the philosopher and educator who originated the "great
books" program at St. John's College in 1937, observed that "one of the impressive functions of the cosmic idea is to preside over the birth of possible,
new, and good worlds, and to incite new wills to make them actual."

In Leopold's land ethic, we are in the presence of a cosmic idea. It can,
and has, incited new wills to make its promise at least partially actual. But I
would argue that the great irony of the land ethic is that those who embrace

it most fervently—those who love the land—often are among those who obstruct its fulfillment. By and large, land lovers have copped out, arguing for the protection of the land on every socio-economic basis they can think of in the manner of Smith and Bentham and Locke, save the ethical one. We try to find arguments to suit the cynics: those who, said Oscar Wilde, understand the price of everything and the value of nothing.

As the sun sinks in the West in more ways than one, we search frantically for tiny indications that a land ethic, at least a prelusive one, can really exist in America and that it can exist for reasons of obtaining a good life rather than just making a good living.

The closest anyone has ever come to actualizing what we might call a Level I land ethic has been the state of Oregon, under the leadership of its late governor. Tom McCall. McCall died of cancer in January 1983. He was, in my view, the most effective political operative in behalf of American land since Theodore Roosevelt.

Twenty-two years ago, Oregon enacted a legislative package concerning land use in the state. It was designed to stop what McCall cheerfully described as the "grasping wastrels of the land," the "buffalo hunters and pelt skinners," those who presided over the "ravenous rampage of suburbia," and infectious "coastal condomania." He would stop cold, he said (and this is my favorite McCallism), "the sagebrush saboteurs." In a nutshell, Oregon's legislation established an independent state-level body that promulgated statewide land use "goals and guidelines" for application via local regulations. If regulations were not applied locally, then the state government would apply them itself. There were nineteen goals-and-guidelines statements dealing with such matters as transportation, industrial siting, waste treatment, water supply, and farmland. The net was a broad one. Not many square feet of McCall's "beautiful Oregon country" were left uncovered by the legislation.

One goal, dealing with agricultural land, is especially instructive. It provides the basis for "exclusive farm use" zoning—EFU—on most existing and potential privately owned farmland in the state. Though the farmland zones are established locally, the permitted uses are defined by state statute, which provides that any new lot in an EFU has to be large enough to maintain a viable agricultural economy in the area so that families can continue to make a whole living from it. If, therefore, farms average 100 acres in, say, a dairying district, then local governments cannot permit the subdivision of land into parcels substantially less than that amount. So where is the new development supposed to go? Why, inside the UGB—the Urban Growth Boundary—established under the legislation to confine urbanization to areas in and around existing settlement rather than let it ooze all over the landscape.

In my view the Oregon story is important not because of the technicalities of its legislation, but because in one state at least, a government (which is to say, the citizenry) was able to establish convincingly that "the land" is of *public* concern, not simply a matter that can be left to private economic decision. If it seems like a truism that there are public rights to be considered as well as private ones in the management of the land resource base, please remember that only a very small handful of state and local governments of the United States has any kind of policy dealing resolutely with land in any category, much less comprehensively.

These days we are confronted with a growing trend toward the "privatization" of land-use decision making, to employ an obnoxious contemporary term, which together with a rather negative government role, especially at the national level, seeks to influence land-use decisions so timidly that it is scarcely worth anyone's time messing around with it. We do not seem to be able to produce clear-cut statutory policies that provide in the law of the land, laws *for* the land. For example, in one lukewarm piece of legislation, recently enacted, the best we can do for the Barrier Islands, those magnificent shifting dunes with their fragile ecosystems that guard our coastline from Virginia to Florida, is to constrain the federal government—the *government* mind you, which is supposed to be on our side—from not doing anything *itself* to degrade the islands further.

Tom McCall, God bless him, would have none of this pussyfooting around. His approach was Mosaic, with plenty of thou-shalt-nots deriving from a clearly conceived right of the ordinary citizen to have a landscape worth looking at and living in.

But at what a price. In the end, when he was dying, he had, because a referendum had been placed on the ballot to abolish his policies, to convince his fellow citizens once again that their land was precious to them. For his trouble he was told, not for the first time, that his idea was nothing but thinly veiled Marxism, that what our forefathers fought for, our sacred heritage, was being abridged, that he was depriving his fellowing citizens of their constitutional right to destroy the land of Oregon as they saw fit. In 1982, in the midst of this battle, I invited McCall to attend a meeting I had organized in Ohio, and he told me he would come. But later he telephoned; he said that the cancer was kicking up again, taking his strength, and he'd better stay home in Oregon to fight off "the grasping wastrels" once again. He did, and he won: the voters sustained the legislation. But soon after, McCall was gone. We were never to see him again. And his like comes around rarely.

Leaning on champions like McCall reveals a terrible flaw in our perception of how Leopold's cosmic idea is to be made actual, for it is plain to me that the future of the land ethic—if we are to get beyond Level I, even in a single state—cannot rest on the chance that a Tom McCall will meet history in just the right, dramatic way to save the land. And have it stay saved. Let us be honest. There is no real ethic present, no permanent system of values to which we have given our general consent, when the laws expressing it are constantly challenged, vicious arguments mounted, patriotism called into question as it was for McCall himself. The land ethic of the future will not be without its complications in application, but its basic premise must be accepted as being natural and obvious, made manifest simply by "listening to the ground" in the words of the chief of the Western Cayuses. For this, it may be necessary to look not only to the brilliant political apologist and leader, but to the ordinary *users* of the land as well, for they are most in touch with it.

Why should *they* not be the ones to insist on policies for the land's posterity? Indeed, some do, as in the case of Tom Lamm's farmers—though often we do not hear them, so engrossed are we in our hierarchical attitudes about land. But if I were a farmer, I'd rather farm for posterity than for a bunch of bankers. If I were a sawyer, I'd be pleased to scratch what Gifford Pinchot wrote into the housing of my chainsaw, that what America *still* needs to understand is that "trees could be cut and the forest preserved at one and the same time." If I were a herdsman, I would want pastures of plenty to the horizon of time as well as space. If I were a fisherman, I would wish for the heavy-bodied salmon to run freely up free rivers forever, squirming into the far pools of ancient memory.

To assume that individual, small-scale use of the land's resources leads inevitably to its destruction is to confuse a failure of policy with the function of land stewardship by those to whom the land has been entrusted for care. In *A God Within,* Rene Dubos has written of his beloved Ile de France country, northwest of Paris, as a landscape that is not only preserved, but improves. He quotes the poet Charles Péguy: *"Deux mille ans de labeur ont fait de cette terre/Un reservoir sans fin pour les âges nouveaux."* Dubos translates this: "Two thousand years of human labor have made of this land an inexhaustible source of wealth for the times to come."

Thomas Jefferson had confidence in the American people not only as electors of political leaders, but as stewards of land. "I am conscious," he wrote in 1785 to his friend James Madison, president of William and Mary, "that an equal division of property is impractical, but the consequences of this enormous inequality producing so much misery to the bulk of mankind, legislators cannot invent too many devices for subdividing property. . . . The earth is given as common stock for man to labor and live on . . . it is not too soon to provide by every possible means that as few as possible shall be without a little portion of land. The small landowners are the most precious part of the state."

These, the small landowners, and those who would become small landowners, are the people who most validly may insist on morality in land use, in principle as well as policy. It is in their behalf, primarily, that the Bishops have addressed themselves to the land ethic in their pastoral letter.

And yet the future of the land ethic depends no less on the rest of us, as the faithful supporters of stewardship wherever we can find it—in law and in practice. I can't imagine how else it will come about, the actualizing of this cosmic idea, other than in small but vivid increments of individual choice and collective action.

I will lift up mine eyes unto the hills," the Psalmist wrote, "from whence cometh my help." In my former valley, I could still lift my eyes to the San Gabriels, despite the zooming traffic at my feet. The mountains rise abruptly from the settlement below, and when I was a youngster my friends and I would climb the steep folded flank of the first range to a place we called the Lookout. . . .

"Watch out for rattlers," yelled the leader, a wiry ten-year-old with carrot-colored hair cut close for summer, which was perhaps the summer of 1940. The clattering stones reminded him of the sandy-brown snakes that liked to hide among the roots and in the crevices to keep cool.

"Rattlers don't worry me," someone shouted back. "It's the mountain lion."

"Mountain lion?"

"Yeah, mountain lion. You never seen a mountain lion?"

"I've seen Mr. Williams' yellow dog. I bet that's your mountain lion."

"It wasn't no yellow dog that chased the coyotes away."

"Shoot."

"Well, shoot yourself."

We pushed ahead, grabbing at ironwood branches to hand ourselves up the slope, winding through dead yucca spires that earlier in the year, in spring, had shot up six feet from the nest of sword-like leaves, each spire surmounted by pannicles of creamy blossoms, like giant lilies, which they were.

Finally, dusty-dirty, with sweat rivers eroding down flushed faces, we gained the Lookout and our California valley was spread before us.

"Jeez, lookit everything," said the redhead.

"There's the mesa," said another. "See, we're looking *down* on the mesa." It always amazed us, to be above it.

"You mean where the mountain lion scared the coyotes away?"

"Can't you pipe down!"

We knew that if the coyotes were gone from the mesa for an evening or two, they'd soon be back, the moonlight behind them, howling with their muzzles pointed skyward in the yip-yip-yiparoo that covered the sounds of their brothers creeping up on the chicken coops below.

As we looked across our valley, the brightness made it all the closer, like a medieval triptych whose foreshortened perspectives could give a scene a holy quality. The vineyard rows cut into each other at crisp angles, the details of the vine-trunks and the interlacing runners almost visible, even from here. And beneath the gray-green leaves hid the heavy blue and green bunches, like prizes.

"Lookit Mr. Kraus. Lookit!" It was the redhead again, though only a couple of feet from the farthest ear.

Mr. Kraus, for it was he, was cranking up the tractor, which had a bouncy metal seat, smoothed and glinting with wear. The pops and clanks drifted up to us, out of synch with his actions, for he was at a distance. A tiny speck of red appeared as Mr. Kraus straightened up and ran a bandanna across his flat German brow. He was constructed of planes and bands of bone and muscle. With his sons he would be cutting the grapes using linoleum knives honed like razors. They would pile the dark bunches in wooden crates left at the end of each row, thence to be hefted onto the flatbed wagon, drawn by the tractor.

We watched for a while as Mr. Kraus messed with the spark, then we surveyed other quarters. "The school, the school," someone said, directing our attention to it. And there it lay, its Spanish tile roofs enclosing a yard of live oaks whose cantilevered branches could, when school was in session, support a line of children as a telegraph wire supports a line of swallows.

And so we went through the litany of places, freshly revealed by our superior angle of view: the olive trees along school street, the state highway below, the tomato patch—a huge field of ruby fruit—and the orange groves set into the scene like emerald rectangles spread across the middle distance.

To the northwest was Tujunga, and southwest the Devil's Gate, great arroyos among many that guided the waters out of the mountains during the brief season of rain. At other times, the water for the houses and the groves and vegetable crops (vineyards were dry-farmed) came from catch basins fed by water mines, bored in the canyons by the earliest settlers, perhaps even the rancheros of the original haciendas.

In such canyons we would find smooth stones, and carrying them up the mountain would send them humming aloft from the Lookout, into the brilliant air, with David's-slings made of raw-hide thongs knotted to leather pouches that were slit to cradle the missiles. We swung them round and round, faster and faster, and when we released them there was only sound, for the stones would fly faster than the eye could follow, upward in a great arc—a fragment of our place flung into a distant land, perhaps another country whose people would marvel at the mysterious object falling at their feet.

From fragments such as these will a land ethic for the future be created, the fragments of a sensibility and a hope whose origins are in the earth itself. The Kodak carousels of our memory go round and round in the darkened living rooms of America, where images of the land are cast upon lenticular screens. "Oooh. Aaah," say the neighbors. "Beautiful. Just beautiful."

And so it is.

(Spring 1985)

WALLACE STEGNER

This Land

W hen Europeans found it, North America was very sparsely
peopled, and by their standards unowned. Therefore subject
to seizure. To men from a continent where land was a resource and not a commodity, and where it was entailed and primogenitured
and encumbered and parceled out by aristocrats to peasants under feudal
rules of tenure, free or unoccupied land was explosive with possibility. As
Walter Webb pointed out in *The Great Frontier,* only in America has the
word "claim" come to mean a parcel of land. That single word expresses a
revolution in attitudes. The historian who remarked that America's whole
history could be read as one continuous real estate transaction was not too
far off.

Land has been the creator of our wealth and the shaper of our expectations. From the sixteenth century onward we considered the virgin continent
ours for the taking. Some among us feel exactly the same way about the unappropriated remnants that we call the public domain. The value of that
public domain has increased exponentially during the very years when public policy was changing from disposal to retention and management by the
federal government. Earlier raids upon it have been inconsequential and
abortive. But the raid that began to gather force at the end of the 1970s and
that early acquired the name of Sagebrush Rebellion, is not inconsequential.
It could be so important to the future of the nation, and especially the West,
that it might even drive us back to history to learn what the public domain
means and where it came from.

Quieting native unrest with beads, bullets, and treaties not meant to be kept, Europeans claimed whole empires on the grounds that one of their kind had first sighted a headland, or put into a river mouth, or planted a cross. Francis Parkman describes what happened when LaSalle beached his canoes at the mouth of the Arkansas in 1692 and harangued a crowd of Indians in a language they didn't understand. "On that day," Parkman says in a famous passage, "the realm of France received on parchment a stupendous accession. The fertile plains of Texas; the vast basin of the Mississippi, from its frozen northern springs to the sultry borders of the Gulf; from the woody ridges of the Alleghenies to the peaks of the Rocky Mountains—a region of savannas and forests, sun-cracked deserts, and grassy prairies, watered by a thousand rivers, ranged by a thousand warlike tribes, passed beneath the sceptre of the Sultan of Versailles; and all by virtue of a feeble human voice, inaudible at half a mile."

Great expectations, unlimited opportunity. The fabulous treasures that the Spaniards found in Mexico and Peru led all the competing empires to hope for similar jackpots. All of Europe found a treasure of fish on the Newfoundland Banks, and the French found a strenuous treasure of furs in Canada. But most of the New World proved to be worthless unless settled, and so the monarchs who had acquired it by proclamation began giving it away to court favorites or colonizing companies, who in turn either disposed of it as headrights to settlers, or turned it into plantations worked by Indians, black slaves, or indentured servants, many of whom soon fled the coop and went off into the woods and settled on some land of their own by squatters' rights. In a country that, as Jefferson said, was rich in land and poor in labor, land to settle on and work came to be part of the human expectation.

The protracted real estate transactions went on. France lost Canada to the British on the Plains of Abraham in 1759. Twenty years later the American colonies forced England to acknowledge their independence. In 1803 Napoleon sold to the infant United States all that Louisiana Territory that LaSalle had claimed and named. Once started, the Americans spread like impetigo. In 1819 they forced Spain to sell Florida. In 1845 they absorbed the Republic of Texas and thus took over a big chunk of the old Spanish empire in America. In 1846, by the Oregon Treaty, they made good their claim to the Northwest. In 1848, defeated Mexico ceded the Southwest and California and five years later, in the Gadsden Purchase, sold the rest of what is now Arizona and New Mexico. Seventy years after the Revolution the mongrel Republic had spread from sea to sea, and from the 49th Parallel to the Rio Grande. The Alaska Purchase of 1867, and some island loot from Caribbean and Pacific wars, expanded the boundaries but had little effect on the formation of the national set of mind.

Seven of the original thirteen colonies held crown grants to western lands between the Alleghenies and the Mississippi. Six had no such lands. When the time came to sign the Articles of Confederation in 1777, Maryland, one of the six, refused to sign unless New York, Massachusetts, Connecticut, Virginia, Georgia, and the two Carolinas would cede their western lands to the federal government so that all could start equal. Beginning with New York in 1781 and ending with Georgia in 1802, the landed colonies made the cession. Congress in 1780 had defined the policy with regard to the proposed public domain: "Resolved, that the unappropriated lands that may be ceded or relinquished to the United States, by any particular states, pursuant to the recommendation of Congress . . . shall be disposed of for the common benefit of the United States, and be settled and formed into distinct republican states, which shall become members of the Federal Union, and shall have the same rights of sovereignty, freedom, and independence, as the other states."

Three laws were significant in the administration and disposal of that first public domain. The Ordinance of 1785 established the rectangular surveys into mile-square sections and gave one section in every thirty-six to the new states for support of education. The Northwest Ordinance of 1787, among other things, required that all new states formed out of the public domain formally renounce any claim to public domain lands and agree to respect the right of the federal government to dispose of them. That early, there were insurrectionary states-rights feelings that had to be squelched. And finally, in 1789, the Constitution, in Article IV, Section 3, gave Congress power to regulate and dispose of public lands. That authority has never been shaken in any court test.

Nevertheless, there was no intention, then or for a long time later, to retain any permanent public domain or extend federal ownership beyond the small amounts of land needed for military reservations, post offices, and other federal enterprises. Eventually, virtually all of that original public domain was disposed of to state, private, or corporate ownership and in accordance with the 1780 resolution was formed into new sovereign states.

The public domain that was added west of the Mississippi by purchase and conquest after 1803 was of a different sort. It had never belonged to any of the states, and was never ceded by them to the federal government. It was federal from the beginning. The demand today of some that the public domain be "returned" to the states is either ignorant or disingenuous. It could be *given* to them, conceivably; it could never be returned. Except for Texas, which was annexed as an independent republic and hence never has had any public domain, no state west of the Mississippi has ever had title to any of its territory except that granted it by Congress.

From the Articles of Confederation until 1872, every substantive land law dealt with ways by which the public lands should be sold or given away. The year 1872, which saw the reservation of Yellowstone National Park as a "pleasuring ground for all the people," marked the beginning of a change from disposal to retention. But the general policy of disposal was not substantially ended until the Taylor Grazing Act of 1934 and not formally repudiated until 1976, with the passage of the Federal Land Policy and Management Act.

The early land sales were mainly to speculators, and in wholesale lots. Individual settlers hunting land had either to buy it from speculators or go out ahead of the surveys and squat on a piece of the unappropriated continent. In 1841, through the Preemption Law, the government acknowledged the reality of their settlements and let them obtain legal title to 160 acres on payment of $1.25 an acre. A homestead law, many times proposed, was for a long time blocked by the South, which feared the creation of new free states in the West. But in 1862, after the outbreak of war, Congress passed, and Abraham Lincoln signed, the Homestead Act that would give any settler 160 acres in exchange for stipulated improvements and residence. Two years later the Morrill Act made large grants of lands to the states for the support of agricultural colleges, and after the Civil War the Desert Land Act, the Timber and Stone Act, and the Carey Act all continued the effort of the federal government to get rid of its domain. Enormous grants went to railroads, others to the states in support of canals, turnpikes, and other public improvements beneficial to the nation as a whole. Eventually, by one law or another, almost all the land east of the 100th meridian was disposed of.

But west of the 100th meridian, it began to be apparent, the patterns of settlement and the laws of disposal that worked well in fertile country with dependable rainfall did *not* work well. Settlers found it possible to hold on only to land with access to the water of springs, creeks, or rivers, and in altitudes that permitted farming or ranching. In the mining regions, beginning with the California Gold Rush and spreading later into Nevada, Colorado, Montana, Idaho, and Utah, the gold hunters were all out ahead of the surveys. Every gold or silver strike precipitated mass trespass on government land that was not only not policed but literally had no laws. Miners made their own laws, including water laws, and eventually saw them validated. But homesteaders trying to operate beyond the 100th meridian under the Homestead, Preemption, and Desert Land laws had to bet their lives against 160 acres that they could make agriculture pay in the dry country, and most of them lost. Vast areas were either never settled at all, or came back into the government's hands as the homesteaders dried up and blew away. Water was the difference between making it and not making it. The West grew up as an oasis civilization, and that is what it still is. The residual public domain is the unappropriated and long-unwanted land that holds the oases apart.

The individual who saw most clearly what was happening in the West, and who had the clearest vision of how settlement must be adapted to western conditions, was Major John Wesley Powell. He began as a public hero for his exploration of the Colorado River, rose swiftly to become the most powerful scientist and most effective bureaucrat in Washington (he headed both the United States Geological Survey and the Bureau of Ethnology), and ended up a defeated old man, put down by the West he had tried to educate, guide, and save.

His *Report on the Lands of the Arid Region,* in 1878, said more truth about the West in its first three chapters than had been said altogether up to then. Manifest Destiny and the boosterism that it encouraged envisioned a West more densely peopled than the Roman Empire under Trajan and the Antonines, believed that rain followed the plow and that settlement made the climate wetter, saw South Pass as a gateway more thronging than Gilbraltar, held to the faith of William Gilpin that on the dry plains settlers could *dig* both for wood and for water. Powell's *Report* said otherwise.

It asserted what the boosters and promoters were denying, that beyond the 100th meridian agriculture was possible only with the aid of irrigation, which was generally too much for the individual farmer to handle; that much of the well-watered land was too high, and most of the arable land too dry, for the raising of crops; that the rectangular surveys that worked well in humid country left thousands of square miles of potential homesteads in the West without access to water; and that the 160 acres allowed under the Homestead Act, though more than an intensive irrigation farmer could work, were totally inadequate for a stock farmer, who needed at least four sections, 2,560 acres. He thought the system should be changed to allow the formation of cooperative irrigation districts in which the surveys should conform to the terrain, so that every parcel, whether farm or ranch, should have a water right and a portion of irrigable land. Farm size should vary from 80 to 2,560 acres. Reservoirs and canals, impossible for individuals, should be built cooperatively. The federal government, except for providing a system within which homesteaders could succeed, should stay out of it.

The alternatives, Powell said, were already apparent: they were widespread homesteader failure and the monopolization of land through monopoly of water. Using their cowboys as fraudulent filers of homestead claims, cattle outfits were picking up the quarter and half sections containing springs, or land along the banks of rivers and thus controlling whole dukedoms of the public grass. Those homesteaders, "nesters," who had managed to find land where they had a chance, were coming into conflict with the stockmen, who cut their fences, shot their animals, threatened their families, and sometimes fired their haystacks or their houses.

Powell was a sort of early Populist. He was on the side of the Jeffersonian yeoman and the family farm and against the highhanded practices of some cattle outfits, many of which in that day were foreign-owned. His heresy, in the eyes of the Westerners who ultimately defeated him, was that he thought in terms of the democratic health of the society and the health of the resources upon which it must be built: land and water.

His *Report* brought about controversy, but little change. In that same year, 1878, Congress did put a 160-acre limitation into the Timber and Stone Act, but like the similar limitation in the Homestead Act, it was essentially an invitation to fraud. The Forest Service estimates that nearly one-third of the privately owned timber land in the Pacific Northwest was obtained through fraudulent entries—such practices as taking a whole shipload of sailors to the land office, having them file individual claims, and then giving them ten dollars, or a few drinks, for commutation of their claims to the company. In similar ways, such enormous land accumulations as those of Miller and Lux, on the San Joaquin River in California's Central Valley, were steering the West toward monopoly and factories in the field. On the Plains, the trouble between the nesters and the cattlemen came to a head in Johnson County, Wyoming, in 1892, when a posse of cattlemen rode north from Cheyenne to rub out some "rustlers." Some of them may indeed have been rustlers, but some of them were simply homesteaders trying to exercise their rights under American law, and all of them were harder to handle than the cattlemen anticipated. The posse in that "Johnson County War" was made up of ancestors of the Sagebrush Rebels. And Owen Wister, a friend of the leader of that ignoble outfit, cast their principles in bronze. He made the good-guy Virginian, that knight errant on a cowhorse, one of the vigilantes, and wrung readers' hearts with the Virginian's anguish at having to help string up Shorty—a friend, but a cattle thief, and hence subject to summary justice.

By 1888 the West was enduring a severe drought, and western members of Congress known to history as the "irrigation clique," under the leadership of Senator William Stewart of Nevada, pushed through legislation calling for a survey of reservoir sites. Powell, as the man who knew most about western land and water, and as head of the Geological Survey, was put in charge of the new survey, and he leaped at the opportunity to put some of his reforms into effect. He proposed to survey and inventory all the public lands in the West, locate reservoir and canal sites, designate lands as irrigable or non-irrigable, and thus give settlers an opportunity to locate on lands where they had a chance to survive. Senator Stewart's intentions were probably less altruistic, for when he found that by a freakish amendment to his legislation the public domain had been utterly closed to entry, he blew up. His friends in Reno and Carson City, having inside information, could not now file on reservoir sites as they were designated and make a good thing of them. What was worse, there was no quick way of reopening the public domain to entry. Only when Powell had finished his survey and designated western lands as irrigable or non-irrigable would he be required to certify certain areas to the President, who in turn would reopen them. And Powell was apparently going to take years about a task that Stewart had conceived as a quick reconnaissance.

Within a year Senator Stewart perceived that he had embraced a serpent. He became the bitter enemy of his own legislation and of Powell. By 1892 he and his colleagues of the Irrigation Clique had killed the appropriation for the irrigation surveys and cut Powell's Geological Survey budget; by 1894 they had forced Powell's resignation. They had also killed the first farsighted effort to give the West a system under which it could develop without either bitter individual failures or land and water monopoly by large interests. If Powell's plans had been given a chance to develop, the West would have reached a settlement equilibrium a great deal sooner, and the federal presence would probably be less. And it was the West itself, or its oligarchies, that broke Powell.

During 1889, when he and Senator Stewart were touring the West in something like harmony, Powell addressed the constitutional conventions of North Dakota, Montana, and Wyoming. He urged all of them, in planning their states, to lay out their counties not by arbitrary political lines but by drainage divides, so that watershed and timber, grazing-land foothills, and irrigable bottomland would all be interdependent parts of the same unit. He urged what later came to be called the Wyoming Doctrine, which tied water rights to land. And he made very little headway against habit, optimism, boosterism, and self interest. In 1893, addressing the Irrigation Congress in Los Angeles, he told those blue-sky boosters that they were laying up trouble, because there was only enough water in the West to take care of about 20 percent of the land. They booed him, as boosters might boo him now if he should return to tell them that they can't expect to fill the West with new towns, new cities, new resorts, stripmines, power plants, synfuel plants, slurry pipelines, and such goodies, and still have water for the traditional uses that have made the enduring life patterns of the West: ranching, irrigation farming, trout fishing, outdoor recreation, and Coors beer.

The West is full of ghost towns, and may be hatching a new crop. It is also full of vast ranges of what was once good grassland and is now mainly sagebrush, rabbitbrush, shadscale, and dust. (The basin of the Escalante River in Utah once carried 4,000 cattle and 12,000 sheep. Now it carries none.) One of the reasons for ghost towns and deteriorated ranges is that the West has always been subjected to the economics of liquidation. Another is that it is a collection of fragile ecosystems that too few of the people who lived in it understood, or do yet. Still another is that for decades everybody's land was nobody's land and was used without management, restriction, or responsibility.

A policy of disposal has to change if you find out that you can't dispose of something. With regard to the public domain the disposal policy began to change, as we have seen, when Yellowstone National Park was set aside in 1872. It took a big step toward retention in 1891, when an amendment to the General Land Law Revision Act authorized the President to create forest reserves from public lands and thus save at least a portion of the American forests from what had happened in Michigan and Wisconsin. Grover Cleveland and Theodore Roosevelt took full advantage of that authorization, and because only in the West was untouched forest land available their reservations were made west of the 100th meridian.

There were complaints from hungry timber interests, but the forest reserves were by no means imposed upon protesting western states by an authoritarian federal government. Many western cities wanted forest reserves around them to protect their vital watersheds. The Oregon legislature in 1889 *petitioned* the government in Washington, asking that the Cascade forests be set aside. (The request came to nothing because of the resistance of stock and timber interests.) After 1897, western landowners could take advantage of the "lieu lands" clause, and trade poor land within a proposed forest reserve for better land outside. That generated a good deal of local enthusiasm for forest reserves. And it should be noted that the Utah national forests that Senator Hatch wants "returned" to the state were carved out of land that had never been anything but federal, with the enthusiastic backing of both Utah officials and the Mormon Church.

Not that the disposal policy or its states' rights corollary submitted meekly to this gradual conversation. In the 1890s, Irrigation Congresses regularly asked that the unappropriated public lands be ceded to the states in support of irrigation projects—a plan that would have made some sense if the states had been financially capable of swinging such projects. The Carey Act of 1894, in fact, granted up to a million acres to any state willing to irrigate them. Willing or not, the states did not have the ability; historically only California has managed to develop and support a water plan of its own, and most of California's system is based on federally built projects. The Irrigation Congress was not long in understanding the facts of life, and the demand for cession was replaced by a demand for federal appropriations to assist irrigation and protect watersheds. The result was the Newlands (or Reclamation) Act of 1902, which in the next eighty years poured more money into western water projects than the lands they would water were worth.

In the beginning, the national forests had been under Interior, a department with a long history of corruption and land fraud. In 1905, on the urging of Gifford Pinchot, they were moved to Agriculture and put under Pinchot's aggressive direction. The multiple-use policy had not yet developed, and timber cutting on the reserves was minimal; the principal *use* of the forests was for grazing. Pinchot promptly proposed what had never been required before, a grazing fee. It struck stockmen, accustomed to free use of the public domain, as un-American. They refused to pay, sued the Forest Service, and stirred up their congressmen.

By 1907 they had succeeded in attaching to the Agricultural Appropriations Bill a rider banning creation of any further forest reserves in Washington, Oregon, Idaho, Montana, Wyoming, and Colorado without the consent of Congress, which in effect meant the consent of the western-dominated land committees. When the bill came to Roosevelt's desk for signature he knew that a veto could not be sustained. So he held the bill through the last days of his administration, worked furiously laying out new reserves, and only when he had created sixteen million acres of new federal forests, signed the bill that would have prevented him from doing so. Except for about 20,000 acres in Washington that promptly disappeared into the hands of the lumbermen, the reservations stuck, primarily because western public opinion was more for than against them.

Once initiated, permanent withdrawals from the public domain increased in number and multiplied in kind. Getting the Indian tribes onto reservations meant carving out large areas, many of them out of the poorest and apparently least usable land. Though national forests remained more or less fixed, national parks continued to be set aside, some of them out of the unappropriated public domain, some out of former national forests. The Antiquities Act of 1906 authorized the President to create national monuments in areas of great natural, historical, or archaeological value. Wildlife sanctuaries, national seashores and lakeshores, wild and scenic rivers, wilderness areas created under the Wilderness Act of 1964, all represent a strenghtening of the decision to hold onto and manage large sections of the public domain rather than try to dispose of them or let them deteriorate. Apart from the Indian reservations, these withdrawals represent pretty much the cream of the remaining public lands. What about the leftovers, the sage plains, the deserts, the barren mountains where the potential was thought to be almost exclusively minerals and grazing?

Mineral lands especially were of continuing interest to westerners, and the traditional practices of free exploration and entry were well established. When Theodore Roosevelt and William Howard Taft, between 1907 and 1910, withdrew from entry many non-metallic mineral deposits and potential waterpower sites, they encountered immediate stiff resistance. Western legislatures in 1913, 1914, and again in 1919 demanded (the old cry where apparently valuable resources were involved) that all remaining public lands be ceded to the states. They did not get the lands, perhaps did not expect to, but as is often the case in these federal-state disputes they got something just as good or better: the Mineral Leasing Act and the Water Power Act of 1920, which opened the Roosevelt-Taft reserves to exploitation under lease, and gave the states 90 percent of the mineral lease revenues and 87.5 percent from the licensing of power sites.

After that resounding success, states' rights agitation subsided for more than a decade. Why buy a cow when the milk is so cheap? Why take the risk of owning and managing lands that the federal government will manage in your behalf, giving you 90 percent of the proceeds? So in 1930, when Herbert Hoover and his Secretary of the Interior, Ray Lyman Wilbur, proposed to give to the states all the unappropriated public domains, minus its minerals, the states laughed. They already, said Governor George Dern of Utah, had more than plenty of that kind of land. "Why should the states want more of this precious heritage of desert?"

That was in 1930, the beginning of the Depression, the beginning of the Dust Bowl, when plowing, overgrazing, and cyclic drought had turned much of the Plains country into a disaster area. By 1934 the dust had blown clear to Washington, D.C., and converted an old fed-hater, Congressman Edward Taylor of Colorado, into a believer in federal rescue and management. He fathered the Taylor Grazing Act, which organized most of the remaining public lands into grazing districts and closed them to entry under any existing land law. The federal government, represented by the new Taylor Grazing Service, would manage them with the advice and consent of local district boards.

Predictably, some die-hard cattlemen resisted, denying that overgrazing had anything to do with erosion. Congressman Ayers of Montana introduced yet another bill that would have turned over the public domain to the states. But some people learned faster than Congressman Ayers. The appalling evidence of range deterioration through the western states was reinforced by the success of the Mizpah-Pumpkin Creek experiment in Montana, where careful range management increased the carrying capacity from 2,000 animals to 5,000 in six years. The Taylor Grazing Act, with its built-in range rehabilitation financed by the federal government, had broad support. But Senator Pat McCarran of Nevada (they're generally from Nevada, at once the driest and least reasonable of the western states) worked out his method of letting the feds pay for the restoration of the range while frustrating their efforts to regulate grazing: fill out the district advisory boards with local stockmen and keep the Grazing Service budget down to starvation levels. McCarran, one of the best friends special interests ever had, kept the Grazing Service poor and impotent through its short life. After the Grazing Service was fused with the General Land Office to form the Bureau of Land Management, the effectiveness of McCarran's formula did not decrease.

The Taylor Grazing Act virtually closed the public domain and ended the long-lived policy of disposal. But it did not *say* it did and so did not overtly repudiate a bankrupt policy. From the cattleman's point of view, it put the grazing lands in the hands of a bureau that could be milked for benefits while being controlled by its permittees. But the BLM Organic Act, FLPMA, passed by Congress in 1976, indicated an alarming change. It said outright that the public domain would hereafter be retained in perpetuity and managed in the national interest. It gave BLM, for the first time, not only an adequate budget but also greatly expanded powers and an expanded staff. It gave it specific management directives and an obligation to serve not only grazing interests but also other, and sometimes competing, interests such as wildlife management, wilderness protection, and public recreation. It asserted federal sovereignty over local tradition, the integrity of land and water resources over local and sometimes (not always) self-interested freedom of action. Unquestionably, the new hard line of the BLM Organic Act was dictated by a new perception of the national interest as against the regional western interest and by a new perception of the importance of the resources buried under the scruffy grass and inaccessible mountains of the West.

To the BLM Organic Act stockmen reacted predictably: FLPMA has been generally conceded to be the precipitating cause of the Sagebrush Rebellion. A good thing was threatened; federal managers were empowered to manage; AUM's (Animal Units per Month) might be cut; fees might be increased, deliberate trespass might not be condoned. And this at a time when cattle ranching was marginal or threatened with failure, when there were no beef price supports to match tobacco supports or milk supports (and hard-nosed cattlemen wouldn't have accepted beef price supports anyway; they would rather cut off their noses to spite their faces). Some BLM lands were closed to mineral exploration while being studied as permanent wilderness. It could even be that in the euphoria of sudden power, some BLM officials threw their weight around; at least they failed to observe the traditional subservience to local graziers and their politicians. And wildlife, whatever that meant, was held to be a legitimate use of the public domain. When Uncle Sam's elk or deer, wild burros or wild horses used the range, or broke into a rancher's haystacks, he was supposed not to get out his rifle but appeal to the local BLM office, which would probably cite him the multiple-use regulations.

Those were irritations to a traditional, well-organized, and barely economic industry. There was something else, within a year of the passage of FLPMA, that really scared the West and brought a good many allies to the original Sagebrush Rebels. In 1977 Jimmy Carter announced his "hit list" of proposed water projects that he intended to block. Of nineteen projects, seven were in the West, four in the Colorado River drainage basin. His announcement seemed to mean that after seventy-five years of pouring money into western reclamation, the eastern states, which have paid most of the bills, were getting tired of doing so. At the same time, President Carter indicated that he hoped to develop a national water policy. The double threat of reduced federal aid and increased federal participation in water decisions trod on every toe in the West, and the 100th meridian began to seem like a north-south Mason Dixon line. Western congressmen of both parties rose up and aborted most of President Carter's plans and cut his hit list drastically.

However justified it may have seemed as national policy, Carter's move was a political blunder and certainly had something to do with Reagan's 1980 sweep of the western states. On water matters, the otherwise diverse and disunited West is traditionally unanimous, or at the very least states are willing to trade support for the projects of others in exchange for support of their own.

The feds, despite serious mistakes and despite a recent tendency of the Forest Service to defect to the enemy, have always been the West's best chance for survival. They have made some parts of it what they are, and brought some parts of it halfway back from ruin. In its relations with Washington the West has been subsidized, not victimized; the land-managing bureaus have more often been patsies than tyrants.

The grazing fee on Taylor lands from 1936 to 1946 was a nickel per animal unit month. By 1966 it had gone up to thirty-three cents, by 1974 to a dollar. In the 1980s, at something over two dollars in the Jackson Hole area, it is less than half of what comparable private grazing land leases for; and if there are hindrances and restrictions on federal land that are not imposed on private land, that fact should be matched against the controlling fact that there isn't nearly enough private land to serve ranchers' needs. Though less a bargain than they were, the BLM and forest grazing leases are the resource that keeps many ranchers afloat, and there is every prospect that with improved management they will get better, not worse. Moreover, half the grazing fees collected go to the state, and half of the federal half is plowed back into range improvement. Furthermore, the states get big federal payrolls; extra highway aid through public lands; free development of national parks, which in some states are the biggest source of tourist revenue; free management of forests and watersheds, which to cities such as Salt Lake are virtually local parks and playgrounds. They still get half the mineral-lease bonuses, royalties, and rentals, amounting in most western states to several millions each year, and in Wyoming to $39.4 million in 1979. From the Outer Continental Shelf lands in Oregon, once granted to a railroad and on collapse of the railroad reclaimed by the federal government, the timber payments totaled $86.7 million in that same year. Of that, according to the prevailing formula, 50 percent went to the state, 50 percent to the federal government, which in turn invested half of its half in timber improvement programs. Also, all public lands states get many millions in lieu of taxes.

And not only money. That open space that fills your vision and lifts your heart when you drive across the West is federal open space, most of it. Federally owned, protected, managed, federally kept open to almost any sort of reasonable public use. If it brings some irritations from hordes of tourists, it also fills the local treasury, and it gives a large part of the spaciousness and satisfaction to western living. As for wilderness areas, if we had had to depend on the states for their protection, there would pretty clearly be none.

The Sagebrush Rebels, bemused by their own mythology, are fond of asserting that rugged individualism built the West, pioneer grit and self reliance. It is true that the West's history is punctuated with the lives of rugged individualists—Henry Villard, Marcus Dailey, Henry Miller, Jim Hill—but they built such things as railroad empires, land empires, and the Anaconda Copper Company. Who built the West as a living-place, a frugal, hard, gloriously-satisfying civilization scrabbling for its existence against the forces of weather and a land as fragile as it is demanding, was not rugged individuals but cooperators, neighbors who knew how to help out in crises, who could get together to build a school and figure out a way to get the kids there, pool their efforts to search for lost cattle or lost people, and join in infrequent blowouts, dances, and fairs. It was rugged individualists who *raped* the West, some successfully, some not. One remembers Bernard DeVoto's remark that the only true rugged individualists in the West generally wound up at the end of a rope whose other end was in the hands of the cooperating citizenry.

Unfortunately, the West has already gone a long way on the booster road, and federally developed water has made possible a lot of what is called Prog-ress but might well be called something else. A river such as the Colorado is dammed and managed from its headwaters to what used to be its mouth—there isn't a mouth now, the river dies in the sand miles from the Gulf. One keeps remembering that reservoir sites have a predictable life, on the Colo-rado, of not much more than a hundred years, and Boulder Dam was built nearly fifty years ago. One can't help being aware that the closer it gets to its end, the more saline the Colorado's many-times-used water becomes, and that only an expensive desalinization plant allows the United States to fulfill its obligation of 1,500,000 acre-feet of usable water to Mexico.

No western states except those on the Pacific Coast can permanently sup-port large populations. Nor can they support, without drastic consequences, continued application of the economics of liquidation. The extermination of the beaver and the bison, the gold and silver rushes, could be recovered from; the rivers still run, though without the flood protection of beaver en-gineering; the abandoned drifts crumble in the dry hills; the grass, with great effort, can be brought back after decades of overgrazing.

But the contemporary raids on coal, oil, gas, and uranium, the high-pow-ered explorations for every sort of extractable wealth, threaten to destroy the one appropriate, enduring, and renewable future for much of the West, espe-cially of the northern plains and Rockies, which is grass. Industry threatens the integrity of every western town exposed to it, and the thousands of megawatts of electricity from coal that are already being produced or are on the drawing boards threaten both the air and the clean space. Immigrants hungry for just the goodness of life that much of the West still provides en-danger what they come seeking. Much of the West, sparse as its population is by comparison with that of the Midwest or Northeast or even California, is over-populated right now. The rivers are oversubscribed, the groundwater is pumped down—and that is the ultimate bank account. When that is gone a place is in trouble, like a Vermont farmer who has been forced to log his sugarbush in a last desperate effort to stay solvent.

If the West is going to be saved in anything like its present state, it will not be by the states or the oligarchs who dominate most western capitals. It will be accomplished, if at all, by the greatest cooperation possible between state and federal, private and federal, private and state, business and agricul-ture. The Sagebrush Rebellion is a delusion, an anachronism, in some part a selfish attempt at a grab whose consequences the grabbers either do not see or do not care about.

A little less boosterism, a little less mobility (it is graveyards that give sta-bility to towns, and most western graveyards hold only one generation of a family), a little more consideration of the earth, which is all we have to live on, and the water, which is all we have to live by, would become us. The West is not only beautiful and spacious and exhilarating, it is also very fragile. Westerners would do well to examine their own relation to it and learn to live in harmony with it, instead of joining those who, as Aldo Leopold said, are trying to remodel the Alhambra with a bulldozer and proud of their yardage.

If Westerners are uneasy about the future, they have reason. But it seems to this observer that federal control of the public domain and the continuing strength of the federal land-managing bureaus are indispensable parts of the future. Without them, in fact, there may not *be* much of a future.

A note from the editors: In the summer of 1981, when Wilderness *published this article, the "Sagebrush Rebellion" was in full flower, supported both philosophically and politically by Interior Secretary James Watt, Bureau of Land Management Director Robert Burford, and others in the administration of President Ronald Reagan. Among other things, the movement called for the "privatization" of many public lands, either through direct sales or by transfer from federal to state ownership; the primacy of local control over federal control in management decisions; and other notions designed to accelerate resource extraction and weaken or even eliminate most environmental protection for such lands.*

Unsupported by a significant core of power in Congress and at odds with the sentiments of the American public at large, the movement had declined appreciably by the latter third of the 1980s. But the instincts that fired it had not died, and it has since surfaced again, this time in the guise of a "Wise Use" movement that has launched a powerful assault against the federal management of federal lands and every environmental law on the books, from the Wilderness Act of 1964 to the Endangered Species Act of 1973. Its leaders bill it as a "grassroots" movement, but it is largely financed (and often led) by the mining, timber, and livestock industries, and with a growing Congressional base it appears likely that it will continue to play an increasingly significant role in public land management and species protection decisions for years to come.

BRYAN G. NORTON

The Spiral of Life

L ife creates life—a puzzle and a paradox. Left undisturbed, forms of life reproduce themselves and multiply, creating a stunning variety of species and natural communities. When the first European settlers arrived in the New World about 400 years ago, they encountered an untamed wilderness busily engaged in this ancient task of making and remaking life. The settlers immediately began to tame the land, making it useful for fulfilling human needs. And everywhere they went, they interrupted and modified the processes that had generated, over millennia, life's great diversity of form.

Only later did a few visionaries begin to worry that they were destroying something of value. Gradually the idea emerged that communities of life and the processes that formed them have irreplaceable value; over time, a system of forests, parks, refuges, and wilderness areas was set aside: the public lands, which, as Paul Ehrlich notes in his essay for this issue, remain America's last best hope of preserving the biological diversity—biodiversity—necessary to a viable future. The power of the creative force biologists call "adaptation and natural selection" is exhibited in all these publicly owned areas. In a remnant of the great tropical moist forest that once covered Puerto Rico and in an oasis in the Mojave desert; in tiny patches of tall-grass prairie remaining in the Midwest and in old-growth forests of the northern Pacific Coast; in all of these and dozens more, one can see the multiple versions of life's creativity.

In what follows we will briefly explore eight showcases for biodiversity, all but one of which are part of the public lands system. Each has the power to amaze. But if a tour through varied ecosystems is to reveal the mysteries of the creative force, rather than just parade its results, one must do more than visit in awe: one must also examine the processes and mechanisms that generate variety in nature.

Medieval theologians who puzzled about how God could exist eternally and yet be the creator of all things, concluded that He must have created Himself. Had He not created Himself, they reasoned, He would be dependent, unGodlike. This idea supplied the ultimate explanation in the Great Chain of Being—everything else depends on God and is shaped by His will; but God depends only on Himself. God must be a self-moved mover.

The idea of self-generation thus has a long history in Western culture; it is nonetheless surprising to find that it also plays a central role in modern biology. This point was brought strikingly home to me once when I was speaking with an ecologist friend, pestering him to say something, without qualification, on the murky subject of diversity and stability relationships. Finally, in exasperation, he said, "The only thing we can say for sure in this area is that diversity creates more diversity." This is the theory of Robert H. Whittaker, the late botanist and theoretical ecologist who worked at Cornell University. Diversity, he maintained, creates and sustains diversity. It is an elegantly simple idea, hardly surprising once you think of it, and it holds the key to understanding the panoply of diversity encountered in natural systems.

So biology mimics theology. Its ultimate explanation is that life, wherever it came from, creates itself. The force of nature is in this respect Godlike; the earth's community of life is a self-moved mover. This much, as the theologians said, is self-evident. But it is the mechanism by which life generates itself that is so devilishly fascinating.

To understand the apparently limitless upward spiral of diversity, it is helpful to employ some concepts that Whittaker introduced in 1960. Diversity comes in three varieties, or levels. Whittaker called them alpha, beta, and gamma diversity; today they are referred to more descriptively as within-habitat diversity, cross-habitat diversity, and total diversity. Thus, as we visit our eight representative ecosystems, we will not just travel horizontally across the geographic expanse of the country, from Puerto Rico to the Pacific Northwest, but also on a rollercoaster ride up and down Whittaker's three levels of diversity, all of this adding up to a startling variety. The different levels of diversity are worthy of special attention, for it is in the subtle interplay between and among them that we must seek answers to the puzzle of life's self-generation.

We will, for example, encounter within-habitat diversity in Caribbean National Forest, a tropical rainforest where the processes of nature have created a complex web of co-evolved species in dense forests; while at Ash Meadows National Wildlife Refuge, where tiny, almost-isolated microhabitats exist in and around spring-fed desert ponds, we will see the adaptational forces that cause within-habitat diversity to generate cross-habitat diversity; and at Great Smoky Mountains National Park, we'll see how these forces contribute, on a much larger scale, to cross-habitat diversity and to total diversity.

It is usually total diversity that environmentalists tout when they say we should "preserve diversity." The old-growth forests of the Pacific Northwest, among the oldest forests in the world, show the essential role of mature forests in supporting specialized and highly co-evolved associations of species that represent the pinnacle of the evolutionary process. The total diversity of any area, from a backyard to the globe as a whole, is the product of its within-habitat diversity and its cross-habitat diversity. Total diversity is, roughly speaking, the sum total of species existing in a geographical area and the genetic variability embodied in the gene pool of particular species. It therefore represents the stock of potential colonizers in the battle to create and invade new niches. The Yellowstone Complex, consisting of the national park and contiguous national forests, is spread over 13 million acres of publicly owned land in three states. It illustrates how, from microhabitat to macrosystem, the forces of nature create the multi-tiered multiplicity of living things.

We will see also the fragility of such systems. Human-wrought changes threaten the national parks, forests, and refuges. Payette National Forest on the Idaho Batholith exhibits, in the bare bedrock of hillsides stripped by mudslides in 1965, the delicacy of the accommodation life makes with the granite hills there. In Kesterson National Wildlife Refuge, selenium leachate from surrounding irrigation projects has poisoned the water and the migratory waterfowl that visit the refuge. Finally, we'll visit the national park that doesn't yet exist. We will see a few remnants of the tallgrass prairies and a valiant attempt to replace the irreplaceable. The goal is to rebuild, in a tallgrass prairie preserve, a system approaching in intricacy the association of grasses and fires and bison that once covered more than a million square miles.

Just as diversity creates itself, generating an upward spiral, losses in diversity generate further losses, as extinctions and local extirpations threaten other species that depended on their lost mutualists. The upward diversity spiral can thus reverse and begin a downward spiral. In the worst case, nature fails. Species die out in increasing numbers and more and more are threatened in turn. The spiral accelerates downward and eventually the self-supporting forces of life collapse. Only opportunistic species survive. Winds and rain strip topsoil from denuded hillsides—death begets more death.

As humans develop more and more sophisticated tools, as they travel more deeply into areas once uninhabited by technological cultures, the diversity of America is threatened. And here we do not worry only about the loss of one species, though each loss is regrettable, but also about losses in the variety of associations that species inhabit; for it is the variety of associations in which plants and animals participate that forces them to face multiple evolutionary regimens, to develop varied adaptations and, eventually, to create new species.

If natural diversity survives and flourishes here, it will be because we leave some areas largely alone, letting the forces that create and sustain life continue, forever wild.

Caribbean National Forest

The Caribbean National Forest, the only sizeable publicly owned tropical rainforest in the United States, contains 250 tree species, more than any of our other national forests, on less than 30,000 acres. This small remnant of the vast forest that once covered most of Puerto Rico exemplifies the role of tropical rainforests, the most rapidly disappearing biome in the world, in developing and supporting global diversity. The tropical forests are home to at least 40 percent of the world's species while occupying less than 10 percent of the earth's land surface.

Scientists don't yet know exactly why there are so many species of plants and animals in the tropics. Surely it has something to do with a steady supply of sun and rain through all seasons. The lack of seasonal variation frees species from the threat of a cold and resource-poor winter. Under tropical conditions, species expend far less energy in dealing with their environment and turn on one another. The resulting riot of diversity stems from processes called "niche differentiation" and "species packing." Species adapt to narrower and narrower niches along a limiting gradient, such as a variation in food source. For example, up to four species of pigeons, which differ mainly in weight, feed on a single fruit tree in the tropical forests of New Guinea. The successful smaller and lighter birds are adapted to feeding on fruit growing on successively smaller branches outward from the trunk.

The results of this specialization are astounding. Terry Erwin of the Smithsonian Institution's Man and Biosphere Program extrapolated, from species collected in Panama, that as many as 12,500 species of beetles may live in one hectare (2.6 acres) of tropical rainforest canopy. In Puerto Rico, the diversity is less extreme because of the limited supply of species available on islands to invade, compete, and colonize. And yet one finds, here on this small island, remarkable variety, including the only wild living representatives of the Puerto Rican parrot, most of the few remaining Puerto Rican boa constrictors, and countless insects. All depend on the large variety of tree species and their associated tangles of undergrowth. There are so many species in the tropics because life there is freed of the fetters of many environmental constraints. Once freed, the competition is stiff. Incompetent competitors, the weedy species that colonize quickly because they have generalized adaptations, eventually lose out to more specialized and well-adapted species, and these will occupy narrower and narrower niches. To a large extent, this means each species comes to depend increasingly on some other species—the pigeons in the fruit tree, for instance, each of them making a living from a different part of the same tree. Without this single tree, four species of pigeons (not to mention any number of ants and bugs) could not survive.

In a fifty-year management plan issued in 1986, the U.S. Forest Service noted that "a vast diversity of grasses, forbs and other non-wood herbaceous species are present," but "a systematic inventory of understory vegetation has not been conducted in the Forest, and no data are available on understory associations or communities." In short, the agency does not know what it has under its protection or how much could be destroyed through careless management.

That could be a great deal. The intense competition for resources in tropical forests means that there are very few nutrients free-floating in the system. Consequently, forest soils are poor, and topsoil is thin. Because species are so entwined in their adaptations and because the soils are so poor, tropical ecosystems are extremely fragile. The complex interrelationships that constitute and fuel the growth of diversity also make it vulnerable. As species are lost from a tropical ecosystem, others are endangered. The upward diversity spiral is reversed. Species are removed from the system and others, adapted to the vanished species rather than abiotic conditions, falter. A downward spiral is begun and accelerates. The result is seen in places like Haiti and Madagascar: denuded hillsides, dead plains, and soil washing to sea in unrestrained orange rivers.

Ash Meadows National Wildlife Refuge

When the last ice age receded, water was trapped underground and still springs onto the earth's surface not far from Death Valley, sustaining a beautiful oasis called Ash Meadows. Only a few species survived the abrupt changes in climate at the end of the last ice age, but these, marooned with a supply of fresh water, have flourished like Swiss Family Robinsons. In only ten thousand years, an eye-twinkling in evolutionary time, they have created a unique island of life surrounded by a sea of sand.

As the environment changed from moist and cool to dry and hot, most species of fish went extinct. A few survived, however, in isolated spring-fed pools and, like Darwin's famous finches in the Galapagos Islands, they adapted to widely varied local conditions, speciated, and created a laboratory in evolutionary theory. The most celebrated inhabitants of Ash Meadows are the several hundred Devil's Hole pupfish that live in a single population 50 feet underground in a pool in a limestone cavern. These and other desert fish that evolved quickly in desert pools of varied alkalinity, sometimes isolated by only a short distance, appear to support the theory of punctuated equilibrium. According to that theory, evolution occurs in bursts of rapid change, rather than by gradual increments.

Similarly, 200 species of plants, some of them endemic to the alkali barrens of the area and others that differ significantly from their relatives elsewhere, represent a remarkable illustration of the forces creating diversity. Isolated in unusual and varied micro-habitats in a desert oasis, the plants developed unusual characteristics in response to unusual and varied conditions. As collections of plants and animals are isolated from larger breeding populations, they compete for space, colonizing particular micro-habitats where they have a minor advantage. At Ash Meadows, varied alkalinity and water availability create remarkable gradients of habitat in a small geographical area.

Species adapt to particular micro-habitats, and in the process alter the environmental conditions under which the ongoing competition continues there. These alterations provide new opportunities for yet further species, and more and more species find a niche. Each new species also alters the environment for further competition. Initially similar habitats are thereby partitioned into differing micro-habitats with varied opportunities for new colonizers. While initial developments in diversity are mainly within-habitat, evolutionary time leads to an increase in cross-habitat diversity as the processes of competition and co-evolution create greater and greater variety in environments available for new colonizers.

Ash Meadows, which was recently rescued from developers who would have constructed 20,000 resort homes on it, has been preserved after it was purchased by the Nature Conservancy and turned over to the U.S. Fish and Wildlife Service as a wildlife refuge. The Service plans to restore degraded areas and do what is possible to protect the unique and beautiful communities there, which include nearly two dozen endemic species. Perhaps even more importantly, the preservation of Ash Meadows is the preservation of a process—a tiny laboratory where the forces of colonization and competition, of adaptation and evolution, can continue. Such living laboratories are essential if we are to succeed in unravelling the mechanisms by which increasing within-habitat diversity alters local conditions to contribute to greater cross-habitat diversity and, ultimately, to the much-prized total diversity of our planet.

Southern Appalachian Forests

The Great Smoky Mountains Handbook, published by the Park Service, features "A One-day Walk to Maine." In this brief chapter, the reader is encouraged to follow, by foot or imagination, a climb from the "cove" forests of the lowlands to "balds," high areas that support no forest canopy. The trail from cove to bald meanders through every major forest type characteristic of the eastern United States. Increasing elevation becomes a metaphor for latitudinal change, and the reader is first led through second-growth forests of the once-farmed lowlands and then through primeval stands of the southern "cove" forests that blanketed the low areas before the arrival of European settlers. The path leads upward through oak-hickory forests, and then into the more open, sun-drenched pine forests that allow sufficient sunlight to penetrate and nourish a tangled thicket of mountain laurel as undergrowth. Pressing upward, hikers encounter beeches, birches, maples, and buckeyes, vegetative patterns familiar in New England. Finally, after a detour to examine the unique Appalachian heath balds and grass balds, the hike culminates in a spruce-fir forest on a mountain peak—Maine in Tennessee. Great Smoky Mountains National Park is therefore introduced as a living laboratory of cross-habitat diversity. It is no accident that it was here, in 1947, that the young Robert Whittaker began developing his theories describing the self-augmenting forces that create and sustain biodiversity.

Varied terrain, from valley to mountaintop, has provided multiple stages on which the historical drama of ecological competition and evolutionary selection has unfolded. Temperature gradients caused by differing elevations change the composition of the canopy; the park contains about 130 tree species, more than exist in all of northern Europe. Differing temperatures and canopy densities, in turn, provide varied conditions for the struggles among other species, as those with differing tolerances to temperature variations exploit their advantages up and down the mountainsides. Equally important, every slope causes the sun to strike the earth at a different angle, differentially favoring species with dissimilar requirements for sunlight.

Water availability also varies, as some areas are splashed by waterfalls and sprays, the result of heavy rains tumbling down the mountains on the way to the Tennessee River. In addition to affecting vegetative and insect diversity along the way, the varied stream habitats provide a home for seventy species of fish, and the Tennessee River system as a whole has more species of fish than any other in North America.

But environmental variation is only half the story: the Southern Appalachians have been south of the ice and above the sea for many millions of years. Subtropical vegetation flourished here 65 million years ago, while temperate vegetation grew north to the Arctic. As temperatures cooled at the onset of the ice age, and then warmed and cooled several times subsequently, vegetation types receded and advanced, with cold-sensitive species finding shelter in valleys while temperate and even arctic vegetation clung to the mountaintops. The Smokies thus became a patchwork of "refugia," remnant habitats of species with special adaptations that could maintain their existence in small patches because of the variation in temperature and sunlight afforded by the mountains.

Given these two ingredients, varied environmental conditions and a wealth of species (total diversity) available to compete and colonize, evolutionary forces worked their magic through passing time. Species competed and adapted to local conditions and to species already present in varied patches. The competition continued as species adapted to species, developing symbiotic relationships at the same time they altered the environment in which other species competed.

The variegated structure of the forest, with its overstory, understory, and forest floor, features three horizontal planes of habitats, a three-dimensional chessboard on which the game of survival is played. Complex interactions create unique characteristics as species develop adaptations in response to shifting patterns of competition and dependency. As each new species establishes itself, its special characteristics provide opportunities for yet more invading species. As a result of these processes, the park is home to 1,500 species of flowering plants, 2,000 species of fungi, 50 mammals, 200 birds, and 80 species of amphibians and reptiles (including 22 species of salamanders—more than any other place of similar size in the world). They all live in a harlequin environment, with patches overlapping patches, in a wonderland of cross-habitat variety.

Old-Growth Forests

Timber interests disparagingly refer to the spotted owl as "the billion-dollar bird." The populations of this shy and retiring bird have been declining steadily, and the species has become the center of a pitched battle between conservationists and lumber producers, with Forest Service and Bureau of Land Management (BLM) policies as the battlefield. The northern spotted owl depends on old-growth forests of the Pacific Northwest for its survival. These forests have declined precipitously under the lumberjack's saw and now cover only one-fifth of their original 15 million acres, with

most of the remainder existing in national forest and BLM land. The economically pressed forest industry insists that it needs to log the remaining
old-growth forests to stay in business and that the spotted owl is too costly
to save.

But placing a price tag on a predator species like the spotted owl, as if it
were a parakeet in the pet-shop window, may result from asking the wrong
questions. The forests of the Pacific Northwest are among the oldest in
America, and the spotted owl has been integrated by millennia of competition
and evolution into the multi-storied habitat created under the canopy of 200-
foot-high Douglas fir and hemlock; its fate cannot be separated from that of
the old-growth forests as a working ecosystem. A breeding pair of spotted
owls requires anywhere from 2,000 to 4,000 acres of old-growth forest, depending on location. As the forests on which they depend are fragmented, the
owls are only the first of many species to be threatened—perhaps the largest
number of bird species of any forests in the United States, together with such
other creatures as bats, flying squirrels, and martens. These species depend, in
turn, on a rich plant and invertebrate population that is generated from decaying logs on the forest floor. The timber barons call this "waste" and refer
to mature forests as "cellulose cemeteries," but it is in these logs that the spiral of diversity generates more and greater life from death. For the trees on
which the animals depend in turn depend on the animals—redbacked voles
eat the fruiting bodies of fungi on dead logs and excrete their spores on new
sites. These spores grow into fungi that carry necessary nutrients and moisture to tree seedlings.

Even if disturbed and early successional-managed forests have in some
cases more species than old-growth forests (a fact often cited by production-
oriented foresters), the mature forests are essential to the protection of total
diversity because there are highly adapted and specialized species that exist
there and nowhere else. Only in systems where the processes of evolution
have worked for ages, fashioning exquisitely developed relationships among
species, can there develop the specialization required to lengthen food chains
and support species like the spotted owl. Thus, even if open fields and second-growth forests approach or exceed mature stands in within-habitat diversity, they cannot replace old-growth in providing habitat for the specialized
species that have evolved in highly developed systems. It is these species that
represent the vanguard of evolution, and we cannot protect the total diversity
of our nation without saving adequate stands of mature forests. The loss of
the spotted owl would signal the demise of a complex web of relationships,
and the fragmentation that causes that demise will, in the end, lead to the
demise of an irreplaceable, interconnected system. If that happens, our nation
will be, to that degree, impoverished.

The Yellowstone Complex

It is a grand experiment: can wild grizzlies and civilized humans coexist in the same region? The grizzly is gone from most of the rest of the contiguous forty-eight states, and the Yellowstone Complex—which includes the national park, neighboring Grand Teton National Park, and the seven national forests surrounding them—is our last real chance to prove ourselves compatible neighbors.

The average range of an adult male grizzly in the Yellowstone area is more than three hundred square miles. This fact explains why it is at once so difficult and so important to save the grizzlies. The bears are omnivores, often eating berries and roots as well as prey and carrion. Because of their voracious summer appetite and varied diet, the bears roam widely from mountain berry patches to elk and bison pastures to salmon streams. The grizzlies therefore are an important indicator species—if the bears could maintain a healthy and stable population without human assistance, we would know that the varied habitats on which they depend are surviving as well.

But the indications are not good. As more and more vacationers and residents have used the park and surrounding areas, the grizzlies encounter limits on their search for food, and are sometimes killed because they interfere with human activities. Scientists fear that if the present downward trend in grizzly populations continues, the bears will disappear from Yellowstone within decades.

Why is it so important to save the great bears? There are, after all, large and healthy populations in Canada and Alaska, and skeptics, citing the great problems involved in mixing bears, tourists, and grazing livestock, have argued that the Yellowstone bears are not worth the considerable cost and trouble required to save them. Environmentalists and the National Park Service, however, believe the grand experiment is worth the trouble because the Yellowstone Complex, with its splendid large mix of federal parks and forests, may provide a rare opportunity to practice "whole ecosystem management."

We have learned, through a series of tragedies and miscalculations, how little we know about complete ecosystems and how to protect them. In the process, we also have learned the value of a nearly complete system in our quest for a deeper and more effective understanding of natural areas. Early in this century the national parks were thought of largely as "game ranches," areas where wild species valued for sport were protected for controlled hunting within a park or as stock that would wander across park boundaries into prime hunting areas surrounding it. As part of the effort to maximize populations of moose, elk, and mule deer, a concerted predator eradication program was carried out at Yellowstone from 1915 until 1938. Wolves and mountain lions were eliminated by 1930, in the name of the public's desire to maximize game species. Wildlife managers in the twenties and thirties thought that they could replace the predators with human hunters and thereby regulate the game herds. But the disappearance of wolves and mountain lions was followed by the swift overpopulation of elk, moose, and eventually even bison. Starving herds overgrazed their ranges and began to threaten a number of the plant communities in the park. As Aldo Leopold concluded, regretting his part in exterminating wolves from the Southwest, hunting is at best a blunt instrument for managing wildlife. The only precision instrument is a natural predator-prey relationship.

Ecologists use the term "ecosystem" to describe a complex of related communities and their physical environments. The term functions to delineate a temporary and conventional boundary for the purposes of scientific study, isolating one system of interacting species from those that surround it. So ecosystems come in many sizes and often overlap one another. When ecologists speak of a pond or an isolated valley as an "ecosystem," they merely invoke a conventional boundary within which they can measure energy flows—they are well aware that, in fact, ecosystem edges are permeable membranes with energy flowing across them, often in the form of larger animals that wander across these boundaries in search of food. We can say, then, that the Yellowstone Complex, with bears, approximates a whole ecosystem.

Where highly adapted predators like grizzlies range across smaller natural boundaries, they impose a regimen of natural selection and survival of the fittest on grazing species. If we can observe a system large enough to exhibit the interactions of grazing species and the larger predators that intersect the subsystems in which the grazers feed, it may be possible to learn how variety is created in the complicated interplay of the three levels of diversity.

That is Yellowstone's singular value, and the hope is to return it, gradually, to natural control, decreasing the role of human management; and then, perhaps, to reintroduce wolves, thereby re-establishing another link in the essentially interrelated system that worked at Yellowstone before the arrival of European settlers. Rangers at Yellowstone sometimes say that the real resource there is not any particular species, but "wildness." It is an especially valuable resource because of its rarity in the contiguous United States and because of its scientific importance—Yellowstone may present our best chance to study the full, uninterrupted system by which the diversity of America has created and sustained itself.

Aldo Leopold, writing forty years ago, recognized that humans have become the dominant species on the American continent: "Above all we should, in the century since Darwin, have come to know that man, while now captain of the adventuring ship, is hardly the sole object of its quest, and that his prior assumptions to this effect arose from the simple necessity of whistling in the dark." Leopold, who participated in those Southwest predator eradication programs early in his career in the Forest Service, came to realize that, when it comes to the management of natural systems, we are still whistling in the dark. He became a powerful advocate of wilderness preservation and protection of predators, arguing that we must minimize human management of wild areas if we are to have any chance of maintaining self-regulating systems. The trick, he might tell us today, is to edge the Yellowstone system back toward the ideal of a natural ecosystem, delicately "managing for wildness" at the edges, so that we can step back and watch the grand experiment.

Idaho Batholith

The South Fork of the Salmon River, which drains much of the vast Idaho batholith, was once the most productive spawning area for summer chinook salmon in the entire Columbia River basin. The batholith is a huge outcropping of granitic rocks that erodes into streambed gravel and provides ideal spawning habitat for anadromous fish, mainly salmon and steelhead trout, that live in the oceans but are born and spawn in the headwaters of rivers. The South Fork once produced 50,000 adult chinook annually, 55 percent of the population of the Columbia drainage.

Then, in 1965, after clear-cutting and road-building had left the fragile, granitic soils vulnerable, heavy rains and melting snow caused over 500 separate mudslides that stripped mountainsides bare of their mantle of soil and life. A U.S. Senate hearing document described the result of what came to be called "The Big Blow-Out": "Along twenty-five miles of the South Fork, the soil seemed to dissolve and run like wet concrete. Roads slumped and collapsed for great distances. Roads failed high on hillsides, slid down onto others, and set off a domino-like chain reaction that stripped entire slopes of their soil. The forest opened to reveal swatches of naked bedrock, as dislodged trees flowed away."

Most of the soil ended up in the South Fork. Four hundred thousand cubic yards of sediment were dumped into the streambed, and the finer soils mixed with the gravel and changed the ideal salmon and trout habitat. Now, some estimates of the spawning population of chinook are as low as 300 individuals, and steelhead trout are spawning at only 10 percent of their historical rate.

The U.S. Forest Service, in a remarkable act of bureaucratic amnesia, has proposed, once again, heavy logging and road-building in the drainage of the South Fork. They propose to remove 110 million board feet by the year 2005, three-quarters of it by the "tractor-jammer" method, the most destructive allowed by the Forest Service. It is as if they haven't learned two crucial facts implied by the last disaster.

First, the Big Blow-Out shows the fragility of the accommodation that life achieves in certain vulnerable habitats. The unstable soil of the Idaho batholith is largely held in place only by the trees and other vegetation— cover that restrains the decomposing rock from being carried into the streams by rain and melting snow. For its part, the crumbling batholith provides topsoil for the vegetation. If the vegetation is removed, the rocks are more quickly eroded, and the resulting soil-making sediment ends up in streams—crippling the opportunity for vegetative regrowth.

Second, the problems of the anadromous fish illustrate the tight interrelationships that evolve among species in undisturbed areas. The incredibly complex adaptations required to allow fish to be born and mature in freshwater mountain streams, spend their lives in the ocean, and return years later to spawn in the same stream involve a most delicate balance. The fish are so finely tuned to their environment that the size of the gravel in a streambed can determine their viability as a species. Tree removal by tractorjamming, even miles upstream, is not a part of the delicate balance they've evolved over millennia, because those human activities can change the mix of gravel and fine sediment in their spawning pools. The salmon and the trout are, one might say, adapted to the lodgepole and yellow pines on the mountainsides; they won't survive without them. And if the salmon and trout don't survive, then the whole Columbia River system will be damaged—a lesson the Forest Service should have learned in 1965.

Kesterson Wildlife Refuge

"That really spooks them. Except for the coots. They just swim into the reeds and wait until we leave." The speaker, a wildlife biologist, was describing rocket-borne whistles and propane explosives that imitate shotguns. These devices are now used to drive migratory birds out of Kesterson National Wildlife Refuge in California's Central Valley. The irony of this situation, of a supervisor for animal damage control driving waterfowl out of a wildlife refuge, illustrates the difficulty of maintaining suitable habitat for wildlife in this modern age of high-tech farming and the relentless encroachment of human activities on formerly wild areas.

Prior to settlement, the Central Valley of California contained about four million acres of wetlands and nearly a million acres of riparian forests. These areas represented winter habitat or temporary quarters for most of the migratory waterfowl that breed in Alaska and use the Pacific Flyway in their annual migration patterns. Less than 6 percent of the wetlands and 11 percent of the riparian forests remain in the Central Valley; the rest has been converted to intense agricultural use. About 30 percent—91,800 acres—of the remaining migratory waterfowl habitat exists on public lands that, like Kesterson, are managed for wildlife. Nine endangered species, including the blunt-nosed lizard and the Southern Bald Eagle, live in Kesterson, a 6,000-acre refuge of grassy fields, ponds, and brilliant spring flowers.

But Kesterson is a "refuge" no longer.

In 1982, the Fish and Wildlife Service checked the refuge to determine what had happened to the bass and catfish once caught there. They found that selenium, a naturally occurring trace element that is harmless in normal quantities, has been concentrated in the waters of Kesterson, killing fish and other wildlife. Its source is the irrigated soil of rich farms upstream from the refuge, and it arrives there through a canal that drains spent water from the huge Central Valley Project, a massive irrigation system begun in the 1930s and in part still not complete. Heavy dumping of wastewater began in 1981; a year later, bass, catfish and carp had disappeared and mosquito fish contained concentrations of selenium of more than 100 times the normal amount. In 1983, the Service found that 60 percent of the coot nests contained dead embryos and 20 percent of young birds were born deformed, often without eyes or with their brains protruding from their skulls. Thousands of adult birds died from eating contaminated shellfish.

Finally, fearing that federal managers could be prosecuted for criminal violation of the 1918 Migratory Bird Treaty Act, which prohibits the killing of migratory birds, Interior Secretary Donald Hodel halted the dumping of wastewater in a surprise action in March 1985. Since then, legal and political wrangling has prohibited the expensive cleanup that is necessary, and the hazing of waterfowl in an attempt to keep them out of the poisoned waters continues, with limited success.

While the frightening situation at Kesterson is unique in magnitude and urgency, it represents just the "tip of an iceberg," according to wildlife experts. A 1986 report by the Fish and Wildlife Service listed eighty-five national wildlife refuges as having either documented or suspected problems with contaminants, and critics believe even this number is based on an unreasonably optimistic interpretation of the data gathered.

The problems at Kesterson and other wildlife refuges illustrate the difficulty of protecting biological diversity in this technological age. As new procedures, such as mass irrigation and applications of new chemicals, are instituted on a broad scale, new threats to naturally functioning ecosystems occur more quickly than they can be detected and remedied. Irreparable losses of wildlife occur and extremely expensive cleanups are required. Migratory birds are often the first victims because their total habitat is only as healthy as the weakest link in the chain that supports their annual junket to warmer climates. But they are also important indicators: the interlocked ecosystems inhabited by migratory waterfowl that summer in Alaska and winter in Mexico represent an interdependent system of related species and ecosystems that, taken together, constitute much of the total biodiversity of the western portion of North America.

Tallgrass Prairie

When the French explorer Charlevoix saw the great grasslands of the midwestern prairies, he said "Nothing to be seen but immense prairies interspersed with small copses of wood, which seem to have been planted by hand; the grass is so very high that a man is lost amongst it, but paths are everywhere to be found as well trodden as they could have been in the best peopled countries, though nothing passes that way except buffalos, and from time to time some herds of deer and a few roebuck." Before the arrival of European settlers, the tallgrass prairie of interior America covered some 200,000 square miles from the Allegheny Mountains to the edge of the Great Plains, from Oklahoma to the Great Lakes.

In the terms used in these essays, the contribution of grasslands to the total diversity of America is less than that of some other biomes. Prairies are not as diverse as tropical forests; they lack the cross-habitat diversity of montane forests; and they have few species that exist nowhere else. But it is nonetheless important to preserve samples of the once-extensive prairies. As a diverse grassland system that was able to maintain itself both against erosion and against encroachment by trees, the prairies constituted a variety of unique associations of dominant species. Future generations will want to know how they were sustained for millennia.

As a coherent ecosystem, of course, the tallgrass prairie is gone now. In its place is the nation's breadbasket. All that remains of the once-vast prairies are a few scattered fragments, most of them on poor soils that escaped the plow. Still, such reasonable facsimiles provide some hope that the possibility exists to recreate, on a modest scale, the vista described by Charlevoix. There has been a serious discussion of two sites for the reconstruction and preservation of a national tallgrass prairie, one in the Flint Hills of Kansas and the other in nearby Osage County, Oklahoma. Current attention focuses on the latter site, after local opposition made a national park in Kansas politically unlikely. A plan to purchase two large ranches and surrounding easements as the Osage National Tallgrass Prairie Preserve has considerable public support in Oklahoma and is being advocated by the Park Service. The area is dominated by little bluestem, big bluestem, switchgrass, and Indiangrass, and contains approximately three hundred additional species of grasses and forbs. But there remains strong opposition from oil and mineral interests, and the outcome is in doubt.

If we try to fill in the vast hole in the diversity puzzle that was caused by the conversion of tallgrass prairie to farmland, we will have to reassemble an ecosystem from its parts. In addition to preserving one important facet of the total diversity of the continent, the exercise of reconstructing a prairie will illustrate how confoundingly difficult it is to rebuild a functioning ecosystem once it has been fragmented and impoverished. As John Madson says in *Where the Sky Began,* "If we knew everything we needed to know, and had exactly the right equipment and sources of seeds, we might be able to recreate a fairly authentic prairie in as little as a century—although Peter Schramm's best estimate is from 300 to 500 years." [Schramm is a prairie expert from Knox College.] If we undertake this long task, we will have signalled our intent to stop the downward spiral driven by the conversion of whole biomes to human use; and we will have signalled our intent to start back up the diversity spiral.

Conclusion

There is something both pathetic and heroic about the grand enterprise of the biological sciences: through the cooperation of many curious lookers, each of whom sees only a patch of reality for an instant of biological time, scientists must somehow extrapolate theories to explain an endless process. We have only begun to make sense of it all.

This much we know from the geological record: life-forms have increased gradually through most of the history of life, showing a tendency to elaborate themselves in more complex, varied, and interrelated patterns. There must then be some mechanism by which life-forms reproduce themselves and, over evolutionary time, produce new and more complex forms. Left uninterrupted, this mechanism, driven by the forces of adaptation and natural selection, augments itself. It is the self-moved mover of biology.

But we know also that the overall trend toward greater diversity is subject to reversals. The elaboration of life-forms is periodically interrupted by cataclysmic die-offs of species, and by rearrangement of the relationships among them. We are entering such a period because of human alteration of natural systems. The current and projected rates of extinction would involve an extinction event of significant geologic proportions. A great die-off has already begun and it accelerates daily.

The first key to understanding the self-augmenting diversity spiral and its reversals requires an explosion of one's frame of time to cover a process that has continued for at least three-and-one-half billion years. It is natural for us to think in terms of days, years, even generations; we do not adjust easily to thinking in evolutionary or geological time. For example, a recent oil company television commercial that shows the comic spectacle of dinosaurs dying off en masse, falling awkwardly over one another in primordial ponds where they are destined to become high-octane gasoline, represents the compression of millennia into milliseconds. Even at the end of the cretaceous period, when dinosaurs lost their supremacy and were gradually replaced by mammals, paleontologists believe the extinction rate among vertebrates may have been only about one species per thousand years.

We have visited seven natural systems that exist on the public lands (and one—tallgrass prairie—that many *hope* will become part of the public lands). Each represents one patch in the awesome array of the continent's natural systems, one snapshot frame of its total diversity. Interlocked in space and changing dynamically through time, the systems of the continent sustained themselves and created new forms as diversity developed, through a complex interplay of the three levels of diversity, prior to the arrival of European settlers.

When we encountered 250 species of trees in a tiny forest in Puerto Rico, we saw the within-habitat aspect of diversity. At Ash Meadows we found several species of pupfish and many plants evolving quickly as they encountered varied water availability and differing conditions of alkalinity—creating a textbook example of cross-habitat diversity. These two levels come together on a larger scale in the Southern Appalachians, where mountainsides provide infinite variation in temperature and light patterns, producing a remarkable total diversity of plants and animals.

But we begin to glimpse the process that feeds itself only when we see a system, like the vast Yellowstone Complex, sufficiently intact to have potential for self-regulation. Only a system with large far-ranging predators provides natural regulation of grazing species; lacking such regulation, grazing species proliferate and, instead of merely trimming vegetation and providing varied conditions that encourage plant diversity, they overgraze their favored grass and browse. In the process, they decrease the niche opportunities for other species and begin to detract from, rather than contribute to, total diversity.

And thus we see the value of designated wilderness areas and other protected natural enclaves in preserving biological diversity. If such areas are large enough to support an essentially complete system, they also close the circle of competition and adaptation. Within a closed system, where the various levels of the food chain regulate one another, within-habitat diversity contributes to cross-habitat diversity as competing species alter the environ-ment in which other species compete, creating a patchwork of varied habi-tats. The large animals that cross these smaller boundaries exert, in turn, adaptive pressure on species lower on the food chain because a population explosion of any species will encourage an increase in the species that con-sume it, thereby regulating its populations and providing a chance for other species. Within self-regulating systems of this type, the diversity spiral is also closed—each turn in the corkscrew of competition and adaptation is also an increase in opportunities for new adaptations. And each new species contributes in turn to greater total diversity and therefore to the stock of species available to compete in new situations.

The same factors that create more and more interlocked micro-habitats and more specialization also make the diversity spiral vulnerable. Species be-come increasingly interdependent through ecological and evolutionary time. These highly specialized and interrelated complexes of species are therefore more susceptible to rapid alterations in conditions—each species lost threat-ens others that depend on it.

Until we know how to manage a total system, controlling all of its major interactions, we will be unable to manage geographical regions without gradually eroding their total diversity. Humility suggests that we may never learn this much about ecosystem functioning. In the meantime, closed sys-tems that can exist only in protected natural areas are essential to the preser-vation of total diversity and the processes on which it depends.

A disaster on the Idaho batholith provided a warning that the very soils and mountains, and all the species living on them, depend on the trees that hold the mountains together. Threats to grizzly bears and to migratory wa-terfowl are early indicators that the interlocked systems that link Canada to Mexico are undergoing accelerated change, change that is measurable in human time—months, years, and lifetimes. Specialized species are stressed by these changes, and a major readjustment is already underway.

Nature, like some tireless Dr. Frankenstein endlessly experimenting in the creation of life, has now produced a new and ironic twist in the self-pow-ered diversity spiral. In devising *Homo sapiens,* a creature so complex and so clever that it has presumed to try to gain control of the very processes of life, the self-moved mover of biology has created a new era in evolutionary his-tory. Human population growth and new technological abilities are altering natural systems with a rapidity seldom seen in nature. Acting on scanty evi-dence and gerrymandered theories or, worse, ignoring these and acting purely on short-term economic motives, we manipulate and alter systems, seldom foreseeing the consequences.

Human alterations occur so quickly that other species cannot adapt, and we have set in motion a startling downward spiral in the earth's diversity. Experts project that, if present trends continue worldwide, we could lose a quarter of all species, most of them in the tropics, in just the next few decades.

At some point, the downward trend must be reversed, if the human species is to survive indefinitely, but at this point we know far too little to halt it. We do know, however, how to slow the process, how to buy time during which we can learn more of the mysteries of life's processes: we must protect large areas of habitat, areas where the creative and self-sustaining forces of nature can continue; and we must study those processes so that we can act responsibly when we face the accelerating changes to come.

Retaining and protecting the magnificent examples of diversity exemplified on the publicly owned lands represents only a small step toward protecting the biodiversity of the planet. But, more than that, their preservation represents a symbolic recognition of finitude—an admission that, for all our cleverness, our tendency to control and manipulate must be restrained, exercised only at the edges of wild areas and wildlife preserves. The decision to preserve these lands also implies an admission that there exists a greater wisdom than we have yet attained, a wisdom embodied in the processes that created us. If we survive our new-found powers, it will be because we respect that wisdom enough to keep hands off some wild places, to step back and watch the self-generating processes that create and sustain the incredible variety of life.

(Spring 1987)

DAVID RAINS WALLACE

Labyrinth
and Temple

W etlands are subtle things, hard to measure and define. Official
estimates of the original wetland acreage in the coterminous
United States (the lower forty-eight, that is) have ranged
from 127 million to 215 million, or from roughly five to ten percent of
wilderness America. That's a very rough estimate indeed, but then the pioneers weren't counting swamps and bogs as they slashed their way west.
(Survey marker trees have provided some records, but many species such as
elm and ash grow both in swamps and dried places.) Even if they had been
counting, they would have had problems, because wetlands can change size
significantly over relatively short periods, and can be hard to even recognize,
as anyone will agree who has started to walk across a meadow and ended up
in a bog.

Most people can recognize baldcypress swamps, cattail ponds, or tidal
cordgrass marshes, but prairie potholes, sedge meadows, riverbottom forests,
vernal pools, pocosins, and fens can be deceptive in dry years, or dry times of
year, although they are well-documented wetland types. To the casual eye,
most wetland trees, shrubs, and herbs aren't markedly different from dry land
counterparts, and even such wetland peculiarities as the carnivorous sundews
and bladderworts aren't particularly eye-catching. What's more, many places
that aren't well documented as wetlands can get pretty wet at times.

I once worked for an Ohio regional park agency that presided over a
collection of old fields, woodlots, and ravines snatched from the jaws of
suburbia; pretty places but with nothing legendary about them in the way
of swamps. Certainly, none of the parks was *called* a swamp. The administra-

55

tion shied away from such a buggy connotation, preferring "woods," "creek," or, as a last resort, "ponds." I doubt if the parks bulked large in any official wetland estimates. Apart from a few buttonbush pools and creek oxbows, they just weren't very wet for most of the year, just nice tidy woods and fields for suburban strolls.

Then the March rains thawed the ground and filled thousands of unnoticed little holes and channels. Suddenly, the parks were making up for the previous twelve months' tameness by reenacting all the invertebrate and herpetological unruliness of the past billion years. Quiet glades became raucous chorus frog and spring peeper bathhouses, salamander spermatophores littered pool bottoms like discarded shreds of plastic bags, a yard-long snapping turtle gobbled fairy shrimp in an oxbow festooned with egg masses, gray flatworms picked at an orange crayfish carcass. An entire swamp ecosystem had surfaced, as though the ground had dissolved and let up the creepers and crawlers from some prehistoric realm out of Jules Verne.

Of course, they'd simply been there through the dry months, waiting. Such is the nature of our watery biosphere that any healthy bit of terrain will develop wetland attributes with surprising speed given the opportunity. In a sense, the term "dry land" is a misnomer, a phantasm of the dualistic mind. Land and water are not opposites but complements. Land so thoroughly compacted and drained as to be without water is no longer land: it is pavement, or dust.

One could say that most of primeval North America was wetland, at some time, in some way, even the desert, where cloudburst pools that may fill the flats once in a decade promptly produce fairy shrimp and spadefoot toads. A certain degree of wetland is normal wherever water is allowed to seek its unobstructed way and find its undepleted level. I've never been in a wilderness area where wetland wasn't a theme repeated with variations many times in a day's walk by springs, seeps, wet meadows, lake margins, floodplains, fault slips, hanging bogs, sinkholes. The pioneers encountered the theme even more frequently, with delight at the abundance of good springs, with terror at the engulfment of wagons and oxen, as they penetrated a vast hydrological system about whose intricacies we now can only guess, having largely destroyed it with our ditches, canals, levees, sewers, wells, and reservoirs.

Enough remains of the system for us to have a crude understanding of it. The most recent, Wisconsinan glaciation largely caused it, directly or indirectly. By leaving behind great drifts of undulating, pocked, silty, or otherwise water-retaining terrain as it melted, glaciation directly caused the bogs and fens of New England, the upper Midwest, and the western mountains, as well as the swamp forests of the Great Lakes and the prairie potholes of the Northern Plains. It created the intermountain marshes of the West just about as directly as alpine glaciers melted into valley lakes, which then silted up.

Glaciation indirectly created coastal marshes and mangrove swamps by raising ocean levels as the glacier melted; there were tidal wetlands before the ice sheet receded, but they now lie far offshore. Similarly, glaciation helped create the great bottomland swamps of the southeast as fluctuating ocean levels and floods of river-borne meltwater changed drainage patterns. Even desert wetlands aren't free of glacial influence, since many depend on fossil aquifers left over from glacier-forming pluvial periods. Most wetland plants and animals had been on the continent for millions of years before the Wisconsinan glaciation, however, and they reclaimed the soggy barrens it left behind in a geological instant.

Marching northward in the glaciers' wake came much the same wetland ecosystems we have today, minus the odd mastodon or ground sloth: first tundra with its masses of ground-nesting birds among the tussocks and cotton sedges; then the spruce, larch, and poplar bogs of the taiga, home of the stilt-legged, pondweed-eating moose; then northern deciduous elm, ash, and maple swamps, where lived the almost equally aquatic elk; and finally southern deciduous tupelo, gum, and baldcypress swamps, home of that most ancient of wetland creatures, the alligator, effectively unchanged since the pre-dinosaur Triassic Period. Moving from east to west, the post-glacial observer would have seen an even wider wetland transect, from Atlantic cordgrass marshes, to white cedar swamps, to sycamore and cottonwood floodplains, to seasonally flooded canebrakes and tallgrass prairies where the buffalo soggily roamed, to reed-hidden, swan-haunted potholes, to sweetwater marshes at the base of the Rockies, to increasingly bitter and salty marshes in the Great Basin sinks, to tule marshes and alder swamps beyond the Sierra and Cascades, and finally to Pacific cordgrass and pickleweed marshes.

Such transects are mere abstracts of living complexity and diversity, of course. Not only do they inadequately describe common wetlands, they slight the fascinating rarities and oddities: the crocodiles at the tip of Florida, the pupfish thriving in ninety-degree waters of desert oases, the blind minnows and salamanders of subterranean wetlands, the cobra plants and endemic wildflowers of the Pacific Coast's deceptively barren-looking serpentine wetlands, the glacial relict wetlands still sprinkled over the north temperate belt where buried blocks of the glacier planted them, natural refrigerators for spruce and arborvitae, botanical time machines concealing paleontological clocks in their pollen layers, mammoth bones and mammoth-hunter spearheads in their peat deposits.

Some of these, puddles high on mountains or deep in caves, may not seem like wetlands at all. Yet for me it is not so much the location or extent of a wetland that defines the phenomenon as a certain fecund interface of air, water, and soil, and a single puddle can provide that as well as a thousand. I don't think it's possible to overestimate the importance to evolutionary life of that interface. It's likely that life first appeared in shallow waters enriched by dissolved minerals and warmed by the sunlight, and if it didn't, it quickly moved there, as various wriggle marks in Paleozoic mudflats indicate. Since then, the development of land as we know it has been to a great extent a product of interaction between living wetlands and various geological climatic forces. Mountains erode into floodplain swamps and delta marshes, which fossilize into sandstone and shale and then are uplifted into new mountains. Certainly, the mountain-leveling force of industrial civilization would not have evolved without the fossil swamps of the coal measures.

Fifteen thousand years of post-glacial swamps and marshes prepared a North American continent eminently suited to agro-industrial exploitation, which has always seemed a little uncanny and ironic to me. Such a resource accumulation, all that lake and river water to pollute, all that topsoil and groundwater to deplete, seems to hint at some not-very-healthy divine intervention: land as a piggy bank left under a pillow by an overindulgent parent. Of course, the pioneers didn't perceive the trackless, howling Dismals and Limberlosts into which history shoved them as a porcelain indulgence, but they broke them just the same, and we've been spending them ever since.

A television mini-series might be made of the saga of swamp exploitation in America, one of those dynastic epics that carries a large, colorful cast from the squabbles and philanderings of the Colonies to the squabbles and philanderings of the present. It would concern, say, the Fenimans, a Puritan family down on its luck for some entertainingly scandalous reason who comes to Massachusetts Bay Colony and raises cattle on the salt marshes. The Fenimans don't know that salt marsh cordgrasses are four times as productive as twentieth century cornfields will be, but they have a sharp eye for the produce, maybe a little too sharp for their neighbors, whose complaints about numerous, wide-ranging Feniman cattle add a lively note of conflict to early episodes. Conflict doesn't daunt the Fenimans: they raise large hay barns, and larger families.

The salt marshes get a little trampled and eroded after the first century, and the Fenimans move on. A particularly fetching daughter marries into the wealthy Reed family, which is developing rice, indigo, and sugar plantations in the black rush marshes behind South Carolina barrier islands. A particularly imaginative son flees some trouble with Church elders and becomes an Indian trader in western Pennsylvania, enriching himself on the proceeds of beaver ponds. Less imaginative sons move stolidly but steadily west across New England, pasturing stock in sedge meadows, draining bogs, planting bottomland.

The tempo quickens as the French and Indian War is fought over the beaver supply, and the clever son gets even richer than before. The fetching daughter produces another imaginative scion who moves south to Florida with an exotic, unruly collection of slaves and starts a sugar plantation near the mouth of the St. Johns River, where the slaves almost revolt at being forced to eat too many ducks, oysters, and other cheap foods. The stolid sons keep pushing west, fanning out, some north to even boggier Vermont and New Hampshire, some to the hardwood and cedar swamps of Pennsylvania and New York, some south to Virginia tupelos and sweetgums. One loops back to the New Jersey salt marshes, as yet less trampled than the New England ones.

Then disasters strike. The fur trader chooses the wrong side in the Revolution and is lynched by a patriotic mob. His son has to go to work as a trapper for the Hudson Bay Company and disappears into the vast, soggy forests beyond the Great Lakes. Stolid sons are struck down right and left by Hessian bullets. Mohawk arrows, epidemics: the New Jersey branch is completely terminated by the yellow fever outbreak of 1793. Sequestered from the war, the Florida son lives to a ripe old age, but the Seminoles burn him out in 1835 and he dies of apoplexy.

Things improve after that. Manifest Destiny is underway, and the Fenimans find swamps that make the sandy Atlantic shore seem miserly. The Reeds move to the Mississippi bottomlands and get rich beyond their wildest dreams on the accumulated silt of half a continent. Stolid Feniman sons prosper more modestly as they pour west from the Appalachian crest, through the Ohio River bottoms, and into the black land-wet prairies and lake-muck swamps of Ohio, Indiana, and Illinois. These roosts of the passenger pigeon and haunts of the muskelunge disappear into drains and ditches almost faster than the historian can record as demographic momentum carries more Fenimans across the Mississippi to the less level but equally damp and rich moraines of Iowa, Wisconsin, Minnesota, and the Dakotas, where they encounter the fur trader's heir, who has established a post of his own on the Missouri and gets his furs from the Bear River marshes and the Willamette Valley.

Prosperity is never unbroken, or there would be no sagas. War strikes again, and Union troops sack the Reed plantations, turning their most valuable assets into American citizens. Dispossessed sons drift west and pick up odd jobs along the Louisiana and Texas coasts, fishing, trapping, cypress lumbering. A Blackfoot war party terminates the Feniman fur-trading branch. Most of the stolid Fenimans return from the Civil War intact, on the other hand, and since the high, dry plains beyond the pothole country offer little enticement to the unimaginative, they tend to stay home more than their fathers had. This is not always a joy to fathers faced with dividing up homesteads, but they get along more or less comfortably for the next half century, among depressions, droughts, and floods. There are more droughts and floods as more Fenimans install more tiles, plow more bluestem and bulrush, and cut more bur oaks, but this is ascribed to the fecklessness of the younger generation, not the niceties of soil drainage.

Things are a bit more colorful with the Reeds, many of whom have sunk to bayou shacks. The imaginative gene shows up again in one Texas son, who parlays some sharp practices in cattle and plume dealing into a muddy tract of huisache and mesquite along the lower Rio Grande. By the turn of the century, steam technology has helped him to transform it into a booming supplier of urban markets hungry for citrus and fresh winter vegetables.

War is not always a misfortune for Fenimans and Reeds, especially if it happens someplace else. The farm boom of World War I encourages both to expand, meaning more cabbages and corn, fewer wood ducks and black-bellied tree ducks. Farm prices dip in favor of commerce and speculation in the twenties, but the Fenimans ride the decade out comfortably enough, waiting for the good times to trickle down, which perhaps is why few are prepared for the thirties. Drought and Depression hit them hard: they have a tradition of leaving land for better places, but not of land leaving them in dust clouds or county auctions. The experience is traumatic, and the number of Fenimans farming former wetlands in North America begins to decline for the first time in three centuries.

Most drift into Midwestern commerce or industry and soon regain a modest comfort. The imaginative gene shows up yet again as one son, tractored out of a South Dakota farm, hitchhikes to California and gets a job on a gold dredge in the San Joaquin delta. After serving in the Seabees in World War II, he moves to the Bay Area, contracts with some landowners, and starts building G.I. Bill housing on fill. By 1985, he is the richest Feniman who ever lived, with a million-dollar second home overlooking the salt marshes of Stinson Beach.

The sprawling Feniman saga would be lent a certain elegance by its hourglass plot, starting with a few Fenimans and thousands of wetland acres and ending with thousands of Fenimans and a few wetland acres, perhaps none. The salt marshes would have become city dumps and sewage plants, the bogs and sedge meadows would be reservoirs and resorts, the black rush marshes golf courses and retirement communities, the wet prairies soybean fields, the Mississippi floodplains the same, the Rio Grande lagunas a suburb of Brownsville, the San Joaquin tule marshes cotton fields and alkaline settling ponds.

Yet reality is less elegant than dynastic sagas. Millions of Americans might be content to see every wetland acre converted to inheritable currency (28 percent of respondents of a 1979 Florida survey thought wetlands more nuisance than value), but millions of wetland acres remain. It's hard to say how many. Not only are we vague about the original amount and confused about the definition, but wetlands are diminishing so rapidly that this year's total may have little relation to last year's. It's probably fair to say that the coterminous United States had lost well over a third of its wetlands by 1950, and that, at a yearly loss rate of between 380,000 and 450,000 acres since then, it has now lost over half. The Fish and Wildlife Service's 1984 *National Wetlands Inventory* estimates that 54 percent had gone by the mid-1970s, so depending on one's preferred estimate of the original, we now have between 90 and 40 million acres left. That may seem like a lot of swamp, but figures don't address the quality factor. In 1957, wetland biologist Paul Errington maintained that less than a quarter of the original acreage remained fit for waterfowl.

Wetlands persist in America for two reasons. The more historically important one is that they can be difficult and expensive to destroy. My favorite swamp story is the one about the elderly ex-slave who worked on Captain Henry Jackson's dredge when Jackson was trying to drain the east part of the Okefenokee into the St. Mary's River. The old man is supposed to have been the first to ask why Jackson's canal water kept flowing back into the swamp instead of east into the river, a nice variant on The Emperor's New Clothes. Jackson died after dredging only twelve of the estimated three hundred miles of canal required to drain the Okefenokee, and it took him seven years to do that. It would have been a temporary blessing to local Fenimans even if he'd succeeded, since the Okefenokee is a giant peat bog on white sand, and its "reclaimed" soils would have succumbed to fire, erosion, and southern heat even faster than the Everglades' limestone-based mucks. Wiser successors, the Hebard Cypress Company, built tracks on pilings, skimmed off the big timber, and left the swamp to the waterfowl, the alligator poachers, and the New Deal.

The second reason has arrived late, but is presently the most important one, and likely to remain so. Some people value wetlands for qualities other than cropland or building potential, an esteem that has grown less quickly and conspicuously than love of forests, mountains, or even deserts but still has deep, if eccentric, historical roots. William Bartram, the sometimes neglected grandfather of American wilderness appreciation, showed a virtually unqualified admiration for eighteenth century Georgia and Florida swamps, although he had to endure fevers, hurricanes, and twenty-foot alligators. "What a beautiful retreat is here!" he wrote of the St. Johns River country, a remnant of which is preserved in Florida's Lake Woodruff National Wildlife Refuge, "blessed unviolated spot of earth. . . . What a beautiful display of vegetation is here before me! seemingly unlimited in extent and variety."

Bartram also displayed a classic case of the schizophrenia that can afflict wilderness lovers in societies largely indifferent to their enthusiasm. After devoting some exhilarated passages to the Appalachicola River bottoms, "the most extensive Cane-break that is to be seen on the face of the whole earth . . . the most magnificent amphitheatre or circus perhaps in the whole world," he proceeded dutifully to state the obvious: "under the culture of industrious planters and mechanics . . . almost every desirable thing in life might be produced and made plentiful here. . . . Corn, Rice, Indigo, Sugarcane, Flax, Cotton, Silk, Cochineal, and all the various esculent vegetables."

Fifty years later, John James Audubon wasn't even schizophrenic about Florida swamps and their discomforts. "I have been deceived most shamefully about the Floridas," he wrote, "scarcely a bird is to be seen, and those of the most common sort . . . the eternal labyrinth of waters and marshes, interlocked and apparently never-ending, the whole surrounded by interminable swamp—all these things have a tendency to depress my spirits."

Between schizophrenia and depression, American swamp preservation got a wobbly start, and advanced haltingly. In 1853, Thoreau might proclaim "my temple is the swamp," but in 1869, John Muir would get "tangled . . . like a fly in a spider web" as he tried to walk across "thorny, watery" Florida and would nearly die of malaria. The specter of fever haunted every nineteenth and early twentieth century naturalist. Mary Austin walked around the Mojave Desert with aplomb, but when it came to the marshes west of the Sierra, she showed a shrewd faintheartedness. "Last and inevitable resort of overflow is that tulares, great wastes of reeds . . . in sickly, slow streams. The reeds, called tules, are ghostly pale in winter, in summer deep poisonous-looking green, the waters thick and brown, the reed beds breaking into dingy pools, clumps of rotting willows. . . . The tulares are full of mystery and malaria. That is why we have meant to explore them and have never done so."

Such ambivalence made the righteousness that worked so well for Muir in the Sierra difficult to tap in the cause of swamps. While Yosemite and Yellowstone were drawing nationwide admiration and protection, state legislatures were selling off the Okefenokee and Everglades at prices like 26.5 cents an acre. The federal government had virtually abdicated any authority over wetlands, first through Chief Justice Roger Taney's decision that submerged lands beneath navigable waters were state property, then by simply giving away huge tracts in the Swamp Lands acts of 1849, 1850, and 1860. The Sidney Laniers and Gene Stratton Porters could write movingly of wetland loveliness, but somehow it wasn't awesome or substantial enough for nineteenth century preservationist instincts, obsessed with cliffs and geysers.

People finally began protecting swamps not for the swamps' sake but for what was in them. Audubon may have found little of interest in Florida's "eternal labyrinth," but later ornithologists found much, and the first effective wildlife preservation movement coalesced around the slaughter of egrets and other wading birds by the turn-of-the-century plume trade. A realization that the birds' rookeries and feeding grounds would have to be protected as well as their hides led to the first swamp preserves as the Audubon Society began leasing and patrolling cypress strands and mangrove hells.

A much bigger group of wetland birds, with a much bigger group of admirers, also was wearing thin at the turn of the century. From the humblest farm boy to President Theodore Roosevelt, American sportsmen had grown up to view almost unlimited waterfowl bags as a birthright, and it must have seemed like subversion when the flocks began to dwindle. Yet it couldn't be blamed on anarchists, or even market hunters; the evidence was too concretely there in the duck club photographs festooned with feathered carcasses and in the ditches and culverts that increasingly defined the countryside. Such considerations must have been in Roosevelt's mind when he established the first national wildlife refuge in 1903, although that was a seashore rookery rather than a duck marsh. Duck marshes looked too much like potential homesteads in 1903, so Teddy spoke softly.

The next two decades saw progress toward wetland preservation as well as accelerating wetland destruction. Francis Harper, naturalist and Bartram scholar, thoroughly explored the Okefenokee and brought it public attention in books. Another unassuming explorer, landscape architect Ernest F. Coe, did the same for the Everglades by tirelessly lobbying for preservation. Will Dilg, founder of the Izaak Walton League, was one of the first to perceive the vital relationship between wetlands and water quality, and promoted the first big wetland national wildlife refuge, the Upper Mississippi. The man who probably did the most for wetlands in the twenties was duck-hunting newspaper cartoonist J. N. "Ding" Darling, whose drawings of trampled potholes ringed with blazing shotguns must have been worth thousands of words.

The federal government had gotten back into the wetlands game with the Rivers and Harbors Act of 1899, but not for the sake of preservation. On the contrary, the job of ditching and dredging had proved too much for the private and local sectors, so the pork barrel began its ponderous roll, throwing up levees, spoil banks, and dams in its wake. With presidents who equated government with business interests, with the Corps of Engineers drowning swamps along navigable waters, and the Bureau of Reclamation draining them inland, there was little enough wetland conservation, much less preservation, at the federal level.

Even Ding Darling's popularity probably wouldn't have prompted much federal action for wetlands if the financial bubbles of the twenties hadn't burst, dropping land prices and discouraging speculators. As drought dust settled in fiscally stagnant air, new things happened. The Migratory Bird Conservation Act of 1929 and the Migratory Bird Hunting and Conservation Act of 1934 provided funds through congressional authorization and duck stamp sales for buying back some of the wetlands the government had previously given away. Most of these were duck marshes as was to be expected, but not all.

The U.S. Biological Survey, the beginning of today's U.S. Fish and Wildlife Service, our main wetland manager, started out emphasizing the economically productive aspect of its acquisitions (the Fish and Wildlife Service still emphasizes it), but its mandate was not really that simple, fortunately. A new specter had risen from the swamps by the Depression. Extinction may not be as frightening in the short run as malaria, but its implications are not unlike those of a deadly, wasting disease. The passenger pigeon and Carolina parakeet were already extinct in the twenties, but it had still been possible to imagine them surviving in remote swamps. These were, or seemed, the wildest remaining places, and they did contain other frontier echoes—whooping cranes, ivory-billed woodpeckers, limpkins, Everglades kites, Audubon's caracaras, Bachman's warblers. The twenties were the last gasp of romantic expansionist euphoria, however (as opposed to today's hard-eyed variety), and the Depression's gritty dawn seems to have prompted a general, if tacit, recognition that there wasn't much left to find in swamps, but a great deal to lose. It is hard otherwise to account for the sudden public willingness to save places like the Everglades and Okefenokee, both of which were authorized for federal protection in the thirties.

The people didn't save enough. If the public sector had protected northeastern Louisiana's 120-square-mile-Singer Tract of Tensas River bottomlands in 1934, an area less than one-fifth the size of the Okefenokee, we might now have descendants of the estimated seven pairs of ivory-bills that lived in the tract then, along with panthers, red wolves, and Bachman's warblers. Unlike the Okefenokee, the Singer Tract still contained much valuable timber, and by 1943 the ivory-bills were gone, along with the "overmature" trees they depended on for their borer beetle diet staple.

A lot more than ivory-billed woodpeckers was gone or going in the 1940s and 50s. Errington considered this the major period of prairie pothole destruction. In 1949–50 alone, 188,000 acres were drained with federal assistance in Minnesota and the Dakotas, countless more privately. Duck populations were down to a third of their nineteenth century numbers that year. By the 1960s, Iowa and Illinois wetlands were 95 percent drained, and Great Lake marshes had declined by 71 percent. Most wetlands with agricultural potential had fared about the same. California's once vast valley wetlands were 90 percent reduced, and southern Florida, alternatively parched and drowned by a century of ditching and by vast Army Corps of Engineers flood control and reclamation projects begun in 1947, had lost 90 percent of its wading birds in a generation. Coastal marshes suffered almost as badly from navigation channel dredging and filling and urban sprawl. Long Island lost 30 percent of its marshes in the decade from 1954 to 1964.

DDT and other persistent biocides entered the picture in the forties and fifties, with results that seem predictable in hindsight. Wetlands not only were sprayed for mosquito control but received poisoned runoff from uplands and towns. After twenty years, Long Island marsh soil contained thirteen pounds of DDT per acre. Populations not only of eagles, ospreys, and waterfowl but of fish, shrimp and crabs declined. The pesticides combined with more traditional effluviums such as sewage, heavy metals, and waste petrochemicals to produce corrosive wastelands like the Hackensack marshes I recall from childhood, wherein the stench made breathing difficult.

Yet pollution may have helped teach us a lesson. In its insidious way, striking quietly at the bases of food pyramids as well as the tops, it demonstrated that wetlands must be valued for healthy muck—bacteria, algae, dead grass—as well as for ducks, since muck makes ducks. It demonstrated that wetlands must be valued for themselves. As ecologists such as Errington and the Odums began paying close attention to the inner workings of muck, they found some unexpected things, not only that salt marshes are more productive than cornfields, but that floodplain forests are efficient regulators of stream flow, that swamps store water with less evaporation loss than reservoirs, that marshes purify wastewater, that most commercial and sport seafoods breed not in the sea but in tidal marshes and estuaries, where their fry and larvae feed on cordgrass detritus, that is, on muck.

Weighty discoveries, but they did not sink quickly into the complacent jello of postwar prosperity. *Silent Spring* may have been a bestseller in 1962, but Congress took a decade more to pass, much less enforce, significant pesticide control and water quality legislation. Luckily for some wetlands, postwar prosperity wasn't expressed only in home and car sales. People wanted places to go in their new cars, and it was getting harder to find them as home sales soared. Even boggy open space looked good to a generation that had grown up without traditional fears of fevers and miasmas, so swamps finally got firmly, if quietly, hitched to the recreation bandwagon. Public pressure forced a reorganization of the Duck Stamp program to increase land acquisition in 1958, and, even more importantly, the Outdoor Recreation Resources Review Commission was established. It was the Commission's 1962 report, *Outdoor Recreation in America,* that prompted the creation in 1965 of the Land and Water Conservation Fund, which probably has done more to perpetuate local wetland preservation than any other public institution. When I worked for the Ohio park agency, Land and Water Conservation matching funds helped it acquire the only remaining pothole marsh complex in the area and the only relatively pristine, undammed floodplain.

Wetland preservation underwent a modest heyday in the 1970s, when the Land and Water Conservation Fund tripled in five years, the Fish and Wildlife Service made plans to acquire an additional 1.9 million acres to keep waterfowl populations at historical levels, and an American president came right out and said: "the Federal Government will no longer subsidize the destruction of wetlands." Even privately owned wetlands got a boost from Section 404 of the Federal Water Pollution Control Act Amendments of 1972, which required the Army Corps of Engineers to start regulating filling of wetlands shoreward from established harbor lines (a subsequent court decision widened federal authority to include all U.S. waters).

Wetlands finally joined canyons and mountains in becoming the subjects of nationwide preservation campaigns. The Everglades and adjacent Big Cypress swamps escaped conversion into a jetport and sacrifice area for Greater Miami, and central Florida wetlands were not gutted by a barge canal. The Big Cypress became a 570,000-acre National Preserve, and other stretches of cypress, sawgrass, mangrove, cordgrass, leatherleaf, and pitcher plant became not only parks and wildlife refuges but wilderness areas as well, inaccessible not only to dredges and draglines, but to outboards and airboats.

Nobody knows how much wetland there is under wilderness designation because the managing agencies haven't tried to count it. Any wilderness is likely to contain wetland, as I've said, but since the wilderness preservation system encompasses only two percent of the coterminous United States, the designated acreage certainly is small in proportion to the original, or even the remnant. It also is concentrated in agriculturally marginal areas such as the sandy southeastern coastal plain and the granitic Boundary Waters, and there are problems even with that, since fishermen can get just as passionate about outboards as hunters can about ORVs. The country's biggest freshwater swamp, the Atchafalaya, has no designated wilderness, nor do the remnants of many other once-vast morasses—California tulares, prairie riverbottoms, Midwestern lake plains.

Rather surprisingly for a statistics-loving civilization, nobody knows how much wetland there is in *any* protected form, wilderness or otherwise. The Forest Service, Bureau of Land Management, and National Park Service all manage substantial wetland acreage, but only the Fish and Wildlife Service has attempted to quantify its holdings, and it appears to have doubts about those. Its 1977 *Proceedings of the National Wetland Protection Symposium* cited twelve million acres of FWS-controlled wetlands in the coterminous United States but its 1984 *National Wetlands Inventory* seemed to cite only seven million (with an additional twenty-nine million in Alaska). If our ignorance of federal wetland is deep, our ignorance of state, local, and private is abysmal. Few conservation bodies at those levels count their wetlands either, and who would put the figures together if they did? They tend, furthermore, to get tangled up in federal programs because so many local projects have been pursued with matching funds.

Of course, the 1970s weren't any millennium for wetlands, which continued disappearing as rapidly as ever, succumbing to soybean culture, peat or phosphate mining, monoculture forestry, condominium development, and other economic fads. The Mississippi Basin states indulged in a veritable orgy of soybeans during the farm price boom, and reduced their bottomland forests to five (or three) million of an original twenty-four (or twenty-five) million acres. Timber companies converted a half-million acres of North Carolina pocosins (elevated shrub bogs specializing in Venus flytraps) to large-scale agriculture. Urban expansion in northern and central Florida shrank wetlands so drastically that the climate seems to have become cooler and drier. The Sunbelt boom also stressed Southwestern riparian ecosystems already troubled by irrigation and grazing. Despite brave words, the Carter administration did not stop federal subsidization of wetland destruction: the Garrision Diversion project of North Dakota and other boondoggles shamble on.

Unfortunately, the seventies seem a little like the light at the beginning of the tunnel now. The federal role in wetland preservation has declined since 1980, to say the least, although not as drastically as James Watt promised when he put a moratorium on further acquisitions for refuges and parks, attempted to develop refuges, and tried to use park acquisition funds for park construction projects. Subsequent interior secretaries have been more circumspect about niggardly acquisition and management budgets, but the budgets haven't been much better than Watt's, and would have had a similar effect if Congress hadn't increased them by factors that seem enormous in comparison (anything seems enormous in comparison to nothing) but are modest by 1970s standards.

The acquisition slowdown has been complemented, of course, by the regulatory slowdown. Although environmentalists beat back the Gorsuch/Burford EPA and the Corps of Engineer's 1982 attempt to abdicate its wetland responsibilities, generally sluggish and lenient administrative attitudes have not been lost on developers, and if causes get buried in piles of documents, effects are becoming increasingly visible. I've noticed more malls and condos sprouting on San Francisco Bay fill in the past couple of years than in the previous decade. After surviving a power plant and a refinery, the endangered salt marsh harvest mouse is once again under attack, by a golf course this time, and oil companies continue illegal discharges into Bay wetlands.

The scattered, often inconspicuous or evanescent character of wetlands makes the effects of the Reagan slowdown hard to calculate. There still are fewer big name wetlands than canyons or mountains, and wild places that don't make good copy are easy to whittle away. While Watt's attempt to cut off authorized funds for Big Cypress Preserve was decried, square miles of Gulf Coast bottomland silently became soybean fields and housing tracts. We hear about them later, when denuded rivers flood out new property owners.

In the end, the Reagan administration won't be judged for what it did— its petty squeezing of nickel-and-dime budgets, its Scrooge-like withholding of authorized funds—but for what it didn't do. After the wide public acceptance of an environmental agenda in the seventies, an eighties administration had a chance to save, or even restore, significant samples of neglected wild ecosystems. Read what Fish and Wildlife biologist Brooke Meanley had to say in 1972 about the Arkansas River bottomlands downstream from a place called Arkansas Post: "When I went to that area, I always had the feeling that I had stepped back two centuries into the past. There was a sense of wildness there that I never felt in the heart of the Okefenokee, the Great Dismal Swamp, or the Everglades." It seems doubtful now that future Americans will be able to share that feeling in that place.

A lot of credit is due private and local conservation bodies for attempts to fill the federal vacuum. With a little tax-deductible help from industry, the Nature Conservancy has initiated effective programs to acquire wetlands in southeastern river bottoms, migratory waterfowl flyways, Atlantic barrier islands, and western deserts. An estimated half of Conservancy projects are water-related. Under Governor Bob Graham, the state of Florida has begun a bold attempt to reverse some of the damage done to its hydrological system in the past forty years. The "Save our Everglades" program has prevailed upon the Corps of Engineers to plug some of the ditches that drain life from the national park's borders, and proposes to acquire large wetland acreage for protection and to rebuild Alligator Alley and the Tamiami Trail to increase southward water flow and reduce wildlife mortality. Graham has said the program means "to provide that by the year 2000 the Everglades will look and function more as it did in 1900 than it does today," which somebody had to say if the Everglades was not to continue deteriorating into a dried-out, pantherless stretch of Brazilian pepper.

Only Washington can make the Florida program work, however. The water management system that is strangling the Everglades is congressionally mandated, and only congressional action can change it significantly. Local and private conservation can't obviate the fact that North America is subject to one of the most powerful central governments in history. If that government chooses to neglect air and water quality in favor of Star Wars technology, not even the most carefully managed duck marsh in the remotest county in the most environmentally conscious state will escape the consequences of those choices. If groundwater pollution doesn't get it, acid rain will. No swamp is an island.

Fortunately for those making the choices, the consequences won't become clear until the last acre of exploitable wetland is filled, drained, or poisoned in the mid-to-late twenty-first century. Wetlands are less dramatic in their destruction than forests or rivers. They tend to die by inches, a peat fire here, a fish die-off there, an oxidation failure here, and they may continue to provide wetland benefits such as streamflow regulation or groundwater retention long after they have ceased to be complete, or even discernible, wetland ecosystems. After the cattails and rushes have been plowed up, the spongy peat persists. Only when the apparently dry land is committed to "highest" use, to pavement and foundations, do the benefits finally stop, and then they may stop fast, with the speed of flood or wildfire.

It will be a chancy experiment, this replacement of a system that has persisted since the Paleozoic Era, this revolution from land to pavement. Failure will be accompanied by human suffering on a large scale. We can get an inkling of that scale by considering the history of China, which has (or had) ecosystems eerily similar to ours: glaciated mountains and grasslands releasing heavy silt loads into rivers that then flow down through vast, soggy plains. China has (or had) the only other alligator species in the world. Long ago, the Chinese valleys were deforested, and the rivers were confined by levees and canals administered by a strong central government. Without broad, forested floodplains to disperse over, silt built up in the river beds, raising them above valley level. When levees failed, as they did when the central government failed, the rivers flooded so powerfully that they sometimes changed course over hundreds of miles. One such flood, of the Yellow River in 1931, killed 3.7 million people.

Of course, that was before modern engineering. China is harnessing her rivers with concrete now, just as we have, and harnessed rivers can't do such things, can they? Consider the Mississippi where it strains at the Army Corps of Engineer's Old River Control Structure that keeps it flowing toward Baton Rouge and New Orleans instead of flooding into the Atchafalaya Basin, population 140,000. The river emptied into Atchafalaya Bay once, and it appears to have decided to do so again—pretty soon, probably. Silt is no great respecter of high technology, accumulating impartially behind dirt or steel-reinforced concrete.

Population growth is the generally accepted cause of such predicaments, but I think they are as much rooted in perception as history. Land and water are not really separate things, but they are separate words, and we perceive through words. We see a river as separate from its swampy floodplain, but the floodplain sycamores and cottonwoods are ecologically as much a part of the river as its deepest channels. The cordgrass marsh is part of the estuary, the cypress bay is part of the lake, the pothole marsh part of the cornfield, the leatherleaf bog part of the cowpasture. We need a wider vision of things, and we don't have to go to outer space to get it. Goethe provided one two centuries ago when he showed us greedy altruist Faust draining tidal marshes with demonic helpers, displacing elderly cottagers in the process:

> *Human sacrifices bled,*
> *Tortured yells would pierce the night*
> *And where the blazes seaward sped,*
> *A canal would greet the light.*

"Thus space for many million will I give," brags Faust, but Mephistopheles is digging him a grave instead of a ditch, and has the last word:

> *But all your work is done for us,*
> *Your dams and dikes will do no good*
> *For you are cooking Neptune's food;*
> *That Devil of the Seas will dine quite well.*
> *In every way you're doomed to fail.*
> *With the elements we've sworn to prevail,*
> *And wash it all away to hell.*

(Winter 1985)

CHARLES E. LITTLE

The Old Wild Life

I am staring at Monte Dolack's twilight painting of a mother wolf and three cubs going yip yip yiparoo at the rising new moon over Yellowstone, the new moon that holds the old moon in her arms, as Coleridge would say. They are standing on a rock outcrop, these painted wolves, and below them a wide alluvial valley spreads from canvas edge to canvas edge, steam rising here and there from the hot springs that seethe just below the thin crust of this caldera. The river, which stands for all rivers of the region, meanders peacefully into the distance with a moose posed in the foreground shallows and a dozen buffalo agraze on the far bank. Dusk is gathering quickly, the last light catching the high clouds over the mountains. Yellowstone dreams. Primal. Whole. Complete.

The painting, whose unapologetically sentimental style may not be to everyone's taste, was commissioned by Defenders of Wildlife, the conservation organization that has spearheaded the drive to get wolves back into the "GYE"—the Greater Yellowstone Ecosystem, as it is called—and improve their chances for survival in two other large wilderness ecosystems, in northern Montana and central Idaho. Defenders has published the work as a poster in order to raise money to pay off ranchers who can show they have lost livestock to wolf predation—or "depredation" as some call it, using a more freighted word, as if the wolves were acting out of malice.

We will return to these matters after a bit. They are important, but less important in many ways than what this painting actually depicts, however well or badly. It depicts a wolf family in Yellowstone, where no wolf family has existed for half a century. The painting is of some future time when the wolves will be *put* there, in Yellowstone, by *mankind.* Not God, or accident, or outcome of evolutionary dynamics, but by men and women consciously deciding, probably for the first time in three million years, to reintroduce a major big game predator into a range from which human beings have expended a great effort to rid forever such a scourge.

Should the reintroduction come about, and there is no doubt in the minds of most that it will, the event will signify in a way that few other environmental reform actions of this century ever have. Perhaps the only comparable achievements, from a pure ethical point of view, are the establishment of the National Park System itself and the later passage of the Wilderness Act—both of which transcend ordinarily ratiocinated public policy and move into a realm scarcely touched by legislators, or even fully understood by them: a kind of uncomplicated reverence for what William Faulkner has called "the old wild life."

Let us be clear. The reintroduced wolf will be as elusive as the mountain lion and the grizzly bear. As a reinstated member of the triumvirate of large Rocky Mountain predators, he will be rarely seen (though sometimes heard) by visitors to the park and its surrounding hiking areas and camping grounds.

Why then even bother with the wolf in Yellowstone? Could it be that by reintroducing the wolves, those old enemies, we hope, paradoxically, that we will become more fully human?

The story begins (at least as I would imagine it) one fall afternoon in the mid-1930s when a Yellowstone park ranger astride his favorite chestnut mare spotted a paw print in the first snow of the season. He dismounted to take a closer look. No doubt about it, it was a wolf. You hardly saw them any more, but by golly there it was. Probably denning hereabouts. In the old days they'd find the dens in the spring and shoot the pups right then and there, kick the dirt over 'em, and that was that. And that was the law, too. The very law that set up the National Park Service to begin with made it clear: to destroy any "detrimental" animals and plants in the parks. And what was more detrimental than a wolf?

The ranger followed the tracks, now plain, now obscured over rocky ground, until at last, with the sun low, glinting beneath the scudding clouds, something entered the corner of his eye. Could it be the neck ruff of a gray wolf? He guessed that whatever he saw was perhaps two hundred yards across a swale. He dismounted quickly, pulled his Springfield thirty-ought-six from its scabbard, chambered a round quietly, and crept into an alder thicket. He held his position for a moment, testing the wind. It was in his face, praise be. Then he climbed softly up a slope that concealed him and that would put him above the wolf and maybe fifty yards closer at the same time. Some minutes later, he came out into an open grove of lodgepole, and looking down saw the wolf, its fur, thickened up for winter, tinted orange by the lowering sun. The wolf was poised with one foot off the ground, exquisitely balanced and muscle-ready, staring hard at the place the ranger had been, as if to begin a dash the moment he saw any motion. If the wolf were startled, the ranger knew sure enough he'd lose him. Even an old wolf could run all day at twenty or twenty-five miles an hour if he had to, could outrun any critter there was except maybe a griz over short distances. They were about as scared of bears as he was.

As the wolf stood, the ranger laid his rifle stock against the rough bark of a lodgepole. He adjusted for windage and elevation, clicked off the safety, sighted at the wolf's shoulder down the blue barrel, and squeezed the trigger. After the rifle crack, the wolf leapt up, and a split second later came the shrieking bark. It was a fair shot, a solid shot. The wolf fell to the ground squirming, unable to run. Hit his backbone, most likely, paralyzed him. The ranger ran down the slope, splashed across a stream, and found his quarry. Turned out to be an old female, about eighty pounds, now just lying still, watching him approach out of her yellow eyes. She thumped her tail, her head lifted slightly. Without pausing, the ranger, now half a dozen yards away, took aim and mercifully put a bullet into the wily old brain, just behind the ears. The head jerked, lowered, and the yellow light went out.

When the ranger rode back into his station, long after sundown, he gave a whoop. The wolf carcass was strapped on behind the saddle and everyone came out to admire what he had done, examining the old gray female by flashlight. They did not know it then, nor did he, but none of them would see another gray wolf in Yellowstone Park again, neither in day nor at night unless, perhaps, it was in their dreams.

In a 1944 review of a book about wolves, Aldo Leopold provided a capsule history of gray wolf extirpation in the United States. They were "incredibly abundant in buffalo days," he said, but then, in the 1870s, were decimated by the demand for their fur, just at the time Yellowstone was established as the first national park. "It appears that the Russian army at that time used wolfskins for part of its winter uniform and thus levied tribute on all the world's wolfpacks"—including the packs of the big gray wolf that roamed throughout the northern Rockies. The fur-trade wolvers used poison, not wishing to puncture the pelts with bullet holes.

After the white man nearly exterminated the buffalo and had vanquished the Plains Indians whose economy depended upon them, the wolf might have been in almost as much trouble as the Sioux. As it was, the buffalo were rather quickly replaced by cattle and sheep as a food source for the wolf. And so, Leopold said, they held their own, even though they were avidly hunted for bounty. In 1914, the U.S. Biological Survey, predecessor of the U.S. Fish and Wildlife Service, discarded federal bounties (though others remained) in favor of salaried trappers in an all-out effort to control predators. After that the wolves were all but "wiped off the map," said Professor Leopold. "I personally believed, at least in 1914 when predator control began, that there could not be too much horned game, and that the extirpation of predators was a reasonable price to pay for better big game hunting." But, as he had written elsewhere, "I was young then, and full of trigger-itch."

So, it took fifty years to wipe the gray wolf off the map of the Yellowstone country. And then fifty years, so it would seem, to decide to put him back. A long time, but not as long as it might have been, for wolf hatred is close to the surface in many of us. The salient and scientifically accepted facts of the case are these:

• For humans, wolves are about as harmless a species of large wildlife as there is—certainly safer to be around than a bison or a moose or a black bear, never mind a griz. There has been not one documented case of any human being in North America ever having been attacked by a healthy (i.e., non-rabid) wild wolf. When a wolf encounters a human, it flees.

• Wolves, at least in the Rockies, do not come down like Abyssinian hordes and feast on sheep. Or cows or calves. They much prefer elk and deer. In northern Minnesota, where wolves have lived interspersed with livestock since the time of settlement, the average loss has been five cows per 10,000 (one twentieth of one percent) and twelve sheep per 10,000 (a bit over one tenth of one percent).

• Wolves do not multiply to the degree that they deplete their natural food supply. Their numbers are governed by the prey base, not the reverse. Therefore they do not eliminate a prey such as elk, which is also the prey of hunters.

Nevertheless, even Aldo Leopold, during his trigger-itch days, killed wolves every chance he got (indeed, his famous description of the dimming light in the eyes of a dying wolf in *A Sand County Almanac* inspired my own tale of the last wolf in Yellowstone recounted above). Leopold's mentor, the great William Temple Hornaday, father of scientific wildlife management, wrote in 1914: "Wherever found, the proper course with a wild gray wolf is to kill it as quickly as possible." In the distinguished eleventh edition of the Encyclopaedia Britannica (the last "scholarly" edition, published in 1910–1911), we learn that from time immemorial the wolf has been "the devastator of sheep flocks," and that "as is well known, children and even full-grown people are not infrequently the objects of their attack. . . ."

Given the unimpeachable misinformation of the experts early in this century, it is close to a miracle that the wolf has survived at all in the United

States. In England, gamekeepers and shepherds succeeded in extirpating wolves during the reign of Henry VII—1485–1509. In the view of some, the mythic wolf—the ravenous, vicious beast of fables ranging from the Werewolf to the Three Little Pigs—has come down to us from the Middle Ages when starving wolves roamed the countryside during the time of the Black Plague.

After the gray wolf had been cleaned out of Yellowstone, the long wolfless era ensued. The elk, unpreyed upon, multiplied and, as Leopold came to believe, degraded its range to a state of near-catastrophe (although this point remains in dispute). Coyotes, once relatively rare, multiplied, too, partially filling the niche left by the wolf, which kills the competing coyote whenever it can. The bears may have multiplied, as well (although reliable statistics aren't available)—not naturally but because of garbage-dump feedings arranged for the amusement of the visitors. When the science of ecology was finally discovered by public policy in the late 1960s, the dumps were closed (rather too abruptly it turned out), and the bears declined precipitously. They had grown too used to human food and sometimes threatened the humans that were to provide it. Such bears had to be killed, until at length there were scarcely more than a hundred grizzlies left in Yellowstone by some counts.

And so, by the 1970s, not only were the wolves gone, the bears were declining. Among the big three predators, then, only the mountain lion, also stressed and never very plentiful yet able to move into and out of hunting grounds at long distances from one another, seemingly had a chance to survive in the region of this greatest and oldest of our national parks, Yellowstone.

But an agent of change was at hand, a legislative *deus ex machina:* the Endangered Species Act of 1973.

The Endangered Species Act says that when a species is listed as endangered (or threatened, which means likely to become in danger of extinction if present trends continue), you've got to do something to get it *off* the list. Among the remedies: ban (or restrict) hunting and killing, protect and improve the habitat, reintroduce the species into suitable former range. From its earliest version, the act has listed the Rocky Mountain gray wolf (*Canis lupis irrimotus*) as endangered. And since the Greater Yellowstone Ecosystem, a former habitat for the wolf, is practically perfect for the purpose ("The place cries out for the wolf," says the renowned wolf biologist David Mech), the reintroduction of the gray wolf to Yellowstone would seem virtually mandatory, Q.E.D.

Yet, as many will remember, during those early days of implementing the Endangered Species Act the snail darter and the furbish lousewort were most often in the news. The wolf, though mentioned, became no *cause celebre*. Perhaps even those conservationists who proclaimed a solidly scientific, coolly rational view could not fully escape from the layers of acculturated wolf-aversion.

Ordinary folk, of course, had no compunctions about overt expressions of fear and loathing. Ethologist Roger Peters, in his 1985 book, *Dance of the Wolves*, which recounts his studies of wolf behavior in northern Michigan, found human behavior to be equally fascinating—and vile. He tells how a pair of fishermen who, discovering a female wolf near a favored spot, returned to their jeep, excitedly grabbed a rifle, and killed the wolf. They drove back to town with the dead animal, and once arrived trussed the carcass with rope, tying one end of the rope to the rear bumper of the jeep. "All that evening," writes Peters, "they dragged it up and down the main street of Axe, until nothing was left but a dust and blood-caked swatch of black fur. They stopped at every bar but could not pay for their drinks. They were men of the hour; they had killed a wolf."

Wrote David Mech in his 1970 book, *The Wolf*, "If the wolf is to survive, the wolf haters must be outnumbered. They must be outshouted, out-financed and outvoted. Their narrow and biased attitude must be outweighed by an attitude based on an understanding of natural processes."

According to Hank Fischer, the Northern Rockies representative of Defenders of Wildlife and the point man for the wolf recovery movement, the recent turnaround in attitudes about the wolf in Yellowstone has been nothing short of astonishing. The first official effort to comply with the mandates of the Endangered Species Act was begun reluctantly and with a palpable lack of enthusiasm when the Fish and Wildlife Service belatedly assembled the first team of biologists in 1977 to take a crack at a recovery plan. The draft of the plan issued the next year was so vague about the whole business of reintroduction that it might have been a hurried term paper, not a blueprint for resolute action. It was approved (in 1980) anyway—though its weaknesses were so obvious that conservation organizations, scientists, and others asked that the plan be immediately revised, with the missing details of reintroduction included. The federal authorities agreed, and, amid growing controversy in the region, began working on a revised recovery plan in 1982, having just completed an ecosystem-oriented plan for the grizzly bear, which I shall return to later.

Now that government agencies seemed to be taking wolf reintroduction seriously, stockmen, hunters, and doctrinaire anti-environmentalists enlisted powerful members of Congress from the three affected states—Wyoming, Montana, and Idaho—in an anti-wolf campaign designed to reach deeply into unconscious wolf-fears. So effective was the campaign that the then-director of the National Park Service, Russell Dickenson, denied that any effort was being made to restore the wolf to Yellowstone.

It was then that pro-wolf groups—a growing number that by now included not only Defenders of Wildlife but The Wilderness Society, the Greater Yellowstone Coalition, the National Audubon Society, among others—realized that if there were no strong countermeasures from the conservation community, any hope that the wolf could soon be returned to Yellowstone would be dashed. In an inspired move, they persuaded Yellowstone Park Superintendent Robert Barbee to permit Defenders to sponsor an exhibit in the park called "Wolves and Humans." Created by the Science Museum of Minnesota, the exhibit was seen by an estimated 250,000 Yellowstone visitors during the summer of 1985. Among the most impressed were National Park Service employees themselves, who along with other government officials say that people were genuinely fascinated by the idea of wolf reintroduction. Nearly three-quarters of the visitors polled in Yellowstone during the summer when the exhibition took place said that they would favor a return of the gray wolf.

Fischer believes that the great shift in attitude about the wolf began with this exhibition. But more political troubles lay ahead. The revised plan was quite specific about where wolf recovery should take place—in the Selway-Bitterroot wilderness of Idaho, the Glacier Park-Bob Marshall area of northern Montana, and in the Greater Yellowstone Ecosystem. It called for the introduction of ten breeding pairs of wolves (imported from Canada) into each of the three areas, presuming that these pairs would then create ten packs of five to ten animals each. Under the Endangered Species Act, the northern Montana and Idaho animals, as existing endangered species, were automatically protected from hunting and killing—no administrative decisions were necessarily required to affirm that status. But in Yellowstone, where reintroduction was needed, three different habitat zones would be established so that management issues could be dealt with. In zone I, prime habitat, the wolf's welfare would be paramount. In Zone II, a so-called "buffer" area, wildlife managers would remove problem wolves or take other steps to assure that the animals did not unduly interfere with livestock operations. In Zone III, wolves could be more freely controlled (i.e., killed), but only by employees of responsible government agencies.

The National Park Service and the Fish and Wildlife Service eventually gave the plan formal approval in 1987. Immediately, William Penn Mott, the new director of the National Park Service replacing Russell Dickenson, ordered an environmental impact statement (EIS) for Yellowstone as a means to move the reintroduction schedule along as quickly as possible.

But the anti-wolf forces were still well-organized. Senators Malcolm Wallop, Steve Symms, Alan Simpson, and James McClure inveighed against the plan, as expected, along with many members of the House representing affected areas in the three states. Stockmen and hunters' groups persuaded state legislators that the wolves would cause great economic hardship to the region, even though conservationists could produce scientific evidence that the impact would surely be negligible. Moreover, state wildlife agencies were opposed because they were given only a minor role in the management of the imported wolves.

Perhaps the most effective opponent of the recovery plan was the highly respected Congressman Richard Cheney of Wyoming (later Secretary of Defense), who sent a blunt letter to Interior Secretary Donald Hodel. "I just wanted you to know," wrote Cheney, "that I am every bit as committed to preventing government introduction of wolves to Yellowstone as Bill Mott is to put them there. If he wants to fight, I'm ready." Whereupon Director Mott blinked, announcing that the recovery plan was thenceforth "on hold."

This turn of events introduced a new phase in wolf politics. In 1988, annoyed at bureaucratic inaction and the ability of wolf opponents to thwart the provisions of the Endangered Species Act, a Utah congressman named Wayne Owens offered a bill, quite off his own hat, that cut through all the nonsense and required, simply, that the wolf be reintroduced forthwith. Owens did not believe that his ideas would just sail through Congress, become law, and solve all the problems. He did hope that it might somehow get the reintroduction process started again. And in this respect, he succeeded. Hank Fischer of Defenders, and a good many others who were impressed with Owens' initiative, convinced the congressman to revise his bill so that instead of mandating reintroduction, it would call for an environmental impact statement, as Mott had suggested, as the more politically palatable approach.

After making the rounds on Capitol Hill, pro-wolf lobbyists were able to convince the House to appropriate the money needed to carry out an EIS, but when it came to the other body they bumped into what might be called the Rocky Mountain Curtain of anti-environmentalist senators: Symms, Simpson, Wallop, and McClure. In their meeting with McClure, whose environmental record was generally abysmal, conservationists found that while the senator was unwilling to support the EIS approach, he *would* back a special appropriation of an equivalent amount for what came to be called the "Yellowstone Congressional Studies." On the one hand, it would appear that McClure had cleverly introduced a stalling tactic. On the other, the congressional studies might be a way to lay to rest the old shibboleths that a hundred wolves in Yellowstone would wipe out all livestock operations in three states, demolish the sport-hunting business, and reduce the region to a condition of economic collapse.

As it turned out, the possibility of compromise was significantly enhanced by Montana Congressman Ron Marlenee, whose vituperative ravings against the wolf made even McClure's somewhat reluctant willingness simply to *talk* about reintroduction seem positively statesmanlike. "Montana needs wolves like we need another drought," said Marlenee. He compared wolves to "cockroaches in your attic," which would breed madly and fan out across the countryside devouring sheep and cattle by the thousands. The invective made a moderate pro-wolf position appear sweetly reasonable.

When the congressional studies were completed, the antagonism lessened somewhat (except for Marlenee and a few others). Moreover, Defenders mounted a new public relations initiative to follow up on its successful "Wolves and Humans" exhibit. This was the creation of a Wolf Compensation Fund that would reimburse any rancher who had lost livestock to wolves. The program started where the wolves already were, in northern Montana, as a kind of test. After three years of operation, Defenders has paid out some $9,000 for five cows, fourteen calves, nine sheep and one electric fence.

In 1990, McClure introduced his own bill, suggesting a very limited program of wolf release at Yellowstone and considerable latitude on the part of state-level wildlife agencies to limit the population. It was promptly opposed by pro-wolfers. Meanwhile, the House approved the money for an EIS study, but once again McClure blocked the initiative. Then, as part of an Interior Department appropriations bill, a new compromise was struck: money would be set aside for a "Wolf Management Committee" made up of representatives of the National Park Service, the Fish and Wildlife Service, state wildlife management agencies, commercial stock-growing interests, hunting interests, and conservation organizations. Hank Fischer is one of the ten members.

Ron Marlenee, true to form, complained in his own curious idiom that "the committee has been stacked with a pre-determined bias to reintroduce the wolf"; that "the Secretary [Lujan, of Interior] has been sold down the river"; and that "if Hollywood made a movie of what's been going on . . . they'd have to title it 'Dunces with Wolves.'" The committee nevertheless got down to work to get at the exact details of how (not whether) the wolf would be restored in Yellowstone and in the two other Rocky Mountain areas. They are to have their final report ready by May 1991.

"When do you think the first wolves will be released in Yellowstone?" I asked Hank Fischer.

"In the fall of 1993," he answered.

"Really?"

"Well, I really do hope so."

There are those who speculate that the wolves might just reintroduce *themselves*. Gray wolf populations are reported to be slowly moving down the Rockies and already are south of Missoula in Montana. They might just make it back to Yellowstone on their own—in which case, they would be fully protected under the auspices of the Endangered Species Act. Whatever may eventuate in this regard, the recovery of the wolf will have everything to do with the recovery of the bear in an indirect and yet crucial way—and the wolf in turn might well have an effect on the recovery of the bear, as we shall see. The point is that the gray wolf is the beneficiary of a new kind of thinking about wilderness areas in general and Yellowstone in particular that has emerged largely because of a better understanding of the ecology of the grizzly bear. In the old days when Yellowstone grizzlies were scarfing up plate scrapings, bacon grease, and coffee grounds at the garbage dumps they were, essentially, a zoo animal, protected and fed within the park, even as they were killed on sight outside the boundaries. Then came the famed "Leopold Report" (1963), the work of a team of scientists led by Aldo Leopold's son Starker, which said that the large national parks ought to be "vignettes of wild America."

Following this dictum, Yellowstone park officials began closing the dumps and in the early 1970s inaugurated a policy of "natural regulation" to deal with wildlife. The griz was on its own. The only trouble was, the critter didn't know it, resulting in a sudden increase in "human-bear" conflicts, wherein bears went after campers' food and sometimes the campers themselves. The bears not only had gotten over their fear of humans, they had lost the knack of foraging for food and carrion in the age-old grizzly-bear way. In a human-bear conflict, humans sometimes lose—parts of their bodies, sometimes their lives—but serious injury and death are extremely rare. By contrast, the bears *always* lose, for repeat-offender problem bears are summarily executed by National Park Service bear-management teams.

Clearly, with problem bears being dispatched within the park and other bears often being killed illegally outside the park (despite earning their "threatened" status in 1975 under the Endangered Species Act), the numbers of Yellowstone grizzly bears, which is an isolated "island" population incapable of regeneration by individuals wandering in from other areas, declined precipitously. The drop in numbers stemmed from a combination of growing pressures; still, it is said that at least a hundred Yellowstone bears were killed in the two-year period 1975–1977. According to Frank and John Craighead, leading experts on the grizzly, for one reason or another its population declined by 45 percent during the 1970s. No one knew how many might be left—fewer than 200 certainly, maybe quite a bit fewer.

In 1979, in his book, *Track of the Grizzly Bear,* Frank Craighead suggested that Yellowstone Park could not in itself serve as the area in which the bear might make a comeback. In fact, grizzlies routinely roamed through an area then totalling some five million acres, not just the 2.2 million acres of Yellowstone. What we needed, he said, was to recognize the reality of what he termed, for the first time, the Greater Yellowstone Ecosystem, and to base bear-recovery plans on the actualities of the ecosystem rather than the artificialities of park boundaries. Nevertheless, when the first grizzly bear recovery plan for the Lower 48 states was issued by the Fish and Wildlife Service in 1982, it recommended that only those areas occupied by bears at the time of their listing as a threatened species in 1975 be identified as recovery areas, even though the areas were much smaller than the animal's prior range.

A revision of the 1982 recovery plan released in draft form in October 1990 did little to relieve doubts that the grizzly population might soon stabilize at some viable level in the GYE. Based on the authors' assumptions (much disputed by conservation groups and members of the scientific community), the revision announced that the crisis had passed and the grizzly was all but recovered. Moreover, since the authors concluded that bears have a good deal of "habitat tolerance" (also disputed), the revision abandoned the old "occupied habitat" designation in favor of a pre-determined "recovery area." The recovery area would be divided into eighteen "bear management units." The plan's proposed bear population goal within this area was given as "15 females with cubs (FWC) over a running 6-year average; 15 of 18 Bear Management Units (BMU's) occupied by females with young from a running 3-year sum of observations, provided that no two of the unoccupied BMU's are adjacent; and known mortality not to exceed 7 total or 2 adult females annually on a running 6-year average."

There is no efficient way to translate this goal into ordinary speech except to say that when it is met there will be, according to the Greater Yellowstone Coalition's Louisa Wilcox, no more bears in the GYE than there are today—about 200 (although estimates vary from a low of 170 to a high of 350), which in the view of most conservationists is too few. Further, the recovery area is too small, since it is based on the area used by bears in the 1970s when the population was at an all-time low. Critics also point out that the plan doesn't even deal with actions to protect bear habitat from clearcutting, oil and gas exploration, and hardrock mining. Bear mortality, they say, is still high—nine grizzlies were killed in Yellowstone in 1990. And finally, because of the slow reproduction rate of bears (especially for

Yellowstone's "island" population, where inbreeding may further reduce the reproduction rate), the plan uses unrealistically short time frames for analysis. Numbers of females with cubs are averaged over a three to six-year period when, says the Greater Yellowstone Coalition, "recovery success needs to be measured in decades."

David Wilcove, former Senior Ecologist for The Wilderness Society and supervisor of several Wilderness Society studies of grizzly bear management, summed up the revised proposal this way: "Mostly, it is a plan of small ambition. And a small ambition is not enough to restore a healthy grizzly population to the Yellowstone ecosystem—or anywhere else in the conterminous United States. We have to expand the recovery zone into a larger part of the ecosystem and establish protected dispersal corridors to other bear habitat areas as well. The grizzly's a big animal. It needs big country, and big thinking."

Back to the wolf for a final word. It's probably too much to hope for, and certainly there's no great scientific agreement on the point, but maybe the wolves can help out a bit in grizzly recovery. While the bear will kill other animals, it is only a sometime predator, preferring berries and other vegetation much of the year, and often settling for the kills of other animals rather than killing anything itself when the hunger for flesh is upon it. The trouble in Yellowstone, of course, is that few other animals can provide kills for the bears to eat—the occasional mountain lion or an especially accomplished family of coyotes in rare instances, but not often. Once some wolf packs get established in the back country, however, as Olaus Murie found in his 1944 study of wolves in Alaska, some of the wolf-kill—of elk, deer, moose—can feed the griz, who'll chase the wolves off a carcass any chance he gets.

Doug Peacock, in his marvelous book, *Grizzly Years: In Search of the American Wilderness* (1990), describes a similar phenomenon based on the activities of the "magic pack" at Glacier. "I saw the remains of seven deer carcasses," he writes, "in the immediate vicinity of sweetvetch patches used by bears. Grizzlies had visited every single wolf-killed deer at some point. Deer hair was in nearly every bear scat. Something symbiotic was going on there with wolves and griz. Reintroducing wolves to a place like Yellowstone might make for a lot of extra grizzly food." That's the way the old wild life is supposed to work, of course. The ecological vision seen for Yellowstone is of something symbiotic going on, a predatory loop that simply does not include man, except perhaps as an observer of outcomes.

In *A Sand County Almanac* Aldo Leopold wrote: "A deep, chesty bawl echoes from rimrock to rimrock, rolls down the mountain, and fades into the far blackness of the night. It is an outburst of wild, defiant sorrow, and of contempt for all the adversities of the world. . . . Only the mountain has lived long enough to listen objectively to the howl of the wolf."

Doubtless true. But we are trying, Professor Leopold. Perhaps one day a tiny bit of the mountain's wisdom will find its way into our flawed plans and policies to help get the bears and wolves together again—as they have lived naturally for eons. And then the healing may truly begin in a great and wonderful wilderness ecosystem where, as Monte Dolack's painting suggests, a new moon is rising.

(Summer 1991)

A note from the editors: Hank Fischer's hopeful prediction that wolves would be reintroduced to Yellowstone as soon as the fall of 1993 was off by a few months. At this writing (December 1994), fifteen Canadian wolves are scheduled to be placed in holding pens in the Lamar Valley of Yellowstone National Park in January 1995 (fifteen more are going to Idaho in a similar program). After six to eight weeks during which the wolves will be allowed to adjust to their new surroundings, they will be released. National Park Service biologist Mike Phillips has high hopes: "If a wolf can't make a living in this country, he can't make a living anywhere. They're going to do just fine, but it's going to take a few years and people have to be patient." Livestock interests are still trying to fight a holding action against the plan, but it appears to be a losing battle.

CHRISTINA BOLGIANO

Concepts of Cougar

In the beginning was the lion. Images of leonine power are as ancient as
the first scratchings on cave walls and as ambiguous as the Sphinx.
Lions roam through the Bible, emissaries sometimes of God, sometimes
of the Devil. From Aristotle's attempts at empirical description to the fanci-
ful symbolism of medieval bestiarists, the lion embodied both the noblest
and the most savage traits of humankind.

Lions had been gone from Europe for more than a millennia by the time
Europeans discovered the New World. Bears, wolves, and several species of
small wild cats remained, so the analogous animals on new shores were easily comprehended. Large cats, however, were completely foreign. From Co-
lumbus on, explorers wrote of lions, leopards, tigers, "ounces," panthers and
"pards," confounding real and mythical animals of the Old World with the
jaguars, mountain lions, and ocelots that are unique to the New. Of these,
only the mountain lion ranged throughout both hemispheres, including the
thirteen colonies. The assimilation of this unknown creature into the collective American consciousness transpired through the workings of what Aldo
Leopold called "the mental eye." It is our "perception of the natural processes by which the land and the living things upon it . . . maintain their existence," Leopold wrote, that determines our reaction to them. Or, as Barry
Lopez put it in *Of Wolves and Men,* "we create wolves" in the eye of our imagination. In the course of four centuries, the American imagination has created of the mountain lion the most terrifying, the most contemptible, and
the most magnificent animal in the American wilderness.

My own mind's eye has fashioned an idea of mountain lion over a period of many years. I can barely remember, as in a dim haze of prehistory, when I was perplexed by the cat of many names. Who were those mysterious and vaguely threatening animals called cougar, puma, panther, catamount, and wild cat? Slowly I etched out a single cat in my mind, the chaos of images resolved into the quintessence of feline grace. The image is with me still: Mountain lions move through my dreams, leaping, bounding, scrabbling over rocky cliffs, padding down sandy streambeds.

The confusion of my early imaginings mirrored distantly the initial confusion of colonists. The idea of lions was so intriguing at first that skins of the elusive creature were sought through friendship or trade with Native Americans. Gradually it became clear that the sleek, stealthy cat that screamed instead of roared, and that never had a mane, was not the lion of fable. Curiosity withered as the thin, short-haired pelts proved of little value in the fur industry. Busy on the frontier, Americans simply substituted one mythical image for another. By the 1670s, settlers were consistently calling their cat a panther. Panthers were vague concepts that for centuries had been inextricably mixed with leopards. Both animals were generally symbols of evil: the leopard was bloodthirsty; the panther, treacherous. In its lithe body form, its solitary nature, even in the spots that mark it as a kitten, the American mountain lion resembles rather closely the animal we call a leopard today. It was as a panther, sometimes rendered as "painter" in backwoods slang, that the animal became known throughout most of the eastern United States.

Once Americans recognized that this animal was not the lion of myth, a certain disappointment set in. Virginia gentleman William Byrd II expressed the ludicrous in the conflict between myth and reality in 1728 when he called the panther the "absolute monarch of the woods. . . . However, it must be confessed, his voice is a little contemptible for a monarch . . . being not a great deal louder nor more awful than the mewing of a household cat." Eventually the mild, almost disinterested response of panthers to pursuit earned them the label of cowards too abject even to defend themselves. In the world of myth, this was the opposite pole from the courageous lion.

Panthers seem to occupy extremes in the various mythical worlds of Native Americans as well. Sometimes the same culture produced images that embraced both the threat and the beauty of the cat's rippling power. The Southeastern mound builders, for example, incised the dreadful Underwater Panther on shell cups and pottery. This was a monster composed of cougar, snake, and other animal parts that arose from water to hunt on land. Yet other portrayals of the animal are eloquent with beauty. Notable among them is a wooden figurine unearthed from Marco Island, Florida, that has the sinuous lines, round eyes, and delicate nostrils of a living panther. It sits on its haunches in a human posture, graceful and appealing, almost supplicating.

Some Native American cultures produced images that seem reverential, such as the cougars carved from boulders in New Mexico. In others there are hints of uneasiness, even dislike. A Nootka Indian in the Pacific Northwest called the cougar the one animal the Indians did not understand. Charles A. Eastman, a mixed-blood Sioux from Minnesota who graduated from Dartmouth, published in 1904 an explanation of wild animals from the Indian viewpoint that described the great cats as "unsociable, queer people. Their speech has no charm. They are very bashful and yet dangerous, for no animal can tell what they are up to. If one sees you first, he will not give you a chance to see so much as the tip of his tail. He never makes any noise, for he has the right sort of moccasins."

White settlers absorbed this distrust of the animal's secrecy. They also adopted the Indian taste for cougar flesh, comparing it to mutton and veal. Turnabout was not fair play, however, from the white point of view. Not that panthers ate people with any regularity. Less than half a dozen pioneer deaths have come down through the records as attributed to panthers in the first several centuries of settlement. Panthers preferred hogs. In 1705 the surveyor John Lawson, shortly to burn at an Indian stake for his trespasses, called panthers "the greatest enemy to the planter of any vermine in Carolina." The accusation gains some credence from the accuracy of Lawson's other observations about the panther: that it climbs trees with "the greatest agility imaginable," covers its kill with leaves, purrs like a cat, and is easily treed by "the least cur." This one paragraph contained most of the details that formed the core of knowledge about the animal, as animal, for more than two centuries.

A science of natural history was emerging from a ferment of ideas, but zoology was ignored and panther folklore blossomed in its absence. Naturalists embellished their meager store of facts with rumors and anecdotes. Popular magazines distorted a few accurate biological details with tall tales. Certain motifs emerged: screams like a woman in pain, ambushes from tree limbs, follows humans as prelude to a cowardly attack from the rear, covers sleeping hunters with leaves for later consumption, drinks blood, black in color like the devil's beast. Over and over, the panther was characterized as remarkably cruel and bloodthirsty, the terror of all other creatures except, perhaps, the grizzly bear (and a few stories had panthers vanquishing even them). The culmination of all negative images into one criminal cougar occurred in the mind of Theodore Roosevelt. Although justly credited with placing the new conservation movement on the national agenda, Roosevelt displayed a neurosis about predators in general and cougars in particular. In 1893 he began writing of cougars as beasts "of stealth and rapine . . . craven and cruel . . . as ferocious and bloodthirsty as they are cowardly . . . with evil yellow eyes." This was the mental image that had resulted by Roosevelt's time in the virtual extermination of the eastern panther, except in the inaccessible swamps of southern Florida. For decades more, it inspired the implacable predator-control programs in the West that killed lions by the tens of thousands.

So it is remarkable to find a paean of pure aesthetic ecstasy bursting forth only twenty years after Roosevelt's first essay on the cougar. Charles Livingston Bull, a popular turn-of-the-century magazine artist, painted a gray lion on a snowy mountain ledge, its muscular body surging upward to swat at two ptarmigan. "Oh, the beautiful, splendid, supple, graceful, powerful, silent puma!" he wrote. "I would rather watch and draw and dream about it than about any other living thing."

At about the same time, Ernest Thompson Seton was gaining immense popularity with his sentimental stories of animals that appealed, for the first time, to the sympathies instead of the sensationalism of a mass audience. As wildlife management began to establish itself as a scientific discipline in the 1930s and 1940s, the place of predators in the natural world was grudgingly acknowledged. After Aldo Leopold described his flash of understanding of "the fierce green fire" in a dying wolf's eyes, acknowledgment slowly grew into popular appreciation. Like wolves and grizzly bears, cougars began to appear benignly in books, on television, and in movies to an urbanizing audience hungry for a link to the natural world. Nowhere is the change in perception so tellingly revealed as on Madison Avenue. From cars to shoes to knives, cougars today sell a fast, sleek, and sexy power, a steely strength, a matchless beauty.

These positive images did not, of course, drive out the negative ones. Several distinct perceptions of the American mountain lion coexist today, a phenomenon that Harley Shaw calls "concepts of cougar." Shaw did field research on lions for the Arizona Fish & Game Department from 1970 until his retirement in 1990. His recent book, *Soul Among Lions,* is an odd one for a scientist. In addition to the expected biological explications, there are intimations of morality and even mysticism. Shaw scrutinizes the motives of each of the lion's major constituencies: Deer hunters, trophy hunters and their guides, ranchers, preservationists, researchers. "Biologists often reflect the species they're studying," Shaw once mused, "and lion researchers tend to be silent, solitary, and distributed at low densities over large territories."

Despite any innate reclusiveness, lion biologists from the twelve western states and several Canadian provinces with confirmed lion populations have managed to congregate three times in the last fifteen years. Shaw hosted the Third Mountain Lion Workshop in Prescott, Arizona, in December 1988.

Official representatives from British Columbia, California, Nevada, Wyoming, Colorado, and Texas reported that lion numbers in their regions were either increasing or were already greater than in many decades. Changes in public attitudes were credited as fully as the elimination of bounties in the 1950s and 1960s and the gradual reduction of sheep farmers, the lion's most virulent enemy in the West. Maurice Hornocker, venerated as the dean of lion research because he inaugurated the current era of telemetry studies in 1965, has suggested that across the West cougars have increased by 20 to 40 percent. Nowadays, when Hornocker gives a talk, he titles it: "Mountain Lions: A Carnivore Success Story."

Others, including Shaw, argue that no field evidence exists to verify the "gut feeling" on which some biologists base their judgment that lions are thriving. Increasing numbers of lion sightings might well document the growing numbers of people in lion habitat rather than lions, and sightings are notoriously inaccurate anyway. The strongest consensus to come out of the third workshop was that field methods for counting cougars were the most pressing research need.

So cryptic are the cats, so inextricably merged into the boulder-strewn or brush-choked landscapes they inhabit, that even after more than twenty years of research biologists still can't answer a basic management question: How many lions are out there? Enough knowledge has accumulated, however, to redefine panther folklore. Lions do scream like wailing women; they also whistle, chortle, chirp, purr, and meow. They have been known to follow people, for a motive that seems appropriately described as curiosity. No black mountain lion has ever been found in North America.

Radio collars have illuminated the mystery of what lions do in their secret lives, which turns out to be a combination of restless, random roaming through their home range and a lot of sleeping and lazing around after a kill. Even the ultimate mystery, the kill itself, is yielding to knowledge. Unlike wolves, who seem in some subtle way to choose their prey for pursuit, cougars wait in hiding to make a short rush at any animal that happens by. Lions do not ambush from tree limbs, because they could not get leverage for a death grip on the throat or neck; their hind feet must be firmly fixed on the ground. Deer and elk are staples, but lion predation seems generally to affect herd size very little, perhaps only mitigating the more extreme fluctuations that might otherwise take place. Kills are dragged to a protected spot and scratched over with leaves or twigs; it is highly unlikely that any living human being was similarly treated. Lions also eat porcupines, raccoons, rabbits, rodents, reptiles and birds, but people, perhaps because they stand upright on two legs, are not viewed as regular items of prey. And cougars eat very little livestock, although an individual rancher in good lion habitat can lose high numbers of sheep, or, less frequently, cattle.

Although attacks on humans have increased in recent years, probably because more people are invading lion habitat, such incidents are still extremely rare. Usually the offending lion, tracked down and killed, is found to be too young or too old to catch anything fleeter. Some culprits have shown unmistakable signs of recent release from human captivity. Children, because of their small size and irrepressible motion, are particularly vulnerable. In lion country, it is wise to keep children close by, and if you meet a lion face to face, hold your ground, pick up your child, and make yourself as big as possible. Running seems to trigger the cat's hunting instinct.

Lions desire solitude so deeply that they will spread themselves thinly across the landscape even when food is abundant. Kittens stay with the mother for one to two years, but thereafter show little need for the company of their own kind. The amount of territory a mature male lion needs depends on many circumstances of terrain and varies from 50 square miles in the oak woodlands/chaparral communities of California to 400 square miles in the wet prairies of the Everglades. Territories are occasionally shared by cats of the same sex as well as opposing sexes, although when this occurs the animals almost never meet. Mates consort for only a week or two.

All of the above are rank generalizations; it is difficult to say anything terribly precise about the cougar as a biological concept. In every different research situation, lions have responded in different ways. But it is clear that the general portrait of the cougar that is emerging from biological studies does not easily accede to the overwhelming tendency in our culture toward anthropomorphism. Anthropomorphism need not be a bad thing. The belief that animals feel some approximation of human emotions generates much goodwill, and it may even be true. Cougars, however, are more difficult to portray in human terms than bears, who have been teddified for almost a century, or wolves, whose admirable family life has recently been popularized. Maybe this will make it harder for lions to become truly accepted over the long term, although the fact that Americans now own more cats than dogs may signal a greater tolerance of the independence and aloofness traditionally ascribed to felines.

Acceptance of the cougar reached an apotheosis in California in June of 1990, when voters passed a permanent ban on trophy hunting of mountain lions known as Proposition 117. Lions had not been killed for fun there since 1972, when the legislature approved the first of several temporary moratoriums in response to citizen concern over diminishing populations. (Hunting of lions that killed livestock continued and is permitted under Proposition 117.) Few knowledgeable people today dispute the assessment of the California Department of Fish and Game that lions have increased since 1972, although there are many good reasons to quarrel with the department's specific calculation of 5,100 lions. It was the very fact that tenable populations of lions still existed in California that helped make the ban so attractive. "Must we wait until a species is on the brink of extinction?" asked Sharon Negri, cofounder of the Mountain Lion Preservation Foundation, a nonprofit organization based in Sacramento. In the few years since its inception in 1986, the Foundation has grown to 38,000 members and was a major grassroots force in securing the passage of Proposition 117. "There's something about the mountain lion that goes to the hearts and minds of Californians," said Negri, who was executive director of the organization during the Proposition 117 campaign. "We've lost our grizzlies, wolves, condors, and jaguars. The mountain lion is our last majestic predator. It's the symbol of the old, wild California that we revere." To the mythic power of that symbolism the Foundation added the clarity of science. Brochures, fact sheets, advertisements, and videos portrayed the compelling beauty of the cougar while citing scientific research that "debunked the myths of the lion as a vicious killer that threatened livestock and people."

It was inevitable that the California Department of Fish and Game, supported in part like every other state wildlife agency by hunters' license fees, should recommend a regulated lion-hunting season. It was to defeat this proposal that Proposition 117 was developed. Several theories currently being bandied about postulate reasons to hunt lions. One hypothesizes that removing resident adult lions will open up territories to young animals who would otherwise be pushed into the least desirable territories, which often verge on human settlements where lion-human conflicts are likely. To date, no studies support this idea. Another theory claims that lions uncowed by a seasonal scourge of hunters and dogs through the woods will more readily attack humans, although there have been no more attacks in California than in states where lions are routinely hunted. On the other hand, hunting is indisputably the single greatest cause of death for cougars anywhere. Once good hounds pick up its trail, a lion has very little chance of escape. The irresistible impulse to climb a tree, born perhaps with eons of competition with wolves, makes lions terribly vulnerable. Hunters shoot an animal that is sitting on a limb, composed and calm, peering down at the yelping dogs below. Because Californians view the cougar with a new form of desire that can be gratified only by living trophies, this scenario was rejected.

As if in counterpoint to the New Age vision in California, the cougar is reviled as the biggest little varmint in Texas. The only state that refuses its lions even the minimal protection of game status, which brings hunting seasons and bag limits, Texas allows lions to be shot at any time for any reason. No reports are required. Not long ago a gracious, fragile old lady of 90, who has ranched in west Texas since Pancho Villa raided it, told me how much lovelier that sere landscape would be without a single lion in it. Hers was a cattle ranch, and I asked how many head she had lost to lions over the last three quarters of a century. The answer was none. "But what right do lions have," she asked, "to kill the beautiful deer I love to see?"

Conservation groups tried several times during the 1970s to persuade legislators to change the lion's legal status from varmint to game animal, but were stymied by sheep ranchers. Game status is hardly a panacea for protecting an animal, but it would undoubtedly raise lions considerably in the management priorities of the Texas Parks and Wildlife Department. The current position of the department is that lions are doing so well on their own, as demonstrated by sightings in areas where lions were shot out years ago, that no further study is necessary. Although the department supplied brief reports to each of the three lion workshops, data tables and bar graphs in the published proceedings show Texas as blank lines and wide open spaces.

If California and Texas represent extremes in a continuum of cougars, Florida represents the fulcrum point. The last few dozen disease-ridden, parasitized, incestuous Florida panthers (subspecies *Felis concolor coryi,* on which the eastern name of panther has devolved) survive tenuously in the southwestern part of the state. The theme of habitat loss that colors discussion of lions everywhere turns black and ominous here. The multiagency recovery team is riven by dissension over the captive breeding plan now being implemented and confused by the legal implications of new genetic proof that "pure" Florida panthers have hybridized. Yet there is unanimous agreement that technical and biological problems are not the crucial issues. The fattest and healthiest panthers live on private lands west and south of Lake Okeechobee. These are dry uplands, where pine flatwoods, tangled islands of hardwoods, and the wandering edges that delineate them from surrounding cattle pastures produce far more deer than the wet prairies of public lands in the Everglades and Big Cypress Swamp. It helps that private landowners tend to post their property against hunters, who can drive panthers out of their home ranges even if they can't legally hunt the animals (and a small number of hunters will poach panthers regardless of the law). On the other hand, panther researchers, who might confirm the presence of an endangered subspecies that needs large expanses of undeveloped habitat, are also refused access.

Development of wetlands is being increasingly regulated in Florida, but the dry uplands are up for grabs. Although wildlife habitat everywhere is being assailed, the development of Florida has become a paradigm for the paving of America. The state's population has doubled since 1960, and an estimated 1,000 people continue to arrive every day. Smoke from landclearing fires smudges the horizon. Trucks laden with rolls of sod for new yards always seem to be blocking the road in front of you. The southward push of the lucrative citrus industry, with its square miles of regimented trees separated by barren strips of mown grass, promises panthers no respite from endless acres of suburbia. "We fully understand that less and less private land will be available to panthers in the future," says Dennis Jordan, coordinator of the recovery effort for the U.S. Fish & Wildlife Service. In a region where land prices are astronomical and the terrain requires some of the largest panther home ranges yet documented, the problem cannot be resolved by the traditional fee-simple acquisition of critical habitat. "We know," Jordan continues, "that public land agencies could never hope to acquire all the habitat that is used by panthers even today, much less what is needed to maintain genetic vitality in the future." The need to involve private landowners is inescapable and urgent. "There must be some landowners who love the land and want to keep it the way it is," Jordan says, "and we've recommended that a program be formulated that would investigate such things as conservation easements and long-term leases. It's going to take a lot of strategizing." Convincing landowners that panthers are as valuable as oranges or winter homes will take little less than a revolution in thought.

There is a segment of society willing to precipitate such a revolution. Audacious as ever, Earth First! has begun to demand that lions (as well as wolves and other extirpated species) be restored to the Appalachians through a system of large, connected preserves. Wildlife experts I've questioned agree that there is no biological reason, now that white-tailed deer have reached superfluity in many second-growth Appalachian forests, why lions couldn't thrive there. Introduced lions could probably weather even the deep snows of the Adirondacks, according to a 1981 study sponsored by the state of New York and the Fish & Wildlife Service, but not the "high level of man-induced mortality." Even in the most isolated areas of Adirondack Park, the report concluded, the roads, dogs, and guns fatal to so many western lions would be too dense to permit lion survival.

Yet for decades there have been dozens, perhaps hundreds, of people every year who, having glimpsed some sort of dusk-colored shape, are convinced that lions roam the crowded east. By the late 1970s the proliferation of sightings, some of them by highly creditable observers, had prompted the Fish & Wildlife Service to mount a field search. "Reports were so frequent when I first started my study," says Bob Downing, who led the search, "that I really thought some had survived." But after years of wide-ranging searches, Downing and assistants turned up only a couple of possible cougar tracks and one suspect scat. They couldn't even document any cougars killed by cars, an assumed source of death even for sparse Florida panthers. Probably the handful of plausible sightings originated with cats released by owners overwhelmed when the kitten they bought grew up, or by escapees from circuses. Although there were hints that the native eastern subspecies, *Felis concolor couguar*, might be filtering into the Lake States and New England from Canada, Downing came to believe that it was "virtually impossible" for a viable breeding population of native eastern cougars to have persisted in the United States through the last 50 to 100 years.

The question of whether the eastern subspecies exists is not merely a matter of aesthetics. There is considerable doubt whether the Endangered Species Act, as interpreted by the Fish & Wildlife Service, would embrace lions brought to the east from one of the stable subspecies in the west. Without federal support, state wildlife agencies are unlikely to attempt restoration. Unless the Fish & Wildlife Service takes the lead, then, there's little hope that the ghostly panther will materialize in the east.

In the meantime, people keep seeing panthers. Among my neighbors in the Allegheny foothills are several who become quite irate when I gently suggest that what they saw was most likely a dog or a deer. It is as if an honor has been bestowed on them, one they refuse to relinquish to mere reason. Whatever they actually saw, they insist on perceiving a vision of a wild America they thought their forebears had destroyed. Sometimes at dusk I step out of my house and look toward the rocky slope where one of the last panthers in Virginia was shot. I wonder how it would be to know a panther crouches there again, yellow eyes gleaming, muscles taut, utterly focused. How it would be to accept the risks with understanding and respect, in return for the rightness. A dank breeze slides down Cross Mountain and a chill rises up my back. It would feel, I think, like freedom.

(Summer 1991)

NORMAN BOUCHER

Smart as Gods

I n the Everglades, so much depends on the forbearance of alligators. The largest reptile in all of North America, *Alligator mississippiensis* is most easily observed in winter, the season of shrinking sloughs. The resting time. You can see them on the borders of canals and freshwater pools, where they appear to have plopped down, exhausted, as though their short legs could not possibly have hauled that ample bulk another step. On land at least, an alligator seems like an extravagance of nature, a profligate accumulation of mass. The broad mouth hinges open like the hood of a car. Often the only movement is in the eyes.

During late winter and early spring, when the Everglades are at their driest, and fish, the chief food of alligators, are most difficult to find, these inscrutable reptiles use the brawn of snout, legs, and tail to bulldoze down through the peaty Everglades soil. Water, never far from the surface, pools in these gator holes, and the fish and invertebrates that collect in them soon draw wading birds such as egrets, herons, ibis, and storks. In June, a month or two after mating in these oases, female alligators plow mud and rotting plants into mounds along the sawgrass ridges, then lie across the top and drop eggs by the dozen into a hollow they've worn in the center.

The rain falls and the water rises. The females wait. Even in the best of years, the Everglades are a capricious place, where months of summer rain bring abundant water to the sawgrass and months of winter drought take it away, confining most food to the deepest bowls in the underlying limestone. In the dry season, most Everglades animals are wanderers in search of this receding nourishment, for in this place water determines what lives and what dies.

In building their nests, alligators respond to an instinct honed over millennia, a precise gauge of how many inches above the June level of water their eggs must lie to remain safe. The landscape dictates their urges. In drought years, when low water means fewer fish, the alligators may not nest at all, while in flood years the nests may be inundated and the eggs drowned. But natural cycles are tuned to the long run. When the muffled cries in the mounded peat stimulate the females into digging the hatchlings free, chances are that the Everglades they are born to is an Everglades rich again in food.

Or so it was when alligators were the reigning engineers. In the last century they have been steadily displaced by human ones, whose vision has greater scale, it seems, but less understanding. Since the early 1900s, more than half of what was once Everglades has been drained and developed. Here, where the tropical and the temperate meet, gator holes have given way to vacation homes, while sugar cane and winter vegetables have replaced the pond apple and sawgrass that once grew in this "reclaimed" soil.

But human engineers have not yet stopped the summer rains. Before the arrival of developers, the rain filled Lake Okeechobee to the north until its waters' spilled over its banks and flowed southward at a snail's pace in a shallow sheet 50 miles wide. Now the human engineers shunt this water away from south Florida and direct it instead to a variety of compass points, driving it along 1,400 miles of canals and levees with some of the largest pumps in the world, eighteen of them to be exact, pumps capable of sucking water off the land at a rate of more than 20 billion gallons a day. To protect the human investment, the water is channeled by the shortest and quickest route to the sea, or it is spilled into marshes away from the man-made world. Overseeing the master plan is the U.S. Army Corps of Engineers. Assisting it is the South Florida Water Management District, which draws up the daily schedules and graphs. Its motto, "PROTECTING THE EVERGLADES SINCE 1949," adorns the doormats in its West Palm Beach offices.

The motto derives from a requirement that the system of flood control also allow for the protection of fish and wildlife as well as for the delivery of water to Everglades National Park. Often, however, fulfilling this requirement undercuts what Florida taxpayers have always considered the more important ones: controlling floods, supplying water for drinking and irrigation, and even facilitating navigation. To this day, the engineers and hydrologists haven't worked out the kinks. In times of little rain, water has been withheld north of the Park, while in times of flood it has been sucked from the settled landscape and discharged in sudden destructive surges to the southern Everglades.

In 1963, for example, the Corps of Engineers completed L-29, a levee and canal along a section of the northern border of Everglades National Park. As it happens, the early 1960s were a time of fierce drought in south Florida, and the levee choked off the last of what little water was arriving from the north. Alligators, already on the decline from overhunting, particularly suffered. Back in 1958, one researcher had counted 130 alligators in a one-mile section of the Park's Shark River Slough; when he returned to the same section in 1966, he could find only three. Two years later, another scientist calculated that one million alligators had once lived in the area now occupied by the Park; now, he concluded, there were only 10 to 20 percent of that. Panicked resource managers scurried through the sawgrass, trying to find water for this vanishing wildlife. Using dynamite, they blasted gator holes in the bedrock.

Park officials begged for water. As a result, Congress in 1971 ordered that a minimum amount be delivered monthly to the Park. Canals leading south were widened to facilitate the process. The problem now became too much water. The scheduled deliveries worked during some months, but at times of heavy rain the Park got huge additional slugs of water that had been removed from areas where it threatened farms and cities. Alligators, which had begun to increase in numbers after being declared endangered in 1973, now had trouble producing young. Their nests, so carefully positioned according to timeless reptillian calculation, were inundated and lost. They are in danger still, although to what precise extent remains unclear.

John Ogden's responsibilities require him to worry about alligators in the Everglades, but he worries more about wood storks. A small, sturdy man with a full gray beard, Ogden is a senior wildlife biologist at the South Florida Research Center at Everglades National Park. Like most wildlife biologists in south Florida these days, he spends much of his time indoors, reviewing data, reading reports, writing papers, talking to lawyers, and organizing symposiums—all of which he does in an office crowded with papers, skulls, and books in a section of the Park that is one of the last outposts of the Florida panther.

Ogden's own research for the Park Service, and before that the Audubon Society, has focused on the wood stork as an indicator species for the health of the Everglades ecosystem. He once told a reporter that he has snapped more than a thousand tags onto the wings of wood storks. He has concluded that the birds are abandoning Everglades National Park in ever greater numbers for more suitable, if less protected, habitat to the north, a trend that has been accelerating since the 1970s. In fact, Ogden has found that the number of storks nesting in the Park has dropped by 80 percent since the 1960s. Unless its habitat returns, Ogden believes, the stork will soon no longer nest there at all. Although the wood stork, a large bird as ungainly when perched as it is graceful when soaring, is an endangered species, Ogden is convinced that the true significance of its decline in Everglades National Park is that, to varying degrees, other species of wading birds are following it. He estimates that the population of all these birds had declined by 90 to 95 percent over the last half-century.

"This place isn't exceptional anymore," Ogden says rapidly in a voice sweetened by a slight Tennessee twang. "I've been here 25 years, and the change in that time has been just overwhelming. The pace of degradation since the 1960s has drastically increased to the point where this entire ecosystem is in the process of collapse."

"Ecosystem collapse" can be difficult to observe in a landscape as rich as the Everglades, but Ogden provides a graphic description. "This has always been an extremely complicated system," he says. "On its own, it was a predictably unpredictable system with tremendous seasonal variations." Dry seasons and wet seasons existed within a larger cycle of drought and flood. Over the flat landscape several habitat types developed: open ponds; sloughs with aquatic plants such as water lilies floating on the surface; wet prairies with emergent vegetation such as rushes poking through; uniform expanses of sawgrass; scattered stands of baldcypress; bay heads and willow heads; hardwood hammocks; forests of slash pine; and along the estuaries of the coast, some of the finest mangrove forest in the world.

All of these plants—as well as the animals dependent on them—evolved in response to tiny changes in levels of water and, to a lesser extent, salinity. A slough, for instance, may be only a few inches deeper than the standing water on a wet prairie, and in dry years the salt water off the coast may reach farther up the creeks, extending the coastal system. As if this topographic variety weren't baroque enough, the Everglades are as fluid in time as they are in space. Their hydrology is always shining, so that in dry months, a wet prairie may not be wet at all, and sawgrass, which a month or two before was standing in an inch or two of water, may burn down to the soil. In drought years, the peat itself may catch fire.

Faced with such a landscape, animals must learn to adapt quickly. Alligators become engineers, for example. One reason birds do so well in the Everglades is their mobility. When one pool dries up, they can fly to another. Like alligators, many species adjust their nesting habits to water levels. Wood storks are masters at this. Historically, they nested during November and December in Everglades National Park, at the early part of the dry season. At that time of year, many higher elevation marshes near the deeper sloughs still had water and fish, and the storks could feed there when not tending their eggs. Gradually, as the season progressed, the peripheral marshes dried up, and, in response, the storks moved their feeding to the deeper sloughs. The timing worked so that the stork chicks appeared near the end of the dry season, in March and April, when fish, concentrated in the remaining pools, were at their easiest to catch.

Aside from the rain that falls within its boundaries, nowadays the only water in Everglades National Park is the water that the government sends there. With wildlife protection such a low priority, the predictably unpredictable has become, over the last 45 years, simply unpredictable. The Park is so dry in November and December that the peripheral marshes have no fish in them, and the storks have adapted by postponing their nesting. They now must wait to form colonies until February and March, when the deeper sloughs become shallow enough for fishing. Unfortunately, this means the chicks emerge in May, June, and July. In most years, enough rain has arrived by then to disperse the concentrated fish, and, as a result, adult birds can no longer efficiently collect enough food for their young. These are the months when the landscape signals wood storks to abandon their colonies. Left behind, the unfledged chicks starve.

"The first time we realized this was happening," said John Ogden, "we built a pen outside the research center here to see whether it's possible to raise the chicks. It is. But it was an experiment driven more by emotion than by common sense. When we then released the chicks, they had become so accustomed to humans that they showed up begging for food at tents in the campgrounds. More importantly, we realized we were releasing them into what was now a hostile environment, so they probably wouldn't survive anyway." After that, Ogden and his colleagues let nature, as altered by the south Florida Water Management District, take its sad course.

Everglades National Park is widely regarded as the most endangered in the National Park System, and there is a general recognition there that it cannot be saved unless its keepers can somehow exert more influence over policy outside its boundaries. In past years, simplistic solutions had disastrous results, as in the late 1960s, when scientists believed that all the Park needed was as much water as it could get. Michael Soukup, who is the Park's research director and John Ogden's boss, argues that support for restoring the Everglades is rising, and both state and federal officials are beginning to envision solutions that are wider in scope. "If we thought the Everglades could be sustained within the Park's boundaries, we'd do it," he says. "But you just cannot have a naturally functioning ecosystem that stops there. This is the place that's teaching the rest of the National Park System that stopping at the boundaries doesn't work." When most people talk about the Everglades, they are referring to Everglades National Park, but even though its 1.5 million acres makes it the second largest national park in the contiguous United States, it represents less than 20 percent of the original Everglades. Even more remarkable, the Park's vast areas of estuary and mangrove mean that it actually contains fewer acres of freshwater Everglades than do the 1,344 square miles (860,000 acres) of wetlands stretching to the north and northeast of the park boundary.

You cannot truly comprehend the extent of this landscape until you see it from above. Last August, at the end of a particularly wet rainy season, I was flown by helicopter over much of this area. My hosts were representatives of the Florida Sugar Cane League, a trade group made up of Florida's largest sugar growers, who are often portrayed as the Everglades' worst enemy. A few weeks earlier, Florida's Department of Environmental Regulation and the South Florida Water Management District had settled a bitter lawsuit brought in 1988 by the federal government. In it, the United States charged the state with failing to enforce its own water quality laws by allowing farmers to pump water from their fields into the northern Everglades.

Just south of Lake Okeechobee, on what was once Everglades marsh, is a 700,000-acre tract known as the Everglades Agricultural Area (EAA). It is the home of a $1.5 billion farming industry led by U.S. Sugar, which, in addition to sugar cane, also grows millions of heads of lettuce in the EAA every winter. (U.S. Sugar also makes all of the salads sold in fast food restaurants in Florida.) In order to raise these crops in south Florida, growers must irrigate them in the dry season and protect them from floods in the wet season. For storage, they have used Lake Okeechobee, drawing water from it for irrigation and, more importantly, pumping excess water from their fields into it. But when the Lake showed signs of eutrophication several years ago, growers were forbidden from pumping as much water back into it. Instead they now discharge much of it into 1,344 square miles of Everglades that are collectively known as Water Conservation Area (WCAS) 1, 2, and 3.

The problem with this water is that it contains phosphorous at levels that ecologists believe cannot be absorbed by the Everglades ecosystem. When the WCAS were set aside in 1947, the year that the vast system of flood control canals was devised in south Florida, engineers cleverly thought that floodwaters could be stored in them during the wet season and pumped out again for irrigation and drinking water at other times of the year. The plan also provided for protecting the wildlife in the WCAS, which, after all, constituted the bulk of remaining Everglades habitat. In fact, since 1951 most of WCAI, the northernmost piece of Everglades left, has been managed by the U.S. Fish and Wildlife Service as the Loxahatchee National Wildlife Refuge.

Beginning about ten years ago, managers and scientists at Loxahatchee began to notice troubling changes at the refuge. Measurements around the marsh, together with research conducted by the South Florida Water Management District, revealed that phosphorous from EAA water was fertilizing the ecosystem. The most important effect was the breakdown of periphyton, the algal first link in the Everglades food chain. As phosphorous became established in the peat, the mixture of plants growing in it was becoming altered. Sawgrass, which is in fact a sedge ideally suited to low nutrient soils, was in some areas crowded out by cattails, which not only prefer higher levels of nutrients but deplete precious oxygen and water at far more rapid rates.

Estimates vary, but refuge staff now say that 24,000 acres of the WCAS have been affected. Loxahatchee, they believe, has in effect been acting like a 145,000-acre cleansing marsh, in which plants and microorganisms have been extracting phosphorous from the runoff before the water is sent south, where lower, but still abnormally high, levels of phosphorous have been detected at Everglades National Park. By allowing sections of the Loxahatchee ecosystem to become inexorably transformed into a more conventional marsh, and by allowing this polluted water to reach Everglades National Park, the United States claimed that the state and the District were failing to protect the Everglades—despite the motto on doormats in West Palm Beach.

The South Florida Water Management District responded to the suit by hiring the most expensive lawyers it could find. Over the next two years, it spent almost $6 million on lawyers who argued that, despite the District's own studies, nutrient loading was not a problem in the Everglades. The lawsuit brought the state and the District wave after wave of bad publicity from local, national, and even international media. Suddenly the entire world seemed aware that the Everglades were dying. After Lawton Chiles became governor earlier this year, he startled the District's lawyers on May 20 by declaring to the federal judge, "We want to surrender."

By mid-July, the state had negotiated a settlement agreement with the federal government that sets specific phosphorous limits in water entering both the Park and Refuge. Reductions are to be achieved in two ways: by farmers better managing their crops, and by the acquisition of almost 35,000 acres of EAA cropland to serve as filtering marshes, or "Stormwater Treatment Areas." Agricultural runoff will be held until enough phosphorous is removed by the plants and soil to allow the water to be discharged into the WCAS.

The growers, predictably, are outraged by the agreement, and, as of this writing, are trying to block it in state court. ("Oh, yeah," quips Carol Browner, Secretary of the Florida Department of Environmental Regulation. "We get sued every day by sugar. I call it 'suit du jour.'"). In the helicopter and on the ground in Miami, I listened to the farmers' arguments. Robert Buker, a vice-president of U.S. Sugar and the chairman of the Florida Sugar Cane League's environmental quality committee, insisted that the growers are being set up as politically correct scapegoats, that the real problem with the Everglades is not water quality but *quantity.* "This water quality problem is being portrayed as the locomotive drawing the train that's destroying the Everglades," he says. "It's not the locomotive, it's one of the cars." Governor Lawton Chiles describes the farmers' response as "defeatist." He says, "I was a U.S. Senator for 18 years, and they thought I was better than sliced bread. When I was campaigning for Governor, I told the farmers that number one, we're going to save the Everglades. I'm just doing what I said I was going to do."

Now that the quality of Everglades water has been more or less assured, environmentalists in Florida are intent on pushing forward the most ambitious attempt ever to rescue the Everglades ecosystem. "Over the long run, you can have pure water and still lose the Everglades," says Paul Parks, director of the Foreverglades project for the Florida Wildlife Federation and the former head of enforcement for the Department of Environmental Regulation. The talk now has shifted from saving the Everglades to restoring them.

Pressure for restoration comes from the Everglades Coalition, an alliance of national and state environmental groups (including The Wilderness Society) that was formed in 1985 to support then-Governor Bob Graham's Save Our Everglades program. Unlike most other large wilderness areas in the United States, the Everglades are managed by an unusually complex array of state and federal agencies, and the Coalition, with its wide range of membership organizations, has provided environmentalists with a mechanism for influencing all parts of the public process. Content at first with advocating such traditional steps as expanding Big Cypress National Preserve to the north of Everglades National Park and creating the Florida Panther National Wildlife Refuge. Coalition members have gradually realized that only a more comprehensive approach will prevent the loss of the Everglades. Coalition members like Jim Webb, The Wilderness Society's Florida Regional Director and a former Deputy Assistant Secretary of the Interior, have become convinced that the Everglades can be saved only through fundamental reform of the entire system of water management and delivery in south Florida.

On the scientific side, ecologists and hydrologists are acutely aware of their history of blunders. There is now the acknowledgement that the Everglades are in trouble not only because of agriculture, but because officials for every state and federal agency with management responsibility over them erred at one time or another, often out of ignorance, sometimes out of conscious and tragic choice. There is among researchers a certain excitement in the air, a sense that the knowledge of what the ecosystem needs in order to thrive again is now within reach. Hydrologists in particular now see the possibility of reintroducing "sheet flow," whereby water moves through the entire system in a wide swath rather than being pulsed into it at certain points. Wildlife biologists such as John Ogden are convinced that if the hydrology can once again resemble what it was before the canals and levees altered it, not only wood storks but many other animals will return in numbers to Everglades National Park.

This new era of good feeling for the Everglades has transformed old foes into allies. The restoration of sheet flow into Everglades National Park is being designed by the U.S. Army Corps of Engineers, the very agency that some environmentalists traditionally see as the source of the most serious problems. This sheet flow project grew in importance recently when officials realized it could help correct two of the most disastrous mistakes in the history of the Everglade's decline. The first was the drawing of the Park's boundaries. When the Park was established in 1947, most of the best land for development lay to the east, and to keep this real estate from being preserved, the northeast boundary was drawn straight through the heart of Shark River Slough, the great, sweeping channel for water into the southern Everglades, and critical habitat for wildlife, particularly in winter.

The second mistake had been the drying out of WCA-3B, located in the Shark River Slough just northeast of the Park. When the flood control project was built in south Florida, water was found to be leaking into the bedrock below this corner of the WCA. To prevent loss of this precious resource during the dry season, two levees and canals, the L-67 complex, were erected, effectively drying out WCA-3B and further reducing sheet flow to the south.

In 1989, Congress passed the Everglades National Park Protection and Expansion Act, authorizing the purchase of over 107,000 critical acres to the east of the Park, including a large section of Shark River Slough. This action was the first step in redrawing the Park's boundaries to reflect ecology rather than politics. Meanwhile, the Corps was developing plans to breach L-67 and allow water to flow once more into WCA-3B. By raising a portion of the Tamiami Trail that passes through the Slough, the Corps will then allow the sheet flow to proceed into the new eastern expansion of the Park and then curve toward the southwest into its midsection. By the turn of the century water will reach the Park by following the same route it used before humans ever set foot in the Everglades—if all goes well.

But simply clearing the route does not mean the water will flow in the right quantities at the right time. There are still all those canals and levees and culverts, and pumping stations to negotiate. It's easy for everyone to agree—as they do—that the timing and quantity of flows should be patterned on rainfall, but so little data exist on the pre-settlement Everglades that no one is sure exactly how it all used to work. "The hydrology stuff," says Paul Parks, "is going to make the pollution stuff look simple." It is so complicated in fact that only a computer could figure it out—and that's exactly what has happened. One Corps project just getting underway is the refinement of a computer model of rain-driven hydrology developed several years ago at the South Florida Water Management District. A breakthrough of sorts occurred with it two years ago when Thomas MacVicar, the model's original designer, modified it to produce a rough model of how the hydrology of the system would work with all the canals and levees removed. The program is being further sharpened while the Park Service and the Corps introduce habitat values into it in the hope that eventually these hydrological models will allow them to predict, on a precise and detailed scale, just how a certain housing development, say, or a certain pattern of water flow will affect the ecology of the Everglades.

Of course, even computer models are only as good as the assumptions of the people designing them. It will be years before there is anything approaching unanimity on many of them. "To restore hydrological flow to the Everglades," says Jonathan Moulding, ecologist for the Corps' Shark River Slough project, "you have to know three things: the volume of water, how it moves, and its timing. We've done a pretty good job of analyzing how it moves, and we've got a pretty good idea of how it moves in time. But volume is the piece we know little about. We just don't know how much water moved down the system historically, how much was lost by evapotranspiration. So what we're doing is designing these projects to give us maximum operational flexibility—what I call the guess-and-test method."

The obstacles to a large-scale Everglades restoration are as impressive as the technology being used to design it. Restoration costs money, for one thing. Cleaning the marshes alone will cost an estimated $300 million, and computer models and infrastructure work are also expensive. And then there is still the problem of conflicting demands for a limited supply of water. At least one South Florida Water Management District official, for example, has raised the specter of water shortages in Miami if the Everglades is allowed to have all the water it needs. One troublesome aspect of the water settlement agreement is that it may end up reducing the quantity of water available to the southern Everglades while nutrient-rich water is being held in the treatment marshes to be cleaned.

Finally, although a number of federal agencies cooperated to an unusual degree on the water quality lawsuit, there will no doubt be more disagreements. For several years now, the U.S. Fish and Wildlife Service has been objecting to the plan to restore sheet flow to WCA-3B, for instance. The water that has been denied WCA-3B through the years has tended to collect in the adjoining WCA-3A, and this deep water has attracted a population of critically endangered sail kites to the area. The fear is that breaching the levees will lower the water, prompting the kites to leave. The Park Service's response to this objection is that a fully restored water flow to Everglades National Park will eventually revivify traditional kite feeding areas within the Park, and this will more than offset the loss of the artificial habitat that has developed in 3A. The U.S. Fish and Wildlife Service is nervous about taking that chance.

All of these problems raise difficult questions about exactly what restoring the Everglades will mean. What is truly Everglades habitat in south Florida? What is truly wilderness? "We have this debate among ourselves in the environmental community all the time," says Paul Parks. "Is restoring 'The Everglades' really possible? Or is it better to concentrate on what we already have, like Everglades National Park, because everything else has already been too trashed to bring back?"

John Ogden's wish is to push for the largest conceivable restoration while still remaining flexible. "We say our goal is to restore an ecosystem," he says. "But realistically we know that, because of the irreversible loss of large parts of the ecosystem, ecological restoration is possible in only the 50 percent that's left. Yet our job is to push as hard as we can. We're down to five percent of the wading birds in the Park. Maybe if we push really hard we can get back to 15 or 20 percent. It may be too late for much more."

Given the history of management failures in the Everglades, this vision of restoring the system will almost certainly fail unless the agencies in charge of routing and apportioning water in south Florida can overcome decades of shortsighted approaches. There are hopeful signs—the Corps' work on the Shark River Slough project, Governor Chiles' appointments to the South Florida Water Management District board, for example—but one does not need to spend much time in District or Corps offices to sense that this is still new ground for these public servants, that their instinctive response to any new political wind, an instinct honed over decades of bureaucratic habit, is a guarded caution.

Yet, as Jim Webb points out, south Florida today is a radically different place than it was in 1947, when the Central and Southern Florida Flood Control Project was designed. Four million people now live along the Gold Coast of south Florida and by their sheer numbers have displaced farming as the most important economic and political force in that part of the state. Not only have they often expressed their desire to see the Everglades protected, but the source of the drinking water for many of them is the Biscayne aquifer, which, as it happens, is fed by a wet, healthy Everglades. Yet with minor adjustments, the system of flood-control canals is still managed according to the world as it existed in 1947. "The conflict," Webb says, "is essentially between people who need the Everglades system to be dry at its headwaters—mostly farmers—and everyone else." Now that the flood control system is physically complete, Webb suggests, the District and the Corps need to modify its structure and operation to bring it into harmony with the realities of the 1990s.

For instance, the loss of nearly a million acres of Everglades habitat to both the creation of the Everglades Agricultural Area in 1947 and to the draining and development of peripheral marshes since then has eliminated huge expanses where water was naturally stored and then slowly released into the system. Without replacing these storage areas, restoring the mechanism of sheet flow to the Everglades will be futile. Not enough water will get there. Water might be diverted from canals that now shunt huge quantities from Lake Okeechobee to the Atlantic Ocean and the Gulf of Mexico, but where would it go? Where are the marshes to store it? A fainthearted, piecemeal approach to restoration will likely keep questions like these unanswered for too long, and the result could be hundreds of millions of dollars wasted in a poorly conceived plan. "What it adds up to," Webb says, "is that we need a new water management system—call it the 'Everglades Project,' something to protect the economic life of this region in the twenty-first century and the ecosystem on which that life depends. Such a project will have to be designed *with* the natural power of the Everglades and not against it. The effort is as necessary as it is difficult and expensive. It will take time, and we don't have much."

But maybe enough. There is no other habitat in the world quite like the nascent Everglades, and there has never been a project with the breadth of this Everglades restoration. It represents a turning point, a public recognition that we can go too far in letting a vast wilderness decline and that we now have an opportunity to prove that scientists and environmentalists and even bureaucrats can for the first time return an entire ecosystem to health—even if it must be kept alive on a kind of mechanical life-support. The future of wetlands in much of the world may depend on getting this one right.

(Winter 1991)

FREDERICK TURNER

In The Highlands

In the mellow fall of the American Southeast in 1867, the lone hiker, John Muir, saw mountains for the first time in his twenty-nine years. He had known hills before—the gentle Lammermuirs in his native Scotland and then the modest undulations in his part of Wisconsin. But not mountains. On September 10th, he climbed steadily upward for six or seven hours in the Cumberlands, "a strangely long period of up-grade work," he noted in his journal, "to one accustomed only to the hillocky levels of Wisconsin and adjacent stress."

The Cumberlands were fine, and he would never lose the sense of exhiliration he got when for the first time he had the prospect from a mountain summit. Still, the best was yet to come there in the Southeast, and Muir instantly knew himself in the presence of true majesty when, four days later, he beheld the smoky, gauzy expanse of the Unaka range of the Southern Appalachians. The next day he often interrupted his climb to "take breath and to admire." On September 16th he talked with a mountain dweller who told the hiker he could take him to the highest ridge in the country, "where you can see both ways. You will have a view of all the world on one side of the mountains and all creation on the other." On the 18th he got that from a summit on the Tennessee/North Carolina border. "The scenery," he wrote, "is far grander than any I ever before beheld. The view extends from the Cumberland Mountains on the north far into Georgia and North Carolina to the south, an area of about five thousand square miles. Such an ocean of wooded, waving, swelling mountain beauty and grandeur is not to be described." Nonetheless, in characteristic fashion, he could not forbear at least a preliminary attempt to do just that: "Countless forest-clad hills, side by side in rows and groups, seemed to be enjoying the rich sunshine and remaining motionless only because they were so eagerly absorbing it. All were united by curves and slopes of inimitable softness and beauty." The mountain forests he now beheld wrung from him the first of what were to be hundreds of enraptured sputterings about mountain forest glory: "Oh, these forest gardens of our Father! What perfection, what divinity, in their architecture! What simplicity and mysterious complexity of detail!"

Not many months later Muir saw the Sierra, and he gave his heart to it forever. Still, the memory of this primitive encounter remained deep within him so that thirty-one years later, now rich and famous, he would leap at the chance to revisit the Southern Appalachians, writing his friend, Charles Sargent, that the prospect of a return to them "stirred up wild lover's longings. . . . I don't want to die," he continued, "without once more saluting the grand, godly, round-headed trees of the east side of America that I learned to love and beneath which I used to weep with joy when nobody knew me."

John Muir was hardly the first to be awed by the Southern Appalachians. Long centuries before, the Cherokee had come into them, though when Muir beheld the mountains that fall, the Cherokee had been deported to the flat and treeless territory of Oklahoma. They had left behind their remembrances of their forest home in the myths and legends that hung above the valley lands, coves, and slopes like that misty suspiration of the region's billions of trees and flowering plants.

They said their homeland had been shaped by the wing beats of the Great Buzzard as it had flown low over the warm, moist, and still malleable earth in the primordial days when Earth Island had first emerged from the seas. Wherever the Great Buzzard's wings struck the earth there was a valley, and where they turned up there was a mountain. The other animals, watching this, began to be afraid that the world would be all mountains and valleys, so they called the Buzzard back. But not before he had shaped a world where mountains were the dominant feature.

They said, too, that in this long ago world men and beasts and plants conversed together but that eventually the arrogance of the humans became so great that the animals conspired to wipe them out. Only the intervention of the plants saved the humans from annihilation. From that day the Cherokee reverenced the plant world, from the loftiest tuliptree to the low-lying touch-me-not, for all the plants had properties that were important in the grand scheme, and many were medicinal.

The first white expedition into the Southern Appalachians was De Soto's in 1540. He was lost, of course, which explains why he called the mountains "Appalachians," for that was the name of a tribe the bewildered explorer happened to remember from the Gulf Coast. About the only thing the expedition's chroniclers recorded of the Southern Appalachians was their height and their impenetrability—natural enough, since the Spaniards chronically wanted to be somewhere else in this disappointing New World other than where at the time they happened to be.

Something less than two centuries later whites were still complaining about these mountains that seemed always in the way of Progress. Trying to run a boundary line between Virginia and North Carolina, William Byrd of Westover found his efforts balked by the high, sudden rise of the Southern Appalachians. In some exasperation he wrote in his journal that "Our country has now been inhabited more than 130 years by the English, and still we hardly know anything of the Appalachian Mountains, that are nowhere above 250 miles from the sea." But their mystery was no mystery to him, only a great inconvenience.

They were anything but that to William Bartram when he wandered into them in the spring of 1775, in the midst of a four years' botanizing trip from Philadelphia. In Bartram the Southern Appalachians found their first white lyricist—and their only one before John Muir—a man who wanted nothing from the mountains except to experience something of their wonderful geological and botanical diversity. He was properly awed in the presence of these huge climax forests where he moved silently through groves of black oaks thirty feet in circumference at eye level, beeches and sweet gums 150 feet high, chestnuts, hickories, and northern red oaks that formed so dense and umbrageous a canopy that the forest floor was only here and there spotted with sunlight. "Incomparable forests," he called these, "magnificent high forests," "superb" in their stately, untouched groves. At a summit he beheld "with rapture and astonishment, a sublimely awful scene of power and magnificence, a world of mountains piled upon mountains." Those privileged to have seen some portion of the Southern Appalachians will well understand in reading Bartram how these mountain forests can quickly bring one to the limits of language.

I have seen them in the spring when the blaze of the rhododendron makes you wonder, as Bartram did, whether the slopes might be afire. I have seen them in summer when their characteristic haze softens the most rugged lineaments and the streams, almost wholly hidden by the luxuriant vegetation of their banks, gurgle with a seductive softness over dark stones. In winter I have stood in the wild mystery of the mountaintop "balds," knee-deep in heath that would not be out of place in Canada or Scotland; or in a stand of virgin tuliptrees in the Joyce Kilmer Memorial Forest where the great columnar trunks rose together into a thatched tangle, and there reigned a solemn, windless silence within. Here indeed is an evident majesty that would compel a kind of fealty from even the most prosaic and arrogant of visitors. Or so one would think.

These forests are remnants of those vast, broadleafed ones that covered much of the earth millions of years ago, so that looking upon them the white men—had they but known—were in fact being granted a glimpse of the way part of the planet looked when the continental land masses of Europe, North America, and Africa were joined. In the very few stands of virgin trees left in the Southern Appalachians today it is still possible to be confronted with the living evidence of that otherwise unimaginable time. But you don't have to search these few places out to find yourself in the presence of something just this side of eternity, for along almost any sizeable creekbed here you are likely to be looking at rocks far more ancient than the forests. About 200 million years ago the earth's crust began a gradual process of thrusting, buckling, and crinkling that produced these mountains and in so doing exposed older layers of rocks that now were heaved atop younger ones. Thus the phenomenon on view at Cade's Cove, Tennessee, for instance, where you can look upon exposed Ocoee rock some 500 million years old.

For myself, I find existential encounters such as with the hoary rocks of the Southern Appalachians almost self-annihilating after a while, as if regarding the grainy, weathered surfaces of these survivors of the days of creation—granite, schist, gneiss—were to stare, prisoner-like, at the impenetrable wall of Time itself. As a way of comprehending the uniqueness of the Southern Appalachians I feel more at home in thinking about the astonishing variety of life these mountains foster.

As the Southern Appalachians, we are speaking here of the southern Blue Ridge Mountains, the Great Smokies, and the ranges that cut across these: the Black Mountains, the Craggy Mountains, the Unakas, the Cowees, Natahalas, Balsams, and other, lesser, ranges. With Great Smoky Mountains National Park at its heart, this region includes the six surrounding national forests, totaling more than 3.5 million acres of federal land. Within this tumbled, high-piled world exists a densely patterned quilt of micro-habitats that weave together into an ecosystem unrivaled in its complexity anywhere else in North America or in Europe. This same quilt contains within it life forms representative of regions from the Canada Life Zone to the Southern Piedmont.

Consider the variety of this cursory inventory:

Mosses: over 400 species, nearly a third of the total for all of North America.

Mushrooms: 2,000 species within the confines of the Great Smoky Mountains National Park alone.

Salamanders: more than a dozen species, some so isolated in habitat that they have actually taken different evolutionary paths. The Yonahlossee salamander, for instance, is found only east and north of the French Broad River in southwestern Virginia and in North Carolina, and the Peaks of Otter species only on two small mountains in the Blue Ridge range. It is probable that other species are still out there awaiting discovery.

Bogs: home in the Southern Appalachians to species of plants and animals otherwise associated with far more northerly latitudes; they are found in the bogs here because they fled south ahead of the glaciers and then discovered they could survive quite well in this cool, lavishly watered environment—snowshoe rabbits live in Southern Appalachian bogs alongside Nashville warblers, hermit thrushes, and purple finches. Here, too, are found firs, like *Abies Balsamea*, more commonly associated with Maine and such other species as American larches and blue spruce.

Aquatic fauna of the region's myriad streams and rivers—the Rappahannock, Monongahela, Peedee, Tennessee—the tangerine darter, the spotfin chub, hornyhead chub, bluehead chub, river chub, rosyside dace—fifty species of fish and 300 aquatic species in all.

Birds: 159 species, including the increasingly rare golden eagle, the threatened American redstart, and the wild turkey, which has been making a strong comeback here.

Mammals: ninety species known to have lived here within historical times.

Flowering plants: over 1,000 along the Blue Ridge Parkway and 1,400 identified in the Great Smoky Mountains National Park.

Finally, and most gloriously, trees: more than 130 flowering trees and fourteen native conifers—as many total species as are to be found in all of Europe. Here are boreal forests in the mountains' higher elevations, northern hardwood forests on the cool, well-drained slopes: oak/hickory forests in warm, exposed areas, beech maple forests in cool, moist areas; pine/oak forests and northern riverine ones along the watercourses. Richest of all are the Appalachian cove forests wherein you might find as many as thirty species of trees: white basswood, Carolina silverbell, tuliptree, yellow buckeye, sugar maple, red maple, yellow birch, beech, white ash, bigleaf magnolia among the canopy trees; eastern redbud, box-elder, and sourwood among those of the understory. And beneath these, an almost bewildering crowd of shrubs—rhododendron, mountain laurel, flame azalea, fetterbush, wood anemone, mayapple, white trillium, American ginseng.

What a world is here, we might exclaim with the Cherokee and with Bartram and John Muir! What a precious gift!

When the news of discovery of the New World became widely known in the old one, and it became evident that this was not the fabled Far East but instead something different and unexpected, then it was said that the New World was a divine dispensation granted humankind, a second and final chance to begin again in this new Eden and this time to get things right. Here, mysteriously arising out of the gray wastes of the ocean, was a gigantic garden, and surely no part of it was more special, more stunningly diverse, more radically New World than the Southern Appalachians.

Unhappily, the fate of this portion of the new dispensation was prefigured far more accurately by the attitudes of the De Soto expedition and Squire Byrd than by Bartram and Muir. When in the wake of the French and Indian War in 1763 white settlers began to filter into the domain of the Cherokee—many coming down the Great Philadelphia Wagon Road into the rich bottomlands, others migrating inland from the coastal plains of Virginia, the Carolinas, and northern Georgia—then began that careless, arrogant process of despoilment that everywhere characterized humankind's stewardship of the New World. Many of these settlers were Scots or Scots/Irish, a fact worth remarking on since Scotland and Ireland were notorious in the Old World for the primitive rapaciousness of their land ethics. Raised in cultures with almost no traditions of wise usufruct, these Scots and Scots/Irish immigrants and their descendants helplessly recapitulated in the Southern Appalachians what they knew of land abuse.

As the best lands were entered upon, settlement crawled slowly upward into the mountains where the whites began a shifting and often shiftless existence on the precipitous, thin-soiled slopes. The most expedient evident method of clearing the land was to cut what trees you had to, then girdle the peripheral ones, leaving them to rot and fall. Then the planting of the corn fields. Quickly these little patches were worked into exhaustion, and then the settlers would move on elsewhere to repeat the same sorry process. When one mountain white was asked if he didn't weary of these endless removes, he answered, "Hell no. When it comes time to move, all I have to do is piss on the fire and call the dog." This hardscrabble existence produced over the years a rough, colorful, violent regional culture that astonished those few outlanders like Muir who happened into it. Part of that violence was directed against the land itself, a habit of hard, hasty, wasteful usage that evidenced itself with a fateful regularity down the generations.

By the end of the nineteenth century the more accessible portions of the region's forestlands had been cut over, mountain slopes that should never have been plowed had eroded away, and even some of the best bottomlands had been worked out and had become meager pastures.

Everywhere settlement advanced the game was quickly thinned out, and some species were hunted into extinction. The woods buffalo was the first to go, this around 1800. Shortly thereafter it was the turn of the elk. In the natural way of things the losses of these large, hoofed mammals and the drastic thinning of the deer population drove the wolf and the mountain lion to increasingly desperate reliance on the settlers' domestic stock—and with predictably fatal consequences for these predators: the mountain lion all but disappeared by the middle of the nineteenth century (though there persist reports of a few cats left in the Southern Appalachians), and the wolf was gone by the turn of the present century. The deer was almost gone by this same time. When author and naturalist Horace Kephart entered the Southern Appalachians in 1904, about the only large mammal that was hanging on in numbers remotely resembling those of the pre-settlement era was the black bear that stayed within the almost impenetrable forest interiors. Even small creatures now began to suffer significant losses, especially those species that caused the settlers inconvenience: wild turkeys that damaged corn fields, and raccoons, foxes, and weasels that raided chicken coops.

Still, the great, the crowning glory of the Southern Appalachians—the mountain forests—remained pretty much intact, though broken here and there, as I have said. To Horace Kephart in 1904 these forests looked about as unbroken and shaggy as they had to Muir in 1867. Then Muir had said this was "the most primitive country I have seen. . . ." And so it looked to Kephart, who found people in the mountains who had never been to a town nor seen a railroad, this when for the past seventy years in the rest of America the train had been a recognized symbol of Progress. All this changed in the first decade of the twentieth century with the coming of the northern lumber companies, some of which had long since obtained title to the better stands of timber from settlers glad enough to sell a patrimony that had proved stubbornly disappointing.

These companies had by this time pretty well logged out the pineries of Maine and the great stands of Wisconsin and the upper Midwest. The Southern Appalachian forests thus represented the last large-scale, commercially attractive stands east of the Mississippi—another sort of dispensation and last chance—and the companies went at them with will and ingenuity, logging the more accessible bottomlands first, then moving up into the higher elevations with their tooth-wheeled locomotives, their dynamite, their splash-dams, clear-cutting an area and then, like the mountain whites, pissing on the fire and calling the dog. The W. M. Ritter Company was typical, no better or worse than the rest. Beginning in 1910, Ritter mowed down the forests around Hazel Creek, Proctor Creek, and Walker Creek in western North Carolina and took out over two billion board feet. Then the company was gone with the wolf and the elk, leaving behind a blasted, denuded landscape. It was, Hazel Creek native Duane Oliver said, "a war against the forest," one in which the locals were happy to participate since the company's wages had bought them, in the short term anyway, a standard of living they had not previously enjoyed. Oliver said the Hazel Creek people were aware that the company's operations were leaving their mountains "ugly and ragged things," but "no one protested, for the economic benefits outweigh the aesthetic." One timber man bluntly described his company's attitude to Horace Kephart: "'All we want here,'" the man said, "'is to get the most we can out of this country, as quick as we can, and then get out.'"

By the first decade of the present century the Southern Appalachian forests had become fellows to all the others east of the Mississippi, and the condition of these once-magnificent places was grim indeed, so thoroughly had the settlers and their heirs and successors, the lumber companies, done their work. Surveying the history of the eastern forestlands, a report issued by the Conservation Foundation called them "the lands that nobody wanted." Accurate to a point, though it would be more accurate—and damning—to have called them the "lands nobody wanted any more." They had been that badly abused.

And yet, abused, cut over, burned, and eroded as they were, there were compelling reasons why the federal government should now have taken an interest in them. For one thing, forests were becoming fairly widely recognized as naturally efficient regulators of water-flow levels in regional streams and rivers. For another, second-generation growth was beginning to mature in those places that had been logged out earliest, and here and there were stands of virgin timber the loggers had missed or not yet gotten to. In the Southern Appalachians the former virtue was dramatically illustrated—if only in the negative—when heavy spring rains in 1907 angered the Monongahela along its course through a West Virginia now stripped of its hardwood groves. The resulting floods caused $100 million in damages, an astronomical sum for that time, and a significant one even in our own. Robert Zahner of Highlands, North Carolina, a retired forestry professor and a preeminent authority on the life and history of the Southern Appalachian forests, said the first steps to establish national forests in the region were hardly coincidental with the devastation caused by the flooding of 1907. "These mountains are the headwaters for virtually all the major streams of the Southeastern United States," he said. "They [the federal government] simply had to do something to preserve and insure regulated water flows for all those towns and cities. People talk now about the timber in these forests when really their most important natural resource was water."

In 1907 no forest reserves, as they were then called, existed east of the

Mississippi, and so if any were now to be created, they would have to be purchased by the government from private ownership rather than carved from large blocks of the public domain as had been the case in the West. This fact was to prove in the short run a considerable difficulty when establishing eastern national forests, while in the long run it has remained a source of difficulty for forest managers, since all the national forests in the East are peppered with inholdings and otherwise fragmented.

Nonetheless, in the wake of the Monongahela flooding the time was as right as it ever would be for the introduction of federal legislation authorizing government purchase of lands for the establishment of national forests in the East. Acting on the recommendation of the National Conservation Commission, Representative John W. Weeks of Massachusetts introduced a bill in July 1909, "to enable any state to cooperate with any other state or states or with the United States, for the protection of the watersheds of navigable streams, and the appointment of a commission for the acquisition of lands for the purpose of conserving the navigability of navigable rivers." Weeks' bill provided for an appropriation of a million dollars for the current year and two million for each succeeding year to 1916, these funds earmarked for the purchase of Southern Appalachian forestlands as well as some in New Hampshire's White Mountains.

Tellingly, the Weeks proposal quickly stirred up a hornet's nest of opposition in Congress, and during the next two years it occasioned, according to public domain historian Roy M. Robbins, "more bitter wrangling . . . than any other conservation measure" to that point in time. Its opponents attacked it on the grounds that it was unconstitutional and that its covert goal was forest conservation, not water flow regulation. Nevertheless, the Weeks Act, as it came to be known, became law in 1911, and under its authority some Southern Appalachian forestlands now gained federal protection with the establishment of the Pisgah National Forest (1916), the Nantahala and the Cherokee (1920), and the Sumter, Chattahoochee, and Jefferson (1936). A further important measure for the biological health of the region was the creation of the Great Smoky Mountains National Park in 1934, thus sparing from the saws of the Champion Fibre Company and smaller outfits remnant stands of virgin forestland in the very biological heart of the region.

Now began the restoration of the Southern Appalachian forests along with those others rescued under the same federal legislation. In all these forests the Forest Service instituted an ambitious program of replanting and soil conservation. They implemented tough and comprehensive fire protection methods. Best of all, they left the forests' stands of second-generation trees to grow undisturbed toward full maturity. "The rehabilitation of the eastern national forests," wrote the authors of the Conservation Foundation report, "ranks as one of the most remarkable conservation achievements of this century."

In the Southern Appalachians, the Forest Service has taken a justifiable pride in its record of conserving and bringing back the forests under its jurisdiction, and it is still reminding its regional critics of how trashed these tracts were when it assumed stewardship. But these days there are more and more critics and fewer and fewer non-agency champions of the Forest Service's work there, and the agency itself is sounding more and more shrill in its defense of its current policies and future plans. More and more, too, it has resorted to playing with numbers in an attempt to explain practices that many in the region find either bizarrely misguided or cynically shortsighted.

Robert Zahner dates the end of the agency's wise stewardship in the Southern Appalachians as occurring some time in the decade following World War II, when housing shortage pressures, felt nationwide, became translated into pressures to up the cut in the Southern Appalachians. Nationally, the accelerated cuts following the war are indeed striking: annual national forest timber sales leapt from 1.5 billion board feet in 1951 to 8.3 billion a decade later to 11.5 billion board feet in 1971. There was also a concurrent rise in logging road mileage on national forest lands: from 36,000 in 1940 to 106,000 in 1970. The managers of the Southern Appalachian national forests shared fully in the making of these trends, and so did they also in an increasingly heavy reliance on clearcutting as the harvesting method of choice.

But as alarming as these nationwide trends were—and remain—when they are considered along with the fact that all too often the Forest Service was losing money on its aggressive new timber program, the situation plainly called for remedial legislation. Which is what it got with the enactment of the Multiple Use-Sustained Yield Act (1960), the Wilderness Act (1964), and the National Forest Management Act (1976). While they had additional purposes as well, these three pieces of legislation may usefully be viewed here as attempts to correct the Forest Service's increasingly pronounced tilt toward full-throttle timber harvesting at the expense of all other facets of forest management. Thus far, it must be said they have not accomplished this corrective, for the evidence plainly points to the fact that the agency's operative standard of "use" has continued to shrink so that it bears uncomfortable comparison with Wendell Berry's now-classic definition of the land exploiter, who, Berry says, "asks of a piece of land only how much and how quickly it can be made to produce. . . ."

Nowhere have Forest Service critics been more vocal, more active, or better organized than in the Southern Appalachians, and precisely because an increasingly broad spectrum of the regional population has become aware of what a richly diverse landscape they live in. In Virginia, in North Carolina, in Tennessee, South Carolina, and in northern Georgia another kind of forest has sprung up in recent years and grown to a swift and urgent maturity: local volunteer conservation groups formed in opposition to Forest Service policies and long-range plans—Cherokee Forest Voices, Western North Carolina Alliance, Chattahoochee ForestWatch, Friends of the Mountains, and many other groups began speaking for the land in ways no whites there had ever done before.

In the fall of 1989, Peter C. Kirby, Southeastern Regional Director of The Wilderness Society, articulated some of the major concerns of these regional conservation groups in testimony before Wyche Fowler's Senate Agriculture Committee's Subcommittee on Conservation and Forestry. In a stinging, fact-studded lecture, Kirby made the incisive connections between the Forest Service's announced plans for sharply increased timber harvests, its aggressive program of new road construction, its practice of timber sales-below-cost, and the mounting threats to biological diversity on these lands. All of these trends, Kirby pointed out, were national in scope, but all of them were at the same time felt with particular keenness in the Southern Appalachians.

Moreover, the road construction costs play a large role in the endemic pauperization of the budgets devoted to soils and water, recreation, and fish and wildlife. In the past three years in the Southern Appalachians the amount spent by the Forest Service on new road construction exceeds handsomely the *combined* total spent on these other components of multiple use.

Don Rollens, recently retired as supervisor of the Cherokee National Forest, said he regarded new road construction as a "pseudo issue." "We construct these roads with great care," he told me, accepting as apparently axiomatic that they should be built at all. "They're constructed so they'll have minimum impact on the forest floor. We make sure we have ample filter strips, water bars, narrow widths (only twelve feet wide). These are not highways we're talking about. They're minimum standard roads."

"Not mentioned by Rollens," Peter Kirby notes, "is the sorry record in these mountains of road construction that disqualifies areas from wilderness designation—not to mention silting up prime trout streams, opening up bear habitat to poachers, and so much erosion that entire hillsides have been known to slide away." If the Forest Service should have its way, within the next half century these national forests would have almost two miles of road per square mile of land. And this does not even consider the state, county, and private roads that already course through the forestlands. Further: you would still have to confront what might be the road system's most serious, negative long-term effect: the further fragmentation of the forests, the destruction of existing wildlife corridors, and the creation of new forest edges along which wildlife processes are often adversely affected.

Forest Service Plans for the Chattahoochee, Cherokee, Jefferson, Nantahala-Pisgah (managed as a single unit), and part of the Sumter National Forests have all been challenged by regional conservation groups, and with good reason. In the six-forest region they called for a doubling of the annual cut by 1996 over the average annual levels of the previous decade, and a tripling of it by 2020. In the furtherance of such a substantial increase in harvesting, the bulk of the forests is opened to logging, primarily through clearcutting, and to related road construction. The agency is by law (the National Forest Management Act (NFMA)) obligated to determine in its management plans those lands on which timber harvesting is physically unjustifiable, yet in the plans for the six forests *not a single area* was so listed, this despite the fact that a significant portion of these mountainous forestlands is characterized by steep slopes and thin, fragile soils. Under the same NFMA the agency is required to determine acreage on which it would be economically unfeasible to log. In the six-forest area a trifling seven percent of the land base was so judged, and this in the face of three contravening facts: 1) much of the timber in these forests is considered by contemporary commercial standards to be of relatively low quality; 2) for the Southern Appalachian timber industry, national forests provide only about ten percent of the region's annual supply, the rest coming from private lands; 3) while sale volume from national forest lands has gone steadily up, average prices for federally owned timber have gone steadily down. Small wonder then that the regional conservation groups have expressed an amazed outrage. The only truly puzzling matter is what prompted the Forest Service to frame such harvest forecasts in the first place.

Not quite so puzzling—once you consider the interior "logic" under which the Forest Service appears to be operating—is the issue of new road construction. If annual cuts are to be increased to anything approaching the planned targets, then it follows that the agency's already outsized road system would have to be expanded to provide access to the timber. Expanded by an additional 3,263 miles. If completed to such a specification, the six-forest system would be 8,214 miles in extent, a distance longer than from Denver to New Zealand, from Atlanta to Tokyo. In his testimony before the Fowler subcommittee, Peter Kirby claimed the construction of logging roads caused "more environmental damage than virtually any other element of the timber program. . . ." These roads, he continued, "scar scenic mountains, silt up streams, intrude into remote wildlife habitat, pave over hiking trails, disrupt backcountry recreation, and destroy potential wilderness."

They are also very costly: nationwide about half the money the agency spends on its timber programs goes to road costs. In the Southern Appalachians with their steep grades the costs of road construction are even greater than elsewhere, running to about $40,000 per mile.

From a strictly economic point of view—which is what the Forest Service often urges when it is criticized by conservation groups—these roads, the ones already in existence and those on the books, have deservedly been styled "roads to red ink." They are just that since here the Forest Service fails to so much as break even on the operation of its timber program. In Fiscal Year 1988, the total loss for the six forests was $5.9 million; adding in related overhead costs, from both the regional and Washington offices, the total is $9.1 million. The pre-overhead figures for 1989 are just about as depressing: minus $5.7 million. And there are those who claim that even these figures understate the true nature of the losses, since in Georgia and North Carolina the Forest Service adds in the money it makes on timber sales from the flat pine forests of the Piedmont and coastal areas in an attempt to disguise the magnitude of its losses in the Southern Appalachians.

Even those who might condone current agency policies on timbering if these were truly money-making are plainly disgusted with the state of affairs. William Meyer of Tellico Plains, Tennessee, a descendant of the Chickamauga Band of the Cherokee Nation, said he had no trouble at all with the basic concept of the Southern Appalachian national forests as revenue-producing units of the federal government. He said that in furtherance of this he favored a substantially broadened and increased system of users's fees for the forests. But, he concluded, the below-cost-sales operation had "a lot of people around here just fed up. When the Forest Service comes out and says—again—that the national forests are supposed to generate revenues, I say, 'Great!' But when are the going to start producing some? Every year it seems they tell you, 'We've turned this thing around.' Then the figures come out and you see they haven't at all."

The plain facts, then, are these: the demand for national forest timber is low, the grade of that timber is low, and the prices it can fetch are also low. On the other hand, the costs of running the timber program are high. The net result is a good deal for the larger, more affluent regional lumber companies that can afford the expensive cable equipment often required to work the forests' steep grades. For the rest of the region's population it's a deep bath in the red.

These are all obvious matters of concern to the residents of the Southern Appalachians, and they are the major reasons why the Forest Service's plans for the six forests have all been subjected to appeal (and in the case of the

Nantahala-Pisgah plan, sent back by the Chief for reanalysis). But the long-term concern, the threat Forest Service policies and plans pose to the preservation of the region's magnificent biological diversity, has been slower to emerge into public consciousness, more difficult to articulate. Road construction and red ink are more discernible than the slow, piecemeal, often hidden reductions of the life of these forests.

Not, however, to those who make their daily lives so close to the forests that they can see the changes and through them divine the bleak and Spartan shape of the future. Such a person is Elmer Hall, who operates a hostel on the Appalachian Trail in North Carolina. Sitting at lunch in Asheville with Hall and Mary Kelly of the Western North Carolina Alliance, I listened to them talk about the Forest Service's use of herbicides to kill out the native species of undergrowth that compete with commercial seedlings in a clearcut—rhododendron, sassafras, basswood, dogwood. These plants in the turnings of history have now lost their status as native residents and become "undesirables." "Listen," Hall said, turning to me with soup spoon paused in midair, "they (the Forest Service) look upon the forests like a farmer looks upon a cornfield: when he looks out there, he doesn't want to see anything in it but corn, and that's the way they are. Basically, what they want is tree farms. They'll clear-cut, burn, spray to keep out the 'undesirables,' and then create these stands of pine and poplar—early succession species. I'll tell you *nothing* is more depressing and shocking than to encounter one of these areas in the mountains with all its glorious, natural diversity destroyed." People, he said, "come to these forests to get *away* from the homogenized world, and here they find it again."

This latter point is, of course, precisely the one John Muir made when he began crusading for national forests a century ago: that city dwellers were wasting away from lack of what "these grand old forests" could give them. Much earlier, when he had first seen the Southern Appalachians that Fall of 1867, Muir had in fact himself been in flight from the city and what Elmer Hall called the "homogenized world." Working in an Indianapolis carriage factory, Muir with his characteristic perspicacity had understood that the fundamental principles of modern manufacturing—the elimination of distinguishing differences, the paramount need for uniformity, and the interchangeability of parts—were also to be the fundamental principles of modern existence. In leaving the factory for his long walk south, Muir had been renouncing his own part in such a future, and in the forests of the Southern Appalachians he had discovered the complete opposite of what he had left behind.

Now, however, having brought these same forests halfway back to what they were when Muir beheld them, the Forest Service appears bent on once again destroying their integrity and simplifying their arboreal diversity to favor stands of oaks, pines, and poplars. If they do not actually envision tree farms that have the productive regularity of cornfields, as Elmer Hall charged, they evidently do have in mind a profoundly managed landscape that answers more to the bureaucratic cast of mind than to the more complex order of nature. The cutting up of the forests into areas of commercial productivity and the steadfast refusal to manage the six-forest area as an integrated ecosystem are the lazy conveniences of those who see biological diversity as a pseudo issue raised by hysterical tree-huggers.

In fact, forest fragmentation, caused by road construction, clearcuts, type conversions, simplifications, and the district-by-district approach to management, constitutes the major threat to real biological diversity because it tends to isolate nature into islands of increasing artificiality. "Forest fragmentation," Robert Zahner has written, "leads to inbreeding and extinction for those species of the forest interior with limited mobility for migration. Genetic diversity is essential to provide sufficient adaptability within each species to give that species the capacity to adjust and evolve to survive the accelerating environmental changes expected in the next century." The greater the number of what Zahner calls "mature habitat types" in a given landscape, the more biologically stable that region will be. "Optimum regional biodiversity," he continues, "requires continuity of habitats contiguous over a landscape in a mosaic of mature communities." In the Southern Appalachians this translates into allowing those large linked areas of second-generation forests to continue to ripen onward to become authentic old-growth forests with their rich and ordered riot of growing, dying, down, and decaying life. Such areas in addition to the region's thirty-one federally designated wildernesses and additional proposed new wilderness areas would provide all of the requisite conditions for restoring to the Southern Appalachians portions of old-growth landscape.

While it readily acknowledges that under the provisions of the National Forest Management Act it is obligated to protect and foster biological diversity, in actual fact Forest Service practices do something substantially different: they routinely encourage more common, more abundant species at the expense of rarer and more sensitive ones. More specifically, where biological diversity is seen to conflict with the requirements of timber management, the Forest Service has been consistently making decisions sacrificing the former to the latter. White-tailed deer, eastern cottontails, and brown-headed cowbirds are all species that can thrive in forest edges and clear-cuts, and the Forest Service will tell you that their numbers are all up. But biological diversity, as they well know, is not a matter of numbers only. Managing its forests in such a way as to encourage species that have at present no lack of usable habitat throughout the Southern Appalachian region, while at the same time negatively affecting rarer species, is not really protecting and encouraging true diversity. It is instead using the populations of selected species to mask the ever more restricted habitats of rarer ones such as the ovenbird, the American redstart, and the black bear. All of these require large, intact forest tracts of the sort the agency's policies and plans will make increasingly rare in the next half century.

The case of the black bear is as urgent as it is symbolic. The Cherokee, like many another aboriginal group, saw the bear as a mythic creature standing in some special relationship to the spirit world. One of their legends tells how a hunter in the mountains shoots a bear, then follows it, wounding it again and again without being able to bring it down. It is in fact a "medicine" bear, and presently it turns to the hunter and speaks: "It is of no use for you to shoot at me, for you cannot kill me. Come to my house and let us live together." The hunter agrees and for a year lives with the medicine bear, gradually losing his human nature and taking on that of his host. When at last he is found by his people and returned to civilization, he sickens and dies because "he still had a bear's nature and could not live like a man."

Among other things, the legend tells us that the Cherokee found something strangely attractive about the far-ranging life of this shy, reclusive dweller of the forest interior, that perhaps in an unknown way bear life if truly experienced might turn out to be more satisfying than that lived by humans. Now, however, the life of humans in the Southern Appalachians threatens that lived by the black bear, now reduced in territory to something between five and ten percent of its former range. Only on national forest and national park lands and wilderness areas does the bear hang on, a reminder of the primeval days of the tribes and of something even more ancient: of those great climax forests that once were home to the elk, the mountain lion, and the wolf, a time when humankind was not a factor.

For the black bear population the loss of the American chestnut was a blow, since before the great blight, chestnut mast was a staple of the bear's diet. But the creature is amazingly intelligent and resourceful and has until now been able to make do. What it may not be able to survive is further forest fragmentation, the elimination of protective travel corridors, and the increasingly deadly weaponry of its human predators. Dr. Michael Pelton, a black bear authority at the University of Tennessee, writes that the "species' further existence depends on the availability of a diversity and abundance of late successional (greater than 100 years) oaks and alternate fall seedberry species, old growth forests . . . distributed throughout its range (and) limited future road development." In the Southern Appalachians the only one who can hope to provide these habitat requirements is Uncle Sam.

Whether Uncle Sam's Forest Service has the will and the vision to do so remains to be seen. But this much is clear: if the black bear is squeezed out of the Southern Appalachian national forests, then the Forest Service's statutory obligation to preserve and encourage biological diversity there will have been effectively rendered extinct as well, and the nature of the future will have been made evident. Where once we had authentic forests, now we shall have those regimented tree farms of which Elmer Hall spoke—clean, predictable, spiritually empty places where twenty-first century Americans will go to discover the meaning that has lain latent in the words of Thoreau: "From the desperate city you go into the desperate country. . . ."

In that twenty-first century there will be more and more Americans who will resort to the national forests of the Southern Appalachians. Mary Kelly of the Western North Carolina Alliance pointed out that approximately two-thirds of the nation's people live within a long day's drive of the Southern Appalachians, and Forest Service figures for the past decade show a steady rise in the number of visitors to the forests. They deserve better than what the agency evidently has in mind for them. They deserve to experience the luxuriant complexity of this ancient, much abused, yet resilient ecosystem. They deserve to find themselves in the presence of all those mosses, mushrooms, salamanders, and birds, the stunning variety of the cove forests. They deserve the oddly comforting knowledge that somewhere out there, beyond where they will ever penetrate, in the tangled inaccessibility of old-growth forests, the black bear still ranges on his reclusive way, a being who is good medicine for them: a living reminder of what all of the New World once was and what it symbolized to the Europeans who entered into it with the burden of their history and their dreams. This need not become the desperate country. It should not.

(Fall 1990)

A note from the editors: In 1991, Forest Service critics—led by Senator Wyche Fowler of Georgia—succeeded in reducing appropriations for road building by $40 million, the first in a series of annual reductions that lessened the threat of logging in many important roadless areas of the Appalachians. That same year, Congress passed the Chattahoochee Forest Protection Act, which not only designated the Blood Mountain and Mark Trail wilderness areas (neither of which had been recommended by the Forest Service) but established the Ed Jenkins National Recreation Area and the Coosa Bald National Scenic Area. The bill had enjoyed the support of the entire Georgia delegation—including future Speaker of the House Newt Gingrich. Finally, following a successful administrative appeal by The Wilderness Society, the Forest Service was forced to scale back its timber goals for the Nantahala-Pisgah national forests by more than half.

JOHN G. MITCHELL

Love and War
in the Big Woods

pring should be as good a time as any to fly north to the Maine
Woods, if only it were not for the fact that Autumn can be better.
And Autumn is best when the leaves are running yellow and gold
and russet and red and you can see how all these Yankee hardwoods, these
poplars and birches and beeches and maples, weave their incandescent patterns across the black-green tapestry of spruce and fir. I promise you it is
something special to behold on a crystal morning with the pilot floating his
Cessna two thousand feet above the Kennebec Valley, the visibility unen-
cumbered for eighty miles out, the back-seat passenger behind you plugged
into the intercom for instant geographic replay, and a cherished misconception or two beginning to unravel through the lens of the birds-eye view.
And what we see isn't even a quarter of it, barely the tamest edge. To frame
the whole, you'd have to run a line from the Mahoosuc Range off the portside wing to the faraway Meddybemps, starboard; from cockpit north to
Canada. One hundred and eighty degrees of forest, 15 million acres of it, the
biggest forest of its kind left in any one state between the shores of Lake
Superior and the shoals of the Maritimes.

For perspective now—before we get too far over this forest and too deeply
into various accounts of its questionable and possibly perilous future—it
would be well to remember that the Maine Woods are not only big but
wholly unlike any other in the United States of America. We're not botanizing here: we're talking about the history of use and ownership. We're talking
about a forest the accessible parts of which have reverberated to the sounds of
the industrial ax and saw for three centuries. On his way to "Ktaadn," 150

years ago, Henry David Thoreau observed on the Penobscot and its tributaries above Bangor fifty sawmills annually grinding out 200 million board feet of lumber. "The mission of men there," wrote Thoreau, "seems to be, like so many busy demons, to drive the forest all out of the country, from every solitary beaver-swamp and mountain-side, as soon as possible."

Hold on now, Henry David! Those days, there was *no way* for men to drive the forest out of northern Maine. For one thing, the sawyers then didn't have access to feller-bunchers and chippers. For another, the grain in Maine is well-endowed with rain and snowmelt, and spruce and balsam have a delightful ability to seed themselves unassisted, even as most of the hardwood species enjoy the gift of resurrection by sprouting from stump or root. So, as the doublebit lumberjacks lit out for virgin territory, the born-again Maine Woods bounced back to become America's premiere producer of pulp and paper.

But what truly sets these woods apart from any other is how utterly *private* they are. We are talking ownership now, and of the 15 million forest acres spread out below our bouncing Cessna, not even one million are publicly owned. The Feds hold but a fraction of that: a few modest wildlife refuges tucked into the fringes of the Northern Forest, a small lobe of the White Mountain National Forest poking through from New Hampshire, and a slender greenway bracketing stretches of the Appalachian Trail. Almost all of the rest that is public is Maine's, including Baxter State Park in the heart of the big woods.

That leaves some 14.2 million acres in private hands, a bit under half of it held by individuals—thousands of them—and a baker's dozen associations that manage timber for various familial trusts and estates. These are the "nonindustrial" landowners, so-called because they do not own and operate mills, only woodlands. The rest, some 7.7 million acres, is owned by big pulp and paper-making corporations such as Georgia-Pacific, International Paper, Scott, Champion, James River, and Boise Cascade. Proportionally, these lands represent the greatest concentration of industrial forestland in any one state. The presence of the industrials here is the greatest single reason why 40 percent of the state's manufacturing output and 10 percent of its active work force are tied directly to the trees of the Maine Woods. Not surprising, then, that even among some Mainers *not* directly employed by industry there is a tendency to adopt the industry's point of view, especially in matters relating to use of the Maine Woods.

Now I have word through the intercom from the backseat passenger. His name is Jym St. Pierre and he is The Wilderness Society's man in Augusta. He reminds me, as the hamlet of Greenville pops into view on the hard blue edge of Moosehead Lake, that we are approaching the southern outliers of the proposed Maine Woods Reserve, a paper concept advanced by The

Society in the Spring of 1989 to protect about 2.7 million acres of the Maine Woods around Baxter State Park from the kind of development pressures then abuilding across the forests of northern New York and New England. The Reserve idea did not suggest the creation of one great big park or wilderness area, but rather the application of a variety of protection strategies—state or federal purchase (from willing sellers, the proposal emphasized) of certain critical areas, imposition of land-use regulations already in existence, acquisition of conservation easements, and the use of economic incentives, as in tax-code changes, that would encourage landowners to continue growing conifers instead of condominiums. The Reserve idea was not designed to make war on the paper companies and the familial trusts, but to make love with them, if you will, in the interest of an economically, recreationally, and ecologically sustainable forest.

Well, that wasn't the way some Mainers heard it. The way some heard it, this whole Reserve thingamajig was nothing less than a federal landgrab, a scheme to lock the locals and the companies out of the forest and turn it into a romper room for Outsiders. For it was no secret to those who felt strongly about such things that—even with Jym St. Pierre presiding in Augusta and The Society's other New England man and author of the concept, Michael J. Kellett, based in nearby Boston—the *real* home of The Wilderness Society was and is unforgivably Outside, in Washington, D.C.

All of which poses a puzzlement to me as we wing it over Greenville. I am thinking how curious it is that while the disenchanted in Maine fret over a nonprofit idea hatched in Boston, Massachusetts, and Washington, D.C., hardly anyone at all seems concerned by the fact that more than half of the North Maine Woods and a good three-quarters of the proposed Reserve is controlled by forest-industry folks with boardroom votes and Wall Street ideas hatched not in Bangor, Brunswick, or Biddeford, Maine, but in Stamford, Connecticut; Purchase, New York; Philadelphia, Pennsylvania; Richmond, Virginia; Atlanta, Georgia; Boise, Idaho; and—if you throw in some industrial landowners whose mills are located out-of-state—various cities in the eastern provinces of Canada as well as that supreme Outside consumer of North American fiber, the sovereign nation of Japan.

There are so many lakes up here in the Maine Woods—nearly five thousand. From this particular point in the sky the woods appear absolutely spangled with splashes of silver and blue. All these waterfronts, and the mountain views, too. No wonder they call this slice of the pie the Wildland Lakes Region. Give a real estate huckster half a chance in this kind of country, in a riper market for the sale of wilderness ranchettes, and you're looking big trouble square in the eye.

It wasn't all that long ago that the huckster's half chance seemed about to happen. I refer to a corporate raid by the European financier Sir James Goldsmith; to his takeover of Diamond International of matchstick and papermaking fame; to a subsequent reshuffling of Diamond assets, including the sale of a million acres of timberlands scattered across the northern forests of New York, Vermont, New Hampshire, and Maine; and to the frantic scrambling by three of those states to rescue the land from developers. The fourth state, Maine, did not have to scramble. In Maine, almost all the Diamond properties went to other paper companies. As things turned out, a few tree huggers salute James Goldsmith for having given everyone a good scare. For out of that fright came the interstate Governors' Task Force on Northern Forest Lands, which begat the Northern Forest Lands Study, which begat a federally funded Northern Forest Lands Council, which has lately begotten a good deal of political handwringing and public flak, especially right here in the Pine Tree State.

Though recessionary times have temporarily crimped the real estate market, the specter of development still hovers on the horizons of the northern forests. History tends to get cyclical about such things. Today's bust becomes tomorrow's boom. Not that everyone sees it that way. The industry doesn't see it that way. The executive director of the Maine Forest Products Council, Ted Johnston, who is also the leading industrial voice on the Forest Lands Council, tells me the threat of rampant second-home development trashing the North Woods is just as much hot air. Even with I-95 reaching beyond East Millinocket, he says, the region is too remote to sustain a land rush, even in better times.

On the other hand, there is the perspective of Roger Milliken, president of the Baskahegan Company, a family-owned nonindustrial with 100,000 acres of timberlands in Washington County. Milliken sits on the boards of both the Maine Forest Products Council and the Natural Resources Council of Maine, the state's largest environmental advocacy organization, which makes him a bit of a Down East anomaly. He tells me that the sale of northern timberlands for development cannot be ruled out. He pictures for me a struggle between the warm attachment to the land of some nonindustrial types and the cool detachment of the MBAs who are looking over their shoulders, asking how all these trees and acres can be justified at the bottom line. Milliken says, "You know, it doesn't take a whole lot of development to impact what people most cherish about these woods. To me, it's not a question of how *much* development there's going to be, but of how to work out a way to protect the lands and values that are really important—without hurting the landowner."

And there is the perspective of Jerry Bley, the Readfield land-use consultant who sits as Maine's environmental representative on the interstate

Northern Forest Lands Council. Bley echoes Milliken's contention that a few developed sites scattered through the woods can go a long way toward compromising the region's ecological and recreational values. Bley says, "Ten years ago, no one thought it would be possible for someone to buy up 10,000 acres of northern Maine and divide it into large lots and sell them at a great profit to people from Boston and beyond. But that's exactly what happened in the eighties. And that's why you can't predict what's going to happen ten years from now."

And the perspective of attorney Catherine Johnson of the Natural Resources Council of Maine: "The people who say there is no development threat aren't looking at the statistics that are coming out of LURC." LURC is the state's Land Use Regulation Commission, which has zoning and other growth management responsibilities for the ten million acres of Maine's unincorporated northern territory. "The two biggest subdivisions ever proposed for the North Woods," Johnson says, "have come before LURC in the past two years. There is development at the core of the woods, not just along the fringe. It is happening all the time."

The concerns of people like Johnson and Bley are clearly reflected in a Natural Resources Council position paper calling for the creation of a "North Woods Conservation Area" to preserve Maine's "traditional" forest uses, including management for timber production. According to the council's strategy, the conservation area could be established by applying an existing but unused LURC tool, Natural Character Management Zoning, to "a major portion" of these woods. The purpose of such zoning would be to maintain "the natural outdoor flavor and spirit of certain large undeveloped areas" and "to permit only forestry and agricultural practices and primitive recreation." Unrelated developments, such as vacation homes, would not be allowed. Period. Though the council did not discuss precise numbers, the word soon got around that some staffers were thinking in terms of at least seven million acres. Not surprisingly, the idea of a building moratorium on seven million acres did not earn rave reviews among Maine's landowners.

We have landed at Millinocket. And now Gordon R. Manuel, Georgia-Pacific's manager of public relations for Maine, is whisking me off to the office of G-P's Thomas A. Wildman, who presides over the 2.1 million acres of company land that supply wood fiber to the company paper mills here. The two mills (one is a few miles away in East Millinocket) annually produce about 700,000 tons of newsprint, directory paper, and both coated and uncoated specialty groundwood papers. G-P also has land and mills in Washington County, near Calais. It pays state and local taxes in excess of $20 million a year, employs 3,300 workers with a payroll of $168 million, and, to harvest and transport its raw materials, does business with nearly five hundred independent contracts who in turn employ an additional 3,200 people.

With Gordon Manuel and Thomas Wildman at Millinocket, I have time for only a few questions. How are these old mills holding up, I want to know. Manuel tells me they are holding up fine, though it takes a lot of money to *keep* them up. (What Manuel doesn't tell me is that, even as he speaks, contractors over at the East Millinocket mill are working feverishly to repair a ruptured 54-inch effluent pipe that has flooded the plant with untreated sludge, spilled over into the Penobscot River, and forced a shutdown in production that will last the rest of week.) Okay, now how about these big clearcuts I've heard about? "In practicality," says Wildman, "the average size of our clearcuts is down to about 35 acres." There is a forest practices act now that mandates smaller clearcuts, although under certain circumstances some cuts can go up to 250 acres. (In fact, not long before my visit, G-P had obtained state variances for two clearcuts of 746 and 539 acres; only adverse publicity and the threat of a court challenge by environmental groups succeeded in spiking this regulatory end-run.) And how does Wildman feel about The Wilderness Society's proposal for a Maine Woods Reserve? "The first thing I feel," he says, "is that about a million acres of that proposal happens to belong to Georgia-Pacific."

And inevitably I am compelled to ask Manuel and Wildman about reports that G-P is on the verge of unloading all of those acres, and everything else acquired so recently in Maine from Great Northern Nekoosa, for a quick fix of cash. Well yes, there have been discussions. There is not much they can tell me. There will be an announcement. (Two days later, there *is* an announcement. Bowater, Inc., the leading manufacturer of newsprint in the United States, will acquire an 80 percent interest in G-P's Great Northern properties in Maine, with an option to buy up the remaining share after June 1992, and all for a total of $322 million. The announcement is wrought with bad news and good news. The bad news is how volatile the ownership of industrial timberland has become and how vulnerable to market forces a company must be if it can let such an empire go at a price some analysts say is less than half its true value. The good news is that Bowater, a major player in the pinelands of the South and the maritime forests of Nova Scotia, steps up to the Yankee Forest with one of the better corporate reputations in the industry.)

Airborne again, heading up the east side of Baxter State Park, looking over at Henry David's Ktaadn, and a magnificent pile of rock it is. This is wild-looking country, east of Baxter. Wild to the north, too, as we cast our shadow across a nonindustrial forest managed by the Seven Islands Land

Company and angle northwestward toward the Allagash. And by-and-by this course brings us over industrial treetops, International Paper's among several others. Looking down, we don't see much wild. We see logging roads and clearcuts. Clearcuts big and harsh enough to unravel one of my most cherished misconceptions about the Maine Woods. For until this day, I had mistakenly assumed that the blitzkreig approach to logging was something the big industrials reserved for their tree farms out West. I should have known better; the Champion and Boise that clearcut in Maine are the same Champion and Boise that clearcut in the Great West.

Not that I hadn't been properly warned. In Boston, Michael Kellett of The Wilderness Society had told me he regarded industrial forest practices in the Maine Woods to be nothing less than "a slow mining process." He said, "We're dealing with a situation up there that has the potential to dislocate, degrade, and destroy local communities as well as the forest." And this quiet man in the back seat, this St. Pierre, had told me just the other day: "A couple of years ago everyone felt that development was the greatest threat to the Maine Woods. It's still a threat. But Michael and I have done a lot of thinking since then, and looking, too, and we see now that the largest threat, the most insidious threat, comes from the way the big paper companies are treating their lands. They've turned a natural forest into a fiber farm to feed their mills. People keep talking about a 'working' forest. Well, the working forest isn't working anymore. What we should be striving to achieve is a *sustainable* forest."

"Hold on," I said, "The companies claim they've already got a sustained-yield forest."

"Well, they don't," said St. Pierre. "The statistics show that they don't. For some species, we're cutting more wood in Maine than we're growing. We're using up the interest and cutting into the principal."

The literature on timber supply and demand in Maine appears to support St. Pierre's grim assessment. Almost every official state report or research paper out of the College of Forest Resources at Orono in recent years has concluded that inventory levels of most of the important commercial species are certain to decline in the next century if the rate of harvest continues to match the projected demand.

Of course, from the birds-eye view there seems to be more than enough forest down there to make Maine, proportionate to size, the most heavily wooded state in the Union. But the bird's eyes can't see this forest for all the trees. The volume cloaks the quality. After nearly half a century of being highgraded for its best specimens, or clearcut to salvage conifer stands from budworm infestations, parts of the Maine Woods today are borderline puckerbrush and probably not destined to supply the kind of high-quality logs the mills will be looking for in the next century. So here are these studies predicting a quality shortfall for spruce and fir by early to mid-century unless the current rate of cutting is reduced, a major shortage of commercial quality white pine within a decade, and a crunching deficit, after the millennium, of large-diameter sugar maples and yellow birch, mainstays of the economically attractive veneer and furniture markets. According to one analysis by University of Maine researchers Robert S. Seymour and Ronald C. Lemin, Jr., if the approaching hardwood shortfall is not offset by increases in yield and improvements in utilization, "future mill expansions will be threatened, and in some cases present capacity could be jeopardized."

And there's the bottom line. The bottom line says: Listen, Mister Corporate Woodman. Unless you're planning to cut-and-run like your granddaddy did in the nineteenth century, you've got two choices. You either reduce the harvest or intensify the management for increased yields.

Until the spruce budworm outbreak of 1970–1985, intensive forest management to achieve maximum regeneration and higher yields did not command a very high niche among the performance standards of the Maine woodman. The worm changed all that, luring the industry into massive applications of pesticides and ever larger clearcuts, some to be replanted as spruce monocultures instead of left to regenerate through natural succession. More recently, the industry has gone bonkers on the use of herbicides to "release" stands of valuable young trees, such as spruce, that are overtopped by shrubs or less desirable hardwoods, such as poplars. Tens of thousands of acres of the Maine Woods have been treated with herbicides over the past several years. It is said that the herbicides have no harmful environmental effects. It has also been said that the moon is made of green cheese.

Heading for home base. We have crossed over Churchill Lake and Umsaskis, saluted the Allagash, and turned south finally to make a faraway fix on Northeast Carry, that fabled portage at the noggin of Moosehead Lake. Off the portside now, in the shadow of gathering clouds, a huge clearcut like a gray shroud stretches away from Chesuncook. And here are these thin ribbons of gravel that have replaced the rivers in moving the logs to the mills.

Possibly the logging roads have brought greater change to the woods than the clearcuts have. The roads have opened the once-remote backcountry to hundreds of thousands of Mainers and Outsiders who come to these private lands each year to hunt and fish and camp and hike and immerse their boots in beaver-swamp muck. This is the biggest de facto private park in America. The individual and corporate members of the Maine Forest Products Council own, in aggregate, 10.6 million acres, statewide; 10.3 million of those acres are open to public recreation. North-by-northwest of Baxter

State Park—aft our tail rudder now—sits the three-million-acre working forest playground managed by North Maine Woods, Inc., a consortium of landowners including some of the state's biggest industrial and nonindustrial entities. The territory contains more than 2,000 miles of permanently maintained roads and some 300 primitive campsites, accessible to the public for a fee.

And yet who can say how long this benevolence will last? Everyone likes to talk about the long Maine tradition of public access to private land, but hardly anyone wants to speculate about the market forces that are driving landowners to view their assets, and weigh their options, in a different light. "I wish," my friend in the back seat here was telling me the other day, "that people would recognize the paper companies have only one purpose—and it isn't providing recreation or protecting healthy habitats. It's making money. I have no problem with that. Making money is their business. But people should be up front about that. And if, in fact, they are interested in protecting the full range of public values in this private forest, they had better recognize that there is no guarantee they are going to have these values available in the future."

Moosehead under the wingtips, heading home. . .

Now, unplugged from the intercom, I recall other voices pleading for the forest. I recall C. Edwin Meadows, Commissioner of Maine's Department of Conservation and that state's representative on the Northern Forest Lands Council, denouncing public policies that are creating problems out there in the woods. Meadows is saying: "You hear a lot of talk about clearcutting. Well, public policy subsidizes the purchase and operation of large harvesting equipment that requires clearcutting. Workmen's Compensation structure is such that it discriminates against the man in the woods with no more equipment than a chainsaw. The Tax Reform Act of 1986, in changing the capital gains rate, left no economic incentive to hold on to land for the long term. It's silly. Then there's federal inheritance tax. Demographics tell us that 25 percent of the forestland in Maine will change hands through death in the next fifteen years. It scares me, because you know what *that* means."

Steve Schley knows what that means. Schley is president of Pingree Associates, one of Maine's largest nonindustrials, representing sixty families and trusts with control of a significant slice of the north country. I recall Schley saying: "Every time somebody dies we have to pay the government 55 percent of what the individual's land is worth. Just because somebody *died.* Nothing changed on the land. The ownership has simply been transferred to the next family member. But in some cases, the next family member doesn't have the money to pay that tax. In order to do that, he must sell the land." And who can guarantee, I wonder, that the buyer of the deceased's woodland won't be some scheming huckster instead of a Pingree type perhaps, who, in no particular hurry to cash his crop, will be content to grow trees for forty years while sharing their shade with the summer visitors?

Augusta, capital city of the Pine Tree State, dead ahead, and the Kennebec River carving its mighty blue way to the sea. And all those minds under all those institutional rooftops, minds of planners and foresters, bureaucrats and bog trotters, tossing and turning their strategies to assure an acceptable future for the shrinking Maine Woods. Some minds, though not many in Augusta, are trying to figure out how to sell the idea of turning a piece of this private forest into a public one. Some minds are still wondering about The Wilderness Society's Maine Woods Reserve.

Is it still on the table? "Yes," St. Pierre assures me from the back seat of the Cessna. "We're fine-tuning it. It remains a centerpiece of our largest effort for the Northern Forest."

But there is another centerpiece. The Wilderness Society has been working on it in consultation with the National Audubon Society, the National Wildlife Federation, and the Sierra Club. When it is uncorked later this month (October 1991), *Saving the Northern Forest: An Issue of National Importance* will not only articulate the coalition's vision for protecting the wilder woodlands of New England and New York, but will recommend that the strategies include a federal acquisition program, funded in large part by the Land and Water Conservation Fund and dedicated to the proposition that this north country is the place to give birth to a new generation of national forests— forests in which the protection of biological diversity is awarded the highest priority. The vision paper draws no lines to specify where such a national forest might be located. My best hunch is that I've just spent the day checking out the likeliest location through the birds-eye view.

Some folks, I'm told, discern a hidden agenda here—*national* conservation groups, *federal* ownership. But I remember Kellett explaining that the groups are merely giving form to the findings of the Northern Forest Lands Study. "The NFLS report said that these lands are of *national* significance," he pointed out. "We're not calling for the public acquisition of *all* the private lands in the Maine Woods—but we do believe that if the report and the recommendations of the Governors' Task Force are to be more than just so many words, then public ownership—including federal ownership—has to be one of the strategies used. That's not a hidden agenda. We've been saying that for years, because public ownership can best protect the full range of public values involved—healthy forests, stability for timber-dependent economies, and guaranteed access for traditional recreation activities."

Day's done and down we go, circling, setting up for touchdown, the city under us, an alabaster capitol awash in the golden light of a sinking sun.

There are so many different visions for and of the Maine Woods. Here's Jerry Bley, the land-use consultant: "We are in a transition from a time of plentiful resources—enough of everything, for every interest, without a great deal of conflict—to a time of scarcity where there won't be enough to go around without more careful management and planning. And this trend from abundance to scarcity is going to continue. Yes, there may be lulls in the real-estate market and yes, there may be times of a surplus of wood. But overall, the demands of society on the North Woods are certain to increase. And if we just stand by and leave it to the market forces, it will all be gone before we know it."

There is a vision, too, in the eyes of John Cashwell. He is the Director of the Maine Forest Service, a branch of the Department of Conservation. Cashwell is about as familiar with the birds-eye view as anyone can be. He flies helicopters; used to fly them for Georgia-Pacific out of Calais. He is grounded the afternoon I meet with him. We drive over to the state arboretum near his office and walk up a trail through the woods. We sit on a bench. The view in front of us is of a blackberry patch, a gap in the trees, and, beyond the unseen Kennebec, a soft green dome perched atop the capitol building. Cashwell is delighted that all these controversial questions about the Maine Woods are getting debated. He says, "The debate is worth every minute we give it. When debates are public and long, wisdom almost always prevails." I tell him I hope he is right. Then I solicit his vision. As visions go, it is a short one. Cashwell says: "The forest of the future may not be exactly as people would like it to be, but you know what? It will be radiant in the fall and naked in the winter and green in the spring. And it will still be a nice place to be."

Touchdown. And suddenly I am thinking: Okay, John Cashwell, I hear you, and I hope you are right on that one, too. But you know what? By all the sap and cellulose left in the great Maine Woods, it is going to take one helluva lot of hard work to make it happen.

A note from the editors: Since Mitchell's report in the spring of 1992, The Wilderness Society has closed its Maine office and Michael Kellett has moved on to head up RESTORE: The North Woods, a group devoted to the preservation of the big woods. Meanwhile, after six years of study, the Northern Forest Lands Council issued its final report late in 1994. As usual in such matters, conservationists found much to admire and much to dislike in the council's recommendations. The next move, Robert Perschel, The Society's new man in Boston, emphasizes, is to work with Congress toward developing legislation to incorporate the report's best ideas. "If we fail to protect the Great Northern Forest," he says, "it won't be because we didn't know what to do. It will be because our leaders failed to take sufficient action."

DYAN ZASLOWSKY

The Far Bounds

Everything lay quiet again as the six of us—three on skis, I on old
snowshoes as round as platters, and two babies—moved up a gentle
white slope along the Porcupine River in the Gallatin National
Forest, a half hour's drive from Bozeman, Montana. Minutes before, the children had shattered the stillness with their crying, protesting the cold air
that had knifed into the car where they waited as we outfitted for our morning trek. Then they had fallen silent. Jonathan Muir Piedalue Scott dozed in
the backpack his father Michael carried, his body nodding like a bough of
ripe fruit against the frame. Nestled in the Snugli on my chest, three-
month-old Ariel Jane conducted studies. Her eyes roamed the oyster-colored
sky, the sluggish river, and the trees scribbled on its banks, then came to rest
on my face. Back and forth and with much deliberation, she scanned all the
elements of the landscape, made comparisons and drew distinctions. She was
mapping, as infants do, the precise boundaries of her life: *This is me, this is
not me; I leave off here, the rest of the world begins there.* But this will be my
memory, not her's. What we shared is a common birthright, this Montana
wilderness that she surveyed. And I can understand how, in the company of
very small children and timeless natural beauty, it is hard to ignore the future's claim on the present.

My youngest daughter and I were accompanied that day last January by
Michael Scott, head of The Wilderness Society's Bozeman office, his wife De-
nise, president of the Madison-Gallatin Alliance, a local conservation group,
and Joan Montagne, a veteran of many Montana wilderness protection bat-

tles. They brought us to this strip of contested wilderness to show us what Montanans have been fighting to preserve for themselves and the rest of the country. The land belongs to all, they are fond of pointing out, and while the conflicts over the use of the Hyalite-Porcupine-Buffalo Horn portion of the Gallatin and other roadless areas throughout the state may be based in Montana, their resolution will be nationally significant.

Actually, most of the rest of the country has remained unconscious of the controversies that have deadlocked wilderness area designation in the Northern Rockies. The people of Montana, where there are six million acres of roadless lands entitled to wilderness consideration under the 1964 Wilderness Act, have had difficulty deciding what to save for posterity and what to release for development, though they have been working on this for more than four years. In neighboring Idaho, which has far more roadless lands than every state but Alaska, the fate of 9.3 million acres also is quite uncertain. In 1984, the congressional delegations of both states presented wilderness bills that were woefully inadequate in terms of acreage and the constraints placed on it. In Montana, for example, the section of the Gallatin that Ariel and I saw last December may be designated as wilderness but would be opened to snowmobiles and bikers who have strenuously opposed what the magazine *Snowmobile West* labeled, "the encroaching wilderness."

Since 1980, twenty-six states have selected wilderness areas to be protected, and in 1984 the delegations of twenty of these states introduced and won passage of wilderness bills, all of them dipping into the bank of lands identified by the Forest Service's second and still contested Roadless Area Review and Evaluation (RARE II) survey of the national forests. But not Idaho and Montana, in which, if lumped together, roadless lands would cover an area the size of West Virginia—giving these two states the richest stock of wild country in the contiguous United States. Pending the ultimate decision, these lands are protected as wilderness, owing to *California* vs. *Block,* a 1982 court decision holding that the environmental impact statements accompanying RARE II were inadequate. This decision provided the opportunity for citizen appeal of any development in a roadless area until its final status is decided. So far, more than thirty appeals to halt roading, logging, and mining have been lodged against the Forest Service in Idaho and Montana. These holding actions have made timber companies and other extractive industries more eager to resolve wilderness boundaries than conservationists. For, regardless of the ultimate acreage designated as wilderness, it will be only a fraction of what is roadless today.

With their common border and common legacy of Northern Rockies wilderness at stake, it might seem that the two states' problems in completing wilderness selections are related. In one sense this is true, since the arguments against wilderness have not changed much and do not vary from place to place. In the exact conflicts left to resolve, however, and in the manner in which this will be accomplished, Idaho and Montana are very different. The wilderness debates in both states have remained parochial, subject to their own political idiosyncracies. Each in its own way, however, demonstrates the eternal frustration that still accompanies the process of RARE II designation elsewhere in the country—two outsized models of what can go wrong as the nation struggles to deal with the unfinished forest wilderness.

On a summer day in 1983, loggers drove eighty-five semis into Coeur D'Alene, Idaho, and mill whistles at Diamond International and Louisiana Pacific blew for five minutes. The commotion was triggered by the arrival of Idaho's senior Republican, Senator James McClure, to conduct hearings on wilderness legislation. The loggers, who had been invited by their employers to take the day off without pay, were there to urge a speedy resolution to the proceedings. Their jobs, they told Senator McClure and his staff via placards, depended on unlimited access to the national forests. But it was hardly necessary for them to explain their feelings to McClure and his people; the strongest opponents of wilderness designation in the state all along have been led by most of Idaho's own congressional members.

Politically speaking, much in the state had changed since Cecil Andrus, a strong conservationist, served as its governor eleven years before. In his 1976 state of the state address, Andrus had reassured Idahoans willing to listen that wilderness would be protected and that he would not "sacrifice our natural resources for mindless economic development." Andrus, who had entered politics in the late 1960s by fighting ASARCO plans to mine molybdenum in the White Cloud Mountains near Ketchum, kept these promises—but it was as President Carter's Interior Secretary, not as Idaho's governor. Nationally, his name became closely entwined with conservation victories in Alaska, not Idaho. In 1980, with Senator Frank Church's defeat by Republican Steve Symms, Idaho lost its other champion of wilderness. Church had helped draft the 1964 Wilderness Act and had steered the Central Idaho Wilderness Bill through Congress, establishing the 2.2 million-acre River of No Return Wilderness, to which his name was added after his death in 1984. The Frank Church-River of No Return Wilderness Area exceeds Yellowstone National Park in size and is the largest roadless area outside Alaska. Idaho Congressman Larry Craig attempted to undo this honor by proposing last summer to punch a paved road through it, complete with scenic turnoffs and campsites, so that it would be more accessible. Craig's notion might have been laughable, except that its reasoning typified the current attitudes of the state's delegation.

Not only did the Wilderness System lose one of its best friends when

Church was defeated, it also gained one of its most implacable foes in Steve Symms. Symms, who was financially aided in his bid for Church's seat by national right-wing fundraising, declared, among other things, that the Alaska Lands Bill of 1980 "will go down as one of the dumbest things in history." As for Senator McClure, he consistently favored mining interests in particular over any sort of wilderness designation, once lecturing his colleagues in Congress to the effect that the human race never would have spread beyond the Mesopotamian Valley to cover the whole earth had it not "tamed wilderness for man's use."

Given the attitudes of the delegation, state conservationists were prepared for an abominable bill in 1984—though not for one as bad as they got. They had pressed for wilderness designations amounting to about three million acres. The Forest Service had proposed that one million acres be saved; the Idaho Fish and Game suggested 1.8 million acres; The Idaho Wildlife Federation, 4.5 million acres; Earth First! seven million acres; the timber industry, 590,000 acres; and, unsurprisingly, a coalition of mining and agricultural interests submitted a proposal for none. If one had simply averaged out all of these claims, it still would have given the state about 2.5 million acres of wilderness, so when Senate Bill 2457 put forth a proposal of 526,000 acres, it shocked even those who hadn't expected much. The bill was dismissed as "a disgrace" by the state's fish and game director. What made it even more unpalatable was its recommendation that no additional roadless lands could be considered for wilderness for the next 25 years, making conservationists wonder about what would be left by then.

To those who had attended the four public hearings prior to Senate Bill 2457's introduction, it seemed as though Senator McClure had ignored the majority of pro-wilderness testimony. Even in Coeur D'Alene, where noisy loggers had been so visible, the actual sentiments expressed by witnesses had been about two thirds in favor of large wilderness designations. At the Boise hearing, singer and songwriter Carole King, who had made Idaho her home, asked McClure: "How are you going to explain to your grandkids what a wilderness was? How are you going to tell them you sold it?"

A few weeks after the bill's introduction, Congressman Craig had undertaken to explain what "creating more wilderness in Idaho" would mean. He wrote to constituents that it would prohibit trail construction or maintenance and that existing hiking trails would be destroyed. Campfires and woodgathering also would be forbidden in designated wilderness, he claimed. None of this was true, of course, but in the eyes of many a willingness to spread false information and an insistence that no more wilderness be saved only proved, as one longtime conservationist put it, that "our congressmen form an interest group unto themselves." Early in the summer of 1984, the prospect of help from pro-wilderness people outside Idaho seemed likely. To head it off, Congressman Craig urged wilderness opponents to speak up, "otherwise a small but vocal group of preservationists and their eastern friends will determine the fate of Idaho's future for you. I know where you stand on wilderness because it shows up in your letters and responses from the past. But we're not hearing from you now."

Spurned by their own delegation, an umbrella organization of about forty conservation groups called the Idaho Wildlands Defense Coalition found outside help. The coalition approached Congressmen Jim Moody of Wisconsin and Peter Kostmayer of Pennsylvania, and in the summer of 1984 they agreed to introduce a bill calling for the preservation of 3.4 million acres of roadless lands. That summer, Governor John Evans invited Ohio Congressman John Seiberling, chairman of the House Public Lands Subcommittee, and any other interested congressmen to tour the state and render an opinion regarding wilderness preservation. Seiberling, Moody, and Kostmayer accepted the invitation, and after he returned Seiberling said that Idaho could afford to save at least twice as much land as Senate Bill 2457 recommended. On his tour Seiberling also had suggested that the various factions work on a compromise.

But the degree of disagreement was too extreme for any quick reconciliation. In the next two and a half years, there would be no progress, and wilderness remained a major issue in Idaho's gubernatorial race in the fall of 1986, particularly for the candidacy of Cecil Andrus. The Idaho Conservation League handed out 10,000 "Wilderness State" bumper stickers to combat those on the hindquarters of cars and trucks that read, "Cease Mining, Cease Farming, Cease Logging, Cece Andrus." Some hope could be seen in the fact that after an eleven-year absence, Andrus was narrowly returned to the governor's office, having defeated an opponent who ran on a no-more-wilderness-platform. Still, the tight margin suggested that there were plenty of people left who shared the attitude of one of the Republican candidates for lieutenant governor; at one point in his campaign, the candidate had told all Idahoans who favored a large wilderness bill that they might as well pack up and leave the state, because there would be no jobs for them.

Ron Mitchell, a big, exuberant man in his thirties who heads the Idaho Sportsmen's Coalition, has his own unique recollection of the campaign's tension. Last September in Twin Falls, while speaking before a group of wilderness opponents during one of the colloquies he had arranged, Mitchell suffered a heart attack, suddenly perspiring and feeling as though his chest housed an anvil trying to break through his rib cage. An older man in the audience caught him as he collapsed and handed him some nitroglycerine tablets so that he could finish his presentation. This, says Mitchell, who has since recuperated from heart surgery, was an indication of how much anguish the subject of wilderness has stirred in Idaho.

Meanwhile, the wilderness conflict is still far from resolution. While timber industry leaders consented to an increase in wilderness acreage during informal talks with conservationists last winter, they would support such a measure only if development activities on released roadless lands could be shielded from existing environmental laws, thus eliminating the threat of appeals. In addition, industry leaders spoke of devising a statute that would hold the Forest Service accountable for the "community stability" of timber-dependent towns. To conservationists, such conditions were unacceptable. They responded by asking Congressman Kostmayer to submit a 3.9-million acre version of his 1984 bill, which he did in March 1987.

As of this writing, that is where matters stand in Idaho. So the land waits. As it always does.

At the base of the Pioneer Mountains in south-central Idaho, in an area that would have been left open to development under Senate Bill 2457, stands a monument to Ernest Hemingway, whose words grace the stone: "And best of all, he loved the fall, the leaves yellow on the cottonwoods, leaves floating on the trout streams. And above the hills, the high, blue windless skies. Now he will be a part of them forever." Hemingway, Idaho's adopted native son, found much to love about the state, given his woodsman's inclinations. As noted earlier, Idaho represents raw wilderness more than any other state or territory in the country, outside Alaska. With eighty-one separately named ranges, it is the most mountainous state on the continent. Its central portion is the most rugged, consisting of the enormous granitic intrusion called the Idaho Batholith, through which such wild rivers as the Salmon and the Selway twist their course. Small towns cling to the edge of the Batholith but few roads penetrate it.

At Lolo Pass, where the Lewis and Clark Expedition beat its way over the Continental Divide in 1804, Highway 12 is the only paved road in the region; in the entire state there are only 5,000 miles of paved roads. By contrast, the three national forests of the northern panhandle contain more than 6,000 miles of logging roads, a testimony to the industriousness of the Forest Service, if left unchallenged. Through most of Idaho, the spread of mountains and their cold, narrow valleys discouraged settlement. As a result, about 65 percent of the state is federally owned, giving it a public land base second only to that of Nevada. And now it is Idaho's lack of development that is considered one of its chief assets. To a great degree, the state's beauty is unsullied, its wildlife population robust, and its reputation for diverse outdoor experiences growing. Until California passed its own wilderness bill three years ago, Idaho, with 3.8 million acres protected, had more designated wilderness than any state in the Lower 48, most of this in the most rugged parts of the interior.

Yet elsewhere there are numerous places where protection would broaden the "wilderness cocktail" (rocks and ice) image characteristic of much of the state's preserved wild country. De facto wilderness includes a lot of territory besides alpine peaks that has so far remained untouched and eligible for designation, richly variegated habitat necessary for the health and survival of Idaho's one hundred species of animals and three hundred species of birds. When talking to sportsmen in his travels around Idaho, Ron Mitchell avoids using the word "wilderness" if he can. "I don't mention it with some people," he says. "Instead I ask hunters to stop and think about what has happened to their favorite hunting spots because of roading and logging. I talk to them about wildlife habitat, and then they know what I mean." It was as wildlife habitat that Mitchell, a native of Idaho, first discovered what wilderness—or its antithesis—meant. The memory of the landslides of 1965 that ended fishing on the South Fork of the Salmon River in Payette National Forest has never left him, he says. The blowout, considered one of the country's worst wildlife catastrophes, resulted directly from the web of Forest Service roads built on the mountainsides. The destabilized and exposed earth could not withstand the heavy rains and caved into the river. In addition to drastically increasing that kind of erosion, roading reduces the shelter that elk require for security and may drive them away from habitat they have occupied for generations. Studies cited by an Idaho timber industry publication have found that elk won't live within a quarter mile of a road. For these and other reasons, habitat protection has become one of the prime motivations behind many of the most controversial areas recommended for wilderness designation.

Long Canyon, the last remaining unroaded drainage in the Selkirk Mountains of northern Idaho, is a good example. The eighteen-mile canyon is damp and steep-walled, but in its relatively level sections, the accumulation of soil supports an old-growth cedar and hemlock forest. It is beneath such trees that Idaho's endangered woodland caribou (an estimated thirty animals are left) forage for the lichens and mosses that are crucial to their survival. There is beauty here, too. Beyond the upper reaches of Long Canyon is the Selkirk Crest, a scenic ridge that rises from 5,000 to 7,000 feet in elevation and contains more than twenty pristine lakes. Still another area of intense controversy in the northern part of the state is the 240,000-acre Mallard Larkins area. Popular and well-trailed, the crest has been ranked by the Idaho Fish and Game Commission as one of the most critical wildlife areas in the state. Its roadlessness assures the sort of privacy needed to sustain grizzlies, the rare gray wolf, lynx, and the recently identified boreal owl.

In Clearwater National Forest's Great Burn, so named for the fires that swept through the area at the turn of the century, the destiny of a blue-ribbon trout stream called Kelly Creek is yet another critical issue. The Forest Service would like the area logged to maintain the forest's historic harvest levels; sportsmen fear that the heavy ash content of the soil makes it highly susceptible to erosion and stream degradation. The 440,000-acre Payette Crest on the Payette National Forest is yet another place with high fish and game value, but the Forest Service has proposed increasing the cut in the vicinity. The largest remaining roadless tract in Idaho is the 450,000-acre Boulder-White Clouds area, named for the milky quartzite peaks that dominate the summit. Wilderness designation here has been stymied because of the presence of what appears to be a substantial molybdenum deposit. Even so, the market price of molybdenum has plummeted in recent years, which has stifled any immediate pressure to commence mining and kept the area a wilderness in fact, if not in name.

Conservationists often stand accused of using emotion as a weapon over the cold logic of economics. In Idaho, the opposite condition prevails. For in the face of cold economics, an emotional attachment to the logger's folkways is being utilized by opponents of wilderness preservation. Timber representatives assert that wilderness designation already has deprived Idaho of employment in the industry and will continue to do so. "The Eco-freak network is buzzing and the letters are coming in with the impassioned pleas of the stringy-haired, strident-voiced, stern-faced idealists who have their beady eyes fixed, in a myopic stare through their granny glasses on a utopian dream," wrote one of the more impassioned antagonists to wilderness preservation in a letter to the editor of a small newspaper. "People would have to starve or go on the dole, if they did live here, because of the lockup of resources." The statement is melodramatic, though hardly true.

In its 1987 RARE II evaluation, even the Forest Service acknowledged that no timber jobs would be lost in Idaho unless *all* the remaining roadless areas were designated as wilderness (a proposal no one but Earth First! has ever put forth). Furthermore, between 1978 and 1984, the volume of timber offered by the Forest Service for sale on all ten of the state's national forests outstripped the volume purchased by timber companies. According to Richard Rice, a resource economist with The Wilderness Society, a three-year backlog of timber offered but not cut remains. The glut was caused by several years of falling timber prices, lower demand for new housing caused by higher interest rates, and competition—in other words, the kind of economic factors that beset every business environment, none of them having anything to do with wilderness designation. In 1983 the contract price timber companies had previously agreed to pay for national forest trees was so much higher than the prevailing price they requested that their earlier bids be canceled.

Additionally, the Northwest timber industry has steadily lost a large part of its business to Canadian companies that have lower transportation costs and higher government subsidies, and to the southern United States, where timber has become the top agricultural product in six states. In 1982 the South topped the Northwest for the first time ever in its plywood production, according to *The Wall Street Journal.* Twenty-five years earlier, the region did not produce any plywood at all. Tree growing in the South has proved to be more economical because of the region's level terrain and high precipitation, which offer better growing conditions than do the cold, dry weather and the thin, granitic soil and steep grades of the Idaho Batholith. In the South, timber can also be hauled out of the forests and off to the markets more cheaply, since there is already an existing network of roads and the major purchasers are much closer.

Increased competition and a reduced demand for housing are not the only reasons Idaho's share of timber employment has slipped from a high of 20,000. Mechanization continues to nibble away at the number of jobs available in the industry and, in the view of some analysts, is the major force behind declining employment. "The cause of job loss in Idaho's wood products industry is not high wages, a restricted government supply, the Canadians or the recession," declared *Idaho's Economy,* a publication of Boise State's business school, last fall. "The fact is that the process of modernization has changed the industry." The new Potlatch mill in Lewiston, for example, will employ 40 percent fewer workers; a mill rebuilt by Louisiana Pacific after a fire destroyed the old one in 1980 has almost doubled the yearly capacity of its previous mill but employs six fewer workers. The list of companies increasing their production while lowering their personnel goes on.

All this is happening at the same time national forest timber sales in Idaho report the second largest deficits in the nation—almost entirely because of the enormous costs of road building on steep, isolated sites, a cost that the geography of the region mandates. A study conducted by the Congressional Research Service found that in the eleven years ending in 1984, it cost the government more to sell Idaho timber than these sales returned to the Treasury. Year after year, Idaho sat near the top of the list as one of the worst states for timber receipts. In 1982, its losses amounted to almost $18 million: in 1984, the deficit came to $21 million.

The frequency of below-cost timber sales at the expense of wilderness is certainly one of the most controversial aspects of the current debate. "No private landowner would spend ten or even one hundred times the value of his crop to conduct a harvest," fumes Walter C. Minnick, president of Boise-based Trus Joist, a forest products company. "If the government decided to subsidize growing pineapples in Wyoming hothouses, that could become a viable business also," he says. Minnick, an Idaho native, served as deputy assistant director of the Office of Management and Budget under President Richard Nixon before joining Trus Joist. There is no shortage of timber and never will be, he asserts, because of changed demographics: smaller homes and the passage of the baby boomer's prime homebuying years. Despite the fact that Minnick's company is the largest purchaser of high-grade lumber in the United States, he is viewed as a traitor in the timber business because of his criticism of below-cost timber sales, his ardent support of industrial innovation rather than the perpetuation of wasteful methods, and his conviction that wilderness is good for Idaho's business climate.

As far as Minnick is concerned, Idaho's brightest economic future lies in the promotion of its wilderness areas for tourism. "I moved back here for the lifestyle that proximity to wilderness affords," he says. "We are destroying our future by continuing to subsidize timber cutting in roadless areas." The transition will be painful, he admits. Mill-dependent towns will have to become more recreation-dependent, or die. Minnick's depiction of Idaho as a recreational paradise rankles a lot of people. Despite the state's well-established dependence on tourism—sustained without the sort of ballyhoo that national parks in the other western states generate—tying Idaho even more closely to recreation would require a decisive shift in temperament that may be years away. Four years ago, in testimony supporting Senator McClure's acreage, Joe Hinson of the Intermountain Forestry Industry Council (IFIC) called it a "totally illogical assumption" to expect timber jobs to be supplanted by ones in outdoor recreation. "Those robbed of their employment are sawyers, choker setters, heavy equipment operators, millworkers and foresters," said Hinson. "They are not likely to find employment as waiters, salespeople, or guides." On the other hand, conservationists point out, if the market itself will not continue to sustain the industry, the people will simply have no choice—and never mind how much or how little wilderness has been saved in Idaho. Or, for that matter, in Montana—still awaiting its own RARE II wilderness.

Bordering the Spanish Peaks Wilderness Area near Big Sky, Montana, the Lone Mountain Ranch is one of a growing number of outdoor recreation businesses that are thriving here. After our outing along the Porcupine, we stopped at the ranch for steaming vegetable soup, accompanied by fresh ground peanut butter on newly baked bread. Bob Schaap, a Boston computer executive who left that field to retool as Lone Mountain's owner and operator about ten years ago, took our visit as an opportunity to do what he often does when strangers come by: educate them about the need for wilderness. Like Walter Minnick, his timber industry counterpart over in Idaho, Schaap is convinced that the economic future of the Northern Rockies lies with enterprises more like his guest ranch—and enough pristine wilderness to keep people coming back year after year—and not with the massive flatbed trucks heaped with cleanly severed spruce and pine that speed along the Gallatin Gateway, the highway between Big Sky and Bozeman.

While the Gallatin National Forest lost more than $1.5 million on its timber program last year, dude ranches and outfitters and guides dependent on the Gallatin Range for a living pumped almost $3 million into the local economy. "The only reason people come to Montana is to see our clear streams and scenic beauty," says Schaap. "They don't come to see clearcuts and muddy water. When I tell them how much they're losing on all these timber sales, they get mad because they can see how they're losing their land. When you mention tourism to some folks, they think you mean Expos. But we don't need Expos. All we really need is what we already have plenty of." In Montana, it is more customary for natives as well as transplants to speak proudly on behalf of wilderness preservation than seems to be the case in Idaho. Or, so Montanans would have you believe. From a conservation standpoint, "Montanans have done a lot for Montana," boasts Joan Montagne, past president of the Madison-Gallatin Alliance. In many respects this is true: Montana already has about 3.4 million acres of designated wilderness. Even before passage of the Wilderness Act, the state evidenced an uncommon sensitivity to wild country; in 1912 it started purchasing land for game habitat, and when the legislature couldn't afford to buy land, ranchers put up the necessary funds. Today, statewide conservation groups play a vital role in campaigning for large wilderness designations. Chief among these is the 1,000-member Montana Wilderness Association (MWA), which was formed in 1958 and which claims to be the oldest state wilderness conservation organization in the country. It represents a cross-section of interests: teachers, ranchers, outfitters, foresters.

On Wednesdays, local conservationists meet for lunch at the landmark Baxter Hotel in Bozeman, often sitting at a table into which the words "to know solitude is to enjoy freedom" have been carved. The phrase is perhaps only an oblique reference to the need for wilderness, but it obviously has been ingrained in that table for years. In Montana, "Conservation is a growth industry," declares Ed Lewis, who left his law practice in Phoenix to head the Bozeman-based Greater Yellowstone Coalition. And on matters of wilderness preservation there is a strong sense of proprietorship.

Nevertheless, having so much of the populace steeped in the virtues of wilderness has not made Montana's attempts to secure more of it any easier.

Much of the difficulty arises from a political anomaly. Two of the state's four-member congressional delegation—Senators Max Baucus and Congressman Pat Williams—have not voiced a strong ideological resistance to wilderness. The third member and the only Republican, Ron Marlenee, makes up for this benign neglect by being firmly opposed to any more wilderness preservation, though in the eastern half of Montana that he represents, only about 1.5 percent of the land is eligible for protection. Wilderness, Marlenee once observed, is for backpackers who get two weeks vacation or who aren't gainfully employed. Repeatedly, Marlenee fretted in public that expanding Montana's wilderness base would send the message that the state was more interested in "wolves, wilderness and welfare" than in growth. Marlenee does have some aesthetic sensibilities, however, when it comes to his own property. Last fall, when a logging crew moved onto a portion of forest near Marlenee's condominium at the Bridger Bowl ski area, he opposed the fraction of the authorized timber sale he could see from his deck and managed to stop the cut right there.

Marlenee's opposition to wilderness (or that portion of it he cannot see from his condominium) was particularly effective because of the novel approach the Montana delegation used to tackle its task—it was called "consensus," and gave each member the right to veto any or all proposed roadless areas submitted for review. Only one "no" vote was needed to eliminate an area from the bill, creating what MWA President John Gatchell called a most undemocratic situation. "It meant that Montanans who wanted an area protected had to convince four people of its worthiness, while anyone opposed to an area's inclusion had to convince only one person." And that person was never hard to find.

When the Montana wilderness bill was introduced by Senator John Melcher in June 1984, only 50,000 acres of the two million proposed by conservationists were included as proposed wilderness. The delegates also had crafted a new category of land management, the "Special Management Area," and placed about 500,000 acres under this jurisdiction. Much of this acreage had been snatched from what had been known as Senate Bill 393, a law passed in 1977 to protect, as wilderness study areas, some one million acres in nine roadless areas around the state from timber development by the Forest Service.

The 1984 consensus bill was met with utter dismay; for every one acre saved for wilderness, eight were released for development. "Instead of protecting Montana as it is," said Ed Madej, MWA's president at the time, "the congressional delegation, with this bill, has decided that the state has too many clear streams, too many healthy elk herds, too many undisturbed lakes, too many backcountry recreation areas, too many grizzly bears, and not enough publicly subsidized logging roads and clearcuts." The "Special Management" rubric, as it turned out, was little more than a euphemism for "off-road vehicle use," which the Wilderness Act expressly forbids—a restriction trail bikers, snowmobilers, and other ORV users found "inconvenient," according to Russell Jones, assistant editor of SNOWMOBILE WEST. The special management arrangement proposed by the Montana delegation and championed by Congressman Marlenee was an attempt to relieve this inconvenience. Conservationists countered that special management areas for wilderness purposes existed nowhere else in the country and would be a land manager's nightmare. Besides, about 70 percent of the trails in the national forests were already open to bikers. Marlenee stood fast in his insistence that "traditional recreational uses such as trailbikes" should be guaranteed access to such popular spots as the Hyalite Peaks region of the Gallatin National Forest.

The 1984 bill died in Congress, and over the next three years similar bills were stalled because the delegation could not agree on exactly what provisions ought to be made for snowmobilers and bikers. Conservationists were not altogether displeased at the delay, since each new version of a wilderness bill included the possibility of hundreds of thousands of acres being opened to ORV use. Last August, Senator Melcher made one last attempt to pass a Montana wilderness bill through the 99th session of Congress before it ended. "I'm hopeful that we can get everybody lined up because we're down to 25 or 30 sections" of land, said Melcher, referring to the Gallatin Range. Williams and Baucus did not want the area turned over to off-road vehicle users. "Because the Gallatin is adjacent to Yellowstone National Park and very important to elk, deer and other wildlife, and because the future of our state depends so much on that area, that area cannot be jeopardized," Baucus insisted. Marlenee would not budge, even though the Gallatin Range is not in his district. He would not go along with the bill without Hyalite Peaks and the Porcupine drainage open to snowmobilers. He also insisted on the removal of a finger of land from the Absaroka-Beartooth Wilderness Area near Bozeman, asserting that a stretch along the Stillwater River ought to be opened to motorized traffic so that people could enjoy camping beside a "live stream." Without complete agreement, the bill, and the process that begat it, were dead. MWA members were not sorry and last December gave Marlenee their mock Arthur E. Sedlack Award, given for the most outrageous act in defense of wilderness, and named for the Glacier National Park ranger who shot a snowmobile whose owner was trespassing. Marlenee deserved the award, says MWA President Gatchell; his stubbornness "rescued millions of acres of Montana's wilderness." And, it was hoped, gave them a second chance for preservation.

Instead of resurrecting the consensus method, last March Congressman

Pat Williams decided to write his own wilderness bill, in the face of certain stiff opposition from Marlenee. His bill (introduced as HR 2090 in late April) would designate 1.3 million acres as wilderness, 383,000 acres as various types of study areas, and 353,000 acres in five special management areas. Generally, conservationists feel that HR 2090 is much improved over the last two efforts of the delegation but is still inadequate. It would keep the Gallatin Range as a study area, while changing the name to "Land Consolidation Study Area," thus leaving it subject to continuing ORV use— and the kind of abuse that threatens wildlife, causes severe erosion, and intrudes on the exceptional quiet and solitude found here. For the Rocky Mountain Front, the bill would designate as wilderness only half that which conservationists recommended; they want an unbroken wilderness to the edge of the forest in order to protect the game migrations to and from the Bob Marshall Wilderness. Williams' proposal would leave a corridor of undesignated land open for oil and gas development, timbering, and ORV use that would seriously degrade the wilderness and wildlife qualities of both the Front and the Bob, wilderness advocates say. Finally, while the bill would protect the East Pioneers and most of the North Big Hole as wilderness, the West Big Hole would become a "Watershed Study Area," be protected for only five years, and then be released to road building and timbering. The West Pioneers would simply be designated a National Recreation Area, a classification inappropriate for wilderness quality lands. "I've simply made up my mind to join that battle," Williams declared before starting his draft. "We'll see who wins it in the committee and on the floor."

Of all the places the process of consensus had neglected, none was so badly served as the region along the Rocky Mountain Front, the jagged limestone seam that joins the Continental Divide to the Great Plains for 100 miles south of Glacier National Park. Of more than 300,000 acres eligible for wilderness status, Montana's congressional delegation had proposed preservation for about 38,000 acres. The heart of this country is made up of the 1.5 million-acre Bob Marshall, Great Bear, and Scapegoat wilderness areas, which, with Glacier National Park, form a four-million-acre wilderness sanctuary along the northern Continental Divide. The Rocky Mountain Front is probably most famous for its grizzly bear population, and it is the only place in the Lower 48 states where the bear still roams its historic habitat on the plains. It is a prime example of the rich cross-section of life that is associated with what biologists call the edge effect—the meeting of two such distinct habitats as mountain and plain. It is so rich and varied in its wildlife that leading wildlife specialist John Craighead calls it the most important natural habitat in Montana. The Front supports the largest bighorn sheep population outside Canada. The area also holds 3,000 elk, as many as 20,000 deer, and numerous mountain goats. Golden eagles and prairie falcons nest here. Mountain lions are well ensconced, and even the gray wolf has been spotted in the vicinity—last year, a dozen trotted across the border from Canada, presumably driven out by intense mining and logging in British Columbia. Their reinstatement in the area is still shaky, but one female bore a litter in Glacier National Park last year. Game experts believe she was the first wolf to be bred in the western United States in fifty years. For the species to stage a comeback, this remnant band will need more space than that provided by just the national park. The space is there, if protection is extended to five large roadless pockets bordering the existing wilderness complex.

"Protecting the Front is vital to the future of the Bob Marshall," Michael Scott says. "The same game population so evident along the Front in the winter are found in the Bob during the summer. If the Front is lost to development the wilderness and wildlife values of the Bob will suffer irretrievably." Furthermore, wilderness designation for the Badger-Two Medicine, the Teton River High Peaks, and the Choteau Mountain, Deep Creek, Renshaw Mountain, and Falls Creek areas is considered so vital to the tourist economy that the commissioners of Lewis and Clark County, which covers much of the Front, have campaigned for the entire area to be preserved. The commissioners recognized what a recent report by Tom Powers, the chairman of the University of Montana's Department of Economics, would seem to confirm: "While commodity-related job losses would be small (less than eight using a worse-case scenario), wilderness classification would protect and enhance the most important part of the area's economic base that is now tied to national forest lands, the recreation sector." Unfortunately, another name for the Rocky Mountain Front's impressive ridgeline is the Overthrust Belt, a geological phenomenon presumed to be rich in oil reserves. The petroleum industry has tried to keep most of the area out of the wilderness category and has conducted much seismic exploration already. How much oil might be trapped here is, of course, open to conjecture, but by the best estimates of the U.S. Geological Survey, there is hardly enough to meet America's energy requirements for three weeks.

Protection of the 100,000-acre Badger-Two Medicine area, which was released entirely from wilderness consideration in the various bills, has even assumed religious significance. It is here, in a gentle portion of the Front, that traditional Blackfeet Indians go to hold religious ceremonies and seek visions, and it is here that the Forest Service has called for oil and gas drilling—which might, according to the Tom Powers report, result in as few as three jobs for the entire Front, and which would, according to traditional Blackfeet leaders, desecrate the land even if the specific spiritual mountains were untouched. To prevent development, a group of Indians filed an appeal with the Forest Service to keep all 100,000 acres of the Badger-Two Medicine area pristine, asserting that "to imply that only the peaks are sacred is to imply that only the altar in a church is sacred and the rest can be torn down." The Indians have joined with conservationists to press their case. More than 350 marched in front of the Forest Service office in Missoula on behalf of the ancient Blackfeet attachment to Badger-Two Medicine, which suggests that the area will not be given up lightly.

Another place where Montana conservationists believe wilderness status is crucial is the Big Hole River country of Beaverhead National Forest. Unlike other Montana rivers, which are too muddied by spring runoff to be fishable—largely because of timber operations in their watershed—the Big Hole runs clear, its fame as one of the best trout streams in the West a tribute to its unsullied watershed. Since 1977, however, the Forest Service has wanted to offer much of the land of the Big Hole drainage for logging, and its land-use plan calls for more than 1,800 miles of new logging roads—all subsidized by the taxpayers. To stop this, the Beaverhead Concerned Citizens submitted an alternate proposal calling for the designation of a 358,000-acre wilderness area, covering the North and West Big Hole and the East and West Pioneer Mountains.

The Gallatin Range, the Rocky Mountain Front, and the Big Hole country exemplify the breadth and value of Montana wildlands. Together these areas represent only about one-sixth of the roadless lands at stake. But they are by no means the only special places in Montana whose fate depends on the state's delegation and the will of Congress. "Our task," Doug Scott told his MWA colleagues last December, "is to build the case for wilderness preservation in Montana in such a way that the decisions that will be made by Montanans will be as far toward the cutting edge, as far toward the agenda for complete protection as we have the skill to press the political dialogue." This, of course, is the language of conflict resolution, a description of the noisy process called democracy as it rattles and scrapes along, honing an approximation of the will of the people. With babies along on a peaceful day in a place where the sky and mountains and rivers seem to flow on forever, it is maybe better to keep in mind Ivan Doig's words evoking what Montana is and should always be. Properly considered they are words that resonate in Idaho, too—and in all the states possessed of an unfinished wilderness: "Here are the far bounds. All the extent anyone could need," he wrote. "Now live up to them."

(Summer 1987)

JOHN DANIEL

The Long Dance of the Trees

Eighteen years ago on Washington's Olympic Peninsula, eager to penetrate the depths of western wilderness, I veered off the Hoh River trail into rainforest. The spruces and hemlocks closed around me. Ferns sopped my pants, branches slapped at me. Thick vines sloped across my way, clotheslining my brand-new backpack stuffed with enough food for a week. In the solemn forest light I stepped uncertainly, guiltily, each footfall crushing delicate layerings of bright-green moss, moss that covered everything above the ground as well—the enormous trunks and broken snags, the vines, the fallen rotting logs over which I awkwardly clambered. I didn't know where I was going in that slippery strew of life, but I soon realized I wasn't going far. Dropping my pack, I climbed on top of a log some five feet through.

In the sudden absence of my own noise, the huge quiet pressed in. It was raining lightly, soundlessly, no breath of wind, no bird, no animal sound. Something a little unsettling, something tinged with fear, replaced my exploring ardor. Unlike the woods the wide trail had led me through, unlike the fields and fronts of forests I'd sped past while hitchhiking north from Portland, and unlike the bramble-patched Blue Ridge Mountains where I'd hiked as a kid, leafy forests lined with tumble-down stone walls and the ghosts of old mail roads, this place was undefined by man. This wet green riot didn't know who I was, and didn't especially welcome me. But as much as it disturbed me it also thrilled me, struck a happy thoughtless glow in my gut. I leaned over and stuck my nose into the mossy log, into its sodden crumbling wood-dirt, into the thick black smell of it. To either side of me, all down the log's fifty-foot length, seedlings and saplings were growing straight up out of it. I sat with them a long time, shoulder to shoulder, full of an exhilarated contentment both familiar and strange.

I was in my first old-growth forest—a forest, I learned later, that exceeds even the tropical jungles in its acre-for-acre net production of living material. I didn't have a name for it then, and neither did I make a meaningful connection between it and the forested hills farther south in the state that I was doing my part to shear. That summer, and most of the next, I was a chokersetter for the Weyerhaeuser Timber Company, playing a game of colossal pickup sticks called high-lead logging. After the cutters had dropped all the trees on a slope and bucked them into thirty-foot lengths, the rest of us set to work with our diesel yarder and hundred-foot steel tower and miles of cable, hauling those jumbled logs up the hill to the trucks. They were mostly about two or three feet in diameter, but occasionally we came upon what had been an ancient stand of red cedar, Douglas fir, or western hemlock, the butt-cuts sometimes ten or twelve feet through. Because a choker—a length of inch-and-an-eighth cable designed to noose around logs—would snap like string under the drag of one of those giants, we cradled that kind in a two-choker wrap. Then we cleared out of the way, watching it lurch from its bed and start stubbornly up the hill as the yarder roared, the log plunging and rolling like a huge hooked fish, scattering smaller logs and uprooting stumps and gouging long raw grooves in the wet earth. It was exciting, that violent commotion. We whooped and hollered and cheered the log on, and when the rigging came back we hooked up another, and another, and on through the days until the hillside was nothing but stumps and dirt and thickets of limb-trash.

I was vaguely uneasy with all that destruction, but my uneasiness was overwhelmed by my pleasure in living the logging romance, in wearing suspenders and a tin hardhat, in learning to chew plug and cuss well and drink great quantities of beer. Occasionally, I felt a twinge. One day we ate lunch by a fern-bordered runnel that wound its way down the desolate slope and splashed over rocks where we sat. It looked all wrong in the clearcut's noon glare—muddy, misdirected, out of place. I tried to imagine it as it once must have been, how its small splashing might have sounded in the shadowy groves of Douglas fir, how the elk might have stopped to drink and passed on. The stream had once been part of the forest's mysterious life; now it was a trivial oddity, discolored and tawdry, scarcely audible above the diesel's idle.

Weyerhaeuser laid waste to those Washington hills, and in the process they wasted nothing. We spent many cold minutes grubbing choker-holes under mud-buried logs. If a rotted log looked close to half good, we choked it. If a chunk was thicker than six inches and longer than eight feet, we choked it. The hooktender—boss of the crew—prowled the barren slope behind us for pieces we should have sent up the hill. Waste is against the logger's religion. Wood left on the ground will never become lumber or paper, never become money, and the same applies to standing timber left past its prime. To the wood products man an old-growth forest, with its many dead and dying trees, is an over-mature forest, a decadent forest, a forest in decline doing no human being any good. As a Reagan administration official remarked in 1984, "Old-growth forests remind me of an old folks home, just waiting to die."

He said that because when he looks at trees he sees board footage. He sees rotation cycles and allowable annual cuts, he sees lumber and houses and an ill-defined picture of progress that he takes to be the future because it has been the past. To be fair, since clearly he is a man of poetical instincts, he probably sees some beauty in ancient trees, and he probably appreciates that woodpeckers and other creatures nest and feed in them. But he doesn't see, or if he sees he doesn't appreciate, the slow exuberant dance the forest does through time. He doesn't see the intricate webwork of fungi that strands through the ground, drawing its food from the roots of trees and helping the roots draw food from the soil. He doesn't see the red-backed vole that eats the fungi's fruiting bodies and disperses their spores, sheltering itself in downed rotting wood. He doesn't see the spotted owl that eats the red-backed vole, hunting in the dark through thousands of acres of trees, nesting high in a standing snag and feeding her owlets, this brood and all her broods, as the Douglas firs keep growing and growing, each in its turn going down, melting into ground, sheltering the vole and feeding the fungi and holding the cold meltwater in its fragrant sponge.

That is one movement of one forest's dance. Countless such movements looping together form the elaborate equilibrium that is old-growth forest, or forest that has developed free of catastrophic disturbance over a long period of time. It expresses itself differently in different regions, from the coastal groves of California redwoods to the shrinking pine forests of eastern Oregon to pockets of Douglas fir in the northern Rockies to what is left of the North Woods of the Great Lake states to a few hardwood patches in New Hampshire's White Mountains to sixty-five acres of virgin white oaks in Franklin Township, New Jersey, within sight of the World Trade Center. Outside Alaska, old growth in America is mainly a scatter of small remnants. Ninety-five percent of the forests that originally flourished have been humanly altered or have vanished. Only in the Pacific Northwest do extensive tracts of old growth remain, most of them in the Douglas fir belt that runs the west slope of the Cascade Range through Washington, Oregon, and northwestern California.

Old growth in that region is distinguished from young and mature forest by its vigorous diversity of tree species and sizes, including massive Douglas-firs up to nearly three hundred feet tall and thirty feet or more in circumference at the base. Beneath these spiring giants grow smaller trees—western hemlock, red cedar, bigleaf maple, and other shade-tolerant species. The trees together form a canopy of several layers that diffuses light into an ample soft radiance; here and there, shafts of sun penetrate directly to the forest floor. Because shrubs, herbs, and seedling trees are usually sparse and patchy, the forest seems spacious, deep to the eye. Everywhere, more various even than their living progeny, are the generations of trees gone by—the standing dead with dry needles still intact, limbless snags, rotting stubs coated with moss, and downed logs and limbs of all sizes and states of decay.

The part of one tree in the forest dance may take well over a millennium to perform. The Douglas firs begin as seedling pioneers in an area opened by fire or other disturbance, growing quickly for a hundred years, more slowly for another hundred. During that time each tree looks much like the others, a stand of uniform cousins, but after two centuries a combination of genetic inheritance, competition with neighbors, and the scarrings of storm and fire shapes each tree into a distinct individual. Pocked with cavities, the trunks tilt at various angles; often the top is broken, and one or more branches have turned upward and taken over the tree's growth. The bark is deeply furrowed, mossy, and often charred near the ground.

A five-hundred-year-old Douglas fir has a tall crown of short, irregularly spaced branches—often flat, fan-like sprays growing out of the broken stubs of older branches. The crown may carry over sixty million needles, with a combined surface area of thirty thousand square feet. Practically every surface of the tree is colonized by lichens and mosses, over a hundred separate species in all, which fix nitrogen from the air and draw minerals from rainwater, storing the nutrients and slowly contributing them to the entire forest through leaching and litter-fall. The upper surfaces of large branches become ecosystems of their own, accumulating a soil of organic debris that supports entire communities of plants and invertebrate animals. In all, over fifteen hundred species of invertebrates can inhabit the canopy of an old-growth stand, as well as such vertebrates as the red tree vole, which often lives for many generations in a single tree. In winter, the multi-layered canopy keeps the ground clear of heavy snow and open to foraging by various animals. The water content of the canopy—264,000 gallons per acre—softens the effects of winter weather, providing stable-temperatured habitat for species such as deer and elk.

A Douglas fir's life can span a thousand years. When it dies, its role in the forest continues and amplifies. Dozens of species of birds and mammals use standing snags—and large snags especially, which only old-growth forests can produce—for nesting, courtship displays, and sources of food. Specific animals require snags at specific stages of decay, and old-growth forest provides the entire range, just as it provides an array of downed logs, from intact wind-thrown trees to barely perceptible linear mounds on the forest floor, the remains of five hundred years of gradual decay. Logs are used in even more ways than snags: they are cover, bedding, lookout, pathway, food source, and food storage for hundreds of varieties of birds, amphibians, and mammals. Several species, including the marten, fisher, goshawk, and northern spotted owl, are found almost exclusively in old-growth forest. For some forty others, old growth is preferred habitat, where they reach their highest population densities, and hundreds more use it for specific purposes at certain times in their lives.

Many plant species as well find their optimum habitat in old-growth forest, and some probably require it for survival. Nurse logs, like the one I sat on in the Hoh Rain Forest, are a characteristic feature of old growth. The rotting wood of downed trunks provides a receptive site for the germination and growth of young plants and trees, and for one of the most remarkable relationships of the old-growth system. Mycorrhizal fungi colonize the log and attach themselves to the seedling tree roots in a bond that means life to both. Tapping the roots for their stored sugars, the mycorrhizae enzymatically break down nutrient compounds in the rotting wood that the seedlings are incapable of processing themselves—chemically, they crack the nut and present the kernel to their hungry hosts. Long after the nurse log has merged into ground, sometimes leaving a straight colonnade of adult trees, the fungi continue to pass nutrients from soil to roots.

The mushrooms and truffles that appear on logs and in the duff, eaten and scattered by small mammals, are the fungi's reproductive bodies—all that shows of the gossamer webwork pursuing its commerce underground. The old-growth economy works mainly out of sight. Rotting logs are the fundament of that economy, powering and stabilizing the entire system through their slow decay. Energy, nutrients, and organic material that were gradually gathered by living trees are gradually released for the use of other plants and animals. More nutrients are added through litter-fall and leachwater and the nitrogen-fixing of bacteria in the rotting wood. Water itself is conserved in the ground debris, more effectively there than in the underlying soil. In streams, the dams and diversions formed by logs and limbs restrain the erosive power of water and create pool habitats such as spawning gravels for salmon. By slowing the passage of organic matter they allow for its complete processing, and thus the flourishing of entire food chains.

Conservation is the genius of the old-growth economy. Nothing is wasted, but unlike the frugal logger who takes everything out, the wisdom of old growth keeps everything *in*. My characterization is only a sketch of what is known, and what is known—nearly all of which has been learned in the last twenty years—is probably only a fraction of the system's full complexity. But if many details are still missing, one large fact is clear: the death and dying that so depress the government official are actually part of a continuous cycling pathway of life, dead life going down to the darkness of soil and new life rising to the sun, looping streams of energy that look to us like stillness and sound like the most profound quiet. To the official, the forest is a wasted commodity. To John Muir, who a century ago intuited a great deal about the workings of old growth, it was a self-renewing fountain where his spirit could drink. "One is continually reminded," he wrote, ". . . of the infinite lavishness and fertility of Nature—inexhaustible abundance amid what seems enormous waste. And yet when we look into any of her operations that lie within reach of our minds, we learn that no particle of her material is wasted or worn out. It is eternally flowing from use to use, beauty to yet higher beauty. . . ." And, in *John of the Mountains:* "The woods are full of dead and dying trees, yet needed for their beauty to complete the beauty of the living. How beautiful is all Death!"

Clearly Muir's is the richer view and most enriches us. But the government official, within the purview of his specialized mind, sees clearly. He would break the long dance of the trees because humans require the products they yield. Because I write these words on the stuff of trees, because I sit on dead trees to write them, because it is dead trees that carry John Muir's thoughts across a hundred years to my eyes, I cannot discount the official's vision. We need to cut trees. We need lots of trees. And sometime very soon, while there is still time to meaningfully choose, we need to decide where the line should be drawn between our consumptive human economy and the ancient economy of the old-growth forest.

Once, except for the disruptions of fire and other natural disasters, it was all old growth. And ever since John Smith and his settlers arrived in Virginia to find "faire meadows and goodly tall Trees," we've been steadily engaged in cutting it down. The great white pines, which often soared over two hundred feet, were the tallest and the first to fall. Thomas Morton, an early colonizer of Massachusetts, wrote to England that the New World supported an "infinite store" of the pines. Felled for boards and boat planks and flawless masts for the king's navy, they were quickly gone. The mixed hardwoods that shouldered the pines formed a wild so unbroken, the legend goes, that a squirrel with a sense of purpose could have travelled from the Atlantic to the Mississippi without touching ground. Few settlers facing that vast woods had the foresight of William Penn, who ordered one acre of trees left standing for every five cut. We pursued our future, and the endless forest was left in fragments, eaten by axes, intentionally burned when ash was more valuable than lumber. Through the nineteenth century timbering boomed as our busiest trade, finishing off the eastern forest and then the north woods of Minnesota and Wisconsin and then the southern pines and hardwoods and then setting to work in California, where John Muir saw sequoias blasted down with gunpowder, the great trees half-shattered into useless splinters. And today across the Northwest and the Rockies, less wastefully but every bit as wasting, the clearcutting continues, reducing what is left of the primeval North American forest to unstable soils, thickets of brush, and orderly planted ranks of cloned and docile trees.

Historically, and to this day, we have harvested much more timber each year than the amount replenished by growth. We have felt little need to discipline ourselves—the trees have been available, big and ready for falling, still endless-seeming. Logged areas in the Northwest were replanted haphazardly, or not at all, for the first half of this century; only in the last forty years, as sustained yield has developed as a goal if not a fact, have efforts intensified. Rotation cycles vary from forest to forest, from site to site, but planted trees in the Northwest generally require at least seventy years to reach harvestable size. As second-growth crops mature on private lands, timber corporations are pressing for higher and higher annual cuts on the national forests and the other public lands—the lands that contain practically all that remains of old-growth forest in the Lower 48 states.

And the corporations are getting what they want. Though strictly forbidden to do so under the National Forest Management Act of 1976, virtually every national forest in Washington and Oregon is selling timber above the sustained yield level—23 percent above, according to Forest Service data for twelve of the forests. But the numbers mean less than the look of the hills. Though in some forests the devastation is no longer successfully screened off by strips of trees, the view from the interstates and main highways is usually misleadingly benign. Only those who fly over the Cascades, or regularly climb the high peaks, or spend a lot of time driving the back roads, have a chance to see how the brown patchwork mange of clearcuts grows and grows, how the spaghetti-squiggles of logging roads reach deeper and deeper into the last enclaves of unbroken green. Except for designated wilderness, which protects mainly high-elevation areas of little commercial interest, few of those enclaves are safe from cutting. And some of them are more than endangered,

I learned as I drove through Washington state's Olympic and Gifford Pinchot national forests with Chuck Sisco, a biologist for the National Audubon Society who worked ten years for the Forest Service. "Twenty percent of those trees you see are already gone," he told me. "That's the amount in the timber sale pipeline at any one time. They're as good as cut."

The logging country we toured provided ample evidence that not only too much land is being sheared, but also the wrong kind of land. In Olympic National Forest, Sisco had to weave his four-wheel drive pickup through stretches of rock and earth debris that had tumbled down from clearcut slopes that can best be described as cliffs. I remembered setting chokers in similar terrain and having to scramble hand and foot to reach precariously perched logs. It never occurred to me then what now is painfully clear: these mountainsides will never bear forest again, not old growth, not any significant growth of trees. With nothing to secure it the soil is going fast, slumping and silting up the streams below, leaving terrible wounds in the watersheds. These slopes were logged with no thought for what the land could bear. They were logged to make cash of their trees, a one-time bonanza centuries in the making. They weren't harvested, they were mined. And unlike Weyerhaeuser's land, these mountainsides belong to us all.

Clearcutting damage is not always so conspicuous. A mild incline cropped of its old growth and planted in bright young Douglas firs is not an unpleasant sight. Deer and elk are fond of the browse such spaces provide, some of it planted by the Forest Service. Two or three trees or snags have usually been left for birds and small mammals. Sites of this kind, very common on the public lands, will raise a kind of forest—a single-species forest of uniform trees, a forest designed by man to serve the human economy. "Cornfields." Chuck Sisco contemptuously calls them. "We may have lots of trees, but we're not going to have a *forest*." The ecological characteristics of old growth take at least 175 years to begin to develop in Douglas fir country, much longer to reach their full bloom. The planted clearcuts will be harvested in less than a hundred years, as soon as the trees finish their surge of adolescent growth. And even if they were managed on a longer rotation cycle, it is becoming increasingly clear that current logging practices will prevent old growth from ever restoring itself.

When fires—like those that blistered much of the Far West in the summer and fall of 1987—or other natural calamity injures a stand of old trees, the forest economy is curtailed but not destroyed. Usually some big trees and snags are left intact, providing habitat and stabilizing the soil. Much of the damp debris of the forest floor also survives, continuing its slow discharge of nutrients to the roots of the new forests. But in a clearcut, stripped of every stick of standing and downed wood, nature's bridge to rebirth is gone. Pioneer plants such as red alder that pump nitrogen into the soil of disrupted sites are routinely killed with herbicides. And most important, the underground forest of mycorrhizal fungi dies out when the trees are cleared and returns very slowly, or not at all if the site is isolated from intact old-growth source areas. "It's very hard to recreate old growth *de novo*," says Jerry Franklin, Chief Plant Ecologist for the Forest Service's Pacific Northwest Experiment Station, Professor of Ecosystem Analysis at the University of Washington, and the foremost pioneer among old-growth researchers. "The inoculum isn't there—the mycorrhizae, the vascular plants, the invertebrates, all the organisms and interactions that we're just beginning to find out about. Once it's all gone, it's very difficult to get back."

Franklin does feel that the Forest Service is responding rapidly to some of the findings of old-growth research. Progressive managers here and there in the Northwest are bringing a heightened ecosystem awareness to the concern for commodity production that has reigned supreme since the 1950s. More woody debris and more living material are being left in cutover areas, for instance—a sign that the Germanic preoccupation with order and cleanliness that has dominated American silvicultural practices from the beginning may be starting to give way to what Franklin calls "planned disorder," the wise disorder of the old-growth economy. Foresters are more open to experimenting with selective logging and longer rotations. And they are beginning to pay attention to the research of Tim Schowalter, an entomologist at Oregon State University, who has found that planted single-species forests are vulnerable to calamitous insect infestations because they lack the predator-insects that control such outbreaks in old growth. Maintaining the insect balance, by preserving old growth and by planting cutover areas with a more diverse flora, may prove to be a valuable management technique.

Such developments bode well for the future of the managed national forest lands. And as Franklin points out, it is the producing lands that will form the crucial context for whatever unmanaged old growth we decide to preserve: "The commodity lands are going to be the bulk of our landscape, and if we sterilize them we've lost the battle. It's not just a set-aside issue. We need healthy biological diversity throughout the system." Other scientists agree, including Chris Maser, a leading old-growth researcher formerly with the Bureau of Land Management and now a private consultant. "If we want sustained yield we need a sustainable forest," says Maser, "and that means two things. One, set aside old-growth preserves—and unmanaged young and mature stands that will become old growth—as models of what a healthy forest is. And two, restore the commodity lands by stimulating old growth there as best we can. The health of the ecosystem comes first, the harvest of material second—we've had our priorities backward. But we've been manipulating the Douglas fir system for less than a century. It can be restored, if we start now, while we still have enough old growth to learn from—ten years from now may well be too late."

Both Franklin and Maser, though they cite the need to apply the findings of old-growth research to improve the entire ecosystem, caution against an assumption held by some in the timber industry and the Forest Service that old growth itself can be humanly created, through genetic tinkering and management techniques, faster than it develops in nature. Given that we can and must create healthier commodity forests, forests in which some old-growth characteristics are retained, we can't manufacture the genuine article with all its known and unknown functions of habitat, watershed, nutrient cycling, and genetic diversity. Trees, to cite the industry cliché, are a renewable resource—but old growth isn't. "We're really just learning what old growth *is*," says Jerry Franklin. "Twenty years ago we didn't understand what rotting logs did. We were missing the significance of six-foot diameter logs. What are we missing now? I'm very doubtful about the chances of growing something we don't fully understand. If society decides it wants to have old growth, the most important strategy now is to retain it."

And so the questions: how much should be preserved, in tracts of what size, and where? And the related pragmatic question: how much *can* be preserved? The Forest Service, for all its current progress in forestry techniques, has not moved quickly toward answers, or even toward addressing the questions. At the present pace of logging, practically all old growth on national forest lands will be gone or seriously damaged within forty or fifty years, and some say sooner. Estimates are difficult because no one knows with any certainty how much is left, including the Forest Service. Of twenty-one national forests in Washington, Oregon, and northwestern California, only one—the Willamette, in central Oregon—has undertaken a detailed and comprehensive inventory. Others have done some mapping, but they routinely classify old growth together with "large saw timber," "mature conifer forest" and other such categories, despite the findings of Jerry Franklin and others that mature forest and true old growth are distinct ecological systems with widely different characteristics of nutrient cycling and wildlife habitat. These inflated inventories are in some cases further distorted by the inclusion of timber already sold and cut. The result is an impression of ample old growth on paper, but in fact there is much less than either the timber industry or the Forest Service claims, and it is going fast. In arranging timber sales the Service targets old growth first—because it is viewed as over-mature wood that must be cut or lost, because it often occurs in accessible valley bottoms, and because it yields fine-grained and nearly knot-free lumber.

Eighty percent of national forest old growth is available for logging. It is disappearing at over one square mile per week.

And the volume of the cut is only half the story. Since World War II, national forests in Douglas fir country have been logged primarily by a dispersed clearcut system that checkerboards the landscape with 25 to 50-acre clearings, leaving patches of forest of about the same size or somewhat larger. The intent was to minimize damage to the forest, but the result has been to chop it to pieces, injuring its capacity as wildlife habitat, and jeopardizing the remaining trees themselves. Though the edges and breaks that riddle the formerly continuous system temporarily favor game species such as deer and elk, those animals quickly overuse remaining timbered areas and old-growth-dependent species disappear under the pressure. A fragmented forest loses its wind-protection as well, leaving remnant patches susceptible to blowdown—witness the Bull Run River drainage in Mt. Hood National Forest, where windstorms leveled 3,400 acres of extensively cut and roaded forest in 1983. What size of patch is big enough to survive as a viable ecological unit? Not forty or eighty acres, thinks Jerry Franklin, not even three hundred if surrounded by clearcuts. In many cases "we've been thinking in terms much too small," he says. "We probably should be thinking of five or six hundred acres at least." And entire drainage basins, he suggests, are ecologically the most sensible units to retain.

To this point, the Forest Service stance on the issue of what to preserve has focused on a single old-growth-dependent species, the northern spotted owl. Field studies indicate that populations of the owl are declining rapidly, as logging shrinks and fragments its habitat; it may be poised on the brink of population collapse. Charged by law with the perpetuation of vertebrate species native to the national forests, and well aware that if the owl becomes a federally listed endangered species it could virtually shut down logging in the Northwest, the Forest Service has proposed the setting aside of 550 spotted owl habitat areas in Oregon and Washington and 200 in the Douglas fir zone of northwestern California, each containing up to 2,200 acres of old growth. Environmentalists, armed with the data of biological researchers, argue that the acreage is too small and the number of areas too few to ensure the owl's survival. Equally controversial is the Service's estimate that implementing its plan would cause a five percent reduction in harvest levels and the loss of 760 to 1,330 jobs. That estimate, The Wilderness Society has pointed out, is based on potential rather than actual harvest levels and thus is wildly skewed. Calculated on the basis of average cuts over the past ten years, the Forest Service plan would eliminate no jobs at all.

The greatest distortion, however, is not in the numbers but in the Service's formulation of the issue as owls versus jobs. At stake is the health and survival of not only spotted owls but the entire Douglas fir ecosystem of the Northwest—the natural economy on which owls and watersheds and the region's human economy all depend. Spotted owl are a valuable indicator of the plight of that system, but it will accomplish little to set aside preserves for them while the forest all around remains available for destruction. If the land at large goes, so will the owls; as Chris Maser observes, the surest way to guarantee their extinction is to draw a political line around them. And eventually, as the land at large goes, the people will follow the owls. A medicine that targets only one element of the ecosystem will fail. Ecological doctoring requires holistic approaches, and surely none is more important than the immediate protection of what large, unbroken old-growth tracts remain in the riddled forests.

But the Forest Service is placing the future of those tracts in doubt. Compelled by the National Forest Management Act, the Service is issuing comprehensive plans that will shape the management of all its forests for the next half century. In the Northwest, the plans may decide the fate of old growth. The plan for the Olympic National Forest calls for cutting 123,400 acres of old growth over the next fifty years—over half of what remains in the forest. In Oregon's Siuslaw National Forest, 69 percent of the remaining old growth is scheduled to fall. In northwest California, the draft plan for the twin Shasta-Trinity national forests opens half of their old growth— some 200,000 acres, including several major roadless areas—to the chainsaws. Clearcutting in such volumes would irreparably fragment any forest that was spared, destroying the ecological integrity of the system. Under the Shasta-Trinity formula for forest "diversity," only five percent of the forest would need to be maintained as old growth—a formula opposed not only by conservationists but also by the California Department of Fish and Game and even the state Attorney General's office.

Most Northwest forests have only recently begun to release draft plans; none so far reflects significant concern for preserving old growth, or significantly slows the cut. I was in The Wilderness Society's Seattle office last fall when the draft plan for the Siskiyou National Forest arrived. Its four volumes plus maps made a stack some twelve inches high, weighing at least fifteen pounds. Jean Durning, The Society's Northwest Regional Director, and Bob Freimark, Regional Associate, had ninety days to read, assimilate, and develop a response to that daunting pile—ninety days already scheduled to overflowing with their work of research, testimony, and lobbying on old growth and other environmental issues. The Siskiyou, with its complex of Douglas fir and evergreen broadleafs such as tanoak, madrone, and canyon live oak, is unique in the region and in the world. In one of its roadless areas, the North Kalmiopsis, protesters have lain in front of bulldozers and camped in the big trees in desperate attempts to save them. That they have felt moved to such actions has a specific connection, I suspect, to the twelve-inch stack released by the Forest Service—the fate of a distinctive forest sealed in fifteen pounds of virtually impenetrable print, ninety days for comment on the future of millions of years of evolution. The Service without question, put a great deal of serious work into its plan, but public comment on that work clearly is not a priority. The Service has a direction, and believes in it, and doesn't want it disturbed.

That direction is a compromise between its best tradition as steward of the forests and the pressures it receives from the timber industry and Congress to allow more cutting than it should. The forests of the Northwest produce one-third of America's wood products, and the most efficient way to keep the pump primed with raw logs is to build roads into accessible valley bottoms and clearcut the prime old growth and move on. Perhaps less efficient, but considerably more farsighted, would be to limit sales to mature saw timber—trees 95 to 160 years old—and isolated patches of old growth that have lost their ecological viability. Such a policy would not necessarily reduce the harvest level on the forests but it should. Sometime soon, the Forest Service and the country are going to have to deal with the reality that we can't continue to cut more wood than the land is capable of producing. When it estimates the total available timber on its holdings, the Service arrives at inflated figures by including marginal lands, lands that won't grow trees again, and even rock outcrops and meadows that never did grow trees. Basing harvest levels on this paper inventory, it sells accessible old growth to reach those levels—a prescription for a ransacked forest. To assure a sustained yield of timber into the twenty-first century, as both the law and pure good sense require, the Forest Service will have to lower its annual cut.

The forthcoming plans do lower it by a very small amount and for that reason were stymied for months by appeals from the timber industry. The corporations argue that reducing harvests would mean fewer jobs, a depressed Northwest economy, and a shortage of wood products to the nation. They are partly right about the symptoms but wholly wrong about the causes. Between 1979 and 1986, jobs in the wood products industry in Oregon and Washington plummeted from more than 133,400 to fewer than 101,600, while lumber production *increased* from 11.15 billion board feet to 12.28 billion board feet—25 percent fewer workers produced 10 percent more lumber. It is clear that sawmill jobs are disappearing in the Northwest, but it is just as clear that the disappearance has no relation to timber supply. The main immediate cause of the job falloff was a vast increase in mill efficiency, a result of the 1979–82 recession. The problem won't be solved by continuing the wholesale cutting of old-growth forest.

And neither will continued cutting revive the booming timber economy of the past, because the Northwest *does* face a reduction in timber supply—a reduction that will happen whether old growth is preserved or not. The heart of the problem is the private timberlands. Industry chose to liquidate most of the old growth on its own lands by the middle of the century, planting crops of new trees that are now about forty years old. Because most of this second growth won't be harvestable for some time, and because industry has little mature timber to fill the gap, economists predict a drop-off in the timber supply of 30 percent by the end of the century—the exact amount will depend on how much of the shortfall the Forest Service agrees to make up. Two additional factors will worsen the predicament. First, the timber companies are already cutting some of their maturing second growth—the trees expected to yield timber early next century. And second, the primary market for those logs and for industry's remaining mature and old-growth logs is not the United States but Japan. Forty percent of Washington's timber production and 20 percent of Oregon's go overseas, because export brings an enormous profit and feeding the domestic mills does not. Chuck Sisco has seen docks on the Olympic Peninsula loading export logs twenty-four hours a day next to empty sawmills—a fast buck for the industry, still fewer jobs for millworkers, and a serious deficit in our future supply of wood.

By law, no raw logs from federal lands can be exported, but logs subjected to minimal trimming can be and are being shipped to Japan. And every log exported from private land, though not immediately depleting the national forests, will eventually increase the pressure on the Forest Service to continue to allow excessive cutting. The timber industry is selling its future supply and counting on access to publicly owned trees to fill the gap. Claiming necessity, the corporations will continue to clamor for the right to liquidate the last of the old-growth forests. They will cite consumer demand for wood products, but they won't cite their own avarice and poor judgment.

Historically, in the East and the Lake States and the South, timber has been a nomadic and consumptive industry, moving into a region, stripping the trees, and moving on. The Northwest is now at the tail end of the boom of that boom-and-bust pattern. The region is experiencing an inevitable transition from an old-growth to a second-growth economy, and from an economy in which timber is king to one that is more diversified and stable. Old-growth forest could play an important role in the new economy, which will include tourism and outdoor recreation as substantial components. That role would pose different dangers to the forest but if properly managed would not destroy it. Broadly speaking, the Northwest and the nation face a choice about how the economic transition will be handled. We can delay it a few decades by consuming the last of an irreplaceable resource, owned by all

Americans, or we can seek creative strategies for easing the change with the fewest possible losses to both the human economy and the ancient economy of the trees.

At present, the losses are high in both. Too many trees are falling, mill-workers are losing jobs, spotted owls and other animals face possible extinction, and the land itself is slipping away into the rivers and streams. The Forest Service is to blame, and Congress, which annually sets a higher harvest target than the Service seeks, and the timber industry, for its shortsighted self-interest. But ultimately they are agents of us and our appetites. We have prospered for four hundred years by extracting wealth from the land, wasting the plenty we possessed. We need to question now, before answers are forced upon us, whether we and the land can afford that kind of prosperity, whether the economic growth we hold sacred might actually be a self-centered adolescence we must put behind us. In the Douglas fir forest, rapid growth gives way after a hundred years to slower growth and then an equilibrium of growth and death, gain and loss, the forest's wealth conserved and carefully recycled. Each member of that community is supported by what the land in its health allows, a diverse and vigorous commonwealth sustaining itself through time. It is a way of living more stable and more sensible than our own, a way of living that we could be instructed by, if we could stop ourselves from turning it into two-by-fours and more tract homes.

John Muir wrote: "We all travel the Milky Way together, trees and men." Reversing our anthropocentric tradition, he places trees before men and joins the two in a single "We," a single interdependent band of pilgrims. Muir understood, not merely with his intellect but with the full vitality of his imagination, that trees and humans are bound together in one planetary matrix of life, realizing itself over billions of years. We are here together, sharing origin and future. The forest's particular kind of wild, like the other wilds of Earth, refreshes us because it reminds us deeply of who we are.

Something happened to me, something that has helped me grow, in the stillness of that Olympic rain forest. And something happened to me at ten thousand feet in California's White Mountains, too, in the airy groves of Bristlecone pines. Some of them over 4,600 years old, the oldest of all trees for which dates are known, they grow in a few colonies surrounded in sky, their roots clenched deep in crevices of stone. Wind-scoured, split open by lightning, showing more bare grain than bark, they still put out sprays of stubby, five-bunched needles. Each tree is a complete record of what it has been, dwarfed and gnarled but fully formed, fully present in the world. In their age as individuals you can see their age as a kind—the long trail of seed that brought them to their few mountaintops, in much their present form, from a time before the birth of the broadleafs, from the time when plants were first colonizing land. On rocky peaks across the Great Basin the Bristlecones go on, answering snow, sun, and centuries with the measured speech of their bright brown cones.

Aldo Leopold, walking among his Wisconsin pines in winter, received from their snowy ranks "a curious transfusion of courage." I felt that in the Bristlecone forest—a community adapted to a hard location and developed to distinction, to a complex and perfect rightfulness. I felt there, as I had felt in the rainforest, as I have felt in the cathedral groves of Douglas fir and the sunny forests of puzzle-barked pines, an overwhelming sense of place. All old-growth forests, in their different ways, are distinctly placed, and are made of distinct places. A stand of charred and mossy sided Douglas firs is thick with place; a "Hi-Yield" forest of uniform young trees is not. The muddy runnel in the clearcut that twinged my conscience eighteen years ago wasn't a place when I saw it, but it had been. Near a camp I visit each summer in south-central Oregon, by Cougar Peak, a stream slides down a shallow valley into Cottonwood Lake. Climbing alongside it, you pass from a grassy bowl scattered with aspens into a woods of big white firs and ponderosa pines. It is not a striking forest, no one view of more interest than another, until you come to a great pine fallen across the stream. A shallow pool has formed behind it. Streamwater has saturated the log and slowly found seepways through it, spilling out the downstream side and carving the grain over time into a delicate mosaic of scallops and whorls. Mosses, ferns, and tiny yellow flowers grow out of the log, fed by the steady trickling, bright and shaded in the filtered light. You stop there, you listen, you touch the spongy mosses, you peer into the log's crevices, you sit a while if the mosquitoes aren't too bad. That over-mature tree, with all its wasted board footage, has in dying given birth to a place.

In time the log will rot through and the little cosmos of the pool will revert to flowing stream. Heard or unheard by humans, other trees will fall. Other pools will form, like the earlier one and different. The firs and pines will grow and go down, grow and go down. Seedlings will rise where light allows them, doubled over beneath snow, springing up with the melt, raising themselves through the turning of seasons alongside the dead trunks melting into ground. Insects and woodpeckers will nest in the snags, deer will carefully step their way, the cougar will stalk and make its kills, high branches will play the song of the wind as clouds cross the sky, and all of it changing in the hands of time toward whatever it will become. In forest, Earth speaks a peculiar profusion. Planned by no human and no god, it is a birthing ground of possibility—a part, in Wallace Stegner's phrase, of the geography of hope.

And hope arises in surprising forms. In another forest, a forest I haven't seen for a very long time, tall broadleaf trees interweave on a great flatland, blending themselves into one spreading crown, broken by patches of grassy plain. There is stillness upon it—but as in all forest, stillness contains the movements of life. Birds flick through the leaves, small animals are at home on the trunks and limbs, and something else moves, something that has lived in these trees for fifty million years. In that distance of time, slowly, its paws have blossomed into supple fingers and thumb. Slowly its eyes have aligned in the front of its head, so that each graspable branch stands clear as it swings and leaps the high pathways. Slowly the monochrome two-dimensional world has flared with color, deepened with the clarity of thing and relation—green leaf, red fruit, and the long tawny grasses where already this creature is feeling itself drawn, the long ground it will travel on its way to the winning of the world.

We are the children of those African trees. Whatever we are, they helped make us. We sense when we enter a still depth of forest what Emerson sensed in the Concord horizon, something as beautiful as our own nature—something, indeed, of our nature itself. We travel the Milky Way together, trees and humans, and before we destroy what is left of the ancient forests we might pause to ask whose limbs we are lopping, whose skin we are stripping, whose bodies we are severing from their roots in the ground. We might pause to ask, as our past perishes in the screech of saws, if we aren't at the same time clearcutting our future from the face of the earth.

(Spring 1988)

GEORGE WUERTHNER

Dimming the Range of Light

Introduction

I
t was the Spanish settlers of California who gave the range its name, one that rolls off even Anglo tongues with an uncommon sweetness— Sierra Nevada. But the Spanish had a way of putting names on the land with quite as much precision as romance, and what they saw, looking across the rich, grassy, sunlit interior valley at the massif rising up behind the rolling, oak-studded foothills in the east, was what they described with direct simplicity: "jagged, snowy mountains." It was left to a later explorer to discern the true poetry of these mountains and give them another name no less sweet: They were, he said, the "Range of Light, surely the brightest and best of all the Lord has built. . . ."

The explorer was, of course, John Muir, and his description is from the conclusion to *My First Summer in the Sierra,* still one of the most engaging of all his works. It was written—based on journals kept at the time—forty years after his first encounter with the mountains in 1869, yet it still glimmers with the magic of discovery. "From garden to garden, ridge to ridge, I drifted enchanted," he wrote, "now on my knees gazing into the face of a daisy, now climbing again and again among the purple and azure flowers of the hemlocks, now down into the treasuries of the snow, or gazing afar over domes and peaks, lakes and woods, and the billowy glaciated fields. . . . In the midst of such beauty, pierced with its rays, one's body is all one tingling palate."

Every human being who cares anything at all about the natural world has one place that is the home of his heart. The Sierra Nevada were that for

Muir, as they have been for millions of people after him, some of whom know the range only through his writings and those of others, some of whom know it nearly as directly and intimately as he did. And even for those who have not known it at all, the range has been an important part of the national estate. It is the single great geographic fact of California, and it has been invested with the magical ever since it raised the last terrible obstacle between the wagon trains of the westering years and the promise of California's valleys, then redeemed itself in 1848 by revealing the presence of more gold than human history had ever imagined.

That gold doomed the scores of individual Indian cultures that had survived the Spanish and later Mexican settlement of the region, obliterated as well the culture of the *Californio*, made California a state, helped win the Civil War, inspired the building of the first transcontinental railroad, made possible the settlement and exploitation of the entire intermountain West, and changed forever the economic structure of the nation. It also set in motion the continuing conflict between the machine of progress and the great garden of the Sierra (to borrow from Wesley Marx). For the power and glory of gold, towns and villages were implanted amid the oaks and sugar pines of the mountains; holes were punched thousands of feet down through ancestral rock; rivers were dammed and their courses turned to get at their naked beds; flumes were built to snake down through the mountain canyons, carrying water at an increasing velocity to the nozzles of howitzer-like hoses, from which the water was turned against the hills, blasting them into mud that poured into the rivers that tumbled from the mountains and flowed out into the valley, crippling salmon fisheries and smothering downstream farms with silt.

Over the next century-and-a-half, even after the last of the gold had been dug, plucked, and washed down from the mountains, the machine continued. Towns were established, wagon roads and highways constructed, cattle and sheep brought in to graze, entire mountains stripped of their forests, a tourist industry embraced and expanded, and bigger and bigger dams built, the water used now to nourish the enormous agricultural "factories in the field" of the Central Valley. We stopped long enough to set some of the range aside as parks and wilderness, but the fact of the matter is that this enormous natural phenomenon today is as threatened as any major ecosystem in the country. To discover the dimensions of the problem, *Wilderness* sent writer George Wuerthner into the Range of Light in the summer of 1993 to take a look around and talk to those who have used it, studied it, and worried about it—especially those who live there, work there, and find the home of their hearts there. This is entirely appropriate. Muir would have approved of Wuerthner's report, I think, but he would have found little comfort in it. Considering what we have wrought in his blessed Range of Light since his death, he might be moved to repeat his old lament against sheep—but probably with another species in mind: "The dusty, noisy flock seems outrageously foreign and out of place in these nature gardens, more so than bears among sheep. The harm they do goes to the heart. . . ."

—T. H. WATKINS

A Range of Superlatives

Aficionados of the Sierra Nevada are fond of pointing out that these mountains make up North America's longest continuous range outside Alaska. An enormous, complex block of fractured, upthrust, and eroded granitic, volcanic, sedimentary, and metamorphic rocks four hundred miles long and anywhere from fifty to eighty miles wide, the range extends unbroken from arid slopes dotted with orchards of Joshua trees in the Tehachapi Mountains of the south to the dense green forests surrounding the volcanic peak called Mt. Lassen in the north. It totals more than 28,000 square miles, or 18 million acres, making it only a little smaller than the state of Maine.

If it is the nation's longest mountain range, it also is its most lofty. Rising from a little above sea level in California's Central Valley, the Sierra Nevada climbs more than two miles into the sky, culminating in 14,495-foot Mt. Whitney, the highest peak in the contiguous United States. Whitney is not alone in its glory. In the so-called "High Sierras," that 150-mile-long glaciated and lake-studded region between Yosemite National Park in the north and Cottonwood Pass in the south, more than five hundred peaks thrust 12,000 feet or more; thirteen of these exceed 13,000 feet. Hundreds of small glaciers, including the most southerly glaciers in the United States, are hidden in the nooks and crannies of these crags.

The wall of peaks wrings moisture from every passing cloud, and the higher elevations of the range receive more snow than anyplace in the Lower 48 states outside the Pacific Northwest. A number of snowfall records have been set here since records began to be kept in the nineteenth century, including the 32.6 feet that buried the town of Tamarack in 1911 and the 86 feet that smothered Donner Pass during the winter of 1982–1983. Still, the Sierra Nevada enjoys more sunshine than almost any other mountain range, particularly in the summer, when only about 3 percent of the annual precipitation occurs. Overall, it has one of the mildest climates associated with any major mountain range in the world, which is why it has been described as the "gentle wilderness."

The litany of superlatives continues: Lake Tahoe, very near the geographic center of the range, is 1,685 feet deep, making it the tenth-deepest freshwater lake in the world; Kings Canyon, which has been carved 8,240 feet into the original granite, is, according to some, the deepest canyon in the United States. Yosemite Falls, which drops 2,425 feet in a series of leaps and cascades, is the third-highest waterfall in the world and Yosemite's El Capitan is the largest granite cliff face anywhere. Mono Lake, just east of the range, is the oldest continually existing large body of water in the nation. And growing among the unglaciated ridges of the Sierra Nevada's middle elevations are the magnificent trees called *Sequoia giantea*, the Big Trees, the largest living things on earth, some of them more than thirty-five feet in diameter, 300 feet high, and thousands of years old. Finally, the southern portion of the Sierra Nevada makes up the second-largest roadless area left in the conterminous 48 states: 2.8 million acres at the heart of what is called the "High Sierra Wildlands Complex." Only the complex of unroaded wildlands that includes and surrounds Idaho's Frank Church-River of No Return Wilderness is bigger.

More than two-thirds of the Sierra Nevada is in the public lands system—52 percent in nine national forests, from Lassen in the north to Sequoia in the south; 10 percent in Yosemite, Sequoia, and Kings Canyon national parks; and another 7 percent in scattered holdings of the Bureau of Land Management. Nineteen wilderness areas totalling more than 3.3 million acres have been established in the forests and parks. In addition, segments of a number of rivers have been designated wild and scenic, including portions of the American, the Feather, the Merced, and the Tuolumne. Concern over the fate of the Sierra Nevada has been at the heart of the conservation movement for more than a century: The Sierra Club was founded in 1892 to ensure its protection, and some of the most important conservation battles of the twentieth century—from the unsuccessful fight to keep the Hetch Hetchy Valley unflooded to the successful one to keep resort development out of the Mineral King Valley in the 1970s—concerned the Sierra Nevada.

Now a new confrontation is shaping up, one whose complications will require a largeness of vision to match the scope of the mountains themselves. Jim Eaton of the California Wilderness Coalition suggested part of the problem when he pointed out that most of the parkland and wilderness designations in the Sierra Nevada encompass lands only in the higher elevations. "We've done a good job of protecting a lot of rocks and ice," he said. "That's not necessarily bad. These lands are scenic and have high recreation values. Nevertheless, by focusing all our efforts on the dramatic landscapes, we've wound up doing a poor job of protecting the biological diversity of the Sierra."

Much of that diversity already has been lost. The grizzly bear, once so abundant that it was chosen to adorn the state flag, has been gone since the last one was killed in Sequoia National Park in 1924. Wolves have been extinct in the region even longer. Other species that once flourished have become scarce, including wolverines, fishers, bighorn sheep, Sierra Nevada red foxes, and Paiute cutthroat trout, while every kind of habitat from subalpine meadow to foothill grassland has been seriously diminished.

It is the continuing drain on the Sierra Nevada's biological "bank" that has most conservationists worried these days. Some of the problems can be identified immediately—the automobile congestion that plagues the Yosemite Valley every summer or the loss of water clarity and purity in Lake Tahoe because of sediment and nutrient enrichment from housing developments, for example. But they are relatively localized problems and are not representative of the kinds of threats that are unraveling the Sierra Nevada ecosystem range-wide. John Muir, the original Sierra Nevada activist, would recognize some of the problems immediately; others, the products of a civilization nearly three-quarters of a century beyond his experience, would probably astonish—and most certainly anger—him.

Where Angels Fear to Breathe

Some summer days, you don't even have to go all the way to the Sierra Nevada range itself to experience one of its worst difficulties: smog. You can see it from the middle of the Central Valley heading east toward the mountains, a thick gray-brown smear of poisoned air that does not confine itself to the valley but oozes up into the foothills and on into the mountains beyond. The pollutants are emissions from automobiles and agricultural machinery—sulfur dioxide, ozone, carbon monoxide, and nitrogen oxide. Ozone concentrations in some Sierra monitoring locations have been found to be three to four times greater than those recorded for downtown Sacramento and other urban areas of the Central Valley. Researchers at Sequoia National Park have recorded the highest 24-hour ozone levels of any unit within the National Park System, including urban national parks like the Gateway National Recreation Area in New York.

This is bad for people and deadly for forests. A 1988 study in Yosemite National Park found that 58 percent of the Jeffrey pine had ozone-damaged needles. In the southern Sierra Nevada, where pollution is greatest, nearly all of the Jeffrey pine stands at about the 6,000-foot-level in Sequoia National Park were discovered to have some ozone-induced damage. Ozone is easier to monitor than it is to control, Joe Fish of the Northern Sierra Air Quality Management District told me, because the problem is not some conveniently located source of pollution, like a big coal-fired power-generating plant. "Most of California's big industrial sources of pollution are under control," he said. "When you talk about air pollution in California, you are largely talking about cars. California is a car culture." Jim Eaton of the California Wilderness Coalition agrees. "The problem with California," he says, "is that even if you reduce emission from every individual vehicle—which is happening—we keep getting more and more people into this state and they all drive cars." In the 1850s, Mark Twain suggested that the sparkling air of the Sierra Nevada was the same that the angels breathed. On any given summer day in the mountains now, the angels would more likely be choking.

Hands Upon the Stump

Air pollution is insidious, and its effects on the range often take a long time to reveal themselves. Forest fragmentation is more immediately visible and devastating, especially in the heavily logged northern Sierra Nevada and especially in its impact on the maintenance of a healthy diversity in the remaining old-growth forests. There isn't, as a matter of fact, much old-growth forest left, as I learned from Eric Beckwith in North San Juan, a former mining community in the Mother Lode country northeast of Sacramento. With his father, Steve, Beckwith heads up the Sierra Biodiversity Project. The two men have done extensive computer mapping of the region, noting the occurrence of old-growth forest by habitat type and species, and have become the acknowledged authorities on Sierra Nevada forest fragmentation.

Eric agrees with Jim Eaton that the wilderness designations that have been made in the region since passage of the Wilderness Act in 1964 have done little to protect old growth. "They made an effort to keep heavy-volume timber stands out of designated wilderness," he told me. Many of those stands have since been logged over, and this logging, together with various natural conditions, has reduced old growth tremendously. "Only 10 to 15 percent of the Sierran forests," he said, "are covered with closed canopy old-growth forest stands." This is about the same percentage of what is left of the original old-growth stands of the Pacific Northwest over which so much controversy has developed, and, as in the Pacific Northwest, nearly all of the remaining growth is on public lands. Much of it, Eric noted, "is concentrated on steep slopes in river canyons and other areas highly susceptible to erosion. These are areas one shouldn't be logging."

Those doing the logging, of course, do not tend to agree, and before venturing further into the northern Sierra I took a precaution I had learned while on similar jaunts in my own neck of the woods: I removed the "WILDERNESS—LOVE IT OR LEAVE IT ALONE" and "AMERICA NEEDS WOLVES" bumper stickers from my Toyota pickup and put on my removable, magnetic-backed "I SUPPORT THE NRA" sticker. Driving a small, Japanese-made vehicle was risk enough, though having Montana license plates at least removed the suspicion that I might hail from hated Southern California, or Berkeley, or some other local hot bed of environmentalism.

In this country, logging is king. Small communities like Quincy, Chester, Crescent Mills, and Susanville all have sawmills that, until recently, were operating at maximum capacity. Compared to the wilderness drama of the central and southern Sierra Nevada, with their lakes, mountain meadows, beautiful deep valleys, and alpine peaks, the northern Sierra Nevada is more like New England in character. The land is rolling, heavily timbered, dissected by deep river canyons—a pretty but not a magnificent landscape. There are no national parks or big ski resorts: People here do not ski or backpack much; they hunt and fish. And they cut timber—at least they did before the local industry began to sag. The tone of the region was established by a display in a cafe window in Sierraville. In one part of the window were a couple of relics from the Persian Gulf War—a yellow ribbon near the poster of an American flag that proclaimed, "We Support Our Troops," and a poster of a small boy in a red shirt and suspenders standing in the middle of a clearcut next to a chainsaw and some stumps. His hand was resting on one of the stumps. The poster was labeled "PLEDGE TO AN ENDANGERED HERITAGE," and at the bottom was the pledge itself: "I pledge with my right hand upon this stump that my generation will be proud to be loggers." On the Susanville radio station, I heard a local forester talking about "timber-dependent communities." He was not referring to Susanville or Sierraville or the other logging towns of the region. He was talking about Los Angeles. Everyone there, he said, lived in wooden houses and couldn't survive without cutting trees.

In such a culture, environmentalists are about as hard to find as snowmobile dealers in Death Valley. Still, with the help of the folks in The Wilderness Society's San Francisco office, I was able to locate a few who agreed to be interviewed. One was Quincy attorney Michael Jackson who has been involved in Plumas National Forest issues for more than a decade. His law office, situated on the ground floor of an older building in the middle of Quincy's main street and just a block down the street from the historic, maple-shaded front of the Plumas County Courthouse, also doubles as headquarters for the local grassroots group, Friends of the Plumas. Until recently, Jackson also served as Plumas County public defender. He is said to be one of the best water lawyers in California.

Jackson is a big, bear-like man with a graying beard, sparkling blue eyes, and a good sense of humor. It is probably this last that has enabled him to survive in Quincy. The first thing you notice when you enter his office is that he has not replaced a window that was ornamented by the bullet holes that pierced the glass just below his name. He considers the window a good conversation piece. The neat round holes serve to remind everyone that relations between those in the extractive industries and those determined to slow that extraction have not, as Jackson put it, "always been cordial." I congratulated myself on having put the NRA sticker on my Toyota.

"The timber issue has polarized this community for twenty-five years," he told me over coffee. "But things are changing, and even the timber industry speaks differently now. Everyone realizes the game is over. The timber people are resigned to the inevitable changes," he adds, "but they still think we're bastards."

As elsewhere in the country, the timber industry here is facing major economic changes—insufficient and sporadic demand for timber, capital flight to the south, mill modernizations that kill jobs. But loggers would rather point to environmentalists as the cause. This, Jackson said, is just not logical. An honest appraisal of past cutting patterns would find it difficult to blame environmentalists for the current decline of the timber industry. For one thing, he told me, the timber is just not there anymore. A big map on the wall of Jackson's office, which looked as if someone had thrown spaghetti on it, told the story. Logging roads curled through every drainage. The roaded and developed public and private lands on the forest were depicted in light green or white. Dark green indicated unroaded and unlogged country, together with "biological corridors" proposed by Friends of the Plumas. Dark green was *not* the dominant color: Less than 10 percent of the 1.4 million acres of Plumas National Forest is unroaded and undeveloped. Yet, the forest plan issued by the Forest Service to satisfy the National Forest Management Act of 1976 had called for *increased* logging.

The map suggests that the current mill closures hitting many northern Sierra communities can't legitimately be laid at the door of groups like Friends of the Plumas. The more likely reason is that the timber industry has been wonderfully effective at getting out every last stick of merchantable wood. There are just not many places left where one can still cut timber without repeatedly exceeding federal and state mandated environmental parameters and regulations.

A recent directive from the California regional office of the Forest Service may make it even harder. Anticipating legal challenges to continued harvesting of national forest timber because of loss of California spotted owl habitat, the Forest Service developed a California Spotted Owl Protection Plan (CASPO), which, among other things, calls for retention and protection of old growth and a two-year moratorium on clearcutting on California national forests.

Not all Forest Service managers accepted CASPO gracefully. A few tried to rush through a number of previously planned timber sales in order to clearcut and road thousands of acres before the rules took effect—in Eldorado National Forest, for example. I learned of this tactic when I talked to Tom Infusino and Craig Thomas of FAWN (Friends Aware of Wildlife Needs) in Georgetown, a small former mining community near Auburn. "Sometime in November of 1992," Craig said, "we were alerted by an agency employee to the possibility that the Eldorado Forest was planning to offer three timber sales without soliciting public comment, as required by law. When we investigated, we discovered that the forest actually had twenty-four green timber sales ready for bid that had originally been laid out in the 1980s. Before we could intervene, fifteen were sold. In total, these twenty-four sales include 150 million board feet—more than one year's ASQ (Allowable Sale Quality) for the Eldorado Forest!"

"None of these sales had the necessary environmental documentation that is needed before they are sold," added Tom. "These were done with no public comment and without revisions to reflect new regulations." In addition, he noted, the cumulative impact of the timber sales was not being considered. "For instance," he said, "on a twenty mile stretch of the Cosumnes River, they had a dozen continuous sales planned that would have practically created a twenty-mile corridor of clearcuts, yet they considered them as separate sales."

"These sales were approved in February of 1993," said Craig, "just a few days before the March 1, 1993, CASPO regulations were to take effect." He seemed to believe that this was not a coincidence.

The Eldorado sales are still under appeal as I write this. Not so salvage sales here and elsewhere. After six years of drought, many trees have died, and the Forest Service is "salvage" logging, a tactic that is exempt from many environmental guidelines and regulations, including the appeals process. On the Eldorado between 1988 and 1992, there were more than 486 million board feet of timber sold under salvage sale guidelines.

"There hasn't been a green timber sale on the Eldorado Forest since 1989," says Craig. "Salvage sales offer an opportunity for an incredible illegal activity to occur. We have salvage sales to reduce fuels. We have salvage sales to reduce disease. We have salvage sales to take out the dead trees after a fire. We have salvage sales that include green trees if a forester thinks they *might* die within ten years. We even have salvage sales to salvage previous salvage sales. There are really no timber stands out there that the Forest Service can't come up with an excuse to log." FAWN and other conservationists are not alone in objecting. In a letter to Forest Supervisor John Phipps, the Regional Office of the EPA reprimanded the forest managers of the Eldorado because of their recent timber harvest practices. Since 1988, the letter said, "overall harvest levels [are] too high for ecosystem sustainability."

Most grassroots activists I interviewed seemed to think such tactics may be the last gasp of the timber beasts within the Forest Service, who are finding it as hard as the timber industry to adjust to an era in which logging will no longer be the dominant use of the forests. "The war is over," Michael Jackson said. "What everyone wants to know now are the terms of surrender."

Return of the Locusts

While the timber industry and the last of the old-line foresters may or may not agree any time soon to terms of surrender in the forests of the Sierra Nevada, there remains an even greater threat to the forests' biological integrity. In 1992, environmental activists from around the state gathered in Sacramento for a conference called Sierra Now. Among the conference's conclusions was this: "Domestic livestock grazing is one of the oldest, most pervasive and destructive manmade environmental problems on public lands in the Sierra Nevada . . . and also the most overlooked and least addressed environmental problem on public lands in the Sierra region."

So it has been for a long time. One of John Muir's principal reasons for proposing the creation of Yosemite National Park in 1890 was to protect the watersheds of the Merced and Tuolumne rivers from what he termed "hooved locusts" (sheep more often than cattle in his day, though he probably would not have tolerated cattle any more happily). Unfortunately for the Sierra rangelands, Muir's views did not prevail throughout the region. According to Eric Gerstrung, an endangered species biologist for the California Fish and Game Department, "Nearly 80 percent of the lands in the Sierra Nevada have some form of livestock grazing occurring on them. Everything from 20-acre ranchettes in the foothills to national forest wilderness acres—it's all open to livestock. There's far more land involved in livestock production than is affected by subdivisions, logging, mining, or any other use."

It does not seem to matter, he says. "There's a lot of public misconception about cattle grazing and a lot of sympathy for the cowboy. It's part of the Old West. Even though we have a lot of scientific documentation that grazing impacts ecosystems in multiple ways, most of this information doesn't reach the public. They have almost no idea how severely grazing affects ecosystems."

I saw the ecological impacts from livestock many times on rambles through the Sierra. One particularly cowbeat area that sticks in my memory was in the Sequoia National Forest's Domeland Wilderness at the southern end of the Sierra, through which flows the South Fork of the Kern River, a segment of which is designated a Wild and Scenic River. I hiked down the river corridor in the fall of 1993. To enter the "wilderness," I had to open and close three fences in rapid succession. Cow pies littered the ground. In fact, in some places, almost the only ground cover left *was* cow pies. Along the banks of the South Fork, almost no vegetation remained. Willows were broken. Banks trampled. Flies were everywhere. The Domeland seemed more like a cow pasture than a wilderness.

My impressions were supported by the facts. A study done on the South Fork drainage as long ago as 1981 found that 90 percent of the streams surveyed even then had fair to poor channel stability and 76 percent possessed actively eroding stream banks. What is more, this is one of the few places where the Volcano Creek golden trout, a "Species of Special Concern," is found. The trout is endemic to the South Fork Kern as well as Golden Trout Creek on the main Kern River. Gerstrung confirmed what I had suspected. "The South Fork is heavily impacted by livestock," he said. "Most of the streambanks are broken down, soil erosion is rampant, and the habitat effectiveness for fisheries is only 20 percent of what it could be. They [Sequoia National Forest officials] are violating their own land-management plan by allowing streambanks to be degraded, but the range people defend the livestock industry, not the fish."

Domestic livestock grazing has other effects, too. Bighorn sheep numbers have declined significantly, in part as a result of the widespread competition for forage as well as a consequence of disease transmitted from domestic animals. In the entire 400-mile length of the Sierra Nevada there are no more than 325 bighorn sheep clinging to life in five herds. What is more, Sierran plant communities are very intolerant of grazing pressure. The native perennial grasses that once cloaked the Central Valley and foothills of the Sierra Nevada are now functionally extinct because of overgrazing and agricultural development. The Nature Conservancy estimates that native perennial California grasslands now cover less than one-tenth of one percent of their former range. Cattle grazing also is considered one of the major factors leading to the lack of regeneration in the foothill blue oak savannas—one of the most unusual and characteristic plant communities in the Sierra. Cattle not only trample and eat young seedlings, but predator control—done to protect livestock—eliminates the natural checks upon rodent populations, which in turn eat an excessive amount of acorns.

All of this is damage enough, but livestock, especially cattle, spell death to riparian zones, those biologically critical thin, green patches of water-dependent vegetation that line streams and rivers. Jim Carlson of the High Sierra Hikers Association (he is a former Forest Service hydrologist and now a private consultant), says such impacts are inevitable. "Cattle concentrate in riparian areas because there's water and shade and the grass is generally lush and green." Livestock strip vegetation from streambanks, trample shrubs and willows, and break down stream channels. The net effect is a loss of stream-side habitat and wider, shallower creeks that are less favorable for fish and most wildlife species. According to the Sierra Now grazing task force, some 3,000 miles of public streams have been damaged by livestock grazing. "This amounts to more environmental damage in the Sierra than that caused by all the mining, water development projects, and logging combined," the task force concluded, adding that it should be considered an ecological disaster of importance equal to the loss of old-growth forests from logging.

Federal managers tend to respond, when they respond at all, by fencing stream corridors. But fences are only good if they are maintained. The California Fish and Game Department recently fenced a section of the Silver Fork, a tributary of the Carson River within the Carson-Iceberg Wilderness, which contains one of the few remaining populations of Paiute cutthroat trout, a threatened species. Even with the fencing, said Gerstrung, cows kept finding their way inside because the fences were cut or gates were opened. In response, he had to hire another employee to keep up the riparian enclosure. "It's a real problem for me," he complained, "because you almost need someone up there all summer long doing nothing but maintaining the fences. It costs me ten percent of my budget to pay for this, and takes away money that could be spent on recovery of the fish itself."

The best solution from an ecological perspective, Gerstrung said, is long-term rest. "You just move the cattle off an allotment and close the gate." Given the political clout of the livestock industry, however, "closing the gate" isn't as easy as it sounds. Few land managers are inclined to take the political heat such a decision engenders. One agency willing to try, the Tahoe Basin National Forest, has suspended grazing for five to fifteen years on the Meiss Meadow allotment in the upper Truckee River watershed beginning in 1995. The allotment, located in the proposed Echo-Carson Wilderness, and home to the endangered Lahontan cutthroat trout, will be rested to permit recovery of vegetation and fisheries. As might be expected, the decision is under appeal. "Every rancher in the state, the Cattlemen's Association, and even the county board of supervisors," Jim Carlson said, "are appealing the Meiss allotment preferred alternative and all over 250 head of cattle that are grazed for less than two months each year." Carlson says the livestock people are afraid that long-term rest may set a precedent. Exactly.

When a Tree Dies

Just as the ecological impacts associated with domestic livestock grazing go generally unnoticed by the public, the ecological impact of fire suppression is largely unappreciated. Historically, the mid-elevations of the Sierra Nevadan forests burned frequently, both from natural causes as well as ignitions set by people. Frequent ignitions reduced fuel buildup and prevented catastrophic fires. Small periodic burns also thinned the forest, killing the smaller trees, reducing competition, and invigorating overall forest health. Many of the Sierran forest species have evolved adaptations to weather such fires, such as thick protective bark or the self-pruning of lower branches. Fires were to the forests what wolves are to a deer herd: They thinned the trees but preserved the forest. We forgot that important fact somewhere along the line, and decades of suppressing forest fires has resulted in ecological ruin. Crowded, choking on their own abundance, the forests are more vulnerable to drought, disease, and insects. The consequence, dead and dying trees, are all too evident in the Sierra Nevada.

I saw some of the worst examples myself while circling the shores of Lake Tahoe in Tahoe Basin National Forest, where tree mortality in some areas now exceeds 50 percent. I stopped by the Tahoe Basin National Forest's Supervisor's office and spoke with a fire management officer. Thinking of the large numbers of people that visit or live in the basin and the limited number of escape routes available should a major fire start and spread quickly, I asked him if he thought they might not have a disaster waiting to happen. "We have a disaster waiting to happen from Mexico to Canada!" he snapped.

He was right, and the problem is not limited to the Tahoe Basin. As people choose to live in the mountains in ever increasing numbers, it decreases the options left available to fire managers. Few public officials are willing to stick their necks out and permit natural fires to burn for fear they will blaze out of control and incinerate someone's home or business. It is just as hard to get agreement to undertake what are called "prescribed burns" in order to reduce the buildup of fuel, not least because of air quality regulations. In much of the Central Valley, air quality is already so poor that any further degradation is considered unacceptable. A fire ecologist in the southern Sierra who did not wish to be named explained the dilemma to me. "It's politically easier to let the fuels build and accept the consequences of a catastrophic blaze than to try to fight the protests that arise whenever we create smoke through prescribed burning or have a fire get away from us. The only way major fuel reductions will occur is when we get some giant fires that consume hundred of thousands, if not millions, of acres. It will happen. It's only a matter of time."

In the Territory of Hope

If a major, devastating fire in the Sierra Nevada is only a matter of time, so is another big fight, according to water attorney Michael Jackson. "The fight over timber and the spotted owl is nothing compared to the battle we're going to see over water," he told me during my visit. It is water taken from the great storehouse of the Sierra Nevada that has made the growth of California possible. An estimated 60 percent of the water stored in all of the state's reservoirs originates in the Range of Light. Almost every river is choked with dams. According to Tim Palmer in *The Sierra Nevada: A Mountain Journey*, there are 467 dams on Forest Service lands in the higher reaches of the Sierra Nevada alone—and more in the foothills. While these dams have created a garden in the desert, and provide relatively cheap hydro power, they come at a considerable ecological cost. Dams and water diversions change historic flows and timing, resulting in fragmentation of aquatic ecosystems, just as logging has fragmented forested systems. One casualty has been California's salmon and trout fisheries. A common joke here is that you can spot a dedicated California fly fisherman because he has a Montana fishing license in his wallet. Today, the few remaining salmon and steelhead runs that still occur are maintained by hatchery production.

Despite the swimming pools that seem to be a fixture of half the homes in Los Angeles, it is not urban dwellers who are the major consumers of water in the state. Irrigation by agricultural interests accounts for 83 percent of water consumption. Not only is much of this irrigation water supplied at subsidized prices by the federal government, it isn't even used to grow valuable crops. Growing cattle feed—irrigated pasture and alfalfa—accounts for the largest share of water consumption in the state. In fact, producing these two agricultural products requires the same amount of water as is used by an urban population of 46 million people—swimming pools and all. "Urban people are beginning to realize they are not the problem," Michael Jackson says, "and they are demanding a more equitable sharing of water."

Most of those urban dwellers reside south of the Tehachapi Mountains or in the other metropolitan complexes, like the San Francisco Bay area. But the mountains themselves are not immune to population growth, a fact that has benefits as well as drawbacks. Today some 619,000 people live year-round in the Sierra Nevada and another 15 million live within several hours' drive. Even more worrisome is the fact that some Sierra Nevada counties have grown by 50 percent in the last decade and six out of ten of the fastest growing counties, in a state known for unbridled growth, lie in the Sierra region.

The growth is both a curse and a blessing. Added growth means more roads, congestion, and habitat fragmentation. However, most of the new residents are retirees, urban refugees, and "footloose" business owners who are, in ever-increasing numbers, moving to the Sierra for a life free of the traffic, crime, and violence that has mushroomed in California's urban centers. These businesses and people bring alternative employment opportunities to rural parts of the Sierra as well as a different set of values—among them a greater sensitivity to and sympathy for the needs of the environment.

I visited American Valley Aviation in Quincy to get some perspective on this growing trend. The first thing you notice as you drive up to American Valley Aviation's warehouse is that there is no sign. I found out why from owner Ken Wiegand. "We don't sell locally," he said. "We supply airplane parts to the U.S. government and sixteen foreign countries." Ken and his wife Mary, both in their late 40s, started American Valley Aviation in the Bay area a few years ago, then moved to Quincy in 1992. They now employ eight local people. Ken grew up in Quincy but left to go to college and eventually worked as an engineer for Lockheed. But life in the crowded, smoggy suburbs became less and less desirable. "I don't know that many people who enjoy living in San Jose," he says. "If they were given an opportunity to move their businesses or their jobs to a safer, clearer, and less hectic place, they'd take it in a second."

For the Wiegands, as for others, technology was the key. "Ten years ago, moving here would not have been an option," Ken says. "But communications have improved to the point that we could locate our business anywhere. As long as we have access to Federal Express, UPS, our fax machines, and phones, we could live on the dark side of the moon. People just dial in and peruse our inventory from our mainframe computer and a dozen fax machines keep the orders coming night and day."

Like many of these business owners, Ken is not overly sympathetic to the local pro-timber stance of everyone from the newspaper to the county supervisors. "We see a lot of people wringing their hands over the timber industry, but the Forest Service doesn't owe this community a living. These lands belong to everyone, not just Plumas County. The old-time locals think they can force the Forest Service to give them their share of the timber, but it's just not going to happen," says Ken. "I look at the demise of the timber industry not as a loss but as a phenomenal opportunity for Quincy to look for other industry. The Quincy area has a lot more to offer than just timber."

Harry Reeves is another urban refugee who also believes that Quincy is in the transition. He left the Bay area where he worked for the Regional Parks Department and moved to Quincy ten years ago. Like many of the people who grew up here, he has to be content to hold a number of low paying jobs to make ends meet, including work as a clerk at one of the local stores. But for Reeves, the quality of life makes up for the loss in pay. He is one of the active members of Friends of the Plumas and believes the timber industry will die not just because of a lack of trees to cut but because changing technology will make many of the current uses for wood obsolete. "Twenty years from now timber cutting won't be an issue," he says. "Virtually all the things we use wood for today will be substituted by other products, recycled materials and materials made from different plants."

It is people like Reeves and the Wiegands, it seems clear, who inevitably will help to change how the Sierra Nevada are experienced and managed in the years to come. But while we wait, the unravelling of the Sierra ecosystem continues even as conservationists struggle to find a way to halt it. Among the ideas that have emerged is a proposal to make the entire southern Sierra Nevada into a "Range of Light" National Park. Others have proposed a Sierra Nevada Biological Preserve that would encompass the entire range. No matter how it is achieved, there appears to be a consensus that some kind of coordinated management of the entire Sierra Nevada is necessary. Management authority for the 18-million-acre Sierra ecosystem is spread across two states (a little of the range slips over the border into Nevada), nine national forests, a million acres of Bureau of Land Management lands, three national parks, eighteen counties, and dozens of local governments—many with conflicting purposes, agendas, and philosophies. There is even fragmentation among environmental groups, with more than fifty local grassroots organizations attending to their own backyard brushfires, trying to slow the Sierra's physical and biological decline.

Coherence, it seems obvious, is much to be desired. That, at least, was one of the other conclusions that came out of the Sierra Now conference held in Sacramento last August, which recommended the creation of an environmental coalition to be known as the Sierra Nevada Alliance. According to Patty Brissenden, co-chair of the alliance's steering committee, the goals of the new organization will be to coordinate grassroots efforts in order to provide an effective advocate for the entire Sierra Nevada bioregion—not unlike the role that the Greater Yellowstone Coalition fills for the parks, refuges, and forests of the Yellowstone region—viewing the region not as a collection of isolated units of public and private lands and entities but as an entire ecosystem of wild and human interrelationships whose integrity can only be preserved if all of its parts are given an equal measure of understanding. "When we try to pick out anything by itself," John Muir, the great prophet of this Range of Light wrote in *My First Summer in the Sierra,* "we find it hitched to everything else in the universe." If he could learn this great truth here, the Sierra Nevada Alliance seems to be saying, maybe a new generation can learn it all over again here—and put the knowledge to use. If so, maybe we can all sing with Muir, "glorious hope lifts above all the dust and din and bids me look forward to a good time coming. . . ."

(Winter 1993)

PAGE STEGNER

The Unperceived
Wilderness

I t is just after noon when I pick up my old travelling companions at the Reno airport: Bud Bogle, a furniture maker and river runner from Davenport, California, and George Wuerthner, photographer, former park ranger, former botanist with the Bureau of Land Management (BLM), former biology teacher, former student of mine, and formerly the inspiration for a jaunt around the Great Basin at its least appealing time of year— November. As they throw their gear in the truck I indulge in some advance whining about the cold, the rain, the wind, the lack of leaves on the cottonwood trees, the likelihood of snow. George insists the conditions are optimum. Although we are not going to get compulsive about boundaries, the BLM wildlands we plan to visit in Oregon, Idaho, Nevada, and Utah have never been the center of America's playgrounds under the best of circumstances (largely because most of America doesn't know what it's missing), but in the late fall they should be completely void of the touring public. "Drive," he says. "Wake me when I get hungry."

And so I drive—from Reno to Fernley, past the Carson and Humboldt sinks and into Lovelock (named after the man who built the stage station there in 1862, not for the motel strip at the end of town), past the Rye Patch Reservoir with its few acres of Humboldt river water, on to Winnemucca. It is familiar turf to one born in Salt Lake City, half educated at the University of Colorado, addicted to Utah and Idaho rivers, and a resident of California. I have crossed the basin and range country so many times in half a century that I begin to recognize unravelled retreads in the ditches along the highway. I have never until now felt proprietary. But some of these empty miles (not nearly enough, I'm afraid) have lately been in the public eye as candidates for protected wilderness status, and I am suddenly curious to see what the stewards of the domain have chosen to include—and exclude. First I wake George to tell him he's hungry.

We leave Winnemucca after an early supper and head north on Highway 95 toward the Fort McDermitt Indian Reservation and the Oregon border. The barren ranges that lie between us and the Black Rock Desert to the west turn sulphurous in the last of the day's light, then fade to silhouettes against the evening sky. The sagebrush begins to lose definition as twilight settles into the basin and the first jackrabbits begin to make their fatal, indecisive appearance beside the road. I reach to the dash to pull on the headlights. Along the horizon ahead there are answering winks from two oncoming vehicles, though how far away in this rarified, clarified atmosphere, how many dips and rises of this deceptively level plain, I have never learned to tell. The radio stations Bud has been fooling with in a doubtful attempt to get the first game of the World Series come from Grand Island, Nebraska, Everett, Washington, San Diego, California, sometimes all three at once, and we are reminded (if we needed any reminding) that this country is designed to trick human perceptions in a lot more ways than the ubiquitous mirage.

At the junction of 290 there is a sign for Paradise Valley and campgrounds in the Humboldt National Forest. Bud and George begin to yawn suggestively, but I am full of Basque restaurant coffee and ignore them. Farther up the road the Fort McDermitt Indian Reservation is similarly marked with signs to tell us where we are and who's in charge. Nothing, however, has ever indicated that we have been traveling through hundreds of square miles of BLM land for most of the day. Public lands. But nothing to welcome us (the public) home here. No Dudley Do-Right standing at the entrance gate to take our three dollars and give us a brochure. In fact, there has been nothing since I descended the eastern slope of the Sierra to suggest we have been trucking about on our own eminent domain ever since we left the outskirts of Reno. One of the most repeated questions asked by out-of-state travelers in the interior west must be "Who *owns* all this?"

Well, *we* own it. We the American people. Before our representatives in Washington began to carve up what remained of the nation's 2.3 billion-acre land mass toward the middle of the nineteenth century (after more than half of it already had been sold off, deeded off, or carted off), the public domain—the public's land—still amounted to well over a billion acres. But Congress ultimately divested much of that in land grants to individual states; some more of it was given to the railroads, to canal companies, to the military; and some was pressed on the Indians we got it from in the first place. We wisely saved some of it in parks, monuments, wildlife refuges, and national forests. And the rest we eventually assigned to the Bureau of Land Management, an entity we created in 1946 out of two (now defunct) agencies in the Department of the Interior: the Grazing Service and the General Land Office. At the moment, this amounts to about 174 million acres in the contiguous states, plus something over 100 million more in Alaska.

BLM territory in the Lower 48 is almost entirely in the West. There is a National Geographic Society map in the back of our truck that shows all this in symbolic color—dark green for forest reserves, light green for parks and monuments, gun-metal grey for military reservations, Wingate red for Indian reservations, cheat-grass yellow for the BLM lands. Even when one knows all the statistics, the map is still a staggering, pre-frontal illustration of how much of the nation is federally owned—one-third—and how much of that third is BLM land. We can hardly drive anywhere between the eastern face of the Rockies and the Pacific Ocean without passing through our own backyard.

It is a desert backyard, much of it, and for those in love with desert—like the three of us in the truck—that alone is reason enough to celebrate this land, cheer when it gets protected, howl when it doesn't. But the BLM has something for every taste and inclination along the lines of wild country, and a lot of it *isn't* desert. Take the hundred million acres or so of rivers, glaciers, arctic plains, forests, and mosquitos in Alaska, almost all of which qualify as wilderness and none of which make it as desert. The Naval Petroleum Reserve on the north slope of the Brooks Range may get less than five inches of rain a year, but because of the permafrost and low levels of evaporation, vegetation in the form of tundra thrives. And when one walks across that tundra, water squishes under the feet. Down in the Lower 48, the old-growth stands of Brewer's spruce and Port Orford cedar in western Oregon's rainforests aren't desert either, as the spotted owls who live there will tell you. Neither is the King Range along the northern California coast; rising abruptly from sandy beaches to summit peaks three and four thousand feet above the sea, it is forested by coastal chaparral and Douglas fir, and averages more than 100 inches of rain a year. Decidedly not desert. The elk and moose and trumpeter swans (not to mention the occasional grizzly) who roam the 30,000 acres of BLM territory on the Montana side of the Centennial Mountains have never heard of shadscale and pickleweed, though they would certainly recognize the paintbrush, columbine, cow parsnip, and aspen that spot the lush meadows beneath Sawtell Peak and Mt. Jefferson. The lodgepole pine and Douglas fir growing in the Garnet Range between Helena and Missoula (site of the Wales Creek WSA) do not thrive in an arid climate. Neither do the moss campion and mountain avens on the alpine tundra of Powderhorn Mountain, Red Mountain, and Handies Peak in the Colorado San Juans—wilderness study areas all.

The BLM logo, reflecting this diversity of terrain, is backdropped by snow-capped mountains from which a sky-blue river flows past a towering evergreen tree. But it would be nice to see some desert there, too, because deserts are where the three of us are mostly heading when, shortly after dark, we cross over Blue Mountain Pass and down into southeastern Oregon. To the west, the long escarpment of Steens Mountain, itself a WSA and a major drainage for the Malheur Wildlife Refuge, spreads like a dark shadow against the star bright sky, and at odd places along our route vaporous mists rise like smoke from unseen creek beds crisscrossing the sagebrush plain. There is a November chill in the air, and I add heat to the lights and the ball game in the truck.

Past the tiny town of Rome, where the highway crosses the Owyhee River (120 miles of it in Oregon classified as Wild and Scenic, and more of it under study for same in Idaho), we pull off the road at a BLM ranger station where Wuerthner and Bogle burrow through the gear looking for ensolite and sleeping bags. I stretch the legs by walking down to the boat launch area above the bridge and stand for a while listening to the frogs and the swirl of silt-laden water as it slides past in the dark, remembering a put-in at this very spot almost a year and a half ago when four of us nearly bought the proverbial farm by running the river in a 15-foot Achilles raft at the highest flood stage in its recorded history. Normally a mild, bump and grind stream along its lower section, there had been a heavy snowfall in the Independence Mountains, followed by freak 80-degree weather, and all of a sudden flows that in April would normally measure 6 or 7 thousand cubic feet per second (cfs) rose to the size and power of the Colorado as it drops through the vastly wider Grand Canyon. The waters crested at 24 thousand cfs on the third day, and I remember the "wild" better than the "scenic" Owyhee.

It is not only parts of the river that are under consideration for protected status, but a considerable amount of solid acreage elsewhere in Malheur County and a total of 2.3 million acres in the state. And next door in Idaho another 1.9 million acres and millions more in uninhabited, unimproved areas all over the western United States, for that matter—though one has to note glumly that the whole preservation process is being pursued with no great enthusiasm by the agency charged with identifying suitable parcels. We wonder, as we hunker down into our sleeping bags, whether this trip to visit a few of these study areas will give us hope or break our hearts.

We breakfast in the little farming community of Jordan Valley, and then, at the edge of town where the pavement turns north toward Boise, we turn east on a dirt road leading through the Owyhee Mountains and into the Snake River canyons of southwestern Idaho. A high plateau called Juniper Mountain rises in the background before us, though we are still traveling through rolling desert tufted with Great Basin big sage, and creased by dry streambeds and stratified benches of Columbia Plateau basalt. Jordan Creek, flowing maybe thirty feet between its margins where we cross it, is lined with bare cottonwoods and the winter lavender of leafless willows, but it is easy to see that cattle have long had total access to the water in this area. The brush and grasses that would normally crowd the riparian zone have been grazed off and trampled into mud flats along both banks.

From a vantage point above the road where we climb to eat out lunch we can see Steens Mountain again, almost 100 miles to the west, rising above its shimmering base to a summit line that is clear as a knife edge in this dry, un-polluted air. To the north, the higher peaks in the Owyhees, some over 8,000 feet, are dusted with early snow. But for us it is still summer-hot in the after-noon sun, and we are grateful for the light breeze rustling the rabbit brush and fescue around our picnic. Wuerthner, a botanist by training (and occasionally by profession), begins a dissertation on the evils of cheat grass in North Amer-ica, and Bud settles back like a big yellow marmot for a nap against the warm rocks. Tiny mosquito-colored clouds drift into the sky from the south. My fin-gers scratch idly in the soil beside me, eventually unearthing a small, rusty sign that says BLM WILDERNESS STUDY AREA. How it got up here I have no idea. The nearest WSA is a few miles to our east, but the bullet holes perforat-ing its surface are a familiar indication of local sentiment toward the informa-tion it imparts. Maybe whoever shot it up carried it around in his pickup for a while before flinging it out where he thought it belonged. In the dirt.

What is this thing, then, this Wilderness Study Area? The Wilderness Act was passed by Congress and signed into law by President Johnson on the 3rd of September, 1964—thirty years ago. Which is a while back. Nevertheless, it was a major piece of conservation legislation, and in spite of its unfortu-nate compromises to a variety of non-preservationist interests, it did, finally, give the Forest Service, the Fish and Wildlife Service, and the National Park Service a clear directive to identify and manage wilderness *as* wilderness. Wilderness areas, the congressional mandate said, "shall be administered . . . in such a manner as will leave them unimpaired for future use and enjoy-ment as *wilderness,* and so as to provide for the protection of these areas, [and] the preservation of their *wilderness* character" (italics mine). In other words, no commercial uses in areas designated wilderness (exceptions, of course, for ongoing livestock grazing, ongoing mineral leasing, and ongoing mining), no building of roads, no building of structures, and no use of the internal combustion engine, including outboard motors.

BLM authority to inventory and study appropriate portions of its territory for inclusion in a National Wilderness Preservation System (NWPS) established by the Wilderness Act did not come until 1976 when Congress passed the Federal Land Policy and Management Act (FLPMA). It was FLPMA that set deadlines for recommendations and required that complete studies be conducted. No rush, of course, although during the ten years since the passage of FLPMA an inventory *has* been taken, and draft or final Environmental Impact Statements were actually completed on 704 of the 861 identified study areas—areas that total 22,898,212 million acres, out of which the agency so far has discovered only 9.6 million suitable for inclusion in the system, less than four percent of the total of all BLM lands. Environmentalists don't like that measly figure much—especially because a lot of them think that there are at least another 25 million acres or so out there that *should* be under study for wilderness but aren't.

We drive on through badly overgrazed country, native grasses like Great Basin wild rye and bluebunch wheatgrass having given away to a dense concentration of sage and an invasion of *Bromus tectorum,* also known as downy chess or cheat grass. It looks tasty, Lord knows, like a nice thick carpet of every bovine's favorite meal, but it is only a pernicious foreign weed. Aldo Leopold called it "ecological face powder" covering the ruined complexion of badly abused hills. We find better country over in Deep Creek, one of seven BLM Wilderness Study Areas in Owyhee County combined under the umbrella of the "Jacks Creek Complex." We have seen absolutely nobody since we left the Jordan Valley yesterday morning and have not passed a vehicle except for a pickup truck lying upside down in a ditch somewhere near a southtrending spur called Dickshooter Road. Finding no corpse in the cab, we take a hike along the streambed marked on our topo map, "Hurry Back Creek." It appears to be fed by "Hurry Up Creek" and "Nip and Tuck Creek," though the significance of these activities to the waterless drainage we explore is not immediately apparent. The area is thick with curlleaf mountain mahogany, a sprawling evergreen with a rough barked trunk and a domed crown, growing larger on this plateau than any of us have elsewhere witnessed. I chew cautiously on a leathery leaf to see if I can ascertain what it is that makes this member of the rose family so attractive to deer and elk. "It's high in protein," George tells me, spoiling investigation.

Jacks Creek is excellent raptor habitat (good for bighorn sheep, too), and for nearly twenty minutes a golden eagle has been circling us, tightening its gyrations in a kind of inverse conical helix until it is hovering almost directly overhead. Prospecting carrion? The white on the upperside of its tail feathers tells us that it is a young bird, less than four years old, but the sex of golden eagles is indistinguishable by any method other than a hands-on inspection. Which doesn't look like it's going to be possible. Deciding we're not dead yet, it soars away across the Deep Creek gorge and disappears.

We are descending the eastern slope and approaching Grand View, Idaho. Juniper Mountain Road becomes Mud Flat Road, which turns into Poison Creek Cutoff, which ends near a Titan missile site on Missle [sic] Base Road just east of the Emigrant Trail and the Snake River. Not far, we note, from the Mountain Home Air Force Base Precision Bombing Range. Talk about reentry. Desertification is almost complete down here anyway, as we can plainly see from the pedestaling around the sagebrush. Might as *well* bomb it. Grazing has stripped the earth naked, except around the sage where animals can't forage, and erosion has left each shrub sitting up there on its little base like something out of Lewis Carroll.

The BLM's land has long been misperceived by the touring public, in part because it has often been characterized simply as desert—a sweeping and misleading classification, to say the least. Much of it, as we have noted, is *not* desert. And even for the part that is, the term "desert" is a generic word that seems to conjure up little more than sand dunes and Lawrence of Arabia to a lot of people who have never been there and seen everything a desert can be. The problem with the generic designation is that it says nothing about altitude, latitude, longitude, drainage; it says nothing about wildlife, insects, avifauna, plant life; it says nothing about whether the animals who live on it (or in it) are grazers, browsers, scavengers, nest builders, burrowers; it says nothing about tar sands, uranium, coal deposits, oil and gas reserves. It does not say a thing for the rivers that meander across flatland or tumble through the carved rock. It does not distinguish between an alkaline basin, a short grass plain, or a slickrock canyon. It can't tell a buzzard from a chick hawk, an antelope from a jackrabbit, a bighorn sheep from a desert tortoise, a fringe-toed lizard from an inch-long pupfish. Not even a hint in it of petroglyphs and pictographs and other relics of the Anasazi—the "people who have vanished." In short, the term does not suggest anything about the multiple flavors desert comes in. Somebody ought to think of a better word.

Heading for the Idaho-Nevada border now. At Wuerthner's suggestion we drive south from the Owyhees, past the canyon of the Bruneau and through the Duck Valley Indian Reservation into the Independence Mountains, where the headwaters of the Owyhee River now collect in a reservoir behind Wild Horse Dam. The shadscale, pickleweed, and four winged salt brush of the Snake River plain give way to juniper-pinon woodlands and then Subalpine fir as we climb to the summit of the Humboldt National Forest. The Jarbidge Wilderness, where three ecological provinces meet (Columbia Plateau, Basin and Range, and Northern Rocky Mountain), lies just to the east, its higher elevations already covered with snow.

We drive southeast some twenty miles to a camp in Lamoille Canyon in the Ruby Mountains. I can remember as a child my family often passing this miserable spine of the East Humboldt Range on our way to Salt Lake City, and my father trying to pry me out of the comic books in order to get me to absorb something of the ambiance of western geography. Years later, my own bored squirming son was similarly unmoved by a parental finger under *his* nose when it was *his* turn to peruse the inhospitable discoveries of Fremont, Joseph Walker, and Lieutenant Colonel E. J. Steptoe. Such preadolescent ignorance still finds credence among those who stick to the lead-footed opinion that the entire Great Basin is nothing but a place to "put the hammer down."

Wrong. But it occurs to me, once we are out of the Rubys and back on BLM lands, that revulsion is an understandable position—for a highlander who will not take the time to look. Take Highway 93 south from Wells to Ely (as we are doing) and the overwhelming impression is of one vast, ochered flat extending for hundreds of miles between transverse ranges of basaltic lava. But if you hang around long enough to let your eyeballs adapt—which is to say long enough for all that hammered, blasted, barren, strata to begin to look natural—you begin to notice subtle distinctions. Color, for instance. You begin to notice that the scrofulous quarter-section of sagebrush you just passed has great variations on a theme and is obviously a lot more than just sagebrush. The straw-colored fringe along the road is bluestem wheat grass, the greygreen is indeed sage but the yellow-green is rabbit brush, and the olive greens over there on the rise are juniper and pinon. The black-olive is juniper; the martini-olive is pinon. Singleleaf pinon. *Pinus monophylla.* Stop the truck, George, we just passed a whole field of *Oryzopsis hymenoides.*

Also we have "Moonrise over Hernandez" happening right here between the Snake and the Schell Creek ranges. Down in the basin the sun has set, but it is still igniting the 13,000-foot top of Wheeler Peak, home of the second oldest living organism on earth (the Great Basin bristlecone pine), and of the only living ice flow between the Sierra Nevada and the Rocky Mountains (the Mathes glacier). The moon, obviously on some schedule of its own, floats in the pink clouds above the mountain and turns Ansel Wuerthner to jelly as he tries to set up his tripod and get that black rag over his head before the whole image goes up in dusk.

Two-thirds of the state of Utah is federal land, of which well over half (or 22 million acres) is administered by the BLM, 3.1 million acres of that in

WSAs—though environmentalist opinion holds that another two million should have been included. There is nothing, of course, to indicate that any of this is even BLM land as we cross the Nevada border and wend our way southeast through the Snake Range and over the Wah Wah Mountains to Milford, Minersville, and Beaver. No signs welcoming us to the PUBLIC DOMAIN, LAND OF MANY USES. Or abuses.

We cut over to the Sevier River through Buckskin Valley where the Old Spanish Trail found its way between the Tushar and Markagunt plateaus, then turn south again to Panguitch. Highway 12 joins Highway 89 at the mouth of Red Canyon, passes Bryce, drops down into the valley of the Paria, and climbs the northwesterly end of the Kaiparowits to a town that will be chiefly remembered in American history for having hanged Robert Redford, conservationist, in effigy. Maybe they didn't like his movies, but they loathed his opinions on coal-fired power plants.

We stop off in Escalante to buy some topo maps and guidebooks at the BLM office. Every citizen in sight seems to be wearing the fluorescent orange of the deer stalker. We are probably the only three people in Utah who are *not* hunters and who are *not* walking around looking like a popsicle (a distinction we may not live to brag about). We ask the BLM official in the office for the latest news on the state's most visible and highly symbolic confrontation between developers and preservationists—a proposal to pave the Burr Trail over the Circle Cliffs and down the eastern side of the Waterpocket Fold to Del Webb's marina at Bullfrog Basin. Be a shame, we say, if the Burr Trail got paved. "Oh yes?" he says. "What's the difference? The way I see it, a goddam road's a goddam road."

Well, no. A dirt road is different from a gravel road, which is different from a paved road. There are two-lane roads, four-lane roads, six-lane roads. There are banked and graded roads, bridged and culverted roads. There are also roads that are none of the above—roads that follow streambeds, ford creeks, climb over talus slopes, get washed out, muddied, impassable at certain times of year. In short, there are roads you can drive your 40-foot motor home on (with your trail bikes and your boat trailer in tow) and roads you can't. The Burr Trail is one you can't—which is a major reason why the Escalante Canyon country, the Henry Mountains, and the Waterpocket Fold remain some of the most exquisite places on earth. Congress so far has refused to approve final funding for the paving project, so with a little luck (and a *lot* of persuasion) maybe the trail never will become just another "goddam road."

We hold this thought as we leave the truck a few miles north of town, shoulder day packs, and follow the Escalante River due west toward Sand Creek and Death Hollow. High redwall cliffs mark the canyon on the south, and the river quietly winds along a broad, gravelly bottom speckled with sage, juniper, and pinon. Ubiquitous cottonwood line the banks, but there are also abundant samples of Gambel oak, canyon maple, box elder, netleaf hackberry. The higher ground is a carpet of Indian rice grass concealing prickly pear and barrel cactus from the daydreaming hiker, and mormon tea pokes its phallic little stalks up between volcanic boulders that have washed all the way down from the Aquarius plateau. Somehow Wuerthner, who leaps and bounds through all types of terrain like a now-you-see-him-now-you-don't dervish, manages to avoid puncturing himself on the *Cactaceae,* but his shuffling companions are not so lucky. I sit in the shade of an overhang for nearly an hour, picking out spines that have nailed my Florsheim to my foot and wondering if the Kayenta Anasazi who lived here some 800 years ago ever had this problem. "They weren't as stupid as you, Kemo Sabe," Bud says. "They bought their Florsheims with reinforced toes."

Late in the afternoon a cold wind begins to blow down off the Escalante Mountains, and a storm gathers in the vicinity of Hell's Backbone. Retreating downriver toward the truck, we stop for a drink at a seep along a south-facing wall and pause, teeth aching from the startling coldness of the water, to look back up the canyon at an ecclesiastical display of sunlight striking through the holes between the clouds. The wind frees dead cottonwood leaves, bright yellow with autumnal color, and flicks them like sparks against the blackness of the approaching sky. Unwilling to turn from this kodachrome spectacle, we stand transfixed until the first spatter of rain rattles off the cliff.

Transfixion becomes endemic as we wander this section of the Colorado Plateau, and while literary attempts to describe it become repetitive, its reality never ceases to astound. It is a reality with easy access. One doesn't need a guide, an outfitter, an internal frame backpack, a Moss tent, or lug soles on the bottoms of one's feet to see it. One needs only a jug of water and a peanut butter sandwich. A little curiosity helps, and a hat. The literal truth is (unfortunately) that one doesn't even have to trek very far from one's car.

At the top of The Hogback between the town of Escalante and the tiny farming community of Boulder, we sprawl on an outcropping below a stunted juniper and peel oranges for breakfast. The first light of day begins to brighten the desert below as we sit, munching, staring across hundreds of square miles of silent, cold, immensely empty, slickrock canyon. The Aquarius Plateau rises to form a 10,000-foot boundary to the north; to the south the sheer scarp of the Straight Cliffs drops to the floor of the Escalante River valley; to the east the triple barrier of the Circle Cliffs, the Waterpocket Fold, and the five peaks of the Henry Mountains hide beneath the glare of a rising sun. Deep in the canyon below the outcrop we can hear the muffled sound of Calf Creek Falls, white noise drifting up from a surrounding maze of fabulous, cross-bedded, multi-colored erosion. Somewhere out there beyond the dun-colored domes and the maroon mesas, the layered terraces, broken spires, Jurassic tide flats, a canyon wren practices his haunting scales against a shaded cliff deep in a sandstone gulch. Those clear, descending notes alone are reason enough to reserve this vast wilderness, and to hope that through FLPMA and the Wilderness Act we can preserve it forever just as it is.

In spite of the obvious intention of Congress to keep a reasonable amount of land unleased, undeveloped, and unexploited, the BLM has systematically subverted the intent of preservation legislation in all its forms. It has illegally manipulated the process of inventorying land for wilderness study in order to eliminate areas of conflict with timber, mining, and energy interests (the subject, incidentally, of a 1985 House Subcommittee on Public Lands oversight hearing on management of the BLM wilderness review process in Utah and other states). In places like Wyoming's Red Desert, the Henry Mountains of Utah, and the California Desert, it has allowed roads to be built into areas under consideration despite a congressional mandate to protect them during wilderness study. It has rushed to issue oil and gas leases in many areas, an enthusiasm that forced Congress to institute an outright ban on such activities in BLM and Forest Service wilderness study areas. It has arbitrarily eliminated millions of acres from the wilderness study process and attempted to justify it with specious excuses and cockeyed record-keeping. And so on and so on and so on.

BLM lands that have been actually *designated* wilderness (as of January 1986) amount to a grand total of 368,281 acres, less than two-tenths of one percent of the total of BLM holdings. And most of those acres were placed in protective custody by Congress in spite of the BLM and the Interior Department, not because of them. The BLM has recommended only 9.6 million acres as suitable for inclusion in the preservation system—only this out of its entire empire, it says, meets the criteria to provide "opportunities for solitude or for primitive and unconfined recreation" and to contain unusual "geological, ecological, scientific, educational, scenic, or historical" values. That's odd. From our vantage point along The Hogback we're looking at about three million acres of solitude in the Escalante Basin alone. Just by turning in our tracks. And if this isn't geological, ecological, and scenic, what is it?

"Wilderness is a resource that can shrink but not grow," Aldo Leopold once remarked, and went on to observe that it takes intellectual humility to understand the cultural value of nature unaltered and unimproved. Nobody ever accused a government agency of intellect *or* humility (or, for that matter, the capacity to manage land), but we have reached a point in our historical development when stale jokes about the "Bureau of Livestock and Mining" and the principles of "multiple abuse" and "sustained greed" no longer serve to mask bemusement with amusement. If we care at all, and many of us do, we can only be stunned by the way our diminished patrimony continues to be frittered away. And angry. Angry enough to sit right here with our jug and our peanut butter sandwich and our monkey wrench until it is saved.

A note from the editors: Since the appearance of Page Stegner's article in the summer of 1986, there is both good news and bad news to report.

The good news is that BLM wilderness has expanded dramatically since he wrote. In October 1990, Congress passed the Arizona Desert Wilderness Act, which not only designated 1.1 million acres of wilderness in BLM areas scattered from Aravaipa Canyon to the Hassayampa River Canyon but added another 1.3 million acres of wilderness in Havasu, Cabeza Prieta, Imperial, and Kofa national wildlife refuges. And four years later, in October 1994, Congress passed the California Desert Protection Act after more than eight years of effort on the part of conservationists. This bill designated another 3.66 million acres of wilderness on BLM land, enlarged both Death Valley and Joshua Tree national monuments and upgraded both to national park status, carved a brand new national park unit—the 1.4 million-acre Mojave National Preserve—out of former BLM land, and added more than four million acres of new wilderness designations in these parks. (Death Valley's new size of 3.3 million acres, by the way, makes it the largest national park in the Lower 48 states.)

The bad news is that much deserving wilderness on BLM lands throughout the West remains unprotected and that Utah's Burr Trail has indeed been paved from the town of Boulder to the edge of Capitol Reef National Park. But there is good news of a kind here, too: the contractors for Garfield County have done such a slipshod job of it, merely slathering a thin layer of asphalt over the old surface, that the road appears to be reverting swiftly back to the natural state; cracks and potholes abound and are increasing in both size and number, posing even more of a threat to vehicular health than the graded dirt surface the asphalt replaced.

JOHN G. MITCHELL

To the Edge
of Forever

On a clear day—and some days come mighty clear in southern Utah—you can see straight out to the edge of forever. Forget it if chance should take you down a slot canyon with walls of red sandstone pinching the view; or out on some mile-high mesa, the pinyons and junipers slapping your shanks. You have to get higher than that, up eight or ten or twelve thousand feet, up on the brow of the Aquarius Plateau maybe, up Powell Point with the tip of your nose sighted in on Kaiparowits country, up in the aspens on Boulder Mountain, looking east across the Circle Cliffs and the snaggle-tooth rim of the Waterpocket Fold, and liking the snow on the caps of the Henry Mountains but wishing they were not in the way because without them the edge of forever would roll on to the Dirty Devil and the great Colorado, to the glacial cirques of the far La Sals, to the gossamer flats of the Great Sage Plain. Out there or over here somewhere, in one direction or another, the maps of such lively places as Death Ridge and Carcass Canyon, Fiftymile Mountain and the Sweet Alice Hills, Fiddler Butte and Tarantula Mesa, Studhorse Peaks and Donkey Meadows and Rat Seep and Hell's Backbone and Choprock Bench and Beef Basin, Robbers Roost and Horsethief Point, Old Woman Wash and Cad's Crotch, The Cockscomb, The Fins, The Maze, The Wickiup, The Needles, The Gulch, The Blues. The Sassy names dance on across the land. Forever is hardly big enough to hold them.

This is a fine sort of country, for wilderness. There are some folks (partisans, to be sure, mostly of the outlander stripe) who will tell you that these buttes and canyons constitute as grand an assemblage of roadless areas as any in America, and, so saying, offer no apologies to Alaska. But why pick a fight over apples and oranges? Southern Utah stands to be counted in its own right. It qualifies. Its backcountry (there's hardly any *front*) has all the necessary credentials for statutory Wilderness—millions of acres of forest, parkland, and public domain ready to put in the uppercase *W* as soon as Congress says the word; a territory once described by writer Edward Abbey as "the least inhabited, least inhibited, least civilized, least governed, least priest-ridden, most arid, most hostile, most lonesome, most grim bleak barren desolate and savage quarter of the state of Utah—the best part by far. So far."

Over the years, the canyon country has survived recurring efforts to tame its wildness. Well, most of it has survived. So far. Glen Canyon did not survive. Glen Canyon was the place no one knew, and because of that, no one now will *ever* know it, for it lies in the deep, deep waters of Lake Powell. Meanwhile plans are afloat to flood the rest of the territory with paved roads, coalfields, slurry pipelines, range improvements, and assorted projects calculated to ream uranium, oil shale, tar sands, carbon dioxide—you name it—right out of the wildest niches of the public domain. And that's only for openers. The worst news is yet to come.

The worst news has to do with some of the people who are trying to call the shots on what happens out there between Boulder Mountain and the edge of forever. Some of these people who would shape the configuration of uppercase Wilderness in southern Utah don't much like the idea of uppercase Wilderness anywhere. Some of them have nothing but contempt for uppercase Wilderness. Some of them run the towns and counties of southern Utah. Some of them belong to Utah's congressional delegation. Some of them work for the Bureau of Land Management of the U.S. Department of the Interior, the agency in charge of most of this land—and of defining what does and does not qualify for the big *W*. Add to that eight years of an anti-wilderness administration—particularly in the persons of Interior Secretary Donald Hodel and Bureau Director Robert Burford—dedicated to the proposition that resource management is one big game of Sagebrush Monopoly and you begin to get the message.

So here I am to fill in some of the details. About the country itself and how it came to be the way it is, and where the lines of wildness and solitude have been most curiously jiggled on the Bureau's maps, and how the Brushpopper came by his name, and why the Bureaucrats are huffing and puffing to blow down Clive Kincaid's house, and what makes Calvin Black of Blanding run, and about Arch Canyon and why one has to do a place like this the right way or not at all, and maybe, too, about the edge of forever, if we should be so lucky to get that far. Let's go.

I. The Five Million-Acre Misunderstanding

There are as many different ways to parse this canyon country as to skin a cat, and I suppose that any one is about as good as the next. For atlas definition, I like to start out on the west side and run my line up U.S. Highway 89, from Kanab more or less to Panguitch, and then string it northeasterly, cross-country, through the high plateaus, past Cathedral Valley and the San Rafael Swell to the Book Cliffs. It is said that the Book Cliffs constitute the longest continuous escarpment in the world, some 250 miles from Price, Utah, almost to Grand Junction, Colorado. But that's too far for our purposes, so I'll leave the cliffs near the Colorado border and drop south along the edge of the La Sal and Abajo mountains until I hit the San Juan River, and then hightail it for sundown across the top of Navajoland back to Kanab. That's the canyon country. Geographers, eschewing the atlas and drawing their boundaries more precisely along the physiographic lines, refer to the general region as the Canyon Lands Section of the Colorado Plateau; the Plateau being that larger province that falls between the Rocky Mountains and the Great Basin and includes, among its other subdivisions, the Uinta Basin to the north and the Grand Canyon country to the southwest. Grand Canyon country, then, should not be confused with *our* canyon country.

So there it is, about 15,000 square miles of slickrock and sand, enough space to bed down Massachusetts, Connecticut, and Rhode Island, with room to spare. Around the edges of this territory are the towns of Torrey, Green River, Moab, Monticello, Blanding, and Bluff—despite their big Mormon families, not even 20,000 people all told. Within the territory are the villages of Escalante, Boulder Town, and Hanksville; the hamlets of Bryce Valley, the marinas of Lake Powell, a few sparsely staffed units of the national parks system, and maybe a dozen ranches—not even 2,000 people. You are talking elbow room, now, like about one pair of elbows to every 4,800 acres.

Aridity is what makes this country tick; aridity, time, and the erosive rivers. Think of it as a great high desert lying in the rain shadow of much higher country roundabout. What falls from the sky on that shadow is not much, fewer than ten inches of rain or snow a year, and nearly all of that is soon sucked up by evapotranspiration. But in the mountains where the rivers begin—in the Wind River Range at the head of the Green, in the Uncompahgre, font of the Dolores, in the San Juans, in the highest Rockies that turn the Colorado loose to gather all the other streams—there the snowfall is prodigious. And the results fascinating, and best described by the man who put this country on the map, none other than the one-armed Major

John Wesley Powell. The summer sun, wrote Powell in an account of his river-borne exploration of the canyon country in 1869, unleashes the snow-pack "in millions of cascades. A million cascade brooks unite to form a thousand torrent creeks; a thousand torrent creeks unite to form half a hundred rivers beset with cataracts; half a hundred roaring rivers unite to form the Colorado. . . . Now, if at the river's flood storms were falling on the plains, its channel would be cut but little faster than the adjacent country would be washed, and the general level would thus be preserved; but under the conditions here mentioned, the river continually deepens its bed; so all the streams cut deeper and still deeper, until their banks are towering cliffs of solid rock. These deep, narrow gorges are called"—now hold on, for few Anglo-Americans then had even heard the word—"canyons."

There are more canyons than a person can count, or name, and they come in all shapes, sizes, and colors. Canyons like cracks, so narrow at rimrock that a man, on the bottom looking up, has trouble finding the sky. Sinuous canyons that writhe and meander. Straightaway canyons, slick as a piston. Awesome canyons a thousand feet deep. Red, white, and blue canyons—blue, or lavender, from a desert varnishing of manganese oxides. Box canyons and side canyons and sides-off-the-side-of-a-side canyons, all with their tails to the high ground, their heads atilt toward the Colorado.

As the country falls away into its canyon, so does it climb here and there to substantial heights above what Powell called "the general level." Or, as another early rover say it, "Why, there's as much country standing up as there is laying down." Standing tallest are the isolated clusters of interior mountains, the aforementioned La Sals, Abajos, and Henrys, each of which lofts a peak or two above 11,000 feet. Geologists call these mountains laccoliths (from the Greek, meaning stone cisterns). In effect, they are volcanoes that never quite blew their lids; instead, the rising lava formed blisters under the skin of the overlying sedimentary rock.

Next in order of presence above Powell's general level are the extraordinary cliffs of the canyon country: the Book Cliffs, already cited, and in places they do indeed resemble a roughcut row of volumes on a library shelf; the Grand Staircase, which begins at the southern rim of the territory with the Vermilion Cliffs and then steps *in seriatum* over the White and Gray cliffs to the Pink Cliffs at the edge of the Paunsaugunt Plateau; the Straight Cliffs, which delineate the eastern escarpment of the Kaiparowits Plateau; the Circle Cliffs between the Henrys and the Escalante country, and the Orange Cliffs west of the confluence of the Green and Colorado rivers. And hardly to be outshone by the colorful cliffs are the upwarps—fangs of steeply tilted and eroded rock, monoclines in the parlance of geology, such as Comb Ridge and the San Rafael Reef, and, most spectacular to my eye, the thousand-foot-high jaw of the Waterpocket Fold. Not to mention some of the more common protuberant features, namely the monuments and buttes, the arches and natural bridges, the little stone fins and shiprock spires that, in aggregate and in combination with the major landforms, give this canyon country an unsubtle texture duplicated nowhere in the world.

With plants and animals the territory comes about as well endowed as one might expect in a land of little rain, though in places the endowment can greatly exceed the expectation. There are barrens to be sure, some moonscapes, stark and brittle badlands where little but lichens will grow. But for the most part, the mile-high general level of the country falls within that great Southwestern botanical zone known as the pinyon-juniper belt. Pinyon pine and Utah juniper, to be more precise. Scratchy yet lovely little trees befitting the sand and the slickrock, resinous and fragrant, widely spaced, usually in mixed stands, and variously mixed up, depending on site and soil, with sagebrush, snakeweed, squawbush, pricklypear, cliffrose, yucca, and buffaloberry, among other attendant species. Down in the canyons, along the perennial streams, one encounters the Fremont cottonwood, the tamarisk (a runaway exotic), and sometimes a garden of wildflowers, hanging upside down from a seep in a sandstone ledge. Going the other way, ponderosa pine and gambel oak poke into the upper range of the pinyon, Douglas fir pops up beyond the ponderosa, and spruce stand sentinel on the lids of those unblown volcanoes.

As for creatures, the territory provides habitat for modest populations of this and that. Mule deer are the predominant large animal and of sufficient number in some precincts to twitch a mountain lion's tail. Yes, there are still some of the big cats left—as many as 2,000 in the state of Utah, in fact—and some elk in the Book Cliffs, and some transplanted bison in the Henrys; plenty of desert bighorn sheep in the wildest niches, and coyotes and foxes and owls and eagles and hawks and peregrine falcons and lizards and snakes, among other good things that fill up their trays on the slickrock foodchain.

But neither wildlife nor wildwood is the main draw here in canyon country. What sets this territory apart—what lures camera-toting pilgrims from the four corners of the earth, what justifies the presence of such five-star national parks as Arches and Canyonlands and Capitol Reef and Bryce Canyon—are the rocks, the cold, inert, unblinking, eroding rocks in all their sculptured and stratigraphic glory. Learning how to read these rocks is the consummate challenge facing every traveler in canyon country, for one can hardly ignore them, or fail to wonder what tales their turning pages have to tell of a time when the whole world sat at the very edge of forever.

And there is this, too, about the rocks: They tend to make a person think big. In the 1930s, for example, more than a few people thought it would be a grand idea if almost half of all of this territory, from the Straight Cliffs east to the outliers of Moab, were placed under the protection of the National Park Service. The idea was to have a park befitting the sand and the slick-rock, a park (actually, a national monument) bigger than any other in the world; and it would be named after the little town, the large canyon, and the eighteenth-century exploratory priest, Escalante. But like most big ideas, this one slipped through a crack, the Depression, and when it came out the other end, it shattered against some tougher ideas such as ranching and mining and damming the glens of the runaway rivers.

Now there is another idea. It is to pick up as many of the old pieces as are still lying around untarnished and put them together again, not as parks but as uppercase W Wilderness. Of course, if there can be another idea, inevitably there must be another crack. This one is called the Utah segment of the wilderness review process of the Bureau of Land Management.

On the last day of January 1986, there emerged from the Utah State Office of the Bureau of Land Management in Salt Lake City, a massive document purporting to represent the Bureau's best thinking—its biggest idea—as to how the lines of proposed wilderness might be drawn upon the maps of its 22-million-acre federal estate. Packaged in six separate volumes, weighing eighteen pounds, and running into hundreds of thousands of words, the *Utah BLM Statewide Wilderness Draft Environmental Impact Statement* remains a kind of "War and Peace" of the canyon country, although no one yet has come to the part about peace. As long as the poles of perception remain so far apart on this issue, no one will.

In sum, the Bureau's best thinking analyzed some 3.2 million acres in eighty-two Wilderness Study Areas, mostly in the southern part of the state. Of these, the Bureau proposed to recommend to the Secretary of the Interior 1.9 million acres in fifty-eight study areas as lands suitable for wilderness designation and the remaining 1.3 million acres as lands "nonsuitable" for wilderness but, by inference, perfectly suitable for just about everything else. The document analyzed certain environmental consequences of the proposal, as well as alternative actions ranging from "No Action/No Wilderness," which would have pleased most Utah politicians, to "All Wilderness/Designate 3,231,327 Acres," which would have sent the politicians right up their walls. Of course a good many conservationists would be climbing walls in either event. To their way of thinking, or at least to the way of thinking of the two-score organizations comprising the Utah Wilderness Coalition, suitable designation for Bureau roadless areas should not begin with 1.9

million acres, or even with 3.2 million. The Coalition had already drawn its own bottom line—and that one stood at 5.1 million acres.

To understand how the Bureau and the Coalition could arrive at such disparate numbers, one must turn back the clock to 1976, a full decade before the Bureau released its draft recommendations. That was the year of FLPMA (*flipma*), shorthand for the Federal Land Policy and Management Act of 1976 (hereafter the Act of '76), which set in motion a number of official actions, including a "wilderness study" process that was supposed to help Congress decide what areas to designate as uppercase Wilderness. These study areas were referred to as WSAs.

Identifying and managing statutory wilderness was not a part of the Bureau's mandate before 1976. The big *W* was for foresters and park rangers to think about. Then the Act of '76 came along and put the Bureau on the wilderness team. The Act directed the Secretary of the Interior to take a careful look at the Bureau's domain, to identify the roadless areas of 5,000 acres or more that might qualify as additions to the National Wilderness Preservation System, to have those WSAs studied intensively, and, after further analysis, to make recommendations for wilderness designation. Under the law, the Secretary of the Interior has until October 21, 1991, to convey those recommendations to the President, and the President then has two years to get them, or some reasonable executive facsimile, to the Congress for enactment.

This should be remembered: Congress gave the Secretary of the Interior no discretion about which lands were or were not to be studied. The Secretary was directed, firmly and clearly, to study every single piece of de facto wild country in the Bureau's control—whether local people liked wilderness or not, whether the local Bureau manager had other plans for an area or not, whether there were minerals or other exploitable resources there or not. Congress wanted to reserve to itself the privilege of making the final decisions. And Interior Secretary Cecil Andrus and the Bureau's chief, Frank Gregg, took that direction to heart, according to Terry Sopher, who then headed up Gregg's wilderness policy staff in Washington and who is now director of The Wilderness Society's BLM program. "Under Frank's direction," he says, "we developed over one hundred pages of wilderness inventory policies and guidelines with one purpose in mind: to ensure that no de facto wildland would be eliminated from the inventory. The state directors were reminded during the inventory that the goal was a pure and professional inventory. No area was to be eliminated unless it clearly and obviously lacked wilderness character."

Still, there were all those decisions to be made out there in the field, and all those cowboys and miners and politicians throwing all that weight around, and those district managers here and there who had little sympathy for the desires of tree-huggers. In Utah it added up to something like this: Acres and acres of de facto wilderness began to vanish from the study process, many of them because district managers decided, however arbitrarily, that the lands did not possess "outstanding opportunities" for solitude or "a primitive and unconfined type of recreation"—and a roadless area, under the Act of '76 and the Wilderness Act of 1964, had to have at least one of these or it could not qualify for the big *W*. Never mind these strict guidelines that came down from Frank Gregg and his people in Washington. And never mind the ostensible reasons for jettisoning all that land. As a number of witnesses would later suggest at congressional oversight hearings and in depositions to the Interior Department's Board of Land Appeals, the very clear and direct reason more likely was to preserve for miners and county commissioners, and for generations of miners and county commissioners yet unborn, the right to exploit the jettisoned areas' resources, for in truth, once the threat of the big *W* was out of the way, opportunities for a primitive and unconfined type of exploitation would be absolutely outstanding.

Macabre tales from the Utah inventory are legion, but to illustrate the sins of omission, perhaps two may suffice. The first comes from the golden pen of the Utah writer Ray Wheeler, in a splendid roundup for *High Country News*. In this account, Wheeler tells of a woman named Debbie Sease (now a lobbyist for the Sierra Club in Washington, D.C.) who accompanied Gary Wickes (then the Bureau's state director) on a tour of roadless areas under review. Sease is quoted as saying: "We stood on the edge of—far as the eye can see—incredibly beautiful, utterly wild land. Miles and miles and miles of beautiful Utah scenery. And I would say, 'Gary, why are you eliminating this?' And he'd say, 'Because there are no outstanding opportunities for primitive recreation.' And I'd say, 'And there's no opportunities for solitude either?' And Gary would say, 'You're right. You can have solitude here, but it's not outstanding solitude.'"

Janet Ross of Monticello offers the second testimonial. Ross is a pedigreed outdoor educator, a leader of wilderness river trips, and nowadays, chair of the board of directors of the Southern Utah Wilderness Alliance, in which capacity she is largely preoccupied with undoing the official sins of yesteryear. For half of one of those years—1979 to be exact—Ross herself worked on the Utah inventory as a seasonal wilderness specialist attached to the Bureau's San Juan Resource Area Office. Her personal account of the Bureau's effort to undercut the process is contained in affidavits on file with Interior's Board of Land Appeals.

"It is my experience and professional judgment," Ross declared in one deposition, "that we did not perform and were not allowed to perform a competent wilderness inventory. The result was that substantial wilder-ness-quality acreage was arbitrarily excluded from further study and pro-per consideration." Inadequate staffing—three employees, including her-self, to inventory half a million acres—was only part of the problem. "From the highest state levels of BLM down through the area office there was little support or interest in the concept of wilderness. . . . Field em-ployees who expressed even mild leanings toward wilderness or particular units were accused of being 'too biased'. . . . The message was clear on two levels: (1) unlike other BLM missions (range, etc.) we were to suppress our commitment to this mission; and (2) our supervisors already had."

In one particular case, Ross and her two colleagues were ordered to evaluate an 80,000-acre unit on Mancos Mesa "entirely by helicopter, as the area was 'too big' to do on foot"—and all of this in a single day. The inventory team recommended that the mesa be classified a WSA. "Due to its vase size and inaccessibility," the team reported, "this area offers great solitude." Nevertheless, the Bureau excluded Mancos Mesa from further review (a decision later reversed by the Interior Board of Land Appeals). The solitude, it decided, while perhaps great, was not outstanding.

The astonishing thing is that so much of the damage was inflicted while the environmentalist Jimmy Carter still sat in the White House. Here were all these tree-huggers in high places at Carter's Interior De-partment on C Street, yet out there in Utah the whole process they had put in place was being busily subverted by the locals. Late summer, 1980: "By now," Terry Sopher remembers, "we were being told by Utah conservationists that they believed that intense political pressures in the region were going to cause the Bureau's state director to dump many de facto wildlands in violation of the law. We planned to review his inven-tory very carefully to see if that was true. We never got the chance."

That was election year 1980. In came Ronald Reagan and suddenly the tree-huggers were being replaced by sagebrush rebels and privatizers, including a ranching man named Robert Burford, who moved into the top spot at the Bureau, thereby sitting at the right hand of Interior Secretary James Gaius Watt—whose appointment had inspired Terry Sopher, till then a career man, to resign in protest. "So that's how it hap-pened," Sopher recalls. "Two million acres of *primo* wilderness never even got into the inventory, and then Burford takes over with a mean anti-wilderness streak. He not only endorsed what had been done in Utah—he wanted them to do even more of it."

In July 1985, after a round of appeals had managed to restore to WSA status at least some of the left-out roadless areas, the Southern Utah Wilderness Alliance, The Wilderness Society, the Sierra Club, and the National Parks and Conservation Association (the nucleus of the Utah Wilderness Coalition) brought forth at a press conference in Salt Lake City their own statewide proposal, conceived in liberated audacity and dedicated to the proposition that a total of 5.1 million acres deserved the big W—including those two million that disappeared through the cracks of the Utah study process. (Note: The statewide figures used here, both the Coalition's proposal for 5.1 million acres and the Bureau's draft call for 1.9 million acres, include several hundred thousand acres of roadless areas in the Greater Zion and West Desert regions, both of which lie outside the boundaries of canyon country as I have defined it.

Unlike the Bureau's fragmented and insular approach to wilderness in southern Utah, the Coalition proposal sought to preserve the canyon country as a single physiographic entity, a macro-escosystem, a great web of protected land such that when you tried to pick out any one unit by itself you found it hitched to everything else in the canyon country, including its national forests (some 700,000 acres) and its national parks, monuments, and recreation area (1.9 million acres, and more than two-thirds of *that* already recommended as additions to the National Wilderness Preservation System). But then Burford's Bureau rolled out its own vision of the territory, its eighteen-pounder, its *Statewide Wilderness* draft, its War Without Peace. Differences of opinion only begin with the statistics.

Consider the Book Cliffs, that world-class escarpment running across the top of the territory. The Coalition proposes more than half a million acres of wilderness here. The draft recommends fewer than 300,000 acres. Three entire WSAS—Coal, Flume, and Spruce canyons—are dropped through a crack. They shatter on the draft's finding that this is an area "known for hydrocarbon potential." Coal, oil, gas. No Action/No Wilderness. In the Desolation Canyon area, where the Green River carves its deep and turbulent passage through the cliffs, where the one-armed Powell lost a couple of oars, where the Coalition calls for designated wilderness, Burford's Bureau gives a "high favorability rating" to the prospects for coal and hydropower—and goodbye to 16 miles of wild river.

Consider the San Rafael Swell, that great eroded uplift with its sickle-blade reef, its Red Desert and Muddy Creek and rainbow badlands. Long considered an area worthy of national park status, the Swell embraces some 650,000 acres of Coalition wilderness. Yet for many of those acres the draft places a higher value on coal, tar sands, and accessibility for dirt bikes and other off-road vehicles.

Moving counter-clockwise across canyon country, we arrive at the sub-region of the Kaiparowits Plateau and the canyons of the remote and wild Paria River. Eight hundred thousand acres of wilderness, the way the Coalition sees it; a bit over 200,000 in the opinion of the draft. Why? Because of coal, again. And maybe a little uranium. And possibly a bit of range improvement, here and there.

Things are looking better in the subregion of the Escalante, though not by much. Here the two sides are fairly close along the main stem of Escalante Canyon, but poles apart in some of the side canyons and up on the benchlands. Apparently because a portion of one key WSA overlaps an area "considered to have a high certainty for the occurrence of large deposits of uranium," the draft recommends No Action/No Wilderness for some 26,000 acres around Scorpion Flat and Brimstone Gulch, acres it otherwise enthusiastically applauds as having high wilderness and aesthetic values.

Swinging east, we'll skip over the Henry Mountains-Dirty Devil complex (saving it for a closer look, later on) and pause instead among the wonders of the Cedar Mesa country, a territory noted especially for its treasure-trove of Anasazi ruins. Some of the major conflicts here go back to the Bureau's inventory, when it declined even to consider as WSAs such gems as most of Arch Canyon and all of Comb Ridge and Harmony Flat. Also at issue are the Dark Canyon and Mancos Mesa areas, where, the Coalition alleges, the Bureau has pinched the potential with "exaggerated claims of impact" in some places, and "understated wilderness values" in others.

And finally, last stop on our way back to the high-noon Book Cliffs, we arrive in the Canyonlands, precinct of exquisite roadless areas abutting the national park of that name (and Arches, too) or tucked into that slickrock maze along the Green and Colorado rivers. Put the W to 481,990 acres, says the Coalition; hold it at 135,365, says Burford's Bureau. If the Bureau prevails, goodbye to wilderness for Hatch Wash and Harts Point and most of Indian Creek and all of the Mill Creek and Negro Bill Canyon WSAs next door to Moab, where Grand County buckaroos sought to preempt any designation by bulldozing jeep trails. But possibly the saddest loss of all would be the evisceration of Labyrinth Canyon, just upstream from Canyonlands Park on the Colorado River. Here the Bureau has seen fit to recommend for designation only a fraction of the total roadless area, bisecting the canyon and excluding its entire eastern flank. "River travelers," the Coalition noted in an early critique, "cannot understand how the west bank is wilderness while the BLM claims the equally natural east bank 'clearly and obviously lacks wilderness characteristics.'" The mystery was easily solved. Right there in the War Without Peace draft was the simple statement that, while no plans existed to construct hydroelectric projects along this stretch of the river, hydropower would have to be rated highly.

One day last spring, in Washington, D.C., I dropped by the Bureau's offices to call on Frank W. Snell, a Utah man who is now program director for the Bureau's Division of Recreation, Cultural and Wilderness Resources. I asked Snell how the Bureau proposed to deal with these multitudinous, juniper-hugging entreaties for wilderness areas far larger than any the Bureau was willing to propose. Snell replied: "We're saying as a matter of practical necessity and legal compliance that we have to get through this process and meet the 1991 deadline. If there were errors—and I don't believe there were any major ones—Congress has the ability to correct them." And then Snell said: "The sides are getting farther apart in Utah. It's in the public interest now to begin to work toward a consensus."

II. The Burr

The idea was to do the country in a week. It was a bad idea. A gadabout person could not do this country in a year, maybe not even in a lifetime if he should measure the doing canyon-by-canyon right down the line. There is too much of it. So you take what you can, where you can, when you can, and hope that enough of it rubs off on you to last until the next time. If you should be so lucky.

My own luck has been pretty good, though it took me long enough to get into the territory to discover what I had been missing. At first I could only sniff at the tamest edge of it. This was in the fifties, when I was gumshoeing for a little daily newspaper beyond the Four Corners in Navajo country. You needed plenty of time, then, to explore *either* country, and one free day out of seven didn't exactly set you up for a proper expedition. But I knew this other country was out there, beyond the spires of Monument Valley and Navajo Mountain, the tribe's holy place, and I promised to post myself across its border some day. And finally got the chance to do that fifteen years later—several sorties, in fact, into the slickrock funhouse around Canyonlands National Park, remanding myself into the custody of that seasonal canyoneer and campfire raconteur Kent Frost of Monticello. And then there was one more journey to the canyons, about the same time that Congress was putting the Bureau into the wilderness business with the Act of '76. That time I had stood at the edge of the Waterpocket Fold and watched the sun rising out of the

Henry Mountains, the shadows reaching out under Tarantula Mesa, the great rift trench of the Fold itself curving down to the red rocks at Bullfrog Bay. It was the kind of morning, at the kind of place, that tightens the skin over one's temples. My temples, anyway.

And now I was going back to do the rest of it, in a week. Pick up a jeep in Grand Junction and skedaddle down the Western Slope; grab some gear and grub and go out to the little airstrip north of Moab and wait for a little plane to bring my big friend The Brushpopper out of the sky. The jeep was my idea and it was a good idea, since we had only a week, but I think it embarrassed The Brushpopper. I'll try to explain why.

First of all, for reasons not germane to this tale, the true identity of my traveling friend must be withheld. Anonymity has to run in one of two directions: either to a pseudonym, or to a nickname. Since I abhor pseudonyms, I had no alternative but to go the other way. And what a hard way it was until, at the end of our first long day, some five jeepless miles up a canyon in the Book Cliffs, my companion took leave of our campsite and disappeared into the pinyons, scrambling, solo, for rimrock. And what the hell had he been doing, I wanted to know when at last, and just in time for supper, he returned from his hike.

"Been brushpoppin'," he said.

"Which is . . ."

"Which is cowboy talk," he said. "Cowboy goes up the side of a canyon after some lost cow, that's brushpoppin'. There was a saying that you could always tell when a cowboy'd been brushpoppin' if he came back with enough wood jammed into his saddle tree to cook dinner with."

So The Brushpopper he'd be, though for some reason he never quite took to the name as eagerly as he pursued the activity. Every chance he got, he'd scramble away from the jeep, into a canyon or out on some ledge. It was as if he were trying to make up for lost time, which in fact he was. Having spent the worse part of his years as a fellow of rather limited ambulatory experience, as an armchair, or barstool, elitist if you will, the Brushpopper had recently undergone a change of life and become—transmogrified—a compleat walker, a seeker of solitude, a bagger of boondocks. Any or all of which does not incline one to be favorably disposed toward traveling about in a motor vehicle, especially in wild country. Moreover, The Brushpopper was painfully aware, as I am, that cityslick boosters of uppercase Wilderness who fly into little airports and then go popping around in jeeps always seem to catch the thickest flak from local-gentry wilderness bashers—their theory being, bygawd, if you want wilderness so much then you should bloody *walk to it*. (The antithesis of this, and I've heard it from more than a few tree-huggers, is equally illogical: Okay, if you hate wilderness so much, and love pavement, then you should bloody well *move to the city*.) Well, you can't please everyone, can you? And besides, we only had this one week.

From the Book Cliffs, we scoot over to the San Rafael Swell and cross its reef through the wash south of Temple Mountain—scarred and battered Temple Mountain with the holes in its sides where they mined uranium for the Manhattan Project, took it right out of the mountain's red-green Chinle shales and packed it off to . . . where? Alamogordo? Hiroshima? Nagasaki? The little black holes in the rock do not suit this country. But it is not too hard out here to get away from them, to turn the corner, cross the head of Wild Horse Canyon and swing down along the edge of the 25,000-acre Crack Canyon WSA and then pull over and leave the jeep and head for the Crack that slices right through the San Rafael Reef, three hundred feet deep in one place, and just wide enough for a horse and a rider with concave knees. Head for—and then stop. There are rainclouds overhead, black as the empty mineheads, and though I have never experienced a flash flood in canyon county, I have heard enough to believe that even long shots should be avoided, especially in a canyon called Crack. The Brushpopper is no dummy about floods either, but I have reason to suspect he harbors a certain predilection for risk. To save face I look at my watch and say we had better be going in any event, if we want to get down to the Dirty Devil by dark.

John Atlantic Burr was born on the briny, bound for the promised land. And that's how he got his middle name. Across the Alleghenies and the wide Missouri, through tall grass and short, his parents bore the twinkling lad all the way to Koosharem in Fishlake country, northwest of the canyons, backside of the high plateaus. Formal histories of the territory hardly give the time of day to John Atlantic Burr; after all, he never grew up to be President or Bishop or a general in the Army, just a stockman, a cowpoke, a six-shooter type who blazed a trail for his cows through the Circle Cliffs. But Old John sure caught the fancy of cartographers, for his name is sprinkled all over the place. Burrville. Burr Trail. Burr Pass. Burr Desert. Burr Point. For all I know, there could be other Burrs that are *off* the map, like the John Atlantic Burr ferryboat that plies the blue waters of Lake Powell out of Bullfrog, where the herds used to drink when the water was brown and the place was Glen Canyon, as, by all that is right and decent in nature, it ought to be yet.

We have come down through Hanksville and off the pavement east of Bull Mountain, in the Henrys, and across the red dust and purple sage of the Burr Desert toward the point—the Burr Point, of course—that overlooks the grand jigsaw of the Dirty Devil. Why Old John drove his stock thisaway is beyond me, if indeed he ever did. Except for the low sage to hold the sand in place, this has to be one of the sorrier cow pastures ever, though I expect it was a bit lusher a hundred years ago, before the free-ranging herds began taking their toll. That was about Burr's time, too, the Eighties. They say his summer range was up on Boulder Mountain and he scratched his trail through cliffs and canyons in order to winter his steers out here or down on the big river at Bullfrog. It was Butch Cassidy's time, too, and the Wild Bunch up at Robber's Roost, on the far side of the Devil, were mavericking strays and making life miserable for honest drovers before turning to holdups and bank heists; so that maybe Burr just put his name down here in the dust, patted his holster, clicked his spurs, and skedaddled for some safer home-on-the-range. Or maybe he didn't.

The Dirty Devil. The legends hold that Major Powell's men named it. Coming down the Colorado, low on provisions, they could see the mouth of this tributary river approaching on their right, and called out to the scouts in the lead boat, "Is it a trout stream?" The answer came back: "Naw! It's a *dirty* devil." That was because of Muddy Creek, which, when it's running, throws a load of badland silt into the mountain-fed Fremont River at Hanksville, and therein becomes the Devil itself. And what an incredible incision so little water and so much silt have made in the rocks—a mini Grand Canyon, one counselor had called it, you just wait and see. Well, we waited and now, here at Burr Point, we see; see the ancient siltstone rimrock suddenly opening into a great abyss, and the Navajo sandstone below, and then a thin bench of red Kayenta, and the long cliffs of Wingate falling down, down, down the Chinle crumbling away underneath, and maybe a streak of Moenkopi bottoming out, and at last the khaki scalpel of the river, twisting and turning, probing for bedrock fifteen hundred feet below our perch.

We have come not only to praise the Devil but to bury it. In a figurative sense, of course. To do the real number, one would have to invoke either an act of God or an irreversible decision by the Bureau of Land Management to gerrymander side canyons, satellite benches, and a stretch of the river itself right out of protective wilderness custody and into the hands of . . . whom? A wild bunch of tar-sands rustlers? Possibly. Who knows? Only Burford's Bureau knows why, as I stand here at the Burr, I can look upstream past Ibex Point and see nothing but Bureau-endorsed wilderness, while across the chasm on Sam's Mesa and for a long way downstream there is nothing but this huge hole in the Bureau's process—no, not a hole, a gravesite big enough to swallow

Sam's and Happy Canyon and The Big Ridge and Fiddler Butte and The Block; can't see it all from here, too far away, but I know they're out there, and just as wild as anything to which the Bureau has given a nod.

On paper, of course, it looks a whole lot better. On the paper of War Without Peace, it looks at first as if the Bureau has tossed in its lot with the tree-huggers after all, for here is a 61,000-acre Dirty Devil WSA with an "All Wilderness" recommendation, and a 25,000-acre French Spring-Happy Canyon WSA in which the Bureau appears to favor 11,110 acres for designation, and finally a 73,100-acre Fiddler Butte WSA in which the Bureau recommends 32,700 acres as wilderness. That's what you get in a cursory glance at the impact statement. But look again. Look again and you see that Fiddler Butte isn't even included in the Fiddler Butte proposal; it has been excised "to reduce tar sand conflicts." Look again and you see that the proposed 11,110-acre French Spring-Happy Canyon Wilderness is a mistake, a slip of some intern's pen (the Bureau says), an entry for the errata sheets (o, so *many* errata). What the Bureau really means to propose for French Spring-Happy Canyon is *zero* wilderness.

But why? Why is so much of this whole Dirty Devil corridor unsuitable for wilderness designation? Why, because of those tar sands. Because Interior Secretary Donald Hodel, one of Watt's successors, has declared mineral development to be the top priority for Bureau lands, and because there is this paper concept called the Tars Sands Triangle, which overlaps much of the corridor. No matter that the conversion of tar sands into oil in the United States is widely considered an alchemist's pipe-dream that is likely to make neither dollars nor sense. If there is the remotest possibility that a mineral or energy resource might be developed some day, Hodel's Interior Department is not about to lock it up and throw away the key. It is going to keep the options open, such that, in this particular case, should tar sands development ever become economically feasible, the Devil will have an altogether different meaning attached to its dirtiness, what with all the injection wells, storage tanks, stream generators, coking plants, and hard-top roads already envisioned by at least one major energy consortium. Now, *there* would be one dirty Devil, for certain.

Tonight, at Burr Point, it is a blustery Devil under a west wind off the snow-capped Henrys, and all those miles of hot, red dust between here and the mountains cannot soften the chill. We have made our camp out of the wind on a ledge below the rim, savaged our rations of tortillas and kabobs, denounced the gerrymanders of Burford's Bureau and saluted the stars. Now the Brushpopper is making noises about descending fifteen hundred feet to the river, just to get warm.

You don't have a flashlight, I tell him.

He'll use the stars, he says. I know he's bluffing. He's all zipped up in his mummy bag, preparing to snore. Not quite. Now he wants to know if I know what.

What, Old Brushpopper?

The sky, he says. The sky has no lid on it.

In olden days, between the demise of the Anasazi cliff dweller and the arrival of the lonesome cowboy, the biggest idea for the canyon country was to find a way to get across it, or around it. Most folks then didn't care much about solitude, nor much about tar sands either, though a handful did care about beaver and gold. The first ones through were a couple of friars, Dominguez and Escalante, sanctioned to explore for a route linking Santa Fe to the precincts of Monterey in California. This was in 1776, about the time George Washington was being routed himself, a world away at a place called Long Island. The friars never reached California, but in their long loop homeward crossed the Colorado at a point now flooded by Lake Powell, and thereby touched the hems of their robes to the edge of the territory. A lifetime later, John C. Fremont of the Army Corps of Topographical Engineers brushed the opposite edge, on the north side. He was looking for a route, too, a mythic river road that would float Manifest Destiny straight to the tides of the Pacific. And a few years after that another topographer, one John N. Macomb, came to discover the most direct route between the new Mormon settlements in Utah and the old Spanish communities of the Rio Grande. Macomb did not care much for southern Utah. He declared he could not conceive "of a more worthless and impracticable region than the one we now find ourselves in." There is no accounting for taste.

The Mormons, of course, put an end to this terrible habit of using the territory as a stepping stone to somewhere else. The Mormons liked the country, and still do. They started poking down this way from the Great Salt Lake as early as 1855. This caused a stir among the locals, first among the Utes and then among the Navajos. But the Mormons were pretty firm about what they wanted to do (and still are), and by-and-by they were dug in along the lee of the high plateaus, and down the wild Paria in places, and out from Boulder Mountain across the northern foothills of the Henrys. To settle the far southeastern corner of the kingdom, the Saints dispatched a train of eighty-three wagons and a thousand head of stock cross-country from Escalante to what is now Bluff, in the Cedar Mesa country. The path today is known as the "Hole-in-the-Rock Trail," because that's what the pilgrims had to do—dynamite a hole in the side of Glen Canyon, a chute just wide enough for wagons, so that they could get down to and across the Colorado, bound for this new promised land. And they got there, too, though it took a whole winter.

Now if the Brushpopper and I had *that* kind of time, we could begin to do the country right. As it is, we have already shot two whole days getting from the Dirty Devil to the Escalante, with no wagons or livestock to slow us down, and no need to blast holes in the rock with dynamite, though some of the people in Garfield County here think a little more blasting might be a good idea, especially along the road we've been traveling. Namely the Burr Trail. People in Garfield don't think much of th Burr as an improvement. I wonder what Old John Atlantic would have to say about that.

To get here from the Dirty Devil, we were obliged to backtrack from dust to pavement and head south, down between the big Henrys and the Little Rockies to Bullfrog, where we marveled at the wonders of the Lake Powell Yacht Club (high and dry and miles from the water to the edge of the Cane Springs Desert) and sundry other amusements of Del Webb Country (Del Webb people being the entrepreneurs of Bullfrog Marina). Then, putting all of that behind us, and none too soon, we proceeded up a graded gravel road, first leg of the Burr Trail, into the Waterpocket Fold. No matter the pressure to be somewhere else, one must spend time with the Fold. It is not to be missed, especially if one can arrange to be at the Strike Valley Overlook for sunup or sundown, as I had that time once before, that time of the tightening of the temples. This time, alas, we missed the sundown show, but we did manage to catch the Fold unfolding under early morning light, and, as before, the view was magnificent: The backlit Henry Mountains—Ellen, Pennell, Hillers, Holmes, Ellsworth—wrapped in blue gauze; those flat-top mesas—Tarantula and Swap—leaning our way; the valley of the Fold with its spine of white rocks—the Oyster Shell Reef—and then the toothy, convoluted, upside-down sandstones defining the monocline's western edge.

Only this time was different. Since my last visit, the Bureau had cast its appraising eye upon the other side of the Fold and decided that the country over there was, insofar as wilderness might be concerned, less than outstanding.

For starters, during the inventory process, the Bureau had sliced from a 140,000-acre roadless area one slim ghost of a study area, the Mt. Pennell WSA, weighing in at some 27,000 acres. Conservationists appealed. The Board of Land Appeals instructed the Bureau to bring the WSA up to snuff at some 74,000 acres. Having done that, the Bureau in its draft environmental impact statement simply threw the whole baby out again, prescribing *zero* wilderness for the Mt. Pennell unit (though another slip of some intern's pen—shades of Happy Canyon—garbled the Bureau's intent; oh, *errata!*). And why no wilderness? Why? Because the Bureau concludes that "Pennell would not contribute sufficiently to the diversity of the wilderness system to outweigh other resource considerations." Which means, there are those miners and cowboys again. And where there are cowboys, there are cows.

From the Strike Valley Overlook, it is easy enough to miss what the Bureau has done to the other side of the Fold, on behalf of the cowman and his cow. The top of Tarantula Mesa, for example, is just a bit higher than Overlook eye-level, so that you need better loft—an airplane will do—to comprehend the meaning of range improvement, as executed by the Bureau of Land Management in southern Utah under the approving eye of old cowman Robert Burford. What it means in the Henry Mountains is the destruction of the pinyon-juniper forest. And all that is needed to convert the forest into pasture is two government bulldozers with an anchor chain strung between them, a bucket of grass seed, and a fistful of *your* tax dollars. In pointy-toe-boot circles, the procedure is known as chaining.

Chaining has already scarred much of the Henrys and their satellite benchlands, and more destruction is on the way. If the numbers can somehow be justified—it beats me how they possibly can—several thousand acres of pinyon-juniper will soon be chained and otherwise "reclaimed" at a cost of $321,000. And the purpose? Why, to increase the mountains' carrying capacity, to provide for some 2,000 additional animal-unit-months (the amount of forage needed to sustain one cow + one calf or 6.2 sheep for a month). This breaks out at about $160 per cow/month, a figure that seems outrageously high. According to Rodney Greeno, issues coordinator for the Southern Utah Wilderness Alliance, the National Park Service is currently buying ranchers out of grandfathered grazing rights right here in Capitol Reef National Park at the rate of $52 per cow/month—less than a third of what the big-spending Bureau proposes to drop for its animal units.

Moreover, there is an astonishing subsidy built into this program. Of the $160 per-unit cost, the Bureau's share (the taxpayer's share) is 60 percent, or $96. The cowman—the permittee, if you will—pays a bit under 9 percent, or only about $14 per unit, and the state of Utah picks up the balance. How about *that?* Remember it the next time you count your change at McDonald's. Thanks to Burford's Bureau, you will already have paid for the Big Mac hamburger—with your subsidy.

Enough of that. The chains and cows are behind us. We have come across the territory to camp at last on a sandbar beside the gin-clear waters of the Escalante. Cottonwoods to the right of us, pinyons to the left. Across the river, a canyon wall as slick as The Ritz. We are at the edge of solitude; not outstanding solitude, mind you, because the trailhead is but a hop and a skip away, and such is the Escalante's five-star reputation, more backpackers are hopping and skipping past our campsite in an hour than we have seen in four days of canyon crawling elsewhere.

Still, it is a salubrious spot—and all the more appreciated since the Brushpopper and I must go our separate ways tomorrow, his time in the canyons cut short by events in the world he left behind. But first, in the morning, we will pack out of here and go to the airstrip outside the town of Escalante and fly over some of the country we missed on the ground. And then I will spend some time with Clive Kincaid, who is the most unwelcome man in the territory. Until Kincaid rose to prominence, the meddlesome and tree-hugging actor Robert Redford held the title of Most Unwelcome (mostly because of Redford's eloquent opposition to a coal-fired powerplant on the Kaiparowits Plateau). In fact, it is said that the good people of Escalante Town would have unwelcomed Robert Redford by lynching and burning him in effigy, if only the folks in Kanab hadn't got the idea first. It was some time after this ripple of ill will that a bolt of lightning struck the Escalante area office of the Bureau of Land Management, and burned *it* to the ground. The Lord works in mysterious ways.

III. The Way to Arch Canyon

So I approached the Sierra Club and The Wilderness Society," Clive Kincaid was telling me that next afternoon on Boulder Mountain. "I'd been working with them a lot as a BLM bureaucrat, trying to involve them in the Arizona wilderness program, and I told them that I was going to be quitting. After a year of the Watt administration I just had to. And they asked me if I would go into the Four Corners Region and determine whether there was any pattern of abuse of policy. So I did that. I left in October of '81 and first went to New Mexico and spent several months and then to Colorado, and then I just drove across the border— I'd never been to Utah before—and kind of went past Monticello and saw those first red rocks and I was blown away. And that's what started this odyssey to uncover what clearly has been a very well-coordinated and direct campaign to corrupt and limit the wilderness review process here in the State of Utah."

We sat on the side of Boulder Mountain, at an overlook off the high road to Torrey, and the whole vast arc of country that once might have been—that still could be—the greatest park in the world unrolled before us in a diorama of a hundred different colors and configurations. From the Moroni Slopes at nine o'clock north, the arc curved behind the high-noon Henrys all the way to the cone of Navajo Mountain, hunkering in a shimmer of haze, three o'clock south. And splitting it all in half, or at least the foreground of our view of it, was the thin red line of the Burr Trail, picking its way out of the Fold through the Circle Cliffs.

We had taken the birdseye view in the morning, in a six-seater aircraft out of Escalante, courtesy of that nonprofit airlifter of ecofreaks, Project Lighthawk, out of Aspen, Colorado. Pilot Bruce Gordon was at the controls, Clive Kincaid beside him with the running commentary; the Brushpopper and I in the middle pew, and Wilderness Society field representative Mike Medberry of Salt Lake City and Gordon's colleague, photographer Andre Ulrych, holding up the tail. We had sought and attained altitude over the Kaiparowits, gazed upon the Paria, the Grand Staircase, the Cockscomb and the Wahweap; east with the wind over the Escalante canyons, Stevens Arch, the Fold, and Tarantula Mesa, where at last we saw what chaining really looks like. It looked like hell. "This is the land of the big mistakes," Kincaid had said from the copilot's seat as we flew from the mesa over the saddle between Mts. Ellen and Pennell. "Someone does something illegal in a WSA and it's called a 'mistake.' Then the BLM reclaims the mistake. Look here. Here's their reclaimed chaining and over there is their reclaimed drill pad. And their reclaimed road. Figure it out for yourself."

Now, sitting with him on the side of the mountain, I had my mind full just trying to figure Kincaid. Who *was* this latter-day Muir-of-the-Desert, this apostate bureaucrat, this whistle-blower? And why were folks on the other side saying such terrible things about him? He didn't look like some wilderness squatter to me—but then he didn't look like an alumnus of the Bureau of Land Management either. He talked, I listened.

He had come out of the University of California at Los Angeles, straight from the campus to a district office of the Bureau in Arizona. He worked as a planning coordinator; his wife signed aboard as the district archeologist. It was the year the Bureau joined the wilderness team. By and by the Phoenix district was looking for someone to handle its inventory, and Kincaid got the job. "Had a wonderful time. A helicopter and airplane at my disposal, and eventually I had something like thirteen people working for me." Then Burford sat at the right hand of Watt. Kincaid bailed out and began his sleuthing for the tree-huggers.

"It didn't take me long to figure out that something very strange had happened in Utah," he said. "Systematically, the Bureau districts had gone about trying to eliminate from wilderness study well-known resource complexes through any machinations they could come up with, whether it was simply saying, 'Well, this is a nice opportunity for primitive recreation, but it's not an outstanding opportunity,' or simply dropping entire areas outright, or excising portions of areas that people for some reason or another didn't question. Anyway, I ended up spending a year of my time and money piecing it together, and it turned out that all those eliminated areas were full of mining claims or coal seams or oil leases or whatever. See, they were smart. They cleared the decks early. They knew to get the problem children out of the way. They tried to do that, and they did."

But why? This hadn't happened in Arizona or New Mexico. Why Utah?

"Utah is Utah," said Kincaid. "Utah was invaded by the United States Army in 1858 to put down the Mormon insurrection. And the inculcated hatred of the federal government because of that is something that will not leave the consciousness of some of these people for another five hundred years, if they're here that long. Look. When I worked for the Bureau in Arizona, nobody wanted to come to Utah. I never understood why. And then I came to Utah myself and met enough BLM people to find out what was going on here. What was going on was that local boys that go to Utah State or some of the agricultural colleges and then go to work for the BLM—they don't want to go to California or Montana or Wyoming. They want to stay right here in Utah. So you had this extension of the local culture into the agency. You had an absence of any kind of pluralism on one hand, and on the other this overwhelming, lopsided cultural layer dovetailing with the political structure of the state. Look at the district managers. Throughout the Bureau, the average turnover of district managers is something like two to four years. In this state, it's thirteen years. A boy comes here that grew up in the neighboring county, went to school in the area, becomes a BLM man, never leaves the district, works his way up, one job to the next, gets into management and stays for his whole bureaucratic career. So. The U.S. Army invaded Utah and the federal government took over all of the land that was the Kingdom of Deseret. But you know what? Ultimately, in their own way, the people here got it all back again. It's really fascinating."

It was *very* fascinating, but we had to get on to other things. So he talked for a while about the Southern Utah Wilderness Alliance, which he helped to launch with a little newsletter published out of Boulder Town, in 1984. The start-up circulation was all of five. Now the Alliance counts a membership of 1,500. And then he spoke of that thin red line below us, the Burr Trail.

The Brushpopper and I had done the Trail, as I mentioned earlier. It is a splendid road, a bit too precipitous for my acrophobic tastes where it climbs the switchbacks up the side of Waterpocket Fold. A bit too slow and bumpy if you happen to live in the lee of the high plateaus and own a powerboat and want to haul it on weekends directly to Bullfrog Marina, instead of taking the long way around, by hardtop through Hanksville and Ticaboo. But it is a scenic road for certain—possibly the most scenic, Brushpopper and I had agreed (and we rarely do), in all of America. And because many folks hold the Trail in the same high esteem, and note that it also happens to cruise past a couple of WSAs, while others would have it the opposite way, unkinked and unwrinkled, with hardtop pavement as smooth as a canvas mat—because of all this the Trail has been on and off the litigious ropes like a punchdrunk contender. Last I heard, the hardtoppers were ahead on points, the courts giving Garfield County a right-of-way on the Trail; but it's still unpaved and the Trail-lovers plan further moves.

And finally Clive Kincaid was speaking of his home, which is down there in the arc somewhere beyond Boulder Town, just off the Burr Trail, and which he built himself, and by the sweat of his brow, of native stone. I had heard about Kincaid's house. It was almost as famous—or infamous, depending on your point of view—as he was. I had asked him why he had left the Wilderness Alliance as executive director, and he said, "The biggest single factor is what happened to me with my house."

The word around the territory—word emanating even from folks who are not altogether admiring of Clive Kincaid—was that the Bureau was out to "get" him, run him out, pay him back for all the trouble he'd caused. So I asked if the Bureau had actually "jiggled" a property line to make it appear he was squatting on public land.

"Yes and no," he said. "They came in and did a survey and it appears that they are correct on one point—that half my house, about six hundred square feet, is on federal land. But what they did to crucify me in the press was to jiggle a *wilderness* line, to make it appear I had built my house in a wilderness study area."

So where did it stand, now, with the Bureau?

"They've given me an order to destroy the house. I'm appealing. Destroy it? I put a hundred and fifty tons of stone in it."

The Bureau's people in Salt Lake City deny that any lines have been jiggled in the Kincaid affair, but confirm that the house will indeed have to be moved or destroyed if the Board of Land Appeals finds in the Bureau's favor. "This has been at least as difficult for us as for Mr. Kincaid," said Bureau spokesman Jerry Meredith, "especially with all these people wrongly accusing us of harassing the man."

With 7,884 square miles, and that doesn't count any of its vertical surfaces, of which there are many, San Juan County is the largest county in the territory, the largest in all of Utah. It is also the poorest county in Utah, at least insofar as one measures personal income and relative numbers of people who fall through that crack called poverty. Much of the poverty is concentrated among the Navajo people, who make up about half the county's population of 12,000 and reside for the most part on reservation lands south of the San Juan River. North of that river, the only major employers are the school systems, a uranium mill outside Blanding, and Hall's Crossing Marina, on Lake Powell. Oil and gas are big in the county—it is the state's leading producer, in fact—but the industry does not produce many jobs. Same goes for cattle—big and consistent, but precious few jobs. Some people say, though not too loudly or openly in local circles, that the last best hope for San Juan County's economic survival is to capitalize somehow on its real wealth—the buttes and canyons and Anasazi ruins that are scattered prodigiously and beautifully across the Cedar Mesa country at the county's core.

To test such an idea against the reality, I had left Clive Kincaid on the side of Boulder Mountain and come the very long way around, through Hanksville the hard-top way, to Blanding, which, with 3,600 souls to its name, is San Juan's largest municipality. In Blanding I called on Harold Lyman, who runs the San Juan Jobs Service Center and is a direct descendant of the Latter-Day Saint who founded the city at the turn of the century. Lyman said, "Every day I sit here talking to people who don't know where their next meal's coming from. And then there's the backpacker. Why, you know he probably flew a jet into Salt Lake City and rented a car and drove down here on a paved highway, and now he wants to hike the Grand Gulch and not be bothered by off-road vehicles." So Lyman had figured me out. Then he said, "The environmentalists are always trying to tell us to develop our tourist economy. And when we try to do that, they object to that, too. Besides, we cannot survive on tourism alone."

A hop down the block at the Elk Ridge Restaurant, I spent some time with Calvin Black, who owns the restaurant and a fine motel nearby, and Hall's Crossing Marina up at the lake, and interests in others things; and is a longtime county commissioner, running this fall for a shot at the state legislature (he's been there before), and a member of Interior Secretary Donald Hodel's National Public Lands Advisory Council, and thinks that the 1.9 million acres recommended for uppercase Wilderness in War Without Peace is just about 1.9 million acres too many. Cal Black is a real veteran of the canyon battles, an articulate and rational spokesman for a constituency that sometimes prefers to foam at the mouth. Once upon a time, Cal Black told Edward Abbey that with so much of the territory locked up in parks, and no jobs available, San Juan County had but two significant exports—empty pop bottles and its own children. That was almost twenty years ago and Black, not without some justification, still believes it.

"Tourism is wonderful," the proprietor of Hall's Crossing Marina was saying, "but—" and now the county commission in him took over—"it is not a good single-base economy. Just look at Garfield County, other side of the lake. Garfield has or is next to the most developed, accessible parks in the state of Utah. Bryce Canyon is in Garfield and Glen Canyon Recreation Area is substantially in Garfield, and I'm not even counting Capitol Reef. Zion and Cedar Breaks are just to the west of them. So Garfield County has the best-known, most-visited parks in the state. Now, there is the epitome of building tourism, and all the benefits that the environmentalists always talk about. Yet Garfield County has not been allowed to have coal development. Limits on oil and gas. Timber sales appealed. All they've got is agriculture, a little sawmilling, and tourism. They now have 50 percent of the population they had fifty years ago, which means they've lost half of their seed and all of their increase. They have the highest average unemployment in the state. If you take out the Indian component in San Juan County, Garfield has the lowest per capita income in the state. Now, if that's what tourism does for you and you can't have anything else, I'd rather have 'anything' else. If I had to make a choice. But what I am saying is that you can have both."

I told Cal Black that most environmentalists probably wouldn't agree with him about the prospects for "having both," but that a few were finally sending out some positive signals on the tourism issue, instead of bleating instinctively every time some local booster suggested a plan to bring more tourists into the territory. Clive Kincaid, for example (though I didn't mention this to Black), old Mister Most Unwelcome himself, had spoken to me of the need to accommodate tourism in a significant way—significant enough to serve as an economic alternative to hit-'n-run resource development. And if that meant paving some road, so be it. And Ken Sleight, the river-runner and pack-trip outfitter and perennial foe of wilderness bashers—even *this* one was talking accommodation. "We've got to help develop the small towns," Sleight told me. "I mean, do they *really* want a small jetport at Hall's Crossing, or at

Blanding? Tourism should be directed at the towns, not Lake Powell. By concentrating on Lake Powell, all you do is turn the towns into piss stops—just like a freeway passed them by."

But I didn't tell Cal Black about that either because Black has no use for Ken Sleight, partly because he views Sleight as a lot of trouble in his own right, partly because Sleight is a good buddy of Ed Abbey, who wrote that seditious book about a monkeywrench gang, and partly because, in Black's view, if it wasn't for people like Sleight and Abbey, San Juan County would have something to export beside empty pop bottles and its own children.

I had planned from the start to save Arch Canyon for the last stop. Everyone—Medberry, Kincaid, counselors to the Brushpopper—had given the place five stars, the highest rating. It just had to be experienced, this canyon that came down through orange sandstones in the Cedar Mesa country between Blanding and Natural Bridges National Monument. Ray Wheeler, a lively wordslinger if there ever was, had whet my appetite with one of his "magic carpet rides" in that newsletter put out by the Wilderness Alliance: "We're skimming south over the level, forested surface of Elk Ridge. . . . Suddenly the land drops away into a breathtaking thousand-foot-deep gorge. Virgin ponderosa line the canyon floor and cling to its walls. Below us are plunging cliffs, narrow ledges, buttes, pinnacles, buttresses, and alcoves. A massive sandstone arch wings by, holding a slice of sky in its armpit. . . . Where the snowmelt funnels down off the rim, we can see a dozen stupendous waterfalls. . . ."

Now how could anyone pass up a treat like that? The canyon's praises had been sung in high places ever since National Park Service Director Stephan Mather posted a scout this way in 1926 to check out some prospects for national monumenthood. "This canyon is one of the most beautiful I have ever visited," the scout flashed back to Mather. "It would be a shame to have it get into the hands of exploiters." But, alas, as happens so often, the good suggestion fell through a bad crack. Impossible, said the crack. It cannot be done because part of the canyon is under the jurisdiction of the U.S. Forest Service (about 13,000 acres of Arch's roadless area are in Manti-La Sal National Forest, about 8,000 under Bureau control). Thus, a line drawn between two federal departments, Agriculture and Interior, became the Catch-22 for Arch Canyon. Agriculture's Forest Service wouldn't consider its share of the canyon for wilderness designation in 1984 partly because Interior's Bureau of Land Management had jurisdiction over the other part of the canyon and had already decided that its 8,000 acres were unworthy of wilderness study.

And the Bureau had come to that astounding decision how? Well, how about partly because Agriculture's Forest Service had jurisdiction over the other part of the canyon?

So I was all set to hit Arch Canyon, last stop and maybe last chance, too, before the exploiters got to it. Mike Medberry had fixed me up with the appropriate maps, had penciled in where one leaves the jeep in a grove of giant cottonwoods and slips in through the slot at the canyon's mouth, and then, farther up, starts scanning the south-facing walls for those thousand-year-old Anasazi cliff dwellings. Just a few hours in from the trailhead, Medberry had said, and I'd start to get the feel of the place. An overnighter would be better, but if you're in a hurry. . . . Get the feel of it and then split for Ken and Jane Sleight's Pack Creek Ranch up near Moab, a western sort of country inn (and five-stars, in my book) that would put me in striking range of tomorrow's flight from Grand Junction. Get the feel. . . .

But wait a minute. After almost a week of hit-'n-run feels for the Book Cliffs and the San Rafael and the Dirty Devil and the Escalante, did I deserve yet another at a place that some folks were calling the jewel in the crown? I mean what would Ken Sleight or Ed Abbey think of some visiting fireman who did Arch Canyon in the elapsed time of a motion picture (and not "War and Peace")? I was driving west from Blanding toward Comb Ridge to try to do just that and suddenly I pulled over and stopped because someone was knocking at the windows of my mind. It was that seditious fellow Abbey, speaking from his introduction to *Desert Solitaire*. Abbey was saying, *Do not jump into your automobile next June and rush out to the canyon country hoping to see. . . . you can't see anything from a car: you've got to get out of the goddamned contraption and walk, better yet crawl, on hands and knees, over the sandstone and through the thornbush and cactus. When traces of blood begin to mark your trail you'll see something, maybe. Probably not.*

All right. I would save Arch Canyon. I would turn around right here and go the other way, to the edge of the territory, to the outliers of Moab, to Pack Creek Ranch and the pavement to Grand Junction, and someday I'd come back. I mean, why not? Sure, there were places—and maybe Arch Canyon was one of them—that might go down the tube for want of protection. But would the Bureau dare risk the lightning? "Time is on our side," Brant Calkin had told me in Escalante. Calkin was bucking for the title of Mister Most Unwelcome, now that he had replaced Clive Kincaid as director of the Southern Utah Wilderness Alliance. A former national president of the Sierra Club, Calkin had served in the canyon trenches as long as Calvin Black, on the other side. "Listen,"

Calkin said. "If I've already outlived some of the bastards, and I have, time *has* to be on our side."

And there was Darrell Knuffke, The Wilderness Society's regional straw boss in Denver. Knuffke had said: "Support for wilderness is growing daily in Utah. Those politicians who stomp their feet and shout, 'No Wilderness!' cannot prevail."

So, all right. If these professional optimists were right, then I could just tuck Mike Medberry's annotated map into my armpit and—someday—come back and do Arch Canyon the right way, though probably not on my knees. I would take a week, slow, walking from pinyon to ponderosa, and maybe every night I would discover what the Brushpopper had seen on that ledge above the Dirty Devil, a sky with no lid on it; and maybe, too, if I was *really* lucky and got into the canyon far enough, I would find where the edge of forever comes down, and finally touch it.

(Fall 1988)

RICHARD REINHARDT

Desert Storm

We met what some would call the enemy eye-to-eye and horn-to-horn, so to speak, on a gravel road across the Rabbit Hills near Mugwump Lake in southern Oregon. The enemy was at breakfast, nipping a tasty selection of crested wheat grass and wild buckwheat from among the tufts of sagebrush. Even cattle, it seems, dislike the bitter tang of artemisia, the principal component of the local browse.

"They look benign," my wife said, keeping her eye on a nearby specimen that she suspected of being a bull.

"They *are* benign," I assured her, "unless you happen to be something they like to eat." Bravely, I met the gaze of a cinnamon-brown heifer who was considering me for dessert. The horn of our car emitted an unimpressive beep.

We honked and nudged our way among the herd and fled in the direction of the Abert Rim, a great flat brow of basalt rock that glowers above a milky, almost lifeless lake. We had barely nicked the lower edge of the country we had come to see and, like Robert Frost, had miles to go before we would sleep. To the north and east lay the Oregon high desert country, thousands of square miles of sage and juniper and lava crusts, cliffs and canyons, dunes and marshes—a huge and complicated territory, larger in area than any of half-a-dozen American states, smaller in population than a minor town, and, to visitors like ourselves, mysterious and paradoxical: unknown yet coveted, rich yet impoverished, isolated yet invaded, ignored yet ravaged by generations of exploitation and misuse. And now, after years of not always benign neglect, the High Desert is the newest arena in the battle for wilderness—a conflict in which the cow plays a major role.

Desert, in any form, is not what most visitors expect to find in Oregon. The prevailing image of Oregon is green, moist and woodsy. (In northern California, where I grew up, we used to refer to rain as "Oregon mist"— missed Oregon, hit California, ha ha.) In reality, the state of Oregon is like *two* states, emphatically separated, east from west, by the Cascade Mountains, a splendid rampart of young volcanic cones that stretches from the northern reaches of California up into British Columbia. The Cascades trap the winter rain clouds that come rolling out of the Pacific and squeeze them like wet sponges. On the wet, west side of the mountains (40-80 inches of rain a year) lies the Oregon of popular imagination—small farms, large forests, wide rivers, modest cities with New Englandish names. To the east (10-12 inches of precipitation) is the other Oregon—dry creeks, gray chaparral, raw bluffs, irrigated pastures, mirages swimming over saline plains. The largest part of eastern Oregon, more than a third of the state, is known as the high desert, although it has little in common with the Gobi, the Mojave, or the Sahara.

Mentally and politically, as well as geologically, the Oregon high desert is part of the Great Basin of the intermountain West, where people and plants and animals are few, summers are short and hot, winters are long and blustery, and rivers lose their way en route to the sea and disappear in salty desert sinks. Its urban center (if, indeed, it has one) is not the far-off city of Portland, but the provincial town of Bend, in Deschutes County, way up at the northwest corner of the region. Its favored gambling hell is Winnemucca, Nevada; its market places are the county seats at Lakeview (population: 2,810), Burns (2,875), and Ontario (9,755); and its history is inextricably entwined with that of southwestern Idaho and northern Nevada—thousands of years of quiet aboriginal life followed by a couple of centuries of desultory exploration, mining booms, Indian wars, range wars, failed homesteads, aborted settlement schemes, and decades of resentful dependence on the federal government.

The Department of the Interior's Bureau of Land Management (BLM) has jurisdiction over 71 percent of Malheur County, 63 percent of Harney County, and 49 percent of Lake County. In several places, the local office of the BLM is the most important industry, the largest employer, and virtually the only game in town.

The southern part of the high desert is what geologists refer to, with Germanic precision, as a *horst* (ridge) and *graben* (ditch) landscape. The *horsts* are blocky basalt mesas, or plateaus, tipped and lifted up by ancient earthquakes and volcanic upheavals; the *grabens* are sediment-filled basins, pulled down by the same sort of seismic disorder. During the misty, muggy, post-glacial Pleistocene period, most of the *grabens* were huge, freshwater lakes. Lake

Abert, our destination on the morning of our first encounter of the cow kind, is the residue of one of those ancient lakes, and the Abert Rim is one of the most distinctive of the *horst* ridges. Both of them were formed by an immense, multi-layered flow of molten lava, which split open as it cooled, leaving a long vertical crack that became a palisade when the land to the east reared up and the land to the west subsided. We found the gloom and pallor of their meeting-place entirely to our liking. We sat near the water on a heap of tufa rocks encrusted with bone-white brine and ate our bread and cheese and sliced tomatoes in respectful silence. The only sound was the hum of small flies, feasting on dried brine shrimp along the shore.

To most people's relief, the area known scientifically as *horst* and *graben* is generally referred to nowadays as the Basin-Range Province of the high desert, a name that seems more suitable to this uniquely western, North American place. Neither *horst* nor *graben* suggests the rich variety of the landscape—the shadowy glacial ravines that slash the slopes of Steens Mountain, the emerald fields of alfalfa surrounded by gray sagebrush in the Harney Basin, the shifting yellow dunes abutting the "Lost Forest" of ponderosa pines east of the Fort Rock Valley, the egrets tiptoeing among the tule swamps of the Warner Basin, shattering the pale, brick-red reflection of Hart Mountain.

The northern province of the Oregon desert, designated the High Lava Plains, is a very different land, scattered with cones and caves, craters and crevices, and blanketed for hundreds of square miles with gray-green sagebrush. The province to the east, edging Idaho, is the Owyhee Upland, a plateau built of layers of volcanic ashes during the geologically recent Cenozoic era, then creased and carved into jagged canyons by the flow of the Snake, the Owyhee, and the Malheur rivers and their tributary streams. In those places where the river-canyons of the Owyhee district widen into irrigated plains, the fields are green with sugar beets, onions, corn, and potatoes, and the ubiquitous sagebrush slinks away on distant hills. People who live here sometimes speak of it as the I-O-N Country—a platter of choice corner cuts of Idaho, Oregon, and Nevada. If the Owyhee canyon lands were to be designated a national park (and many people think they ought to be) the park would be the first to lie in three states.

The geological provinces of the high desert fill three very large, very lonely counties—Lake (8,340 square miles), Harney (10,228 square miles), and Malheur (9,925 square miles)—and a small, arid portion of the neighboring county of Deschutes. In area, the high desert is almost as large as the state of South Carolina, or all of New England excluding Maine, but in the whole of this region there are fewer than 45,000 permanent residents, about a third of whom live in and around Ontario and Vale, at the Idaho border.

Coming into the high desert from almost any direction, strangers become aware of an aloof and vaguely threatening atmosphere. Down at the south edge of Lake County, where my wife and I were sharing our midday solitude with a few million self-absorbed brine flies, the menace is in the disappearing lakes, the scowling cliffs. Coming in from the west, over the high Cascades, one senses the malign influence of the geographic "rain shadow," cutting off the heavenly gift of water. Mile by mile, the landscape changes from moist, ponderosa forest to ashen sagebrush prairie. The pines are shorter, thinner and more widely scattered; and then, all at once, they turn into clusters of dark green junipers, stubby little trees so tough and sinewy that local ranchers say a juniper fence-post can outlast three post holes. Balls of tumbleweed bounce along the highway. The sky is huge and pale blue, streaked with feathery wisps of cirrus cloud and floating thunderheads. It is easy— and quite erroneous—to conclude that this country has been totally vacant and unchanged for, say, ten or twelve thousand years, since the earliest human inhabitants hung out in lava caves along the shores of the great postglacial lakes.

The truth is, of course, that the high desert has been thoroughly, perhaps irrevocably, altered during the past century-and-a-quarter by human settlers and their domesticated animals. Residents of both varieties have always been few in number, but their activities are far-ranging, and the land on which they feed is fragile. Subtle, slow, almost invisible change continues, and in certain areas it threatens to end with the sort of sterile wasteland that some people incorrectly imagine to be the natural fate of arid lands.

Part of the problem is that outsiders, even those who live in the humid portions of the northwest, have never paid much attention to the Oregon high desert. Lewis and Clark bypassed it on their trek to the Pacific in 1805. Peter Skene Ogden, trudging through a couple of decades later, scouting for fur pelts on behalf of the Hudson's Bay Company, took note of the shallow lakes of the Harney Basin and continued on his way; and Captain John C. Fremont, coming up from the south, paused only long enough to bestow the name of his boss, the chief of the U.S. Topographical Engineers, on Lake Abert and its forbidding rim. The pioneer wagon trail to "Oregon" (meaning the Willamette and other fertile river valleys), barely skirted the eastern edge of the high desert, following the Snake River down to the Columbia. As late as 1902, a mining engineer described the region as "so isolated, so non-communicative . . . that its topography, its mineral wealth and its scientific wonders are comparatively unknown."

It was an ideal place, one would have thought, for settlement or plunder—

and so, at first, thought many plucky but badly deceived American pioneers. In the 1860s, prospectors turned up silver in the hills of southern Idaho, and that was what finally got things moving. Land-grabbers scratched out military roads across the rim-rock ridges and the high lava plains, collecting for their efforts alternate six-mile-wide sections of the public domain. Toll roads linking the mining camps to rail lines in Nevada and supply towns in northern California ran through waterless alkali basins and frozen oceans of black basalt. To feed the soldiers and miners, cattlemen brought herds of sheep and cattle on the hoof from Texas and California. The long-time residents of the desert—Paiutes, Snakes, Shoshones and Bannocks, nomadic hunters and gatherers—objected strenuously to the invasion. There were hideous massacres and counter-massacres. The Indians, as usual, lost.

The first cattlemen were dazzled by the richness of the native grasses. In the Silver Lake Valley, thick bunch grass covered a basin well-watered by Buck Creek and Silver Creek. In Christmas Valley, grass grew "up to the belly of a buckaroo's horse." In the Harney Basin, around the present town of Burns, the wild grass was said to grow eight feet tall. Cattle wintered comfortably outdoors, feasting on forage that stood deeper than the snow. Unclaimed, undivided, and uncivilized, the Oregon high desert seemed perfectly suited to the sort of development that the geographer Paul Francis Starr recently described as "the characteristic style of livestock ranching that is romantically associated with brave, laconic cowhands and stubborn, independent ranchers—the ranging of thousands of unsupervised cattle over millions of acres of unfenced, uncultivated and otherwise unwanted land."

Con Shea, a cowhand of the appropriate style, rode into the Owyhee country with a herd of Texas longhorns in 1867 and ranged them over the rough lands east of the Jordan Craters for twenty years until a killer winter wiped out his cows and drove him away. John Devine got started in 1871, soon after the U.S. troops had pushed the last of the embattled Snake Indians out of the Alvord Basin. His Alvord Ranch, which was later incorporated into the enormous holdings of Henry Miller, the California "cattle king," is still in operation. So are the Whitehorse Ranch (1869) and the venerable Roaring Springs Ranch, in nearby Catlow Valley. They jostled around in the great open spaces with such Marlboro-Man neighbors as the Pacific Land Company, the development arm of the insatiable Central Pacific Railroad, which got into cattle-ranching on a million or so acres of Oregon sagebrush and fescue.

The quintessential high desert rancher was Peter French, who came up from the central valley of California in 1872 with half-a-dozen vaqueros, a Chinese cook, and 1,000 head of cattle from the considerable herds of Dr. Hugh J. Glenn, one of the few Californians of any era to have a county named after him. French found in the grassy Blitzen Valley, under the shoulder of Steens Mountain, a perfect setting for transhuman grazing, the kind that requires the seasonal movement of livestock from range to range. He bought a "P" cattle brand and a dozen cows from a disheartened prospector, applied the brand to Dr. Glenn's herd, and founded the P Ranch.

In a decade or two, having nursed the French-Glenn herds through successive droughts and freezes, French had extended his home ranch into several adjoining valleys and had acquired a dozen outlying ranges. At one time, the P Ranch was running 45,000 head of cattle and 3,000 horses on 1.5 million acres of deeded land, plus additional millions of acres of public domain. Once a year cowboys drove the cattle hundreds of miles to the railroad at Winnemucca, Nevada, a three to six-week ride, and shipped them from there to San Francisco. The ranch employed more than 100 men.

But the glory of the great ranches, if that is what it was, lasted for little more than twenty years. In this arid climate, the slow-growing native grasses did not renew themselves from year to year. Instead, the range inexorably deteriorated. Sagebrush and rabbit brush, which do not hold moisture in the soil through the dry season, proliferated, replacing the nourishing perennial grasses. Junipers, which transpire precious moisture from the soil into the air, spread across the lava highlands. Russian thistle (tumbleweed) and cheat grass, introduced perhaps from imported fodder or from the hides or excrement of imported cattle, replaced the native grasses. In the days when bunch grasses predominated, their roots had soaked up the scarce runoff of winter snow and slowly released it, filling small streams even in midsummer; now, the porous ground became as dry as brick in early spring. As for the streams, trampled incessantly by cattle in search of water and tender riparian plants, they ran wild every winter, ripping into their naked banks and carrying away the remaining soil and plant cover.

Herds of sheep completed the destruction of much of the high desert range. Early in this century, there were said to be 3 million sheep in Oregon, most of them cropping the sparse vegetation of the high desert. Basque shepherds from northern Spain drove hundreds of thousands of animals over the hills and valleys of Malheur County. On Steens Mountain, 200,000 sheep gnawed the natural cover of bunch grass down to the roots, laying bare many square miles of dry, red soil atop that splendid basalt ridge and subjecting it to disastrous erosion.

The last, inadvertent despoilers of the high desert country were thousands of would-be farmers, lured in by the promise of free land and opportunity in a time of national economic depression. A revised federal homestead act, promulgated in 1909, offered settlers 320 acres of government-owned land provided they paid a $10 filing fee, occupied the site within six months, and "improved" their claim within five years. Families from many parts of the country arrived, virtually penniless, to accept the amazing give-away. With them came hundreds of land speculators who laid out townsites, promising abundant water, salubrious air, and boundless wealth.

The town of Imperial—eighty acres of waterless underbrush in the high lava plains of Deschutes County—advertised itself as the future rival of Portland and Seattle: "Fertile volcanic soil and a climate with 320 days of sunshine and 12-18 inches of rainfall—suitable for dry farming as is the fertile Palouse Valley of Eastern Washington. . . ."

Incoming settlers found southeastern Oregon a harsh, demanding land with bitter winter storms, brief summers, and year-round winds. At the higher altitudes in Lake County, there were as few as 20 frost-free days a year, and the weather specialized in disagreeable surprises. Frosts came on the Fourth of July, followed by days of searing heat. Lakes flooded, then gradually disappeared, leaving alkali flats that swirled up in clouds of dust, ruining crops and make life miserable for people and animals. Fruit trees froze and field crops dried up and died. Jackrabbits devoured the withered stumps.

It required pioneering fortitude to endure the isolation and the loneliness. A man who grew up on a homestead ranch at Christmas Lake remembers joining his father in a once-a-year trek to Prineville, 200 miles away, to buy supplies. The trip, by wagon, took more than a week.

At the height of the homestead epoch, around 1916, there were about twelve hundred settlers in a dozen small communities in the Fort Rock basin of northern Lake County. Each settlement rejoiced in a post office, and several had hotels. Fremont, which also offered a dance hall and a cheese factory, had no cemetery because, as one of the residents told the raconteur Reub Long, most people would rather be dead somewhere else than alive in Fremont.

By 1920, most of the post offices had closed, and census-takers found the Fort Rock basin almost deserted. Soon, even the names of the villages had disappeared. Up to the north, the site of Imperial was marked by a windmill pumping to a cattle trough. All that remained of the settlers' dreams were decaying cabins, fallen fences, and the scars of an ill-conceived effort at traditional farming: deep, V-shaped gullies, eroded streams, exotic grasses. Most of the homesteads, abandoned, reverted to the government. After World War II, the damaged land came under the control of the Bureau of Land Management.

The fate of the Oregon high desert since the great homestead fiasco has resembled that of other arid places in the American West that have not experienced the benefits of oil wells, high dams, or casino gambling: a gradual intrusion of paved roads and electric power lines, a continued ungrateful dependence on various sorts of government support, emptiness, isolation, and animals gnawing relentlessly at the substance of the public land.

We saw the effects of this half-century of change as we drove north from Lake Abert through Paisley (home of the annual Mosquito Festival and of the ZX Ranch, which runs 30,000 head of cattle on a 1.3-million-acre spread, about a million acres of it public land) along the dusty shore of Summer Lake and the gray fringes of the Fort Rock basin. Mobile homes and satellite dishes have replaced the settlers' wooden shacks. Golf and skiing resorts have brought prosperity, franchised restaurants, and traffic congestion to Bend. The Bureau of Land Management has planted crested wheatgrass for cows to eat in the Diablo Mountain Wilderness Study Area.

There have been less visible historic changes, too, although most of them transpired in Washington, D.C., and other places far from the desert. One was passage of the Taylor Grazing Act in 1934, a long-overdue first step by the federal government to curb the devouring of the West by establishing a permit system to end free and unlimited grazing on public lands. (Within a few years after the ravenous sheep departed Steens Mountain, wildflowers and grasses reappeared on the subalpine slopes of that magnificent ridge.) In 1936 the federal government established the 275,000 Hart Mountain National Antelope Refuge in Lake County, and, at about the same time, acquired Peter French's home ranch and the irrigated Blitzen Valley, annexing them to an existing bird sanctuary on Harney and Malheur lakes to create the Malheur National Wildlife Refuge.

Most significant for the future was passage of the Wilderness Act of 1964, under which millions of acres of the Oregon high desert were designated for study as potential wilderness areas. Although a wilderness designation would not, of itself, curtail existing mineral rights or livestock grazing, it would protect selected areas from the encroachment of power lines, paved roads, buildings, motor vehicles, logging, and certain other forms of exploitation. The Bureau of Land Management, having studied these areas to its own satisfaction, recommended wilderness designation for about a fifth of the lands in question. Left out were many areas threatened with environmental degradation—for example, the 50,000-acre Dry Creek Buttes Wilderness Study Area, a remote region of broken hills and pristine native grasses near the Idaho border, which is a habitat of bighorn sheep and pronghorn antelope. The BLM deemed it to have a "high potential" for gold and silver mining.

For the past decade, however, various Oregon conservation groups have been making wilderness studies of their own. In May 1991, in anticipation of the BLM's report, they announced their own recommendation: a plan to bring more than 6 million acres in eastern Oregon under a new and more stringent form of wilderness protection. Like the California Desert Protection Act, upon which it was patterned, the Oregon High Desert Protection Act would affect primarily government lands; unlike the California act, the Oregon plan was aimed primarily at several hundred thousand "hoofed hellions" on the public land. In Oregon, that means primarily lands now administered by the Bureau of Land Management. The BLM has charge of about 13.4 million acres of public rangeland east of the Cascade Mountains, and nearly all of it is leased to ranchers at a fee per "Animal Unit Month" that environmental groups have long maintained is so low it amounts to a form of "cattlemen's welfare."

Although the consortium of environmental groups was led by the Portland-based Oregon Natural Resources Council, it chose an appropriately rural setting—a recreation room at the Malheur National Wildlife Refuge—to announce its plan. Simple in concept, complex in detail, the proposed bill would:

• Bring more than a million acres of the Steens Mountain massif, the most beautiful and biologically diverse of southeast Oregon's great basalt ridges, into the national park system—half of it as a national park, the remainder as a national preserve, in which licensed big-game hunting would be permitted;
• Create three new national monuments: one embracing Fort Rock and its nearby lava beds; the second, a few miles to the east, protecting the "Lost Forest" of ponderosa pines and its nearby "shifting sand dunes" from the depredation of off-road vehicles; the third at Jordan Craters, a volcanic upland comparable to Idaho's Craters of the Moon;
• Designate forty-seven wilderness areas, totalling more than 5 million acres;
• Expand the Hart Mountain refuge to include the wetlands of the Warner Valley;
• Establish a new National Wildlife refuge at Lake Abert;
• Apply the protection of wild and scenic river status to fifty-four streams totalling 835 miles, primarily creeks in the glacial ravines of the Steens and Pueblo mountains;
• Acquire (eventually) 356,000 acres of private land with high recreational, scenic, or habitat value;
• Phase out, over a ten-year period, all livestock grazing on federal lands that are designated national park, national preserve, national wildlife refuge, wilderness, or wild and scenic river (about 5.9 million acres).

Predictably, it was the proposed phase-out of grazing that drew what the Portland *Oregonian* called "swift denunciations from livestock interests."

Although the sponsoring environmental groups argued that 20 million acres of eastern Oregon would remain available to every sort of exploitation, a dozen ranchers stood outside the Malheur Field Station carrying signs that read: "This family supported by ranching" and "I love it here and don't want to leave." The plan also drew expressions of concern, though not denunciation, from various non-sponsoring conservation groups that were not yet convinced that a wholesale ban on grazing and scattergun conservation proposals were either workable or even desirable in all their particulars. The creation of a preserve on Steens Mountain that would allow for hunting, for instance, was a major concern of Nancy Green, The Wilderness Society's director of BLM programs. "I don't think that having to worry that you might be plugged by some nearsighted hunter should be part of the national park experience," she said.

A year later, the debate on all points was still at a rolling boil, given a little extra heat by the expectation that the Bush administration might be getting ready to announce its wilderness recommendations for the area sometime during the coming summer. None of the environmentalists who gathered for another spring conclave at the refuge in May 1992 expected these recommendations to come close to even the most modest proposals offered by the conservation community, and many people were still calling for the elimination of grazing on those wilderness areas that might make it through the bureaucratic barbed wire of the legislative process.

That sentiment was what inspired Charles Cushman, executive director of the National Inholders Association and the Multiple-use Land Alliance, to organize a protest. Shouting "Cattle Galore in '94" and accompanied by two metal stock trucks full of bawling cattle, Cushman and a platoon of seventy-five pro-ranching activists did their best to disrupt the conference. Environmentalists had already destroyed "hundreds of timber-dependent communities, turning them into ghost towns," Cushman told a reporter from the *Oregonian,* apparently referring to the fight to save old-growth forests in the Pacific Northwest. "And now they are starting on ranching communities. This is a systematic, cultural genocide of rural America." The claim that a new crop of ghost towns had suddenly appeared in the West should have been news to the reporter, but he did not inquire as to precisely which towns had been so heartlessly obliterated by environmentalists or who had done the counting.

One of the environmentalists responded to the protest with poetry, of sorts: "Thank you for coming and bringing the press./A well-informed public will help us clean up your mess./You'll give us some grief, but the conference is full./'Cause we don't want your beef, and we don't need your bull."

It is all too easy to depict the grazing issue in the arid West as a struggle between hard-bitten, stubborn, fiercely independent cattlemen and a few fanatical, ill-informed, city-dwelling conservationists. Letters to the editor greeted the Oregon High Desert Protection Act with this type of argumentation. But there also were critics who contended that the sponsors of the high desert proposal, in sweeping together so many disparate elements into a single plan, had doomed it to fail by antagonizing powerful cattle interests throughout the West.

"Broad-spectrum environmental politics is like a broad-spectrum pesticide," one man argued. "It may hit the target, but it's also going to kill a lot of things that are harmless or even beneficial."

The manager of a Bureau of Land Management office that I had visited in the summer of 1991 called it "Andy Kerr's flamethrower attack."

The Andy Kerr in question was and is the director of conservation for the Oregon Natural Resources Council, a bearded, high-intensity advocate with a gift for creating phrases that crystallize the complex political issues of conservation into short and memorable phrases:

"Livestock grazing has done more damage to the earth than have the chainsaw and bulldozer combined" . . . "There are 65,000 mining claims on BLM lands. What if all of them were used for toxic, destructive, open-pit, cyanide heap-leach mining?" . . . "We ought to require them to top every claim stake with a flashing red light, so people could see what's happening to the public land."

As for the political prospects of the Oregon High Desert Protection Act, which a lot of conservationists continue to oppose and none of Oregon's senators nor representatives has yet endorsed, Kerr shrugged his shoulders when I put the question to him. "It's our job as environmentalists to *change* politics," he said. "Sure, it is a problem. But the point is to bring attention to the high desert, to get national organizations like The Wilderness Society to focus on it."

The strategy, implied in a brochure circulated by the Oregon Natural Desert Association in Bend, is to lure skeptics into the wilderness and send them back as believers. Whether it will win converts to the anti-grazing crusade or not, I can testify that it can make you a believer in the sere and joyous value of the place. It happened to me one day that summer of 1991.

I was driving alone in a rented Jeep that afternoon, up from the shifting sand dunes and the lost forest toward a spot of habitation known as Millican, where I hoped to find the east-west highway. It was an afternoon of restless clouds and cool wind from the north. Great mounds of cumulus fleece were racing across the sky. The road was rough and narrow, and ochre dust swirled up behind the car; but the track was edged like a garden path with tufts of lupin, and there were mounds of saffron-yellow buckwheat scattered in the sage. Rounding a bend, I saw at a distance a roofless wooden cottage, bleached gray by sun and storms, adrift like an abandoned raft in endless, billowing waves. For the next twenty miles I did not see another house, a car, a signboard, or a cow.

When I realized what was happening, I stopped the car and listened to the wind and watched the lupin and the sagebrush tossing at the edges of the road. I got out and picked a twig of sagebrush and tasted it and smelled it on my hand. Peace descended on me like the Dove of Grace. I was stunned by a vision of infinite simplicity. There were no problems without solutions, no questions without answers: this land would live forever, gray and silver and juniper-green, and the world would learn to cherish it. People would come here (one at a time, of course, to keep down the dust and clamor, and preferably on windy, rain-washed summer afternoons); and suddenly they would understand the West and America and themselves, and they would go away soothed and tranquil and restored. None of this had much to do with cattle or cyanide heap-leach mining or bills in Congress; yet, for the moment, it seemed supremely relevant.

I drove on after that, trying to hold onto the vision in my mind. Before long I began seeing the pylons of the interstate power net and pickup trucks with black labradors standing in the flatbeds, nosing the wind. I saw a lot of cows. Millican turned out to be a general store with a parking lot for recreational vehicles. From there I took the interstate and headed back to Bend.

(Fall 1992)

T. H. WATKINS

The Perils
of Expedience

I n the middle of ARCO's Prudhoe Bay oil field operations on the North
   Slope of Alaska, a company "environmental compliance engineer" speaks
   forcefully over the sound of the wind as it whips in off the sun-struck
pack ice of the Beaufort Sea. He is concluding an artful disquisition on all the
measures ARCO has taken, is taking, and will take to satisfy the requirements
of law and ensure the safety of the land and wildlife as the company drills into
and sucks up the "black gold" of the Arctic. What ARCO has learned here, he
emphasizes with pride, will enable it to go one hundred miles east and develop
the Coastal Plain of the Arctic National Wildlife Refuge in such a way that its
presence during the life of the anticipated oil field will be as near to benign as
it is possible for human enterprise to get. He is utterly convinced of this, and
asks only that Congress give him and his company the chance to prove it.

On all sides are big and little pipelines and operating wells and pump
stations and water injection plants and power plants and the stretching gray
levees of gravel roads down which big and little rigs of all descriptions rum-
ble, plumes of dust curling up in their wakes; at no point through 360 degrees of horizon on this great water-logged plain at the top of the world is
there a single stretch where something man-made cannot be seen. But, the
engineer is asked, what about wilderness? If this kind of development, however stringently designed, is put in place on the Coastal Plain won't the
question of wilderness be rendered moot?

"Well, sure," he says. "It won't be wilderness anymore. Not pure wilderness, anyway. But that's a decision the American people have to make. What
do they want and need more—oil or wilderness?"

Five hundred miles south, a normally soft-spoken critic of the Bureau of Land Management's minerals management program twists his tiny plane into a tight turn a thousand feet over the valley of McManus Creek along the Steese Highway east of Fairbanks. Untouched boreal forest and tundra cloak the rolling hills and peaks for as far as the eye can see in all directions—except straight down. River-mining for gold has been going on in the area for decades, and the pilot tips a wing at the tailings piles, diversion dams, artificial ponds, haulage roads, scuttling trucks and crawling bulldozers, abandoned machinery, and other stream-bed detritus and land wreckage that extends up and down the drainage of McManus Creek for mile after ruined mile. "Look at that," he says. "That's what they want to do to the Fortymile River and every other stream they can get their hands on. The *bastards*."

In Fairbanks, Roger Siglin, superintendent of Gates of the Arctic National Park, agrees that gold mining is a clear and present danger—and not just to the Fortymile Wild and Scenic River. He leans back in his office chair and tells an interviewer that a recent court decision validating state claims to all "submerged" river land may be the most important threat facing the land and waters of his park. "The submerged lands issue scares me," he says. "It scares me more than the ATV issue does." He is referring to the use of six- and eight-wheeled tundra-wrecking all-terrain vehicles for subsistence hunting by the Natives in Anaktuvuk Pass—this use itself one of the most troubling problems facing the park's management.

Seven hundred miles south of Fairbanks, Richard Shackeley, a Tlingit Native, sits hunched over his kitchen table in the village of Hoonah on Chichagof Island, Southeast Alaska. While a gentle rain falls and fog oozes over the dark-forested hills of the island, the old man tells of his long life in the village, of the days when deer and bear, salmon and halibut were plentiful, "before they put all them roads in, them logging roads, you know. Now they come in from everywhere to hunt the deer, especially. Too many people, not enough deer."

In his quiet, woodsy office surrounded by trees on a hillside in Denali National Park and Preserve, Alaska's oldest national park and the site of Mt. McKinley, the tallest peak in North America, Superintendent Russell Barry insists gravely that he will remove Park Service tour buses from the only park road if a recreational vehicle campground development on a mining claim brings in too many people to make travel safe. "We're at the saturation level already," he says. "There is going to come a time when the question of who has precedence on the road creates an unsafe condition."

During an Anchorage television news report, a non-Native state legislator is shown addressing her colleagues about the impending federal administration of subsistence hunting and fishing on federal lands. Until now, the regulation of subsistence use on those lands has been the responsibility of Alaska's Department of Fish and Game. She is fearful that under federal management her popular campaign to cripple the regulations that determine who can fish and hunt for subsistence reasons will be thwarted. She appears to be close to tears. "I'm not going to sit by and see my children and grandchildren deprived of their God-given rights," she says, her lower lip trembling.

In his office in a sprawling building just off the New Seward Highway on the edge of Anchorage, John Kurtz tells an interviewer that he is about to retire. He is the U.S. Fish and Wildlife Service's agent in charge of the National Wildlife Refuge program in Alaska. He does not appear comfortable with the fact that his agency is still allowing bear-baiting as a hunting device on Kenai National Wildlife Refuge, something allowed in no other state. "There are many people in the Fish and Wildlife Service," he says, "who feel that that's not the kind of hunting we should be allowing in a national wildlife refuge." He appears to be one of them. "If we're going to allow hunting, it should be of the highest quality—ethical." He is equally uncomfortable about the fact that the Department of Fish and Game has persuaded the Fish and Wildlife Service to continue to allow the trapping of fox populations in the refuge, in spite of the fact that the number of animals is in serious decline. When asked what he would like for the future of Alaska's lands, Kurtz does not hesitate: "I would like to see the Fish and Wildlife Service and other government agencies learn one word in the English language, and that is 'No.'"

In his office in downtown Juneau, Gary Morrison, acting deputy Regional Forester for Alaska, has learned how to say "No": No, he says, the Forest Service is *not* convinced that healthy stream habitat for salmon requires that a 100-foot-wide streamside buffer strip of uncut trees be left after logging operations in Tongass National Forest. "We don't dispute that the streamside riparian area needs to be protected," he says, "but our argument is that we have the wherewithal to go out there and identify specifically on the ground exactly how wide that ought to be. In some places, maybe it ought to be much *more* than a hundred feet, in other areas maybe it ought to be less than a hundred feet for some reason." This in spite of the fact that the U.S. Marine Fisheries Service, citing the weight of twenty years of research and mounds of data, says that one hundred feet is the absolute minimum necessary—and that the Forest Service has no persuasive body of evidence or comparative expertise to contradict the fact.

In Washington, D.C., while the first contingent of American troops is being landed in Saudi Arabia during the latest Mideast Crisis, Alaska's senior Senator Ted Stevens decries the perfidy of Iraq's invasion and takeover of

Kuwait and declares that the federal government must cut the environmental shackles that bind the oil companies of America. Common sense, economic imperatives, and national security, he says, dictate that the Coastal Plain of Arctic National Wildlife Refuge be opened to oil exploration and development immediately so that we need never again fear being held hostage to our dependence on foreign oil.

Also in Washington, a group of conservationists gathers around a table to discuss how best to meet this and other threats to Alaska's natural resources and beauty. The meeting lasts for a long time; arguments flare, voices grow loud, there is some table-pounding. A sense of urgency and frustration is shared by all present. But for some there also is a dreadful feeling of redundancy. Much of what is threatened now has been threatened before. Ten years after passage of the legislation that was supposed to protect Alaska's natural inheritance, the catalogue of ills afflicting the Great Land continues like a kind of threnody. It is an old, wearying fight, and some of those in the room would find wry amusement, if no solace, in the words of scientist Daniel B. Luten almost twenty-five years before: "So long as Americans continue to value both the useful and the beautiful qualities of the landscape . . . for so long will the problems of conflicting demands arise. . . .

"In such dilemmas, we usually speak of compromise. The compromises are never true ones, for beauty does all the compromising. Splitting the difference between utility and beauty again and again ultimately will leave nature next to nothing: half of a half of a half of a half is a sixteenth. . . .

"When will the tide turn?"

The Protocols of Compromise

On December 2, 1980, Alaska, the largest, least developed, and by all measures one of the most geographically diverse and spectacularly beautiful places in the world, was given a conservation measure to match: The Alaska National Interest Lands Conservation Act—ANILCA, or, in simpler usage, the Alaska Lands Act. It began in hope, ended in compromise, and has suffered ever since from the pitfalls of expedience.

The legislation was the penultimate act in a long drama. For more than twenty years there had been a frenetic competition among federal, state, private, and Native (Indian and Eskimo) interests to divvy up the patrimony of Alaska's land, only about 30 million acres of which (out of a total of more than 375 million acres) had yet been set aside as national parks and monuments, wildlife refuges, national forests, or other conservation units. Passage of the Alaska Statehood Act in 1958 had authorized the state to lay claim to 103 million acres—more than one-fourth of the entire state, a bigger gift of federal land than that given any other state government in the history of the nation. By 1980, however, only a fraction of the state's wide-ranging claims actually had been approved and ownership transferred by the federal government.

One thing holding up final approval of the state claims was the question of Native needs and desires. An attempt to satisfy these was made with the Alaska Native Claims Settlement Act of 1971, which stipulated that Alaska's Native villages and Regional Corporations could choose up to 40 million acres of the federal land basket. At the same time, conservationists took advantage of the opportunity the act presented by engineering two significant amendments: Section 17(d)(1) of the act empowered the Secretary of the Interior to set aside up to 80 million acres as potential additions to the national public lands systems; Section 17(d)(2) allowed the Secretary to temporarily withdraw from any other classification another 45 million acres in order to determine what should be done with them.

In the early seventies Interior Secretary Rogers C. B. Morton withdrew most of these lands and put them under the law's interim protection almost immediately. But it took six more years of contention, persistent pressure from the conservation community—especially the Alaska Coalition, an aggregation of leaders and representatives from both local and national conservation organizations founded by The Wilderness Society—and political maneuvering in and out of Congress before the fate of these lands edged toward some kind of resolution. In spite of powerful opposition from Alaska's senators Ted Stevens and Mike Gravel and her congressman Don Young, together with their allies in Congress, chambers of commerce, the oil and gas industry, the mining industry, the timber industry, and others, the Coalition finally managed to fashion an Alaska Lands bill, H.R. 39, which Congressman Morris K. Udall introduced on January 4, 1977. But not even the pro-preservation sentiments of President Jimmy Carter and his Secretary of the Interior Cecil Andrus (who submitted their own version of a lands bill to the Senate early in 1978) and such allies as Congressman Udall and John Seiberling and Senators Henry Jackson, Gaylord Nelson, Frank Church, and Lee Metcalf, could pry any Alaska legislation out of the relevant committees and get it voted on before the expiration of the law's interim protection on December 18, 1978.

Frustrated on the congressional front, on November 16 Secretary Andrus used his emergency powers to withdraw 110 million acres of federal land in Alaska from mining claims and the state selection process for a period of three years. President Carter then invoked the Antiquities Act of 1906 to protect the most critical of these areas by establishing seventeen new national monuments totaling 56 million acres.

243

At best, these actions were desperation measures designed to buy time until all the pieces of the congressional puzzle could be jammed together into something that resembled a coherent picture. The legislation that slowly developed, however, being sniped at and revised to satisfy the demands of Stevens, Gravel, Young, and the pro-development forces who informed and supported them, was less than perfect. It was, in fact, nearly unacceptable in many of its parts. But before suitable repairs could be fashioned, Jimmy Carter was roundly defeated by California Governor Ronald Reagan during the presidential election in November. During the campaign, Reagan had made his feelings abundantly clear with regard to the Carter-Andrus withdrawals of 1978: "Our government in the last year or so has taken out of multiple use millions of acres of public lands. . . . It is believed that probably 70 percent of the potential oil in the United States is probably hidden in those lands, and no one is allowed to even go and explore to find out if it is there. This is particularly true of the recent efforts to shut down part of Alaska."

Convinced that Reagan would never support, much less sign, Alaska lands legislation that protected much of anything at all, the supporters of preservation accepted the picture that was before them and pushed through a flawed Alaska National Interest Lands Conservation Act. And early in December, amid an atmosphere of muted celebration, Carter signed it as one of the last acts of his presidency.

President Carter could (and did) take satisfaction in the Alaska Lands Act, however flawed, because it still was the single most sweeping example of conservation legislation in American history. ANILCA set aside 104.3 million acres, and out of this reservation designated twenty-five new wild and scenic rivers; established twelve new national parks, monuments, and preserves, eleven new national wildlife refuges, the Steese National Conservation Area, and the White Mountains National Recreation Area (both Bureau of Land Management units); added 12.3 million acres to existing national parks, forests, and wildlife refuges; and, in perhaps the most dramatic stipulation of all, designated more than 56 million acres of the 104.3 as wilderness. "What we have achieved in this legislation, imperfect as it is," Edgar Wayburn of the Sierra Club told reporters after the signing, "marks a great milestone in the history of American conservation. The body politic has acknowledged the supreme values of one hundred million acres of primeval land and wildlife. It signals, in part, the coming of age of our country's environmental conscience." But he added, "The act is not an end, but a beginning."

Senator Ted Stevens agreed, after a fashion. "We are not finished, Mr. President," this member of the body politic said during his own ceremonial remarks. "We've really just started." Unlike Wayburn, Stevens was not referring to preservation: "We know that the time will come when those resources will be demanded by other Americans."

The psychology of conflict was still in place, then, when President Reagan took office in January 1981 and began assembling the members of his administrative team, including Interior Secretary James Watt and Assistant Secretary of Agriculture John Crowell (whose responsibility was the national forests). Their reputations as pro-development conservatives preceded them, and three months later Rebecca Wodder, The Wilderness Society's Alaska specialist, outlined those things the conservation community would be watching out for in the Reagan-Watt-Crowell era: "Three major questions are of immediate concern. First, will the Reagan administration issue the rules and regulations needed for properly implementing the act? Second, will the administration put enough money and personnel into Alaska to carry out those regulations? And third, in applying the many sections of the act that allow administrative discretion, to what degree will the administration lean to development rather than preservation?"

Within a matter of months, the answers were apparent: no, no, and development all the way. "Under the guise of implementing the law," Senator Paul Tsongas declared in June 1982 in remarks aimed at Watt, "the secretary is, in fact, undoing the law. Through calculated use of the budget, selective enforcement of some provisions of the law but no enforcement of others, and by suspect interpretation of statutory provisions—the Alaska National Interest Lands Conservation Act is being transformed into the Alaska National Interest Lands Development Act."

Under the relentless management directives of Watt and Crowell (faithfully upheld by their successors), the eight years of the Reagan administration established a legacy for the lands of Alaska that stands as a classic example of nonfeasance, misfeasance, and malfeasance. The point is important, for the legacy did not depart with Ronald Reagan. It remains, a Sisyphean burden that continues to frustrate the protection and intelligent use of Alaska's resources.

Here, then, is some of that legacy:

Year after year, the Reagan administration requested too little money to accomplish the specific requirements of the act to develop and submit management plans for parks, forests, wild and scenic rivers, wildlife refuges, and the BLM's two conservation areas; consequently, necessary planning mandated by the act fell hopelessly behind schedule even when it could be performed at all. Some of the planning is still unfinished.

The administration was just as miserly when it came to financing the study of potential park, forest, and wildlife refuge additions to the National Wilderness Preservation System—studies that the act ordered be undertaken; in 1982, as a matter of fact, the administration requested *no* money for wilderness studies in Tongass National Forest. Consequently, wilderness planning, like other planning, moved ahead at glacial speed.

The administration refused to assign a sufficient number of people to administer all the new conservation units; by the middle of 1983, for example, there had been only twenty full-time employees added to national park and preserve staff to manage more than 50 million acres. The public lands of Alaska are still miserably understaffed.

If the administration was hard put to find sufficient funding for planning and wilderness studies and management staffing, it consistently requested and received generous allotments for such practical matters as minerals management, timber-sale administration, and road building; for Fiscal 1983, for instance, the largest single planning budget item the administration requested was for $9.4 million to finance the Alaska Minerals Resource Assessment called for by the act—more than a million dollars more than the total requested for planning for *all other Alaska departments combined.* As a result, the government soon knew—or at least suspected—more about potential sources of gold, silver, oil, and gas than about the habitat and wildlife that full development of such commodities would destroy or irreparably damage. It was the kind of balance that would come to characterize the administration's notion of stewardship throughout Alaska (indeed, some maintained, all fifty states). Funding for the study and development of commodity resources remains higher than that for any other single consideration.

In June 1981, the U.S. Fish and Wildlife Service issued interim management regulations for the newly expanded wildlife refuge system, at least one of which turned tradition on its head: in the rest of the country, refuges are closed to various uses (oil drilling and the like) until specifically opened only when a refuge manager determines that they are not "incompatible" with the main purpose of the refuge (which, of course, is the preservation of habitat and wildlife); in Alaska, however, a liberal interpretation would encourage such uses. "The Fish and Wildlife Service in Alaska," the regional director told his personnel, "will permit energy development on refuges whenever and wherever development can be accomplished without thwarting the achievement of the major purposes for which each refuge was established." In the political temper of the times, it was a dense refuge manager indeed who did not understand that "thwarting" is a more flexible term than "incompatible." Most proceeded accordingly, and to a measurable degree, "anything goes" became an unspoken watchword. For the most part, that sentiment remains in force.

In a related move, the Fish and Wildlife Service reached a "Memorandum of Understanding" with the Alaska Department of Fish and Game that gave the state agency broad and often unchallenged authority over the wildlife resources of the National Wildlife Refuge System—an agreement that some insisted was a violation of that section of ANILCA stating that the refuges would be administered by the Secretary of the Interior "in accordance with the laws governing the administration of units of the National Wildlife Refuge System and this Act." The Memorandum of Understanding remains in effect—and was paired up with a similar agreement with the National Park Service in 1988.

Finally, in addition to underfunding and understaffing the wilderness review process for the parks, forests, and refuges, the administration frustrated wilderness review for the lands under the aegis of the Bureau of Land Management by more direct action. Except for the lands of the Central Arctic Management Area (CAMA) on the North Slope, ANILCA did not order a wilderness review for BLM lands in the state, including those in the Steese Conservation Area and the White Mountains National Recreation Area. Neither did the act *prohibit* such review, however; in fact, its language gave the Secretary latitude to do so if he wished. Interior Secretary Watt did not wish, and just to be certain that no wilderness reviewing got done while he was in charge of things, he issued a policy directive in March 1981 stating that "no further inventory, review, study or consideration by the BLM is needed or is to be undertaken in Alaska." Policy became order when the BLM itself soon directed that except for the CAMA lands, "all work related to designation of public lands as wilderness in Alaska is to stop immediately." So it did, and so it has remained.

James Watt, John Crowell, and Ronald Reagan have moved on, and there have been three Interior Secretaries, two assistant Agriculture Secretaries, and another President since—but the ponderous inheritance of directives, decisions, interpretations, misinterpretations, and acts of omission they left has so mutilated the structure of land management in Alaska that the highest purposes of ANILCA, like the highest purposes of a wildlife refuge violated by oil rigs and drilling muds, have been thwarted to a fare-thee-well. If the wildlife and natural beauty of Alaska are in trouble today, and they are; if the uneven struggle between preservation and exploitation continues, and it does; if the bewildering numbers of special interests vying for the treasures of the Great Land still demonstrate fury, frustration, and sometimes violence, and they do—if all this still plagues Alaska, it is in large part the responsibility of two administrations that have refused to meet the challenge of the future with intelligence, integrity, and compassion.

But not all that is wrong in Alaska can be blamed on the legacy of the Great Communicator and his successor. Some of the problems were built into ANILCA itself, the residue of those desperate weeks in the fall of 1980 when those who had been fighting for so long to get a law with muscle, purpose, and power were forced to accept less than they had hoped for.

There is, for example, the question of the future of the Coastal Plain of Arctic National Wildlife Refuge, that fragile wild place that lies at the top of the world.

Hostages

Arctic National Wildlife Refuge—known more simply as Arctic Refuge or ANWR—is the second largest and the northernmost of the 437 units in America's National Wildlife Refuge System. It began as Arctic National Wildlife Range, when 8.9 million acres of the region were set aside by Presidential order in December 1960. With passage of the Alaska Lands Act, the range was renamed a wildlife refuge, enlarged to its present size of 19 million acres, and wilderness designation was placed on most of the original 8.9 million acres.

There is no place like it anywhere on earth. Across its center sprawls the immense jumble of the Brooks Range, the northernmost mountain range in the world. On the South Slope of the range the foothills roll gently down to the forested watersheds of the Chandalar, Sheenjek, and Porcupine rivers, principal tributaries of Alaska's greatest river, the Yukon. On the North Slope, the mountains decline abruptly to a strip of rolling tundra roughly thirty miles wide and 125 miles long, laced by the Canning, the Hulahula, the Okpilak, and other rivers running from the mountains to the sea.

The refuge is a unique transition zone between two distinct North American ecosystems—the northern boreal forest, or taiga, and the arctic tundra—and as such is a storehouse of uncommon diversity. On both slopes, the predominant ground cover is tundra, a thick mat of grasslike sedges and lumpy cottongrass tussocks. On the North Slope, the plain is largely arid—precipitation averages only about six inches a year—but in the spring and summer months, bogs, ponds, and lakelets are trapped near the surface because of the permafrost, a thick layer of permanently frozen ground that begins anywhere from six inches to five feet below the surface and extends as deep as two thousand feet in spots. It is a place delicately ornamented with plant life: multicolored lichens are splashed on the rock outcroppings

248

like paint from a careless workman, and sweet pea, forget-me-nots, lupines, avens, cinquefoil, bluebells, asters, and other tiny wildflowers spring into bright punctuations of life during the weeks of sun.

This is the Coastal Plain of Arctic Refuge, and it provides habitat for at least 142 species of birds, millions of which are migrants who return to the plain every spring and summer: arctic terns, golden plovers, pintails, old-squaws, green-winged teals, Canada geese, arctic loons, whistling swans, king eiders, bluethroats, dozens more. There are grizzlies and polar bears, wolves, wolverines, arctic foxes, arctic ground squirrels, thousands of Dall sheep dotting the mountain slopes like tufts of cotton, hundreds of musk oxen moving around like big hairy sofas.

And caribou. The Coastal Plain has been called "America's Serengeti," and not without reason. In addition to the Central Arctic Herd, a population of the big ungulates that resides in the central and western portions of the Brooks Range and on the broader portions of the North Slope west of the Canning River, there is the Porcupine Caribou Herd, whose numbers can vary between 160,000 and 200,000, depending upon the health of the herd in any given year. The annual wanderings of the Porcupine Herd's animals take them from the sheltered winter valleys of the Porcupine River of the South Slope and the Ogilvie Mountains of Canada to the Coastal Plain in the summer to drop calves and stuff themselves with the nutrient-rich forage of the tundra grasses, lichens, and sedges before gathering in enormous aggregations and returning to the mountains in the early fall.

Clearly, a place worth the saving, but even as conservationists began to wonder how they could engineer wilderness designation for it after passage of the Wilderness Act in 1964, an impediment developed. On July 8, 1968, the Atlantic Richfield Company (ARCO) and the Humble Oil & Refining Company (later to become EXXON) announced that a major oil strike had been made on the North Slope at a place called Prudhoe Bay, a little over fifty miles west of the border of what was still to become Arctic National Wildlife Refuge. The state swiftly auctioned off 450,000 acres of North Slope land for more than $900 million, then negotiated a deal with the developers to get a percentage of the value of every barrel of oil that might be pumped up.

In 1973, over the agitated protests of conservationists, particularly The Wilderness Society, President Richard Nixon signed an executive order that granted an 850-mile right-of-way, or "utility corridor," as it was called, through federal lands for the construction of a pipeline to carry the oil from Prudhoe Bay to the little fishing village of Valdez on Prince William Sound, and by the middle of 1977 the first oil from the Arctic Coast was oozing into the bottoms of tankers at the sprawling new Marine Terminal at Valdez.

Within a short time, the state of Alaska, its economy already primed by all the jobs and construction money that had gone into the pipeline and its facilities, was receiving 85 percent of its revenue from Prudhoe Bay oil royalties. (By contrast, in 1960, the state had received only 22.7 percent of its total revenue from *all* resource income, including a pittance in oil royalties.) This was enough not only to make it unnecessary for a state income tax but to help establish a "Permanent Fund" for Alaska that would grow to $10.6 billion by the middle of 1990 and paid annual "dividend" checks to every living Alaskan. The dividend was nothing to sneeze at: it would range between $800 and $1,000 in any given year and reinforce Alaska's traditional fascination with the transient excitements of a boom-and-bust economy—the one legacy that might validate the state's self-promotion as the "last frontier."

If there were nine billion barrels of oil in Prudhoe Bay, the boomers reasoned, there might be quite as many under the Coastal Plain farther to the east. That dream was enough to enable Senator Ted Stevens and the rest of the Alaska delegation to engineer one of the most troublesome of the compromises in ANILCA: Section 1002. This section ordered that 1.5 million acres of the Coastal Plain of Arctic Refuge be placed in a kind of statutory limbo, studied by the Interior Department to determine whether it should be put in the National Wilderness Preservation System, as the Alaska Coalition had urged; opened up for oil and gas exploration and development, as the Alaska delegation, the state government, and the oil companies fervently wished; or left as "de facto" wilderness and managed as such, an alternative favored by not much of anybody.

The "Coastal Plain Resource Assessment" began under the gaze of Interior Secretary James Watt in 1981 and was released to the world under the imprimatur of Interior Secretary Donald Hodel in April 1987. Hodel's covering letter was forthrightly optimistic:

> The Arctic Refuge coastal plain is rated by geologists as the most promising on-shore oil and gas exploration area in the United States. It is estimated to contain more than 9 billion barrels of recoverable oil. . . . Based on the analyses conducted, public comment on the draft report, the national need for domestic sources of oil and gas, and the nation's ability to develop such resources in an environmentally sensitive manner as demonstrated by two decades of success at Prudhoe Bay and elsewhere, I have selected as my preferred alternative . . . making available for consideration the entire Arctic Refuge coastal plain for oil and gas leasing.

Even before the issuance of the report, the conservation community—particularly a revived and expanded Alaska Coalition—had readied itself for the expected assault on the refuge. In 1986, with the full support of the Coalition, Congressman Udall introduced a bill that would have given the Coastal Plain wilderness designation immediately, and while the bill did not move any distance to speak of, it provided a rallying point for the conservationists as they systematically began to eviscerate Hodel's assumptions.

His claim that development had taken place without significant harm in and around Prudhoe Bay was categorically denied, the conservationists citing abundant evidence regarding air pollution (63,000 tons of nitrogen oxides, a little under three times the amount enjoyed by Washington, D.C.); oil spills (at least 17,000); waste pits that leaked drilling muds containing such toxic metals as chromium, lead, arsenic, and manganese; and a severe reduction in natural predators like wolves and grizzlies that almost certainly contributed to an unnatural increase in the Central Arctic Caribou Herd from 3,000 animals in 1970 to 18,000 in 1987.

A good many of the necessary facts to counter Hodel's imaginative hopes for the Coastal Plain could be derived from the report itself. The claim that nine billion barrels of recoverable oil would be found, for example, flew in the face of the report's own "mean" average estimate of 3.2 billion barrels. Similarly, Hodel's assurances that development would be relatively harmless to habitat and wildlife populations was contradicted by a nightmarish scenario of potential harm outlined in exquisite detail by the report's scientists. Bird populations, for instance, could significantly be affected by a number of things, including oil spills, hazardous waste spills, air pollution, noise disturbance, and direct habitat destruction through gravel mining, waste-pond dumping, and the construction of port facilities, airfields, drilling pads, roads, pipelines, and service centers. All animal populations could be adversely affected, the report admitted, including polar bears, grizzlies, wolves, musk oxen, and other creatures of the plain.

None would be more dramatically impaired, however, than the caribou of the Porcupine Herd, which depended absolutely on the presence of undisturbed calving ground and the freedom of movement to graze and to escape the maddening concentrations of mosquitoes, botflies, and other insects that torment the creatures in July and August. The impact of oil field development on as many as 200,000 animals trying to move and feed in a narrow band of territory between the mountains and the sea could be devastating.

Notwithstanding logic, the Reagan administration—and after it, the Bush administration—went on to promote the belief that oil and wilderness could be made to mix in the Arctic Refuge, and the lines of opposition were soon drawn with precision in Congress. Udall's bill in the House was matched by similar bills in the Senate, while Senators Murkowski and Stevens and Congressman Don Young all fashioned and introduced development bills. Meanwhile, Congressmen Walter Jones and Lindsay Thomas cobbled what they described as a "compromise" development bill.

The debate among the supporters and opponents of preservation simmered along without resolution until March 24, 1989, when the oil tanker *Exxon Valdez,* outward bound from the Valdez Marine Terminal, ran aground on an underwater reef in Prince William Sound, spilling 11 million gallons of Prudhoe Bay crude into the water. Aided by a combination of corporate and governmental ignorance, incompetence, confusion, cupidity, and evasion of responsibility, the oil quickly did its work, contaminating tidal flats, estuaries, and island and mainland beaches from Storey Island in Prince William Sound to Aniakchak National Park on the Alaska Peninsula four hundred miles away. It was the worst oil spill in American history, and it killed at least one thousand otters, an undetermined number of seals and whales, and anywhere from 100,000 to 350,000 birds of all species, including bald eagles, peregrine falcons, swans, puffins, murres, cormorants, loons, and 2,927 birds that were so cloaked in oil that no one could accurately identify them.

Suddenly, the oil companies and the Alaska delegation temporarily suppressed their cries for the opening of the Coastal Plain of Arctic Refuge; ARCO and the other companies even went so far as to pull all local magazine and television advertising. "This was a textbook public relations move," Art Davidson noted in his 1990 study of the spill, *In the Wake of the Exxon Valdez* "—even positive messages would have reminded people who they were mad at." Instead, proponents of development concentrated now on refuting charges of incompetence and irresponsibility, celebrating Exxon's brave cleanup efforts and explaining that oil spills were an inevitable, if regrettable, concomitant of progress and that the *Exxon Valdez* spill was not really as bad as the media and the environmentalists made it out to be. Above all, the companies wanted the world and Congress to know, legislation to mandate the use of doublehulled oil tankers in the future and institute financial penalties to ensure that all guilty parties—especially the oil companies—would be subjected to the highest possible liability for future spills was both unnecessary and criminally repressive. Almost the entire independent scientific community disagreed with the notion that for all the mess and inconvenience, the spill was essentially harmless, and for its part Congress vehemently disagreed that oil-spill legislation was not necessary; on August 4, 1990, both houses unanimously passed a strong bill.

Among those voting for the legislation was Senator Ted Stevens, who had confessed his motives in an address before the Alaska Support Industry Alliance on March 16: "The intense media scrutiny these events have received has severely undermined the confidence the American people have in the oil industry," a "talking points" paper prepared for the speech stated. "In my opinion, until we can restore public confidence in our oil transportation system, ANWR doesn't stand a chance. There is only one way to revive public trust—enact tough federal legislation mandating stringent safeguards for transporting oil."

Even before the oil-spill legislation was passed, the industry, apparently operating on the theory that the entire nation suffered from short attention-span syndrome, already had revived its advertising campaign. Given what they saw as the undiluted good that would accrue to the state and its citizens, in fact, the oil companies thought that it would be only fair for the people themselves to pay for the campaign. In March 1990, almost precisely one year after the *Exxon Valdez* disaster, the Alaska Coalition for American Energy Security, an industry-supported "citizen's group," petitioned the state legislature to finance what it described as a "national grass roots and advertising strategy in targeted congressional districts in the Lower 48 states to educate the American public on the benefits of ANWR oil development." The petitioners thought that about $11,243,000 would be a good figure to start with. Alaska Governor Steve Cowper, while not unsympathetic, thought that a more likely figure was just a little over a million dollars, and introduced legislation to that effect. In a rare demonstration of independence, the legislature balked at both proposals.

Notwithstanding the passage of time, public sentiment regarding the development of Arctic Refuge remained an open question that Congress did not feel compelled to address during most of 1990—it was, after all, an election year, and who needed the grief of environmental agitation? Even Ted Stevens had counseled patience during his March 16 speech, recommending that the pro-development forces hold their fire until the results of a National Energy Strategy study by the Department of Energy were released in December. Energy Secretary James D. Watkins, Stevens said, had assured him that the development of the Coastal Plain would be one of the preferred options put forth in the study, and the Senator, in turn, told his audience that he would introduce legislation to that effect in January 1991.

Then, in August 1990, President Saddam Hussein of Iraq lurched into Kuwait, seized its government, took thousands of foreigners hostage, and with brute force changed the positions of all the pieces on the board of global oil politics. Oil imports to the United States seemed suddenly threatened, per-barrel prices for oil immediately shot up, and the Coastal Plain of Arctic Refuge once again was threatened, itself hostage to an eruption on the other side of the world.

Oil companies immediately revived their claims that the only solution to America's dependence on oil from the uncertain Middle East was to exploit

of energy and instead make a commitment to import more and more oil from a region of the world growing less and less stable by the day. "Some would say," Curtis and Freeman wrote,

> that such a program would be the end of consumer freedom of choice. They confuse change with sacrifice. It was a change to develop a vaccine for polio, and it no doubt had a grievous effect on manufacturers of iron lungs. But certainly it was no sacrifice. . . . Others will say that such a program would deal a devastating blow to the U.S. economy. Yet somehow the Japanese, German, Swedish and other economies already do quite well using roughly one-half as much energy per capita as the United States. To think that the technological genius of a nation capable of building a warplane invisible to radar and a submarine silent as a winter's night cannot build efficient cars and buildings is an insult to America.

And if we do not make such a choice, we will not have to look far for where the real sacrifice will occur, conservationists have reminded us: it will take place in the mutely glorious landscape that lies on a fringe of tundra between the looming magnificence of the Brooks Range and the glimmering ice of the Beaufort Sea.

Food for the Soul

As the conservationists and the pro-development folk loosed barbs at each other in preparation for what might be the final battle over the fate of Arctic Refuge come the spring of 1991, there were others whose voices were no less impassioned, if less frequently heard. To anthropologists they were known as the Kutchin, a variegated mix of some 7,000 Athapaskan peoples whose home country ranged from Canada's Yukon Territory on the east all the way to the tributaries of the Koyukuk on the South Slope of the Brooks Range on the west. To themselves, they were the Gwich'in ("*Gwich*in") people, and on August 27–31 about 200 from Native hamlets scattered from Old Crow in Canada to Venetie in Alaska gathered in Arctic Village on the East Fork of the Chandalar River at the southern edge of Arctic Refuge. The subject of discussion was caribou. Every year, as the animals of the Porcupine Herd filter south and east through the mountains after a season on the Coastal Plain, the Gwich'in hunters take their annual harvest of meat and hides and bone, just as they have done ever since those dimly remembered days when their ancestors crossed the Bering Land Bridge from old Chukotka, the easternmost portion of Siberia. But now they fear that the traditions on which they have built so old and durable a life will be erased by the hunger for oil, the caribou populations driven into a long and irreversible decline. Sarah James, a Gwich'in leader, defined their concern with eloquence and precision:

> This is a simple issue. We have the right to continue our Gwich'in way of life. We are caribou people. We still do caribou dance, sing caribou song, wear the hide, use bone for tools, and tell the story. Caribou is how we get from one year to another. Oil development in their calving and nursery grounds would hurt the caribou and could destroy our culture and way of life.

The moral power of their message is great, even if its political power is small, and the voice of the Gwich'in adds an element of antiquity to the singularly modern conflict of values over the question of what is going to happen to the Coastal Plain.

In truth, the conundrum of traditional usages among the Native peoples of Alaska is one that provides a sometimes troubling subtext to the discussion of most public land issues in the state. It is the one element above all others here that gives the struggle between the way of tradition and the way of utility a special character, whether it derives from the Tlingit ("Klinkit") people of Southeast Alaska's forested islands, the Aleuts in the chain of islands that curves westward into the North Pacific, the Athapaskans of the Interior, or the Eskimo, or Inuit, people who inhabit the coastal inlets and estuaries north of the Arctic Circle.

Officialdom has dubbed this way of life "subsistence." By whatever term, it is no simple equation. There are about 82,000 Natives of all categories living in Alaska, and at least 50,000 of them depend on subsistence practices—virtually all of them taking place on federal wildlife refuges, national forests, BLM lands, most national parks, and all national preserve lands. The Natives themselves are not particularly fond of the official name. "I don't like it being called 'subsistence,'" says Lily White, a Tlingit storyteller of the Eagle Clan who lives in the tiny coastal village of Hoonah on the north shore of Chichagof Island in Southeast. "It's our *food*," she says, her dark eyes regarding you soberly through the eyeglasses that seem to be part of the Native costume in Alaska. "When you go to a restaurant and order steak, you don't say you want 'subsistence.' I think it was wrong from the start to call it that. It is what we eat, what we always ate."

To many Natives "subsistence" is a white man's term that denotes poverty and second-class citizenship. But there is nothing bleak and joyless in the Native tradition. It involves so much more than merely hunting and fishing for table food that no single word could be coined that would adequately convey all the levels of history, tradition, religion, and family and commu-

ularly to determine the "take" from any given region in any given year, to make subsistence the "priority use"—and in extreme cases to restrict the allocation of any resource to local people who demonstrated "customary and direct dependence upon the resource as the mainstay of one's livelihood."

The state law had nothing to do with either ethnicity or welfare. Whether Native or non-Native, the only requirement for participation was residence in a rural area in which non-commercial uses of fish and game were found to be "traditional and customary," as defined by a number of specific criteria (length of time subsistence use had been common, consistency of use, and other measures). Of the roughly 110,000 people who lived in 225 such rural areas by the end of the decade, about 59,000 were non-Native, and most of them took part in the subsistence program to one degree or another.

Title 8 of ANILCA accepted the continuance of state jurisdiction over the subsistence program on the new public land units so long as state law and administration conformed to ANILCA's own interpretation. Unlike state law, the language in ANILCA recognized a specific responsibility to the Native population:

> The Congress finds and declares that . . . the continuation of the opportunity for subsidence uses by rural residents of Alaska, including both Natives and non-Natives, on the public lands and by Alaska Natives on Native lands is essential to Native physical, economic, traditional, and cultural existence and to non-Native physical, economic, traditional, and social existence.

In 1982, the federal government validated the state's definition of rural subsistence use as being consistent with the requirements of law under ANILCA. But some sportsmens' groups, professional hunting and fishing guide outfits, and others resented "special treatment" for Natives and those they described as "so-called 'subsistence users,'" and this anti-subsistence lobby soon sprang into action. A state ballot initiative that sought to repeal the subsistence law lost by a wide margin that year, but in 1983 a sportsmens' group challenged the law in court. In *McDowell* vs. *State of Alaska,* the plaintiffs maintained that the rural preference stipulation violated the state constitution. While not fully agreeing with the complaint, the Alaska Supreme Court in 1985 did rule that the state's regulations enforcing rural preference were inconsistent with the state's own law. The Interior Department put the state on notice that it was consequently in violation of ANILCA. The state swiftly revised its law, only to find that the *McDowell* suit was itself amended to challenge the new version.

In the meantime, an assault on the law came from another direction after the Department of Fish and Game ruled the entire Kenai Peninsula to be an "urban" area and hence not eligible for subsistence uses. A group of local

Natives dependent on the salmon fishery in the area forthwith brought its own suit in 1986 challenging the classification. In 1987 a federal court ruled against the claim, but the following year the Ninth Circuit Court of Appeals reversed that decision and the U.S. Supreme Court declined to hear the case.

If that put the status of the state's rural definition under a cloud, an Alaska Supreme Court decision on December 22, 1989, all but obliterated it. In *McDowell* vs. *Collinsworth* the court agreed that the rural preference violated the state constitution. It stayed its decision until July 1, 1990, in order to give the state legislature enough time to revise the Alaska constitution so that the law would conform, but even after Governor Steve Cowper called a last minute special session at the end of June, the snarl of conflicting interests paralyzed the legislature and the job did not get done. On July 1, 1990, the U.S. Fish and Wildlife Service officially assumed responsibility for the overall administration of subsistence hunting and fishing on the public lands of Alaska in accordance with the mandate of ANILCA. With the target now confined to federal law, opponents of subsistence soon threatened to challenge the constitutionality of Title 8 of ANILCA itself.

Unsurprisingly, the Alaska Department of Fish and Game foresaw difficulties under federal supervision. "First of all," James A. Fall, a Regional Supervisor for the State Subsistence Division said on June 19

> the federal agencies have no experience in managing the resources, and for providing for subsistence uses. They haven't *done* it. The state has done it. All the expertise with regard to the populations of fish and game themselves, as well as the characteristics of subsistence uses, is with the state. The federal agencies have a lot of catching up to do, and that's going to take them a while. Secondly, it's going to cost a lot of money, which they probably don't have. If they want to do this well, they're going to have to create a staff that parallels what we've got or contract it out.

Interviewed on June 29, Fall's federal counterpart, Walt Steiglitz, Regional Director for the U.S. Fish and Wildlife Service, disagreed with some vehemence. "A lot of people—conservationists and the press—put down our capability to run this program," he said. "But they seem to forget that we're citizens of Alaska ourselves. We *care* about the state and its resources. And, emphatically, we *have* the capability of doing this." As if to provide support for this statement, the Fish and Wildlife Service published "temporary regulations" for subsistence use in the *Federal Register* that day. These would remain in effect until December 31, 1991—and would become permanent after that date if subsistence administration remained in federal hands.

at the end of June: "Subsistence uses are not authorized in Glacier Bay National Park, Katmai National Park, Kenai Fjords National Park, or those portions of Denali National Park originally reserved as Mt. McKinley National Park.") This mischief, most observers agreed, was less a promotion of the "rights" of Natives to use the area for subsistence than an effort by the state to challenge the jurisdiction of the federal government over these waters in light of the "submerged lands" stipulations of the Alaska Statehood Act (see "Aspects of Mutilation," below). The Park Service responded with restraint. When some Natives showed up with state permits, they were advised that subsistence fishing was still illegal. Most of the people left, and no citations were issued in any case. Since there are no enforcement regulations in place—in spite of the fact that the law is clear—the Park Service held, there was little else it could do.

The Park Service currently is making plans to formulate and put into effect enforcement regulations it can use to close the area to both subsistence and personal use (which allows more generous take limits than either subsistence or sport fishing) when the season opens again in the summer of 1991. Conservation organizations, including The Wilderness Society, have urged the Park Service to stick to its guns and actively enforce prohibition. Local Natives—particularly those in nearby Hoohan—consequently resent the Park Service for what it might do and the agency's conservationist supporters for what they say it *should* do. "It's unfortunate that the state's action has introduced an element of confusion and conflict here that just did not need to be," Allen Smith, The Wilderness Society's Regional Director in Anchorage, says.

This is not a prohibition designed to persecute or discriminate against the Native population but to preserve the natural integrity of the park. Remember, ANILCA says that the general purpose of all conservation units is to "preserve for the benefit, use, education, and inspiration of present and future generations certain lands and waters in the state of Alaska that contain nationally significant natural, scenic, historic, archeological, geological, scientific, wilderness, cultural, recreational, and wildlife values." Consumptive uses for subsistence or commercial purposes in Glacier Bay were specifically addressed—and *rejected*—by Congress in passing ANILCA.

Of Buffers and Board Feet

If conservationists and the Natives of Hoonah cannot find agreement about the waters of Glacier Bay, there is plenty of agreement between them with regard to the forests of Chichagof Island all around the town. "Every time you used to go up the road, you used to see deer, you could shoot deer anytime, you know," says Richard Schakeley, a Hoonah resident all his life. "Now there's roads all over this island and you don't see the deer. We drove more than thirty miles out on one of the roads once, didn't see a damn thing. Logging roads, you know."

Logging roads, indeed. In 1980 there were about nine miles of logging roads in the U.S. Forest Service's Hoonah Ranger District, but according to Alaska Department of Fish and Game studies, that total had grown to 108.6 miles by 1985 and to 273.2 miles by October 1989. One immediate effect has been to make the deer more accessible to hunters—many of them non-Natives working in the various logging camps and sport hunters coming to the island by ferry and floatplane from Juneau, all of whom exploit the resource in direct competition with local subsistence users. In 1988, for example, non-local hunters accounted for 1,269 out of the 1,849 Sitka black-tailed deer harvested on the forestlands nearest Hoonah.

Further, logging practices in the immediate area have had a significant impact on deer habitat. Fish and Game studies show that the total amount of national forest land logged over the past five years has gone from about 3,000 acres to 11,820. Both the level of cutting and the road construction that makes it possible, says Vance Sanders of Alaska Legal Services in Juneau, violate the mandate of ANILCA's Title 8 regarding subsistence and are therefore illegal. Citing that allegation, on behalf of a number of Hoonah's Native residents he has brought suit against the Forest Service to enjoin the agency's timber program. "With this suit," he says, "we're trying to force the Forest Service to seriously think about subsistence for the first time, really. If we win, it will determine how *all* development will have to take place under ANILCA in the future—and it'll show whether or not ANILCA really means what it says."

The Sanders suit is not the only legal challenge the Forest Service is facing in Southeast. Down on Prince of Wales Island, agitation has developed over the question of logging plans, buffer strips, and the continued good health of anadromous stream habitat. Another suit—this one filed by Robert E. Lindekugel for the Salmon Bay Protective Association and the Wrangell Cooperative Association—seeks to enjoin the Forest Service from carrying out timber-sale programs on the island to satisfy fifty-year contracts the agency signed with the Ketchikan Pulp Company (KPC) in 1951.

The plaintiffs do not have any particular quarrel with the contracts—but they do argue with Forest Service management practices that threaten a $28 million pink salmon fishery on which they depend, practices the Forest Service justifies as being necessary to fulfill its obligation to KPC. "This case," the suit says

The controversies over subsistence impact and streamside habitat management are just two more chapters in a long conflict over the working habits of the Forest Service in Tongass National Forest, at 16.8 million acres the largest national forest in the United States. The Wilderness Society, for one, has been subjecting those practices to increasingly relentless scrutiny since at least 1984, when in the pages of *Wilderness* magazine Thomas J. Barlow laid bare the horrendous losses the citizens of these United States were suffering from the sale of timber in the Tongass:

> In a 1983 study, Robert Wolf, forestry expert for the Library of Congress, shows that for the period from 1970 to 1984 the Forest Service spent a whopping $375,162,000 to open the virgin forests of the Tongass to logging companies while charging loggers only $62,615,000. The net result: a loss of $312,547,000 for Tongass National Forest timber management programs. Since red ink in the Forest Service's timber sales activities must be made good from the U.S. Treasury, the destruction of the virgin rain forests of Southeast Alaska is being paid for by American taxpayers.

Since then, the losses have continued to mount relentlessly, each million-dollar debit adding its share to the rising gorge of the national debt on which this nation someday may finally choke. These Tongass "below-cost" sales—the most egregious such losers in a bankrupt management tradition that is common to most of the national forests—provided the core of the arguments The Wilderness Society and other conservation groups began to marshall in an effort to turn a reluctant Forest Service in the direction of reform.

There was more than money at stake here, of course. While it differs slightly in the kind and character of some of its individual plant forms, the tangled green world of hemlock, Sitka spruce, and other forest species that characterizes the richest portion of the Tongass is part of an ecological system that runs from Glacier Bay to southern Oregon, a band of temperate zone rain forests that has no counterpart anywhere on the continent—and possibly the world. Yet little of the Tongass's share of this wild resource is protected; here again, compromises made on the road to ANILCA stymied the best hopes of conservation.

First, only 5.4 million acres of the Tongass were designated wilderness by the act, about half the total that had been sought by the Alaska Coalition. Most of the fourteen wilderness areas that comprised this total protected only tundra, mountain peaks, and glaciers—"wilderness on the rocks," as critics described it—leaving most of the virgin old-growth forests of the river valleys and lower mountain slopes vulnerable to logging. The act ratified the land-use allocations and management directives adopted by the Forest Service in its first Tongass Land Management Plan (TLMP), completed in 1979 and devoted almost in its entirety to a policy of timber extraction over virtually all other uses. This validation carried on the traditions established by the Tongass Timber Supply Act of 1947, a postwar boom measure that had set in motion the development of a large-scale timber and mill economy for Southeast Alaska—and the signing of fifty-year contracts for most of the harvested timber with just two corporations: the Ketchikan Pulp Company (later a subsidiary of Louisiana Pacific), which signed its contract in 1951, and Alaska Lumber and Pulp (ALP), a Japanese firm financed by a loan from the U.S. Import Export Bank, which signed its own Forest Service contract in 1956.

In 1980, the harvest on the Tongass amounted to 452 million board feet, supporting a work force of about 2,700 loggers and millworkers, bringing in $32,474,000 in receipts to the U.S. Treasury, and costing the Forest Service $45,598,000 to plan and administer sales and build the logging roads necessary to timber production. That year alone, then, it cost the taxpayers $13,124,000 to subsidize two lumber companies and keep 2,700 people employed in Southeast Alaska. (By comparison, the federal government spent only $9,552,000 on the General Assistance portion of the Aid to Families with Dependent Children program that year.)

This deficit did not stop Senator Ted Stevens and Mike Gravel or Congressman Don Young or the Forest Service or the timber industry or the timber unions, all of whom pressed for a stipulation in the proposed Alaska Lands Act that would perpetuate the timber program in Alaska. They got it with ANILCA's Section 705, which mandated a ten-year cut of 4.5 billion board feet—or 450 million a year—together with guaranteed funding of no less than $40 million every year to finance the program. Nor did the act touch the fifty-year contracts with KPC and ALP, who continued to enjoy virtual monopolies in their bailiwicks.

It was enough to give a good conservationist (or economist, for that matter) the galloping fantods, and ever since passage of ANILCA there has grown a powerful movement to reform Section 705 of ANILCA, as well as terminate the fifty-year contracts. That movement began its most durable legislative journey on February 2, 1989, when Senator Tim Wirth introduced his version of a Tongass Timber Reform Act. He was followed later that month by Representative Robert Mrazek, who introduced his own Tongass bill in the House. While differing in some particulars, each bill proposed the repeal of Section 705, with its mandated annual cut and its mandated annual appropriation, as well as the repeal of the contracts with KPC and ALP. Furthermore, the legislation would have given five-year protection for 1.8 mil-

perfected in the gold camps of California three hundred years later. A riverbed whose stream has been dammed and diverted, then worked over by bulldozers and earthmovers and jets of water from hydraulicking hoses and flatboat and suction dredges and other equipment, is as thoroughly wrecked a piece of ground as it is possible to find anywhere north of Mount St. Helens.

Through all the booms and busts that punctuated the decades after Alaska's turn-of-the-century Gold Rush, thousands of miles of the state's rivers were subjected to mining, and the language of ANILCA contained little that effectively addressed the problem. Not even the newly established national parks and preserves were fully immune to the potential of river wreckage. The Mining in the Parks Act of 1976 had stipulated that all national parks in the United States were no longer subject to location, entry, and patent under the General Mining Law of 1872 but had acknowledged all existing patented claims, while stating that all actual mining operations were subject to the approval of mining plans by the Park Service. Section 206 of ANILCA embraced and repeated those same principles—and furthermore declared that fair and reasonable access to such holdings through all conservation units could not be denied.

The environmental integrity of the rivers in the new national parks of Alaska, then, depended upon the diligence of the Park Service's monitoring activities—and in 1985 the Northern Alaska Environmental Center (NAEC), the Alaska Chapter of the Sierra Club, and the Denali Citizens Council decided to question that diligence in court. It filed suit, claiming that Park Service approval of many individual mining claims had resulted in environmental damage to park units. On July 22, the U.S. District Court for Alaska agreed, and enjoined the Park Service from approving any further mining plans until it had completed all documents necessary for compliance with the National Environmental Protection Act of 1969—including full Environmental Impact Statements for Wrangell-St. Elias National Park and Preserve and Yukon-Charley Rivers National Preserve; in December, Denali National Park and Preserve was added to the list. In May 1990, all three statements were approved and released in final form. The "preferred alternative" in each of these recommended that all mining claims involved be purchased by the federal government and that the operations shut down. The estimated cost for such purposes came to something between $33.5 and $46 million. In the meantime, the statements promised, all mining plans would be rigidly examined in the light of strict water quality and other environmental standards before being approved.

"Clearly a major victory for the environmental community," Allen Smith, The Wilderness Society's Alaska Regional Director in Anchorage, says.

But the Park Service is just as understaffed and underfunded as it was when all this started to make its way through the courts. How well it can monitor mining operations with even the best and noblest of intentions is open to question. The only sure answer to the problem, obviously, is the purchase of the mining claims. We need to get that underway just as soon as possible.

How much a Congress caught in the perpetual grip of budget agonies might be willing to appropriate even out of the billions available in the Land and Water Conservation Fund remains a critical question—but at least the Park Service has been moved to look upon its rivers as ecological resources, not watery lockboxes full of gold for the taking. Not as much can be said for those rivers luckless enough to flow through Bureau of Land Management lands. The BLM in Alaska always has encouraged mining as the most dominant of the "multiple uses" it is required to provide on the public lands (much as the Forest Service has made logging its dominant use on the Tongass). Just as faithfully, the agency has done a dismal job of regulating that use.

Once again, environmentalists have taken to the courts. On February 10, 1986, the Sierra Club Legal Defense Fund, on behalf of the Sierra Club, the Northern Alaska Environmental Center, The Wilderness Society, and a number of local Native individuals and organizations, filed suit in U.S. District Court, which sought to enjoin any further mining activity on the Fortymile River, Birch Creek, and hundreds of other streams under the jurisdiction of the BLM. Concern was especially strong for the three specified rivers, because all had been placed in the Wild and Scenic Rivers System with passage of ANILCA. "At one time, all three were excellent clear-water float and fish streams," said the Sierra Club's Jack Hession. "Now Birch Creek and stretches of the Fortymile are little more than a 'sewer' for the effluent of placer mines, and Beaver Creek is threatened. In the view of the Sierra Club, what is occurring is a national disgrace." Once again, subsistence came into the equation, according to evidence submitted by Susan James of the Birch Creek Village Council. "Mining has contaminated the village's primary source of drinking water," she said, "limited our subsistence fishing and substantially reduced trapping harvests. The people in the village say that if the pollution does not stop, life in Birch Creek Village as it has been conducted for centuries will."

Similar to stipulations in the suit against the Park Service in 1985, this action asserted that the BLM should be required to prepare full "environmental assessments" before approving individual mines and full environmental impact statements for "multiple mines that may have cumulatively significant effects" on the river environment. The District Court found in favor of

quately be comprehended—certainly not by the people Outside. If, for example, the public land rivers of Montana were subjected to the kind and quality of systematic abuse endured as a matter of course by Alaska's rivers, it is hard not to believe that there would be rioting in the streets of Missoula—or even Helena. "There's somebody calling up every day with a problem that in the Lower 48 would be a major controversy," Rex Blazer agrees, sitting in his tiny, paper-piled office in Fairbanks while the telephone does indeed ring in the background and staff members and volunteers stuff and address envelopes in an equally cluttered room next door.

> But outside Alaska almost no one ever hears about it—and even here it sometimes blows right by the environmental community because we're all so pushed for time and staff and money. I'll call up Allen Smith or Jack Hession and say, 'Can you handle this one?' And they'll say, 'We thought you were going to handle it.' In the end, none of us can handle it as well as we should. We've got all these big issues in Alaska that we can only lose once, and because of the attitudes and the technical regulatory infighting and the emotional, John Wayne-like attitudes a lot of people have up here, it can get pretty ugly.

And the problems continue to multiply. In June 1990 The Wilderness Society issued a report called *The Alaska Lands Act: A Broken Promise.* As an addendum to the specific issues and places discussed here—as well as a working demonstration of the oppression of detail—it may be instructive to take a brief look at what is happening in those additional areas illuminated by The Society's report:

> *Alaska Maritime National Wildlife Refuge.* A major concern here is an almost total lack of funds and staff to manage 33,000 miles of coastline and about 3,000 individual islands (including most of the Aleutian chain), islets, rocks, and pinnacles of the maritime refuge system. This becomes a particular problem with oil spills in the Gulf region. In addition to the oil spill from the *Exxon Valdez,* there were 29 other spills of one kind or another in 1989, two of them involving more than a million gallons. Nor can the Service do enough research to get baseline information on the populations of Stellar's sea lions, sea otters, red-legged kittiwakes, and other creatures vulnerable to damage from oil. Industrial activity—logging operations on Afognak and Kodiak islands, a fish-processing plant at Gibson Cove on Kodiak Island, for example—pose threats, as do continued military exercises in the Aleutians.

> *Denali National Park and Preserve.* Here, in Alaska's oldest park, if Congress does not appropriate enough money to buy both patented and unpatented mining

claims in the Kantishna Hills area deep inside the park—as the Park Service's Final EIS has proposed—placer operations could begin. But recreation development on those same claims could pose an equally damaging threat—and indeed already does. The Kantishna Roadhouse, a 24-cabin Denali Mountain Lodge, forty tent-frame "cabins" and a proposed 200-unit RV park could combine to produce a good-sized village population in the heart of the park every summer. Traffic offers another problem. In order to protect the pristine wildness of this place, there is only one major road in the park (with access to it limited to the single park entrance on the east), and, already, traffic is nearing saturation; in 1989, there were 5,437 shuttlebus trips and 4,443 private vehicle trips out the narrow dirt road, in spite of the fact that the park's general management plan called for no more than 5,084 and 3,664, respectively. Interior Department lawyers have told the park's superintendent Russell Berry that he cannot restrict access along the road to commercial operations on private lands at its end. If he is to keep the impact on wildlife to a minimum and maintain some kind of safety standards on the road itself, he has only one option: to reduce or eliminate entirely the park-operated shuttle-bus system. Other problems in Denali include existing and potential recreational developments just outside its borders and a proposed road to link up with the existing road from the northern side of the park.

Kenai Fjords National Park. Since it includes 410 miles of shoreline along the Gulf of Alaska, this park also is vulnerable to oil spills. As well, it faces potential logging and mining development on 77,090 acres of coastline—about 75 percent of the total park shoreline—from Native corporations that have selected these lands under the stipulations of the Alaska Native Claims Settlement Act. There is some fear that recreation development—including a tramway, a lodge, and day-use facilities—may be developed on the Harding Ice Field, the source of the many spectacular glaciers that flow down the mountains all around this sea-girt park. Finally, the Park Service, understaffed, like everyone else, has difficulty controlling poaching activities.

Kenai National Wildlife Refuge. Within an easy drive of Anchorage, Valdez, and Seward, this is the most popular and accessible of all the wildlife refuges in the state, receiving some 400,000 visits every year by hunters, fishermen, campers, and tourists from all over the world. Here, state utility companies want to build transmission lines across sensitive brown bear habitat and breeding grounds for migrating bird species from the Bradley Lake hydroelectric project to Anchorage. The Fish and Wildlife Service so far has not been able to persuade the utility company to stick to a route that skirts the western edge of the refuge—a contingency that was specifically included in ANILCA. With the cooperation of the Fish and Wildlife Service regional office in Anchorage, the Alaska Department of Fish

Nigu River Valley just north of Gates of the Arctic. In spite of arguments from conservationists that at least another 486,000 acres of adjoining CAMA lands qualified for wilderness and should be included, the BLM recommended that, with the exception of a 64,000-acre chunk of land it has designated an Area of Critical Environmental Concern, these and the rest of the CAMA lands be released for "multiple use"—which is to say, possible river mining, potential oil and gas development, and recreational development.

While they were not specifically enjoined by James Watt from studying and recommending wilderness, the National Park Service and the Fish and Wildlife Service have produced nothing for the agencies to brag upon. Planners for the Park Service studied 19 million acres and recommended that 16 million be designated, but the Interior Department in Washington ultimately reduced that to 4.7 million—and then held up any recommendation. Planners for the Fish and Wildlife Service found 52.6 million acres of qualified wilderness, but Interior officials in Washington cut that to only 3.4 million—and, as with the park recommendation, held things up. The equally reluctant wilderness ambitions of the Forest Service in Alaska have already been discussed.

The Dimensions of Commitment

A decade after the passage of ANILCA, then, the future of Alaska stands on uncertain ground. Overcome by the economies of scale, the bewildering snarl of issues that greet them at every turn, the intransigence of a local population of boomers who make the most backward Two-Gun Desmonds (as Bernard DeVoto once called western boomers) of the Lower 48 look like hairy treehuggers, blocked at every turn by a congressional delegation that appears to have learned next to nothing from two hundred years of American history, and frustrated by agency doubletalk and stubbornness, even the most dedicated grassroots environmentalists might succumb to darker moments of reflection that suggest that saving Alaska may be impossible of solution.

The solutions are there, however, and for the most part are not so different from—and certainly no more revolutionary than—those offered up by the conservation community for the preservation of the rest of the nation's natural inheritance. Funding must be allocated to increase staffs so that adequate regulation and study of wildlife and habitat use can be carried on by all public land agencies. Wilderness recommendations must be expanded to the highest possible levels across the board. Public monies must be used to purchase inholdings and mining claims that threaten the future integrity of rivers and other natural areas. The Memoranda of Understanding that have manacled the federal agencies and kept them from managing the wildlife on the public lands as directed by ANILCA for its own good health and the health of the ecosystem must be rescinded and replaced. The Bureau of Land Management must be yanked bodily into the twentieth century and its love affair with the boom and bust economy of the mining industry ended. A careful path must be steered between the call to satisfy the legitimate subsistence needs of the Native and rural populations and the cry for development on public lands as a panacea to all the ills that plague Native communities. The Forest Service, by act of Congress, must cease its ruinous concubinage with the timber industry and begin to prepare the future of some of the last temperate zone rain forests left on the planet with the sense of stewardship that is its own highest inheritance. The Alaskan national parks must remain primitive, as innocent of modern resort technology as they were when established in 1980. Arctic Refuge must be placed off-limits to development forever and a true and reasonable energy policy for this nation formulated and followed.

But to say that the solutions are no more different from or revolutionary than the coda of goals that characterizes the conservation effort in the Lower 48 states is not to suggest that the task of implementing them is not every bit as daunting as the dimensions of beauty, diversity, and living fragility that are at stake in this Great Land. It will take a level of commitment that the United States has rarely achieved short of war. But it is by remembering the dimensions of the place itself that the conservation community possibly can achieve its vision. For Alaska is not merely unique to the United States; it is not merely unique to North America or even to the Western Hemisphere; it is unique to all the world. In its wholeness and its vulnerability, Alaska must be looked upon by all of us as not just another state but as an international responsibility that it has fallen to this nation to embrace and honor. It is not a marketplace for bargaining, for trading a little development here for a little natural beauty there, or an arena in which we can safely act out the old adventure of killing the future for the sake of present gain. If we sacrifice Alaska to the machinery of abuse, we will have violated the honor of having the Great Land in our care; if we move to save it, however, if we have the strength to reject the weight of our own history, we will have the regard of the family of nations and at least one living reason to describe this as indeed the American century.

Keeping such a hope firmly fixed in mind may be enough to hold back the darkness that accompanies the stubborn persistence of one final question: after ten years of conflict, confusion, nonfeasance, misfeasance, and malfeasance, do we still have time to get it right?

(Winter 1990)

thor-photographer of fifteen books on the American landscape, including *Alaska's Mountain Ranges* (1988) and *The Maine Coast* (1989), both published by American Geographic Publishing, and *Montana: Magnificent Wilderness,* issued by Westcliffe Publishers in 1991.

DYAN ZASLOWSKY ("The Far Bounds"), is a freelance journalist living in Evergreen, Colorado, and a regional correspondent for *The New York Times.* Her work has appeared in numerous other publications, including *American Heritage* and *Audubon,* and she is coauthor of *These American Lands: Wilderness, Parks, and the Public Lands,* first published in 1986 and reissued in 1994 by Island Press and The Wilderness Society in a revised and expanded edition.